GUILTY MEN

GUILTY MEN

CONSERVATIVE DECLINE AND FALL
1992–1997

HYWEL WILLIAMS

AURUM PRESS

PLATE SECTION

We are grateful to the following for permission to reproduce illustrations:
Steve Bell, page 6 *below*;
Financial Times/photograph Tony Andrews, page 2 *below*;
The Independent/photograph Tom Pilston, page 5 *above*;
Ministry of Defence/photograph Chris Fletcher, page 4 *above*;
Popperfoto, pages 3 *above*, 5 *below*, 8 *above*;
Press Association, pages 1 *above left*, *above right* and *below*, 2 *centre*, 3 *centre* and *below*, 4 *below*, 6 *above* and *centre*, 7 *above* and *below*, 8 *below*;
Andrew Shaw, page 5 *centre*;
Universal Pictorial, pages 2 *above*, 4 *centre*.

First published in Great Britain
1998 by Aurum Press Ltd
25 Bedford Avenue, London WC1B 3AT

Copyright © Hywel Williams 1998

Hywel Williams has asserted his right to be identified as author of this work.

The author and publisher wish to thank Lady Empson and The Hogarth Press
for permission to reproduce the verses from 'Just a Smack at Auden' from
Collected Poems by William Empson.

A catalogue record for this book is available from the British Library.

ISBN 1 85410 581 7

Printed and bound by CPD Group, Wales

FOR MY PARENTS

RAYMOND AND GRANWEN WILLIAMS

who have always inspired and encouraged

Waiting for the end, boys, waiting for the end.
What is there to be or do?
What's to become of me or you?
Are we kind or are we true?
Sitting two and two, boys, waiting for the end.

Shall I make it clear, boys, for all to apprehend,
Those that will not hear, boys, waiting for the end,
Knowing it is near, boys, trying to pretend,
Sitting in cold fear, boys, waiting for the end?

Shall we make a tale, boys, that things are sure to mend,
Playing bluff and hale, boys, waiting for the end?
It will be born stale, boys, stinking to offend,
Dying ere it fail, boys, waiting for the end.

Waiting for the end, boys, waiting for the end.
Not a chance of blend, boys, things have got to tend.
Think of those who vend, boys, think of how we wend,
Waiting for the end, boys, waiting for the end.

From 'Just a Smack at Auden' by William Empson
(*Collected Poems*, The Hogarth Press)

CONTENTS

PREFACE

Success, it is said, has many parents, while failure is an orphan. This book seeks to establish paternity – and maternity – for the actions and beliefs that led to the decline and fall of the Conservative Party and Government. In 1940 Victor Gollancz published *Guilty Men*, written anonymously by 'Cato'. Conceived in the shadow of Dunkirk, Michael Foot and Frank Owen's essay in contemporary history sought to portray the appeasing policies and the myopic self-absorption of England's governing class on the eve of its dissolution. It has been a happy inspiration for my own work.

I am grateful to all those who have helped me during the book's preparation. Georgina Capel is the literary agent who haunts the happiest dreams of authors. Sheila Murphy of Aurum Press seized the project with imagination and vigour. Christopher Pick has been the most constructive and sympathetic of editors. I am indebted to Simon Heffer, Simon Sebag Montefiore and Johnny Leavesley for their help and encouragement. Catharine Owst worked energetically on my typescript. An over-riding indebtedness is recorded in the dedication.

Hywel Williams
London, March 1998

RECESSIONAL

Departing Captains and Resentful Kings

THIS IS the story of an incompetent Government, a petulant Prime Minister and an arrogant political party.

The Tories' humiliation on the 1st of May 1997 was the worst defeat in their history as a modern political party. The Government had been widely seen as divided, yet previous divisions between the wets and the dries – between advocates of one-nation liberalism and the free-market economy – in the early 1980s had not stopped the Tories winning the 1983 general election. The truth is that the Tories' fatal division was between themselves and the country they claimed to govern.

The Party luminaries – Michael Heseltine, Kenneth Clarke, John Major himself – never failed to remind the country that their Party was divided, while at the same time warning ostentatiously of the dangers of such division. Indeed, division and fragmentation were part and parcel of the Government's method of governing.

It suited John Major's personality to present himself as a victim of circumstances. This extraordinarily ordinary man, the first British Prime Minister to portray himself as a victim, is at the heart of the Tory horror of 1992 to 1997. He was a true Tory Lenin whose political education from the age of sixteen was almost entirely in the hands of Party cadres. The Tory Party gave him everything he had, and he destroyed it. He was a note-bound Prime Minister dependent on briefing cards for the most mundane of interviews and statements. Since he was of the Party, its increasingly bedraggled, slippered, cardiganed and hearing-aided members clung to him out of affection and blind loyalty.

It is often said that the Tory Party is ruthless with its leaders, but the Party's history since 1945 hardly bears that out. As a national hero, Winston Churchill was allowed to continue as Prime Minister into decrepitude. Only the national humiliation of Suez could get rid of Anthony Eden. Harold Macmillan left because of a medical mis-diagnosis, Alec Douglas-Home departed of his own free will, while Edward Heath had to lose three general elections before his displacement was effected with great difficulty over many months. Only Margaret Thatcher's political assassination can be seen as a brutal act. Major was the beneficiary of the removal of a mannered political diva whose arias had ceased to beguile. The squalid *coup d'état* of November 1990 infected everything he did thereafter. A legitimate order of authority had been broken and, Macbeth-like, he found that the manner in which he gained power meant that its substance eluded him.

Nobody who accompanied John Major to a hospital or a school could fail to be struck by his complete mastery of the personal political arts. He embodied the tactile tradition in modern politics with an enormous, two-handed hand-shake. The superficial warmth of his gaze assured each occupant of each hospital bed that he understood, and sympathized with, each malady and each problem. He would leave behind him a wave of affection and a myriad of contradictory assurances. But a leader is there to take decisions, and when Major came to make those decisions the disillusion among those whose hopes he had aroused was correspondingly the more intense. At the end of a regional political tour the Prime Minister would be found on his own watching himself being interviewed on the local television news programmes. He was the most complete politician of his time but the Tories' most disastrous leader, because so self-absorbed.

Major's most significant achievement was to convince his Party and a large part of the British public of his amiability. But the private reality was often foul-mouthed, irascible and petulant. Hostile to politics as the pursuit of policies, he interpreted his Cabinet Ministers' policy documents as covert applications for colleagues' jobs. The idea that the Government needed some conception of a national purpose eluded him. In this regard he was the mirror-image of the Party he ruled. In the 1990s the Tories degenerated into a Balkanized rabble – a very loose conglomeration of interest groups. John Major treated them accordingly, and they returned the compliment by supporting him as Party leader to the very last reel of their disaster film. Things turned out as they did in the Parliamentary Party because it suited John Major that they should do so. His qualification for high office was that he was a pragmatic ring-master who could tame and reconcile the big Tory beasts and their factions. For this to remain a qualification, factionalism had to continue in the Tory Party, and John Major's skills were devoted to stoking the fires of faction.

This continued to such an extent that the death of Party became one of the big themes of 1990s politics. In 1997 the electorate did not so much deliver a judgement on a party of government as ratify a dissolution that had taken place since 1992/93. If the Tories had ceased to be a political party in the conventional sense of the word, so had the Labour Party. Shorn of its socialism, denuded of its defining creeds and guided by the pungent phrase, the social abstraction and the hope of office, Labour had become less of a party and more of a movement animated by a project – the removal of the Tories from office.

In 1983 T.E. Utley, the Tory journalist, warned against the dangers of bourgeois triumphalism in the Conservative Party. The majorities enjoyed by the Conservatives in the general elections of 1983 and 1987 were enormous by any standard other than that of the 1st of May 1997. However, these majorities were misleading, and obscured the tenuous nature of the

Conservatives' hold on power. Margaret Thatcher was the beneficiary of the formation of the Social Democratic Party (SDP) in 1981 and the consequent split in the left-of-centre vote. Seats that would have returned a Labour member without such a split elected Tories. The SDP reduced the Labour vote while barely affecting the Conservatives'. Britain's natural anti-Conservative majority remained largely intact, while the quirks of the country's electoral system rewarded the Conservatives with disproportionately large majorities in the House of Commons.

Thatcher's language encouraged Conservatives to take a total view of the changes affecting Britain and the wider world. Political liberty could not be separated from economic liberty – the phenomena of freedom were said to be inter-linked. Her language also encouraged that illusion of total understanding, that belief in an inter-connected whole, associated with ideological systems.

Monetarism was just such an ideological construct. Sir Keith Joseph had been a high-spending Secretary of State for Social Services under Heath in the early 1970s. Throughout the 1950s and 1960s he had shared the general belief that governments should intervene and regulate economic activity. Zealotry predominated once he was converted, in 1975, to the belief that inflation was a monetary phenomenon and that a government's essential task in economic management was to control the money supply. In the middle of the economic disasters of 1979–81 he maintained that if the theory dictated that interest rates should rise to 200 per cent, then that was what should happen. When the constraints on the money supply were loosened after Alan Walters' arrival as an economic adviser in Downing Street, economic growth began to take off. From 1981 onwards the monetarist dogma was abandoned but the political dogmas of invincibility and iron maidenhead proliferated.

Thatcher maintained that a radical change had taken place in the way that Britain thought about itself and that the Conservatives were the inheritors. Changes had indeed occurred in economic policy and in business structures, but between 1979 and 1992 the proportion of the electorate voting Conservative remained stuck at 42 to 44 per cent. Thatcher-talk was dangerous because it fashioned a misleading picture of wild-eyed revolutionaries frothing at the mouth as they saw a flood tide of State activity receding. It was also misleading because it led the Tories to believe that they were the happy consequence of an inevitable and irreversible change in the history of human belief and conduct. It encouraged the taking of very large views that did not accord with a more mundane reality. This collective illusion, fostered by rhetorical excess, was one of Margaret Thatcher's worst legacies to her Party.

It is revealing that even after the failure of the 1974–79 Labour Government to control the trades unions, the electorate was still wary of returning to the Conservatives. Margaret Thatcher enjoyed a majority of only forty-three in the 1979 election. Yet the assumption became widespread both within and beyond the Conservative Party that the 1979 victory was a caesura

in political history, an event comparable with the Restoration of 1660, the
1832 Reform Act and the Labour victory of 1945. Arguably 1976 was a more
significant date, with the conversion of Prime Minister James Callaghan to
monetarist economics and the fiscal orthodoxy that no government could
spend its way out of a recession. Neo-Keynesians had left the stage a long
time before 1979.

Margaret Thatcher responded to a change in the public mood and the
intellectual climate to which she, a naturally un-reflective person, did not
contribute. The move towards free-market economics was a widespread
phenomenon of the western world in the 1970s and 1980s. She had done
nothing to establish her own credentials in that department before she became
Party leader in 1975. Indeed, she had been a noticeably high-spending
Education Secretary from 1970 to 1974. The Thatcher Revolution, as she
liked to call it, predated her own eminence. But she was a thoroughly
pragmatic and traditional conservative politician in her ability to pick up the
tunes that surrounded her in the ether and choreograph them as her own. What
was thoroughly un-conservative was her encouragement of the illusion that
the Conservative Party offered a philosophy of total explanation and that that
philosophy had the inevitability of history behind it. In the process, the
Conservatives forgot that, although the political class had changed, the British
people had not.

Some of her Cabinet colleagues agreed with this Leninism of the right,
others disagreed and were quiet. The effect on the Conservative masses was
disastrous. It was important that they believed that they could win elections.
But they were duped by a leadership which told them that their victories were
predetermined by changes in the very structure of British society. Major's
legacy included a pernicious sense of inevitable success reinforced by a 1992
victory won against the odds.

In the 1980s British Conservatives acquired a taste for half-digested
intellectualism. They had always enjoyed, traditionally and self-
deprecatingly, their ascription as the stupid party. Sometimes they might use
the self-conscious intellectual as an *idiot savant*, but they always distrusted
him. With the emergence of a new breed of Tory thinkers in the 1980s, the
stupidity of intellectuals, previously a Fabian phenomenon, became a feature
of Conservative activity. Rather as Catherine the Great fêted Voltaire,
Margaret Thatcher indulged the odd licensed thinker in order to shed lustre on
her reign.

The New Right had seemed to carry all before it in the froth and frenzy of the
1980s. Free-market economics, Promethean energy, impatience with institutional inertia, freedom-rhetoric – all changed the face of Anglo-American
government, underpinned by the Thatcher–Reagan amity. The New Right saw
the fall of the Berlin Wall as a personal tribute to its powers of prophecy. Yet,
within a few years, the victor's palms had turned to ashes. The agenda of the
1990s revealed itself as social, not economic. The consensus, among both left

and right, on the importance of markets deprived the New Right of a platform, and it failed to develop an answer to social discontents. The electorates of the western world preferred to trust left-wing politicians with the implementation of right-wing policies. The clairvoyance of a Blair and the platitudes of a Clinton were the true inheritance of that decade. Governments of the centre-left returned to power in continental Europe, most notably in France in the summer of 1997. The reaction against the harsh economics of a Single Currency, high unemployment and public expenditure cuts had once again made the world safe for 'socialism'.

The rise of the New Right was as international a phenomenon as its fall. It was underpinned by the special relationship between Thatcher and Reagan. She admired him but was baffled by his magnificent indolence. 'It was clear that he hadn't read the papers,' she would say in tones of wonderment after one of their official meetings. The President had a film actor's ability to concentrate on the task in hand for as long as it was necessary. He would then detach himself completely and move on. Each meeting was, for him, like a take on a film set for which a performance was required. Afterwards, it could be forgotten.

Margaret Thatcher, by contrast, was an obsessive scholarship girl. She prepared religiously, did her home-work, and read every paper she was given in order to master a subject.

The sense of a broad and deep Anglo-American unity of purpose that could always be relied on underlay Thatcher's speech to the College of Europe in Bruges in September 1988 – the event that, more than any other, inaugurated the Tories' civil war about Europe. For the first time a Tory leader identified the cause of European integration with the cause of greater government. 'To try to suppress nationhood and concentrate power at the centre of a European conglomerate would be highly damaging and would jeopardize the objectives we seek to achieve.' In a prophetic moment whose realization was only months away, Thatcher anticipated the end of the Warsaw Pact.

> Indeed, it is ironic that just when those countries such as the Soviet Union which have tried to run everything from the centre are learning that success depends on dispersing power and decisions away from the centre, there are some in the Community who seem to want to move in the opposite direction. We have not successfully rolled back the frontiers of the State in Britain only to see them reimposed at a European level with a European super-state exercising a new dominance from Brussels.

American money, through Keith Joseph's plutocratic transatlantic connections, had always been important in the running of Thatcher's favourite think-tank, the Centre for Policy Studies (CPS). Founded by Joseph in 1975, the CPS performed a role analogous to that of the Heritage Foundation in Washington. Both became venerable because of their close relationship with the centre of power. But they also became vulnerable as the times changed.

Under the Bush presidency and subsequently under Clinton, Heritage turned first of all stolid and then marginal: another big American corporation. Smaller, leaner, policy units – the American Enterprise Institute and the Cato Foundation – challenged its predominance.

The CPS also reflected wider, political, turbulences. The contentious figure of Alfred Sherman, its Director of Studies, had to be removed in 1984. He had fought with the International Brigade during the Spanish Civil War and discovered in free-market conservatism the same consoling sense of certitude that he had sought on the left in his youth. His doctrinal rigours alienated many and the Centre's prosperity survived his departure. Its decline started after Thatcher's Bruges speech. Lord Thomas of Swynnerton, the historian Hugh Thomas, resigned as Chairman in 1990 because he disliked the Party leadership's new, strident anti-Europeanism. He was replaced by Lord Griffiths of Fforestfach, a temporizing and ambitious banker who had succeeded John Redwood as Head of the Number 10 Policy Unit.

After Thatcher's fall the Centre decided that it needed access to the Prime Minister if it was to maintain its influence. Major became the patron of a CPS that found its edge blunted by the need to be politic. For a while it obscured the issue by concentrating on education policy – a safe issue since most Tories, including the Prime Minister, agreed on the need for reform. But difficulties could not be avoided. The Centre's board was divided between those who wished to pursue the zealotry of earlier years and businessmen who had grown fat in the 1980s and whose wish for an honour and a quiet life meant that they had no desire to offend the new Tory dispensation.

Dramas consumed the organization. David Willets, its director, made an easy and rapid accommodation with the Majorites on his way to becoming the MP for Havant. Gerry Frost, his successor, was less inclined to do so. Frost's own deputy, the noisily chain-smoking educationalist Sheila Lawlor, ran a campaign against him. Both were of the *enragé* right, but yoked uneasily together, they constituted a lumbering pantomime horse. Lawlor had enjoyed the company of the *bien-pensants* of the right since her arrival in Cambridge in the late 1970s. She found it difficult to adapt to a new political world, and time had withered her political connections. As a defence analyst, Frost had been an important Cold War warrior in the 1970s and 1980s. But looking for soldiers with snow on their boots was not a full-time occupation after the fall of the Berlin Wall. Lawlor eventually leapt the Centre's walls with her heroic simplicities on teaching methods intact. She courted Cecil Parkinson vigorously; he returned her attentions and helped her to establish her own think-tank, Politeia.

Frost was eventually sacked by a pusillanimous board and was succeeded by Tessa Keswick, the doctrinally accommodating *grande dame* married to Henry Keswick of Jardine, Matheson. The Centre survived in quieter pastures. There was less noise than in the past, but neither was there any fury of speculation or connection with Government at an important level. For a Conservative think-tank to survive at all was an achievement. The CPS eschewed controversy. Its Director said, speciously, that it could not commit itself to a campaign against the Single European Currency since that would make the Prime Minister's task in persuading pro-European Tories more difficult. This was to over-emphasize the Centre's importance and to play the characteristic Major game of keeping the 'right' quiet and in a box. Neutrality meant that the CPS lacked a distinctive position and could provide no serious political reason why it should be supported financially.

These Lilliputian dramas illustrated the withering of the Tory intelligentsia's already shallow roots. Thatcher had been good at flattering them and making them feel important. Her vanity had led her to feed the salon intellectual as a rare household pet who could be paraded to impress. Intellectuals with a love of power, such as Paul Johnson, could be relied upon to flatter her in return. When she came up against thinkers of more independent bent, such as Ferdinand Mount and John Redwood, she was dismissive. Like his political counterpart, the Tory thinker was trapped in the Thatcher dependency culture, and her departure left him bereft. The Tory intelligentsia behaved like a sect whose hatreds become ever more virulent as their numbers decrease. Their internal squabbles suited the new Prime Minister's purposes while he continued to exercise his disarming talent for survival.

Distrust of intelligence was indeed an important feature of Major and his circle. The people's John, who had sedulously cultivated the aura of an outsider and arrived at the pinnacle of government, was in reality an insider who shared the traditional English suspicion of the mind. 'You only have to say the words Oxford and Cambridge to see him wince,' said one of Major's political advisers.

Other, less political, think-tanks adapted to the post-Thatcher world. The Adam Smith Institute, with its perkily bow-tied Director Dr Madsen ('Mad') Pirie, claimed the Citizen's Charter as a particular project of its own. Its concern from now on would be with the Majorite project of reforming the public sector. Adam Smith's hidden hands, it seemed, were all very well in their way, but in altered circumstances they could do with a touch of governmental spin. The Institute for Economic Affairs had a twenty-year history of free-market advocacy on a cross-party basis. Its work was done. The Labour Party was no longer socialist, and British political parties now shared a general body of assumptions about what made an economy tick. In Washington the Heritage Foundation decided that it was no longer interested in Britain. The post-war Anglo-American élite, with its shared tastes and interests, its common frame of reference supplied by the experience of the Second World War, had lost its political predominance. The USA had a President whose agenda was dictated by domestic interests, and the country was less interested in the outside world than at any time since the protectionist 1930s. And so in 1995, when Heritage stopped signing the cheques for the Institute for Defence and Strategic Studies, the Cold War and conservative alternative to the Royal Institute of International Affairs with its establishment, Foreign Office view of the world, the IDSS folded.

The think-tanks of the 1970s and 1980s had fulfilled many of the functions of universities. They flourished as the universities became increasingly marginal to the world of politics, power and ideas. Corporatism, Keynesianism, soft-Marxist sociology, structuralism seemed dated survivals within a university world that found it difficult to digest the shock of the new. Resentment and frustration were the Senior Common Room's daily bread as it looked at the world outside and read the signs of the times. The Fabian and leftish intelligences of the first half of the twentieth century – Tawney, Laski, Keynes and the Webbs – thought the universities were central to their work of re-moulding British society. Many Conservatives had now convinced themselves that they also were going to re-fashion Britain – albeit to different ends – and they ignored the universities.

In the 1970s and 1980s, the flourishing think-tanks had been important to the new practising Conservative intelligentsia, men such as Nicholas Ridley, Keith Joseph, Peter Lilley and John Redwood. If the think-tanks were starting to fail in the 1990s, they were doing so because Tory energy was faltering. The think-tanks of the left and centre-left, on the other hand, reflected a new, progressivist energy. Demos and the Institute for Public Policy Research acquired influence and importance. At the centre, the Social Market Foundation (SMF) sought to straddle the ambiguities and uncertainties of the Major era. Its Director, Daniel Finkelstein, had been a political adviser to David Owen, the leader of the SDP, and its chairman, Robert Skidelsky, was the accomplished biographer of Maynard Keynes. It successfully mirrored the shallows of the Major Government, eschewed political belief, and lost itself in technicalities. When confronted with evidence of the modern State's incompetence, the SMF's first response was to ask how the State could reform itself and apply with happier, and more effective, consequences the bandages of better management. The draconian withdrawal of government held few charms for it. On the other hand, Private Finance Initiatives combining public and private capital to build schools, hospitals, roads and bridges were as meat and drink to the Foundation.

So, the merrily contentious discussions and lunches of the Conservative think-tanks were silenced. They reflected, rather than contributed to, the Tory decline, having picked up the signals from Downing Street that their services were not wanted. The useful pin-pricks to an anodyne Civil Service had left. Many Tories were glad of the rest. The problem for the Major Government was that the think-tanks were not replaced by anything else. Politics in Britain after the accession of John Major was an unusually public scramble for office without any accompanying ideological cant. But the Tories had grown used to the age of total explanation as a justification for office. They missed that easy, comforting assumption. It looked as if, when challenged to justify its continued existence, the Government could only say, 'We're here because we're here.'

Thatcher and the think-tank ideologists hoped that their transformation of

Britain would achieve American levels of prosperity. Capitalism, they thought, supplied the United States with its social fabric rather than undermining it, as many European thinkers feared. Margaret Thatcher understood very well how the business of America was business. But she failed to see how Britain, though anti-statist, was an imperfectly capitalist country. Wiser Tories talked of markets rather than capitalism because they knew how uncomfortable the British felt about the word, however much they lived their lives according to its reality. The stubbornly professional nature of English life meant that Thatcher's views lacked resonance within her own country. Capitalism in Britain would always need a veneer.

Major shared none of Thatcher's and Redwood's fascination with the United States and the phenomenon of global capitalism. For Redwood America was a land of milk and honey, a place of abundance and possibility. He believed in Jefferson's prose (borrowed from the constitution of Virginia) about life, liberty and the pursuit of happiness. Major's goals, for himself and others, were more modest – a secure place in an insecure world.

Personally indifferent to American restlessness, Major also presided over a political blunder that alienated the Clinton presidency. During the 1992 presidential election, two members of staff from Conservative Central Office joined the Republican campaign. This was impolitic enough. When, however, it was revealed that Central Office had been involved in trying to uncover evidence harmful to Clinton from his time as a Rhodes Scholar at Oxford, the President and his White House staff responded with a powerful enmity. Clinton retaliated by sending one of his least impressive ambassadors, Admiral Crowe, to the Court of St James, where his rumpled, cardiganed frame did little for Anglo-American relations. Meanwhile, his Secretary of State, Warren Christopher, continued the policy of the early Bush presidency by supporting European integration centred around the needs of Germany.

Margaret Thatcher continued to tour the United States throughout the 1990s looking increasingly like Gloria Swanson searching for the camera in *Sunset Boulevard* and preaching about freedom in cod-Churchillian tones at $10,000-a-head lunches. After Major had successfully persuaded her to give up her seat in the House of Commons, she concentrated her efforts on filling the coffers of her own Thatcher Foundation. Established in a town house in Chesham Place, Belgravia, the Foundation advertised its concern for the new democracies of central and eastern Europe. Its accounts, published in New York, showed that it devoted a very small proportion of its budget to philanthropic work. Most of the money was spent on the Foundation's own running-costs and the substantial needs of the Thatcher secretariat. Her gloom about the lack of political leadership was profound. 'It's a terrible time in the political history of the West,' she once said, 'with most of its leaders being crooks.' She was thinking chiefly of President Mitterand, the conspiratorial survivor of Vichy, but she could see light on the horizon. By 1997 she knew that 'Tony won't let Britain down.'

Her intelligentsia survived, but were cast adrift in Major's new world.

Norman Stone, Professor of Modern History at Oxford, had been close to Jonathan Hill, the Prime Minister's Political Secretary, when the latter was an undergraduate at Trinity, Cambridge, but that was no recommendation at Major's court. Stone's geopolitical ruminations on the rise and fall of nations had entertained Thatcher, but she had found him unsound on Germany and the Germans. For Stone, the problem with modern Germany was that lack of self-confidence and fear of its own past were leading to neurosis and instability. That was why the Germans were either at your throat or at your feet. Britain should be helping Germany to greater self-confidence.

Thatcher, however, shared Redwood's view that the European Union (EU) was the old German problem in a new form. The EU was a German plot to achieve by peaceful means the dominance that had eluded it twice in one century. Redwood's memories from his 1950s Kentish childhood of bomb-sites, of asking his mother whether it would happen again, fuelled his Germanophobia. In Thatcher's case it was a simple matter of agreeing with de Gaulle when the General said that he liked Germany so much he thought that there should be two of them. Stone made no impact on this thinking. As always, for Thatcher the scholar was a *salonnier* to buttress a prejudice. Stone's association with Thatcher, together with his prolific and vigorous journalism, made him unpopular among his Oxford colleagues. By 1996 he had left for the University of Ankara.

The nearest Major came to an official chronicler was Lord Blake. Martin Gilbert, the faithful Churchill memorialist, was a late and improbable entrant in a keenly uncontested field. He accompanied the Prime Minister on some of his visits but had no official role, and the initiative faded away like so many Major projects. Robert Blake, for his part, had for two generations been a loyal portraitist of Tory institutional vicissitudes. The former Provost of The Queen's College, Oxford, and biographer of Disraeli, he was always on hand as a house-trained historian when the Major leadership needed a defence at times of strain. He would have done the same for any Tory leader.

Other Tories in ermine went quiet, or on the run, in the Major years. Some were old, but most were indifferent. Lord Bauer was the LSE economist who did most to popularize the belief that aid to developing countries encouraged corruption, maintained despotism and discouraged economic growth. He believed that Thatcher had failed to use the resources of patronage at her disposal to advance conservative believers. She thought that in ideas, as elsewhere, the free market could not fail to deliver the goods. But Bauer knew markets well enough to understand that they also needed a framework. They were not spontaneous effusions. On this analysis the Thatcher legacy was not strong enough to stand on its own two feet. When Thatcher fell she left no political or intellectual legatee in place. This might have been vanity or carelessness but it certainly led to a market failure – the waste land into which Major moved and made his own.

Lord Dacre, the historian Hugh Trevor-Roper whom Thatcher ennobled, had no interest in a public defence of the Government and would have found it unseemly to offer one. Lord Renfrew, the archaeologist who had been a Conservative parliamentary candidate, had long since joined the ranks of resentful dons who thought that the Tories starved the universities of money.

Among economists, Alan Walters was making money in New York and was out of sympathy with Major. Patrick Minford and Tim Congden, as analysts of markets and their discontents, continued to provide powerful caviare for economically attuned generals. Theirs was a professional influence, and not one that extended to the wider hinterland of public opinion that lay between politics and economics. Neo-classical liberal economists still welcomed the sight of Samuel Brittan of the *Financial Times* descending from the mountain and bearing in his hands the Mosaic tablets of their law. But his powerfully expressed intellectual defence of the Exchange Rate Mechanism distanced him from the diminished tribe of Conservative commentators.

Roger Scruton, as philosopher, musician and fox-hunter, belonged to too eclectic a strand of conservatism to be a convincing and suitable Tory apologist. He was a Tory reactionary animated by revulsion against his own modest upbringing; Majorism could hardly be his creed. Shirley Letwin, an American by birth and English Conservative by adoption, had been energetic, opinionated and successful in the Thatcher years as an intellectual version of Lucille Ball. Her books and teaching at the London School of Economics (LSE) illuminated conservative thought for a generation. For her, the fall of Thatcher was a series of personal betrayals, and she had no energy or inclination to defend a discredited Government. Kenneth Minogue kept a flame of Tory philosophy flickering at the LSE, but a romantic Australian's outsider view of Britain and Toryism meant that he had no interior grasp of the Conservative decline. David Dilks was an important historian and a biographer of Neville Chamberlain, and was also active politically, but a dry sense of self-preservation kept him away from the mire of political influence-peddling.

This left Maurice Cowling, a Cambridge historian and Fellow of Peterhouse, as the only substantial Conservative apologist who could have written convincingly in defence of Major. As an anti-intellectual intellectual, he really did believe that conservatism was simply what the Conservative Party's leadership decided it should be. He was, therefore, well-placed to defend Major – and a common South London background could have added a pleasingly sentimental tone to matters. He had found Thatcher silly, noisy and idealistic, and he approved of an intelligent lowness of tone in a Tory political life which, he thought, should be a cant-free zone. Major was a good example of the kind of politician who flourished in the narrow, self-obsessed world of high politics and low motives celebrated by Cowling in his magisterial histories of the nineteenth and early twentieth centuries. The Prime Minister's career was rather like that of Michael Portillo, Cowling's pupil. They had both been absorbed within Party structures from an early age and had barely encountered an outer, non-political reality. That might not have mattered for a nineteenth-century career, but the demands and the hostility of a media class cast a fascinated and patronising spotlight on the creatures in the political aquarium. The self-imposed limitations of such a form of life needed some justification. Cowling, however, after a few unenthused forays, was disinclined to provide one – as Major might have put it. Rebarbative, mischievous and self-consciously cynical, he lacked the will to be an apologist for Majorite conservatism. Silently, he surveyed the scene from across the Atlantic as a visiting professor in New York, and pressed on with his histories of English religion and politics.

Conservative intellectuals being thin on the ground, the gap was filled by the left and centre-left. Linda Colley's *Britons* (1992) portrayed the country as a historical construct. It had been invented during the eighteenth century and the Napoleonic Wars as a Protestant bulwark against Catholic Europe, and an artificial unity had been imposed upon its diverse constituents, England, Wales, Ireland and Scotland. Shorn of its original justification, the island State was now developing in two directions. Internally, it was devolving into its pre-existing components, while externally it was evolving and being absorbed within a wider Europeanism. This nightmare – a pincer movement on the traditional British State – haunted John Redwood's imaginings, and he saw it developing particularly in Wales, his own area of responsibility.

English Society 1688–1832 (1985) was an attempt by J.C.D. Clark to counter liberal orthodoxy. This history of the seventeenth and eighteenth centuries, suffused with conservative values, failed to reach a wide public. Clark, a former fellow of Peterhouse and then of All Souls and now enjoying the fruits of exile at the University of Kansas, thought that England had survived as an *ancien régime* society until well into the nineteenth century. His eighteenth century was not the increasingly secular, materialist, proto-democratic age beloved of liberal historians since G.M. Trevelyan. These conclusions were too *recherché* to be popularized. Colley, by contrast, was taken up by the *Independent*. Her work was easily assimilated by disillu-sioned, *déracinés* metropolitans. What is more, Clark's conclusions were subversive of conservative, as well as of liberal, orthodoxy. His England was part of a wider European *ancien régime* of rank, hierarchy and sacral kingship. But Conservatives wished to show England as the happy exception, and this was how she appeared in many a Euro-sceptic speech – as a blessed plot of earth protected by good sense, empiricism, the sea and sensible inheritance laws from continental forms of government which, from Louis XIV to Jean Monnet, had emphasized the role of the State in human affairs.

Alan Macfarlane's *Origins of English Individualism* was a more promising source of plunder for the Euro-sceptic conservative forager. Published a year before the Conservatives' 1979 election victory, Macfarlane's book showed an England that, well before the Reformation and the sixteenth-century expansion of capital, gave small landowners extensive property rights. English feudalism had not encouraged the development of large landed estates, as had happened under the feudal system of continental Europe and its associated forms of political control. English property rights had led to the love of one's own parcel of land, of the back-yard and the garden. English variety, eccentricity and stubborn individualism could be traced to medieval tap-roots beneath the modern top-soil.

Macfarlane's book was celebrated in tendentious Tory articles in the 1980s. As late as 1997 David Willetts, ever a successful assimilator of others' views, was using Macfarlane as a source of Conservative inspiration when opposing the dangerous charms of the European social model. But Macfarlane had no successors. When it came to constitutional and political thought Conservatives had gone to sleep by the 1990s. Ferdinand Mount, the journalist and former head of the Number 10 Policy Unit, was the only Conservative commentator to point out the dangers of allowing constitutional issues to slumber, and he was ignored as an increasingly semi-detached Conservative. The Tories' view of the constitution was stuck in the late nineteenth century with Dicey, who, as an Ulster Unionist, portrayed a constitution one and indivisible. They had forgotten Burke's insight that a State without the means of reform is without the means of its own preservation, and they had left themselves cruelly vulnerable to the avalanche when it came.

While the intellectuals declined, political hand-to-hand combat continued unabated. Both parties saw that the real conflict was taking place outside Parliament. When it came to influencing the mind of England, power had moved away from the chamber of the House of Commons into the hands of the media class. Tories believed that their problems emanated from a hostile press – like their leader they regarded themselves as victims. The Party which preached individual responsibility failed to make a connection between the Government's political actions and its electoral consequences. As by-elections, European elections and council elections pounded the message home, so the collective unreality increased. After some particularly catastrophic set of results, Cabinet meetings would avoid discussing the political disaster. A grim-faced Prime Minister would announce that discussion of these issues could not go on for long since the waiting press in Downing Street would assume that they were quarrelling. On other occasions the pretext for curtailment was the need to prepare for Prime Minister's Questions that afternoon – hardly an unusual state of affairs.

Television appearances were a particular torture, as the Prime Minister paid much attention to his appearance and spent an inordinate amount of time on his make-up and hair. Happily, however, unlike Michael Howard he did not carry his own personal powder compact for those difficult late-afternoon interviews.

Occasionally, Major would make a foray into enemy territory. A particularly memorable one took place in February 1996 when Conrad Black, proprietor of the *Daily* and *Sunday Telegraph*, took his political editors to Chequers as the Prime Minister's guests. An awkward discussion resulted in an agreement to give the *Telegraph* newspapers some privileged access to Government-inspired stories. An early fruit was a briefing from Conservative

Central Office that the Lord Chancellor was about to deliver a speech criticizing judges for developing the doctrine of judicial review. Subsequently Lord Mackay, the Lord Chancellor, indignantly denied the story, which the *Daily Telegraph* had given front-page billing, and its political staff were embarrassed as a result.

This was an administration whose incompetence was compounded by its vituperation towards the press. In alienating the world of commentators and journalists the Government took on the most powerful interest group in modern Britain – the media class. That class reflected, fostered and came to relish its conflict with the Prime Minister and his Tories. John Major's hostility was so palpable, his skin so thin, his response to criticism so immediate that he presented a rewarding target. Gus O'Donnell, his first press secretary, possessed Majorite amiability but was not respected by the press corps. O'Donnell's successor, Christopher Meyer, was a career diplomat who had no intention of being dragged down into the quicksands of the failing regime and who resisted too close an identification. Major finally settled for the undistinguished Jonathan Haslam. None of these could cope with the lucid intelligence and ferocity of Labour's Peter Mandelson and Alastair Campbell.

Parliament became peripheral to both Government and Opposition. The Government despised its backbenchers and Labour controlled theirs ruthlessly. A community of interest meant that on a large number of issues – gun control, divorce law reform, Europe – the two front benches shared a unanimity of view that was at odds with their backbenchers' convictions. Stanley Baldwin, John Major's favourite Prime Minister, had led the Tories into a coalition National Government in 1931. The consensus of that government was spurious and appeasing. It amounted to nothing more than the postponement of difficulty. Major's admiration was inauspicious.

The Tories had enjoyed a good press during the 1980s. Fleet Street was no longer at the mercy of the print unions and their restrictive practices, business expanded, and the newspaper proprietors and editors were grateful. Thatcher's combination of hedonism at home and self-assertion abroad was good for business. A new class of commentators and journalists reflected the new climate in their columns and stories.

The Tories encouraged the belief that their election victories were the result of an unusually close relationship with the press. Proprietors and some commentators basked in the warm glow of approval and increased self-importance. Patronage came the way of Lord Matthews of the *Express*, Lord Wyatt of the *News of the World*, Lord Stevens of the *Express*, and Lord Deedes of the *Telegraph*. Grub Street acquired a new authority in the late 1980s as newspapers moved their offices from Fleet Street to Docklands, whose reclaimed lands and new buildings symbolized economic renewal and self-confidence.

A new media class was forged in these years. Vigorous and self-confident, it traded in opinions, beliefs and vivid language. It believed itself to be at the heart of the best, the most crusading and the most iconoclastic newspaper industry in the world. It shared the period's lack of deference, but there were limits to its iconoclasm. It was not very good at turning the spotlight on itself.

It was a true class in the sense that its members came from a broadly similar socio-economic background, lived similar lives, and shared a similar relationship to the means of production. They were the most important part of the intelligentsia in Britain. As the universities' ability to retain ambitious and original minds declined, so the media class expanded. Minds that would have been at home in the Senior Common Room a generation ago now found themselves in newspaper offices. Many shared the heady assumptions of the Tory 1980s and saw themselves creating, rather than reporting, the next Conservative leap forward.

Politicians had for long enjoyed a close relationship with accredited lobby journalists at Westminster. The off-the-record briefing on lobby terms guaranteed anonymity, and the journalistic lunch was an important social ritual in an enclosed world. In its early life the *Independent* had refused to participate in the lobby system's unattributable briefings, believing they led to an unhealthy and collusive relationship between politicians and journalists. This high tone could not be sustained and the experiment had to be abandoned; the lobby system was too strong. The lobby would always survive, but media-class activity now gave a new edge to a culture of commentary in the 800- and 1200-word piece. In both broadsheets and tabloids the reading public showed an appetite for such articles.

After the 1992 election the Conservatives felt more than ever indebted. Their traditional Fleet Street supporters had remained loyal and had mounted vigorously anti-Labour campaigns. The *Financial Times* was an exception. It had endorsed Labour, and nothing amused a Tory, and especially the Prime Minister, more than to remind its journalists that events had confounded it. The Government was happy to acquiesce in the belief that it was 'The *Sun* Wot Won It', but it was also eager to encourage other newspapers to believe that they too had played a unique role in the Conservative victory. The breach, when it came, was devastating in its impact.

From the day on which Britain was forced out of the European Exchange Rate Mechanism (ERM), the Conservative media-class started to train its guns on the Government. In any case, it had political and economic objections to a mechanism that was a stage on the way to a Single Currency and eventual loss of British political control over monetary and economic policy. The media-class as a whole, including its left-of-centre members, shared and contributed to a more general scorn for a Government that had lost control of events, refused to apologize, and now lacked an economic policy.

The *Daily Telegraph* was traditionally the most loyal of the Conservative-supporting broadsheets. Max Hastings, its editor, who had supported Michael Heseltine in the 1990 leadership contest, had always been tepid about Major. Simon Heffer, his deputy editor, was unremittingly hostile. His contempt pre-dated the ERM's collapse, and he had never forgiven the Tories for abandoning Thatcher. For Heffer, Thatcherite economics were important, but, for one of the last Powellites in England, so also was a developed sense of national will and destiny fed by romantic historiography, a native English musical tradition and a post-Christian pantheist's love of the English countryside. He excoriated in personal and moral terms a Prime Minister who offended him on account of his anti-intellectualism, his lack of a sense of public duty and his avoidance of personal responsibility for the mistakes he had made. These Cromwellian and East Anglian asperities were used to edge his editor towards greater hostility. Heffer gloried in the extent of Major's personal animus against him as the first and most powerful of the Government's critics.

George Jones, the paper's political editor, adopted a pragmatic approach on Europe, could not really see what all the fuss was about, and tried to keep open the lines of communication with the Government. Bill Deedes, the benign former editor, was the incarnation of the paper's unthinking Toryism, but events were overtaking both them and that tradition.

By the time Charles Moore was appointed editor in 1995, the *Telegraph* was lurching towards outright hostility to the Government. Despite an old Tory civility and a North London antiquarian bookishness, Moore was part of a new Tory consensus fed by the recovered certitudes of the 1980s. As a serious Anglican who had converted to Roman Catholicism, he found the Church of England a broken reed. As a convinced Unionist, instructed in the rebarbative need to defend Ulster by T.E. Utley, his *Telegraph* colleague and mentor, he thought the Conservative Party was losing its attachment to the North of Ireland. As a high Tory with a belief in the civilizing mission of Britain's historic institutions, he observed a widespread decline in those institutions and the Conservatives' failure to think about the consequences of that decline. Increasingly, he did not understand what John Major and his Conservative Party stood for.

At *The Times* the editor, Peter Stothard, lacked Moore's elegiac affinity with a dying England and his personal sense of Tory betrayal. But he had a profounder intellectual grasp of modern England's democratic restlessness, and was happy to give the Government an increasingly hard time. Hostility to the European Single Currency became an important editorial cause. Simon Jenkins, a former editor, opened up a broader line of attack. For him the Tories had contributed to a crisis of over-government in Britain. Their quangos, their agencies, their itch to intervene and regulate meant that Britain was a centralized State that did not trust its own people to make the right decisions. William Rees-Mogg, another former editor, also decided to join the savagery of the Heffer bandwagon. He offered a critique of the global economy, arguing that high labour costs and low productivity were marginalizing Europe while at the same time creating artificially high unemployment rates in an attempt to meet the strict convergence criteria for the Single Currency.

Mary Ann Sieghart was the paper's New Labour correspondent, and contributed to the overall sapping of the paper's Conservative will. Peter Riddell's political commentaries drew deeply on his historical understanding of Britain's dominant social-democratic tradition in a line that stretched from Gladstone through Lloyd George, Gaitskell and Crosland to Roy Jenkins and David Owen. Martin Ivens, who edited the comment pages, entertained free-trade and anti-statist assumptions. As a putative Citizen Kane on the make, he displayed an increasingly mischievous ability to use the paper's commentary to subvert, annoy and destabilize the elected Government – a long-term project, but worth it. The job of Andrew Pierce, the lobby correspondent, was to keep an eye on the Tories. A disillusioned Tory himself, he found that his eye became increasingly sardonic, and he soon joined in the game of wit and subterfuge – no newspaper used greater *élan* in the task of destroying the Tories. Matthew Parris' parliamentary column was the part of the paper read most eagerly by MPs. The extent of his dislike for Tony Blair offered some Conservative comfort. A friend of the Prime Minister, Parris rather enjoyed the counter-suggestible temptation to refuse to hunt with the pack. But the compassion he extended to the members of the Tory clan was not untinged with contempt.

Ivens continued his campaign at the *Sunday Times* from 1995, but with a more muted voice under his editor John Witherow, whose Toryism was profound and instinctive and whose anguish at the Tory collapse was all the greater. While the provocative historian Andrew Roberts had revived the English art of political biography with his life of Halifax, his column in the paper showed insistently how Major's Tories had cut loose from ancestral moorings and were now adrift in a sea of nullity. New Labour commentaries by Robert Harris and Andy Grice, the paper's Mandelsonian lobby correspondent, were preparing the paper for the dying of the Tory light. At the *Sunday Telegraph*, Dominic Lawson succeeded Charles Moore as editor in 1995. He had already shown at the *Spectator* that he understood better than most the new power of the media class to create and destroy. He was himself a good example of that class in its restless, free-market energy, its intelligence and its contempt for the political estate. Matthew d'Ancona, his deputy editor at the *Sunday Telegraph*, supplied a political commentary whose subtle originalities and absurdist sense became part of the mirror in which the Tories were forced to look at themselves and recognize their collective haplessness.

In Vere Rothermere, Associated Newspapers had a proprietor who lacked Conrad Black's close involvement in the British political scene and Rupert Murdoch's global perspective. Rothermere was happy for his papers to make money in any way they thought fit. Sir David English, Editor-in-Chief of the *Daily Mail* and of the *Mail on Sunday*, had been an intimate part of Thatcher's 1980s successes and remained on friendly terms with Major. However, Paul Dacre's editorship at the *Daily Mail* provided an increasingly hostile account of the Tory stewardship. Europe was an important source of dissatisfaction, but the new social discontents of Britain provided the paper with a powerful new campaigning edge. Dacre felt strongly about the decline of the family, about crime and soft-headed judges as well as about a cumulative loss of national identity. His columnists – the perpetually incandescent historian Paul

Johnson, the demotic Richard Littlejohn, and Simon Heffer, who arrived at the paper in 1995 – probed and provoked these areas of discontent. Because the social canvas was so wide and the issues were so profound, the *Mail* fed and responded to very long-term worries, especially among its female readers. As the paper unearthed increasing evidence of marital discord among the famous and the obscure, as it unravelled tales of personal dishonesty in which its readers could immerse themselves with a delicious *Schadenfreude*, so its condemnation of modern Britain's lack of moral sense became increasingly articulate, as did its tendency to blame Major's Government for all the ills of modern British man and woman.

The *Mail* was the paper Tory politicians most wished to write for. Many were called but few were chosen. The paper would commission two or three articles for the same slot, the final decision being taken at the last moment in solitary communion by an editor famed for his mystical intuitions about the directors' wives of middle England. Increasingly, Dacre's rejection of metropolitan values and fabled ordinariness made him the editor most of Major's Cabinet wanted to meet. He had what they had mislaid, the key to middle England. He was also the editor who was most likely to reject their blandishments and remain elusive.

Moral passion of this order was not so obvious at the *Mail on Sunday*, whose editor, Jonathan Holborow, was fonder of the society of individual Cabinet Ministers. However, in Peter Dobbie, its deputy editor and political columnist, the paper found the authentic voice – irascible, discontented, savage – of the disillusioned Tory jilted by his masters.

As a London newspaper, the *Evening Standard* had an importance that eluded all other dailies. It was the journal that almost all MPs read in their weekday life in the House of Commons. It mattered to the Tories that Stewart Steven, its editor until 1995 and a former Labour supporter, also supported Major through thick and thin. He disliked the Euro-sceptic backbone of the Parliamentary Conservative Party and especially Michael Portillo, against whom he ran a highly personalized campaign with Downing Street's approval. It was a blow to the Tories when he was succeeded by Max Hastings, who felt increasingly detached from the Tories and wanted clearer leadership on European integration. Anne Applebaum's cool, ironic and cultured commentaries gave a Conservative perspective on political life but rarely offered Tory MPs any comfort about their ultimate irrelevance and doom. The *Standard* served a potentially Labour-voting metropolis, and Labour needed its support to swing the outer London seats in its favour. No paper was more assiduously courted by the Party. 'Tell Max', said Peter Mandelson to an intermediary, 'that hunting and field sports are not going to be a problem.'

The *Daily Express* provided a few crumbs of comfort. Peter Oborne had been a Tory iconoclast on the *Evening Standard*, but as the *Express*'s political editor he felt that the scale of the impending catastrophe was so great that rigorous criticism was otiose. He observed the scene with gallows humour. However, Richard Addis, the editor, was a more ambiguous figure than his predecessor, the effusively loyal Nick Lloyd. Addis had been features editor of the *Daily Mail*. He understood the scale of Tory readers' discontent very well and how it related to circulation. He was alive to the crisis in Britain's institutions and the unusual degree of contempt felt by the British for their politicians – especially Tory ones. He could offer the Conservative party naught for its comfort – especially if he was going to improve circulation. The *Express*, the only newspaper to support the Conservative Government, had a falling circulation, while the *Telegraph*, *Times* and *Mail* were flourishing. Criticizing the Conservative Government from a conservative perspective was good for business, and the British reading public had acquired a taste for turning the knife in the wound.

Meanwhile, the *Sun*, mythologized by the Tories, played a waiting game. Trevor Kavanagh, its urbane political editor, was a revered Westminster figure and could read the signs of the times better than most. The *Sun* was also the one newspaper in Rupert Murdoch's British stable that was programmed to respond immediately to its proprietor's wishes. Blair courted Murdoch, and the paper produced increasingly anti-Tory noises.

The Prime Minister's two most urgent journalistic supporters were to be found in the *Spectator*; its readership was less than 50,000, but it remained a distinctive Tory organ. After the 1992 election, Frank Johnson, later its editor, decided that the Tories had to put up with Major and soldier on, stoically, under his leadership. From 1990 to 1992 he had been so critical and sardonic that Major bracketed him with Heffer. When told during the election that a poll showed the Tories trailing by six points, Major responded that, 'Of those six points, three are the fault of Simon Heffer and the other three are Frank Johnson's fault.' Johnson shared with Peregrine Worsthorne, his former chief at the *Sunday Telegraph*, the media-class desire to subvert an orthodoxy. If the Tories and the country had grown to hate Major, then there was surely a market niche for a defence of Major. Johnson shared with Major a truncated formal education and a South London upbringing. As an autodidact he had learnt much at Maurice Cowling's feet. He appreciated lack of belief and a low tone. Laddishly, the balletomane would stand in the breach as Major's patron.

Bruce Anderson, Johnson's colleague, was Major's biographer and intimate. He stood by him and could do no other, although he was sorely tempted when the evidence of a Tory catastrophe became compelling. Noting the absence of a circle of intellectual souls who could lend lustre to Major's reign and enjoy his patronage, Anderson wondered whether Sebastian Faulks, the novelist, would lend his distinction to the membership of such a group of Majorite academicians. To such sad and fawning fantasies were Major's votaries reduced. Anderson had embraced Tory allegiance because the Tories were good at winning. His biography of Major was really the study of a Party that knew how to win and whose sole interest was in power, its exercise and retention. It combined a Tory distaste for ideas with a Leninist regard for power that came easily to a writer with a leftist 1960s past.

This was not a strong base from which to confront the collective scorn of other Conservative commentators and their readers. Conservative critics of the Government in the media class were self-confident, were sure of what had to be said, and knew how to say it. No Government was more savaged than Major's. The only parallel is with the press treatment of Aberdeen's disastrous coalition in the 1850s and its administrative blunders in the conduct of the Crimean War. The *Daily Mail* and *Daily Express* had trained their guns on Baldwin in the early 1930s, but he only became the object of sustained vituperation as a Prime Minister of appeasement after he left office. Vilification of Neville Chamberlain was a posthumous affair. Eden's agony lasted only a few months and did not affect the Government's fortunes once he had left it. Wilson was convinced that the press was hounding him, but he never suffered the sort of sustained barrage unleashed on Major.

The Prime Minister returned hurt to Downing Street and pulled up the drawbridge. He found it difficult to deal with a journalist or commentator who had criticized him. Although he read the press obsessively, he would not effect *rapprochements*. He had a very high sense of his own worth – the soap-box victor of 1992 would confound them all. The more they dismissed him, the more stubborn he became about staying – however humiliating the circumstances. As he instructed Norman Lamont when the Chancellor discussed resignation with him after the ERM debacle, 'I'm not going to resign, and I don't think you should either.' Or, as he told Blair at the Party Conference in 1996, 'Sorry, Tony, job's taken.' It was the cry of the professional politician.

Number's 10's press office was a ramshackle affair and badly staffed. It offered no sense of direction, and the Parliamentary Party was increasingly on the run. The meanest lobby journalist seemed more important than most backbenchers and many a Minister by the end of these years. All MPs and most Tories were now the pawns of a new media class with the bit between its teeth as it patronized Tories, satirized them, and used them as copy for its writings. The media class was mostly richer, and it was certainly cleverer and more influential, than the members of the Conservative Parliamentary Party. Very few of them wanted to be Members of Parliament. They lacked any reason for restraint. The hunt was on.

The plight of the Tory Parliamentarians was not relieved by any sense of corporate esteem. To sit in the House of Commons had been their high aspiration, but this was the age of the death of Parliament. MPs of all parties were being drawn from a narrower and more homogeneous pool of political apparatchiks. The outcome, the professionalization of politics, created a small and isolated political class. Money was also a problem. During the 1990s growing scrutiny by the press and public increasingly restricted the opportunity to earn money outside Parliament. MPs were turning in upon themselves in the Gothic claustrophobia of Westminster. They earned just about enough to keep them in the middle classes, but were dropping out of sight of their more talented contemporaries.

During the 1990s it became very obvious that high ability in Britain, when it was not scientific, was drawn in one of three directions: the world of the City and finance; that of the law; and the world of the word, of the media class. It did not search for seats in the House of Commons. The personal scandals of the period made politicians look ridiculous, and public scrutiny of private lives was a price few were prepared to pay. Public faces in private places were neither wise nor nice.

Backbench MPs were also becoming increasingly convinced of their own impotence and irrelevance except as a branch of the light entertainment industry. They were remote from Ministers and their advisers at a time when the Major administration was increasingly immersed in government at the expense of politics. Power was slipping away to Brussels and European levels of government in a process that was hardly scrutinized in the House of Commons and its committees. British politics had become a trivial occupation for trivial people.

Moreover, large areas of traditional political life had been depoliticized. The great debates of the Cold War era were over. The West had won, CND had disappeared, liberal capitalism and western democracy were the victors. Labour and the Conservatives no longer fought battles over nationalization, State subsidies and privatization. It might not be the end of history, but it was certainly the end of a particular way of doing politics that had been current in Britain since the rise of Labour in the 1920s.

Conservatives were triumphalist about the Party's role in a motor of history that had driven the Warsaw Pact off the map of Europe. But afterwards they found themselves in a cul-de-sac, deprived of a common foe both at home and in foreign affairs. Technical quarrels about how to run the Private Finance Initiative could hardly fill the yawning gap created by the death of ideological struggle. They fell to their internal Party disputes about Europe with venom and zest partly because there was no other great issue to consume their energies.

The truth of the matter, also, was that there was not enough work to keep a Member of Parliament busy. At 651, and 659 from 1997, there were simply too many of them. As long as he had an efficient secretary, an MP could pass the bulk of his correspondence on to a Minister and his officials with a covering letter. He could then return the official reply to his constituent. Much of Government's traditional work had been hived off to agencies and quangos which by-passed regular parliamentary scrutiny. Some members settled for the life of a grander version of a county councillor, giving interviews on regional television and radio programmes. Scrutiny of legislation on select committees satisfied others.

Most, however, lacked the edge to become campaigners for particular issues. Those who had spent years in responsible jobs suddenly found themselves with time on their hands in the middle of the day – to the advantage of the House of Commons bars. Powerlessness increasingly paraded itself as pomposity. More self-aware Conservative MPs, such as

George Walden in Buckingham and Dudley Fishburn in Kensington, decided that the game was up, announced that they would not stand at the next general election, and opted for a life elsewhere. Other MPs, afflicted by inertia, stayed put, bored, discontented and trapped in the oncoming New Labour headlights.

Labour MPs, meanwhile, were kept in check by the increasing certainty of a Labour Government, the hope of office, and a ruthlessly efficient press and party machine. The Labour Party might be committed to devolving government in the United Kingdom, but in its internal affairs it centralized power remorselessly. It understood that the power of the media class exceeded that of Parliament. Labour stories, phrases and briefings were directed to that newer and more glamorous world. When it took office in May 1997 it continued a policy of distancing itself from Parliament and its workings.

The Conservative Government and the Whips office could no longer play on their MPs' hopes and fears. By this time the pool of ministerial talent on the backbenches was drained. What remained was an army of the excluded, the sacked and the discontented. It was a melancholy prospect.

John Redwood's farouche, fastidious and audacious figure mirrored and contributed to these developments. As the Tory Party's Cassandra, he had the gift of tongues, and paid the price for his prophecy. He had been an uneasy member of a Major Cabinet in which personality loomed larger than policy. The Prime Minister was always aware of the importance of having winged members of his Cabinet – Ministers as damaged goods upon whose loyalty he could rely. There had been many such: Norman Lamont, Jonathan Aitken, John Patten, William Waldegrave – these were Ministers whose worth to a brilliantly Machiavellian mind was that they could be used as pawns against more powerful colleagues and who were, in their wounded condition, personally dependent on the Prime Minister. Redwood's Robespierrist purity was annoying on two counts. It had more than a whiff of self-righteous virtue about it. More important, it failed to provide Major's briefing-machine with grappling-hooks to ensure his dependency and compliance. He was invulnerable. This preternatural purity was the cause both of Redwood's strength and of his weakness as a politician. He simply didn't care what others thought about him. He had had a heart by-pass where modern politics' cult of the personality was concerned.

The child was father to the man. Born in 1951, Redwood was the only child, much adored, of a shoe-shop manageress and a self-taught local accountant in Dover. He was a boy at Kent College, Canterbury, a Methodist-run Direct Grant School which stood somewhere between the local grammar school and the ancestral, if reinvented, glories of The King's School in the Cathedral Close. When his father was made redundant in the recession of the early 1970s, he became the assistant school accountant at King's. Redwood went up to Oxford at the early age of seventeen, met his future wife in his first week as an undergraduate, got a First in Modern History, and was elected to a fellowship of All Souls.

His hatred of the label 'intellectual' was more than a canny politician's recognition that the English despise cleverness. Although Redwood was certainly 'clever', he had none of the intellectual's taste for the disinterested exploration of ideas, and he was not, by university standards, particularly well read. His mind was efficient and devoid of agonizing, while his use of language was clear and direct, albeit flat and mechanistic. All Souls barely left a mark on him. He longed for the world of events and for the Midas-fed dramas of the Stock Exchange rather than the cloistered and fugitive academic virtues. He preferred to emphasize his years as a banker with Rothschilds and in business as Chairman of Norcros plc. The key to Redwood was that he had very simple views expressed in a subtle and original manner. For him intelligence was not so much what you thought as the way that you thought it. A powerful mind was used to articulate convictions which were themselves unexceptional. Hence a view of the history of England that was not so far removed from the stories of the Boys' Own Bumper Book of History. Hence, also, a view of the family and its role, of England and her relations with the continent, of the role of money and how an economy should be run, of the Royal Family and the Queen ('a very wise woman, you know'), of the value of truth and honesty, which made sense to the general run of English people.

He liked to regard these views as part of his 'populism', whereas in fact they were simply commonsensical virtues. It was an over-sophistication on his part to categorize these instincts as 'populist' and to run the risk thereby of appearing calculating.

Redwood once said that he had got to Oxford and All Souls by not being afraid to ask obvious questions. A man less easily intimidated would, indeed, be hard to find. He had married young and, with a politician's capacity for emotional disengagement, had very few close friends. This suited him since he had limited curiosity about other minds, although his sensitivity to minor details of appearance and gesture was extreme. He was a man who noticed such things as a slightly frayed collar, scuffed shoes and soiled cuffs. These details could be used in a Holmesian manner to build up a picture of another's character and temperament.

Redwood's relations with Margaret Thatcher had always been cool, and his credentials to be considered a Thatcherite *avant la lettre* were considerable. Privatization was the undoubted success story of Thatcher's premiership, and it had been Redwood's campaign since the late 1970s. It was not until after the great and unexpected victory of 1983 that she was persuaded, and only then with great difficulty, that privatization could succeed. Redwood's view of Thatcher was that she always depended on advice, and was always good at choosing it. She had served in the Cabinet of Edward Heath, the Tories' most *étatiste* Prime Minister, but she was a brilliantly opportunistic politician in a well-established Tory tradition. She recognized the political opportunities of the late 1970s, and adapted and created her own fifth gospel whose holy writ came to be seen as her own. If the authorized version allowed only one mention of John Redwood in her

memoirs, perhaps that is the price advisers invariably pay in the courts of the
mighty.

Redwood's refusal to play the role of courtier, like Kenneth Clarke's,
though for different reasons, eventually cost them both dear when Thatcher
intervened against them before the third ballot in the June 1997 leadership
election. But the coldness was of long standing. Between 1993 and 1995,
when he was in Cabinet, Redwood had seen her as a destabilizing threat and
ignored her. In 1995 she refused to support him in the first leadership contest.
Between 1995 and 1997 he would visit her office two or three times a year and
return with tales of a woman counting her gold and reliving her past. In the
1997 leadership election he phoned her to protest, having read in the press that
she had seen William Hague on the previous day and that the Hague circle was
claiming that this represented a formal anointing. She replied plaintively that
she was meeting all the leadership candidates and would John Redwood like
to see her? Irritated by her self-regard and avidity for a headline, he refused.
John Redwood, like Norman Tebbit, considered himself to be a better
Thatcherite than Margaret Thatcher. Indeed, he mused, future generations
might ask: was Margaret Thatcher a Thatcherite?

Governments need a political rhetoric. The Thatcher years offered competitive
individualism and an ethic of vigour. In the 1990s the Tories lapsed into *fin-
de-siècle* languor without even any compensating aestheticism. The Prime
Minister assumed many masks. To begin with, he was a European at the heart
of Europe. When that failed, he was a Baldwinesque sentimentalist glorying
in old maids, warm beer, Holy Communion and cricket. He then attempted
self-definition as a centre-right politician. At the end he was a one-nation Tory
who had cut himself loose from all Party connections. In one of his last press
conferences on the eve of the general election, he wished to be seen as a
lonely, heroic figure battling for Britain's interests in a cruel international
arena. He was the Prime Minister whose hands could not be tied without
imperilling an undefined, vague national interest. When, in 1957, Aneurin
Bevan had inveighed against being sent naked into a conference chamber,
there were still issues of war and peace to be discussed. By April 1997 all
matters relevant to the European currency had already been settled and
negotiated. The Major posture was a sham.

Why could the Tories not produce language that made sense to the British
people? How and why was it that a once powerful set of political beliefs was
reduced to a vacuous, off-stage noise in British life?

The decline and fall of political parties raise questions almost as complex
as the decline and fall of once great countries and empires. Cavafy described
in his poem 'Waiting for the Barbarians' how those barbarians at the gates had
been 'a kind of solution' because the threat had kept the imperial city and its
defenders on their toes, alert and enquiring without succumbing to
introspection and gloom. Vigorous parties, like purposeful countries, know
how to respond creatively to a threat. For the Tories the threat at the gate in the

1990s was that times had changed, that the British had been changed by them, and that the Party imagined itself immune to the unimaginable touch of time.

Questions of identity, individual, institutional and national, had suddenly become politically important in a new age of anxiety. The British, it seemed, wanted both more and less individual freedom. They liked the economic fruits of chic designer-capitalism, lower taxation and the anti-authoritarian scepticism of advanced societies. They disliked Tories who got in the way of those new freedoms, who intervened, taxed, regulated, and then preached.

But in other areas they thought that individualism was no longer enough. The age was becoming keener on solidarity and communities. When the Tories kept to their old ways and preached the vigorous virtues they were damned quite as rigorously as when they intervened. Their market systems, for example, were thought to be responsible for a bloated administrative system in the NHS which rewarded the middle manager in a Montego dispro- portionately. The British were also disturbed by the fact that their rates of divorce and family breakdown were the highest in western Europe. As marriages waned, so friendship became more important and its meaning widely discussed as the corrective, or complement, to individualism.

In the general confusion, one thing was clear. The Tories had no answers for this awkward age. Like clumsy relatives, they intervened and turned up when they were not wanted, and had nothing to contribute when they were expected. They were either intrusive or absent, their own insecurity mirroring that of the age and masked all too effectively by arrogance and remoteness. Beyond the gates, the electorate needed answers. Behind the gates, the Tories responded with a failure of will, a shallowness of thought and a poverty of imagination. The stage was set for battle.

DARK VICTORY

1992 to 1995

THROUGH GRITTED teeth, Britain elected a Tory Government in April 1992. The Government's first mistake was to view that general election as a great victory won in the shadow of a recession. The truth was that they had been bought on approval and would have to keep their promises. Instead, hubris and paranoia came to predominate.

The Tories polled 14.1 million votes, the largest number ever cast for a party in a general election. But it was a dark and ambiguous victory. The Tories' overall majority of 101 slipped to 21, while their share of the vote fell marginally, from 42.3 to 41.9 per cent, their fourth lowest percentage since 1945. In the 1950s, the Conservatives had won elections with 48 to 50 per cent of the vote, and in 1970 they had taken 46.5 per cent. In 1992, their fourth successive victory was achieved with a smaller share of the vote than in any of the three previous elections.

Labour certainly performed badly. Its 34.4 per cent represented a swing of only 1.9 per cent from the Conservatives to Labour. However, it did well in terms of the number of seats it gained. The real lesson of the election was how well Labour performed in the marginal constituencies. In the Conservative–Labour marginals the average swing to Labour was 3.5 per cent, almost double the national average. The Conservative victory was based on their success in the most closely fought constituencies. They won twenty-one of the thirty-nine seats with majorities of less than one thousand. Their overall majority was twenty-one – but they won their eleven most marginal seats with majorities of under 600. Fewer than three thousand voters had enabled John Major to carry on as Prime Minister at the head of a Government with an overall majority. In the 1992 Parliament Labour's concern with marginal seats was understandably obsessive.

The opinion polls showed an average 1.3 per cent Labour lead, as opposed to the eventual Conservative lead of 7.5 per cent on polling day. The polls' humiliation became part of the Tories' triumphalist croak. However, the Tories' cocksure attitudes obscured an important point. Although the pollsters got the percentage shares of the vote wrong, their prediction of an electoral dead-heat was not that far off. The mistakes in sampling that over-represented the poor and under-represented the professional classes would be corrected over the next five years. The pollsters would ask fewer questions in shopping centres in the afternoon and do more telephone polling.

The council election results that followed a month later ratified the victory, with Labour losing 300 seats and the Conservative gaining 200. But by late September, in the aftermath of Black Wednesday on the 16th of September and the Government's enforced withdrawal from the European Exchange Rate Mechanism, the Government's support had fallen to 30 per cent in the polls. Authority was never regained. How and why did this Government fall like Lucifer?

The rock of Maastricht and the cross of the Exchange Rate Mechanism cast a long collective shadow over the Tories. The Maastricht Treaty was the result of a two-day Inter-Governmental Conference held in the Dutch city on the 9th and 10th of December 1991. After it had been signed by the Heads of Government, the Treaty embarked on a sometimes perilous path of parliamentary and popular scrutiny in the member States before its ratification.

Maastricht was a further development of the principle of a more perfect union that had inspired the original Treaty of Rome. It was a federalizing document in the sense that it presupposed an accretion of power at the centre which could then be delegated to subordinate levels. The principle of 'subsidiarity' was enshrined in the Treaty and stated that action should only be taken at Community level if the objective could not be achieved at national level. However, this was only a principle, and not a legal concept, and it could not be subjected to a legal interpretation.

Nonetheless, the new 'European Union' that emerged from Maastricht was unquestionably a legal entity consisting of the institutions of the old European Community and the two 'inter-governmental pillars', which dealt with foreign policy and home affairs. To the original Treaty of Rome, machinery was now added to formulate a common European foreign policy and to systematize the foreign policy consultations that had grown up among the member States. For the first time, therefore, domestic and foreign policy were brought within a common European ambit. The two 'pillars' were created to meet British objections to the enlargement of the powers of the old Community's institutions. Home affairs and foreign affairs were only to be discussed at inter-governmental level.

At the heart of the Treaty lay the project of Economic and Monetary Union (EMU), a scheme from which Britain had already secured her exemption. All previous European currencies had reflected a pre-existing political unity at national, supra-national or imperial level. After all, currencies need the backing of a Government. Now a currency was to be born, one of whose objects was to be the creation of political unity.

The Social Chapter had long been an object of Conservative suspicion. It emerged from a European tradition of social thought that stressed workers' rights as members of associations and proposed extensive rights for trades unions of negotiation, representation and association. Britain's second exemption applied to this Chapter which was, therefore, excluded from the draft Treaty, while the other member States signed and proceeded with the implementation of its principles.

British negotiators also pressed hard for a measure, Article 171, enabling the Union to fine countries when the European Court of Justice had adjudicated against them. Only later, when storms were aroused by some of the Court's political rulings, did the Government realize that Article 171 could be used against its own interests. For Conservative negotiators, it seemed, even victories could turn into a subtle form of defeat.

Maastricht had not only created a new legal entity called the European Union. It had also given birth to the concept of 'Citizenship of the Union'. European people were now citizens with legal rights by virtue of that citizenship. For Europeans, the children of Hellas, it was another step on the Carolingian road.

The Exchange Rate Mechanism (ERM), which Britain entered in October 1990, was the precursor of the Single Currency project. The mechanism's aim was to link, and thereby stabilize, the value of European currencies. Britain chose to enter at a rate of 2.95 Deutschmarks to the pound to fulfil what was widely described at the time as a 'golden scenario' of falling interest rates, lowered inflation and increased economic growth. An external 'mechanism' replaced British policy as the preferred route to the golden goals.

For the British Government, the ERM's 'discipline' was an essential tool in achieving the Single Currency's convergence criteria as adumbrated at Maastricht. Later, defenders of the system maintained that the system had collapsed because the rate adopted was the 'wrong' one. But, in attempting to fix the necessarily fluid, the ERM had failed to grasp the nature of money and the operation of markets. There could only be the rate which was 'right' for a particular day in currency markets, and a rate fixed in marmoreal solidity was a mechanistic will o' the wisp.

Entry into the ERM had been prefigured by Chancellor Lawson's policy of shadowing the Deutschmark at a level of about 3 Deutschmarks to the pound. Sterling was a buoyant currency in the late 1980s, and its natural tendency was to rise against the Deutschmark and above the ideal, shadowed, level. 'Stabilizing' the currency, therefore and perversely, produced artificially low interest rates. Central banks sold pounds and bought Deutschmarks in order to fight the market's natural tendency. The Bank of England's creation of more pounds added to the money supply. Within the banking system these extra pounds, sold and created, expanded the volume of credit. The consequent inflationary worries led to a rise in interest rates which, by the logic of the infernal circle or of the mechanism's curse, led to increased speculative buying of the currency. This in turn led to the need for more pounds to be printed by the Bank as the battle to keep the pound down continued. The result of this monetary expansion was that inflation rose to 6 per cent by the end of 1988 and to 10 per cent by the end of 1990.

Thus, when Britain entered the ERM it was slipping into a recession caused by the very policy that had been preparing its economy for that entry. If, previously, the pound's tendency had been to rise against the Deutschmark, now it wanted to fall. Whereas in the past the Government's actions had sought to suppress a natural upward tendency by artificial means, now it wanted to boost a natural downward tendency by equally artificial means. This meant high rates of interest that prolonged the recession but were designed to promote speculative buying of the pound. By a vicious twist of the monetary tail, the German economy to whose fortunes Britain had linked herself was expanding in the wake of reunification and was tolerant of high interest rates.

Perhaps, as Margaret Thatcher said in the summer of 1992, there was no such thing as Majorism, but there was a Prime Minister with a personal devotion to both the Treaty and the ERM. Early signs were ominous. On the 21st of May twenty-two Conservative MPs voted against the Second Reading of the Bill ratifying the Maastricht Treaty. They, and others, were further emboldened by the first Danish referendum on the 2nd of June, which went against the Treaty, and by the French decision to hold a referendum. On the 3rd and 4th, almost one hundred Tory MPs signed a motion urging a fresh start to European negotiations. Chris Patten, the former Conservative Party Chairman who, though no longer in Parliament, was still a Major confidant, urged the Prime Minister to proceed with the Bill. He saw that to delay would be fatal. Despite this advice, the Prime Minister took fright and suspended the Committee Stage of the Bill.

As Chancellor, Major had taken Britain into the Exchange Rate Mechanism in 1990. The policy had its successes. By the summer of 1992 interest rates were down from 15 to 10 per cent, and inflation had fallen from 11 to 4 per cent. But the rate of parity with the Deutschmark stood unreasonably high at 2.95. Britain was paying the price for the economic strains of German reunification and the need to keep German interest rates at a high level. All Major's talk that summer was of a strong pound – he wanted the pound to be the strongest currency in Europe. His tone suggested that he did not understand how the ERM worked, why it was harming British businesses and mortgages, and why its role was to prepare for the Single Currency. Politicians live in the shadow of yesterday. The post-war political commitment to full employment resulted from harrowing memories of mass unemployment in the 1930s. Similarly, Major was haunted by memories of British inflation in the 1970s. He saw the ERM as an anti-inflationary mechanism. But he was fighting yesterday's battles with a weapon that formed part of the advance guard of the Single Currency.

Major's retrospective defence would be that he thought the mechanism would be a flexible system with wide bands within which devaluation would be possible. He blamed the German Government for failing to support him in his hour of need. Chancellor Kohl and his ministers had told Major and his Chancellor, Norman Lamont, that they could not lower interest rates because monetary policy was a matter for the Bundesbank – their central bank was independent and they exercised no political control over it. But the idea of an independent central bank immune to political pressure was as much of a chimera in Germany as in any democratic country. Germany's economic difficulties had been created by the Bundesbank's decision to establish a 1:1 rate of parity for the Deutschmark and the Ostmark, the currency of the former East German state, and politics, not economics, had dictated that decision.

When speculators looked at Britain's three million unemployed and thousands of bankrupt businesses that would never return, they concluded that the Government could not possibly continue in this vein. They decided that the policy would have to change – and that they would make money out of that change. Britain would have to withdraw from the ERM, and the thorns of high interest-rates would have to be cut down to stop them choking British business. A wave of selling of pounds on the global foreign exchange markets started on Tuesday the 15th of September, with the pound falling below the lowest permitted level of 2.77 Deutschmarks in New York. Speculators were moving away from the Italian lira, after its devaluation, and closing in on the pound for another kill. The speculative tornado was given an additional whirl by the intimation that same Tuesday by Helmut Schlesinger, President of the Bundesbank, that the pound was over-valued. Britain's interest-rate rises were ineffectual attempts to woo the speculators back into buying sterling. But sterling would be the more valuable to the speculator when it had been devalued by his own activity.

On the 10th of September Major had declared in Glasgow that, 'The soft option, the devaluer's option, the deflationary option, would be a betrayal of our future.' He was also adamant, both in public and in private, that there was no possibility of withdrawing from the ERM. Following the disastrous events of the 15th, the Government's first reaction the next day was to increase interest rates by 2 per cent with effect from 11 a.m. Speculators continued to sell sterling in the certainty of an imminent devaluation. Major over-ruled Lamont's advice that British membership be suspended and accepted the view of Hurd, Clarke and Heseltine that interest rates should be increased a second time, to 15 per cent. But when that failed, Britain's membership of the ERM was suspended. The markets had had their revenge on the conventional wisdom that underpinned the Mechanism. Lamont discussed resignation with Major, who was adamant that neither of them should go. Major would not apologize for the collapse of a policy that just six months before had been described in his party manifesto as 'central to our counter-inflation discipline'.

The Tories endured a disastrous Party Conference in October. Norman Tebbit inflamed populist passions with a prolonged anti-European rant. Douglas Hurd delivered European sermonettes on how the Corn Laws had divided the Party, and Margaret Thatcher published an article in the *European* urging a referendum. Major's talk of 'cold, clear-eyed calculation of Britain's national interests' which were 'first, last and always' seemed empty and posturing. Announcements about improved motorway facilities and wash-rooms added to the impression of a Prime Minister whose habitat was another planet. The press began to publish stories about how he had lost his grip on Black Wednesday and had gone absent without leave in the rabbit warren of Admiralty House, his temporary home while Number 10 was being redecorated.

The following week Michael Heseltine announced a pit closure programme. Thirty pits and 30,000 jobs would go. Many of those affected were members of the Union of Democratic Mineworkers who had supported the Conservative Government in its previous battles. Faced with an enormously hostile public reaction, Heseltine had to capitulate – twenty-one pits would get a full review and Heseltine lost his reputation for an infallible political touch.

Haunted by his Party Conference and attempting to shore up his position, on the 29th of October John Major was telling the 1922 Committee of backbenchers that he was the Cabinet's 'greatest Euro-sceptic'. He knew that the Commons debate on the motion to allow progress to resume on the Maastricht Bill, fixed for the 4th of November, would be difficult. To be sure of winning Major had to make an important concession and agree to delay the Bill's Third Reading. Even so, the Government's majority fell to just three. Among the 316 MPs voting against the Government were twenty-six Conservatives, and a further seven abstained.

A few days afterwards, on the 9th, the judicial inquiry chaired by Mr Justice Scott into the arms to Iraq affair started. This investigated whether Ministers had connived at the infringement of the Government's own official guidelines on arms exports. In due course Major and several other Cabinet Ministers would be summoned before it to account for the actions of the Thatcher Government. The collapse of the Matrix–Churchill trial had opened the possibility that Government Ministers were ready to send innocent men to jail. Throughout his premiership, Major's instict for procrastination led to the appointment of inquiries and commissions which stopped him having to take immediate action but ended in aggravating the original problem.

Within its first few months the Government had established its style – irresolution punctuated by stubbornness. This reflected the Prime Minister's own character. Personality was always a more important fact about John Major than policy. He began his premiership advertising his intention to create a classless society, but sensitivity about class, education and intelligence remained his hallmark.

What kind of man, then, was the Prime Minister, whose personality became so indelibly stamped on his Party and on the Government he led?

John Major's upper-artisan, lower-bourgeois background shared the same social geography as John Redwood's. It was a world in which it mattered enormously whether you were salaried or waged, where social insecurity hung around the lounge, and where origins were never far below the surface. It was the world of Mr Polly and Mr Pooter. Both Major and John Redwood shared a resentful fastidiousness about their backgrounds. Major, *faute de mieux* came to build Coldharbour Lane, Brixton, into an essential feature of his prime ministership. Redwood would wince with an almost physical pain when reading or listening to Major's speeches on the subject. The whole issue operated at far too deep and discordant a level.

Major in conversation sounded exactly the same as Major in a formal speech. There were the same laboured syntax and ponderous circumlocutions that combined to produce the impression of a diligent and upwardly mobile subject of the King Emperor who had learnt his English in a colony during the last years of imperial rule.

Major's concern with his appearance amounted to an obsession remarkable even in the age of media politics. Locked away with a make-up girl for an inordinate amount of time before he was ready to face the cameras, he would pay special attention to his hair, lovingly combing every greying strand into place before the final application of spray. The feature he least liked about his appearance was his hands. They might have been useful for a batsman, but they had aged into large, misshapen, liver-spotted protuberances with a liberal endowment of active follicles.

Once physically prepared to face the cameras, he would rehearse his lines, and often took the trouble to write them down on a sheet of paper which would then go into his breast pocket. After the interview he would check with his aides whether he had said what he intended.

Major's political gifts could be seen at their best when he visited hospitals and schools. He might have been 'extraordinary in his ordinariness', as Redwood once summed him up, but no Conservative politician was better at the political art of the handshake, the gesture, the direct look in the eye solicitous of friendship and support. Some such reasoning underlined the final desperate throw of the electoral dice in April 1997 when he contemplated asking the British people to look in his eyes and trust him.

Major had decided that the press was his greatest problem. Away from London, when a difficult political story was breaking, he would have the first editions of the London papers delivered to him before going to bed. The following morning he would be busy devouring the latest editions of the same papers. He was the textual scholar of the political story, adept at discovering its source among leaky Cabinet colleagues on the basis of the internal evidence and assiduous in recording different nuances of treatment as the story appeared in different papers and successive editions. The self-consciously important intervention of the press office became a customary sight at official dinners. A breathless report of the 10 p.m. news headlines would be intoned into the Prime Ministerial ear. The more self-conscious kind of journalist with a determinedly low view of his own trade found the Prime Minister's veneration for its activities astonishing.

David Evans, the self-consciously outrageous multi-millionaire Cockney MP for Welwyn, was John Redwood's Parliamentary Private Secretary (PPS). A fine teaser of the Prime Minister, Evans worried as well as amused an increasingly perturbed Redwood. Once Evans was waylaid by Major in Downing Street as he was delivering a letter and found himself invited to join the Prime Minister for dinner in the tenebrous presence of Graham Bright, his

PPS. In the House of Commons, Bright hovered outside the Members Dining Room, and reported that they could not possibly go in because the only places available were next to ones occupied by Michael Heseltine and the admirers of that son of mercantile Swansea. After some hesitation and negotiation the Prime Ministerial party found somewhere to sit, and a familiar Major litany of woe started. He would have to do at least two more red boxes that evening. He was exhausted and nobody knew how hard he had to work. 'Why don't you get someone else to do all that reading for you?' suggested Evans mischievously. 'You're Prime Minister and our leader – you don't need to do all that reading.' 'Isn't that sad?' he remarked, telling his story later. Perhaps it was 'sad' in the contemporary ironic sense as well as in the traditional one.

John Major enjoyed government. He also delighted in telling his listeners how necessarily difficult government was. 'You know,' he scolded his Party Conference in 1994, 'running a country isn't like walking down a road' – an original if bizarre analogy. Who, after all, had said that it was? He exuded a well-crafted melancholia about the whole business in a way calculated to generate sympathy. Major liked administrative stability and order. Whereas most politicians live with risk, Major's temperament was more akin to that of the civil servant. Equipped with a different education, he could have become quite a successful one.

Rather like William Hague, his successor as Party leader, he enjoyed a successful working relationship with the higher Civil Service because he had no fundamental objections to the structure and extent of government in Britain. The much-ridiculed Citizen's Charter was a characteristic Major innovation. Limp-wristed and ineffectual, it sought to combat administrative sclerosis by administrative stratagems.

Politically, it suited Major to be considered a victim of the Clarke–Heseltine axis, but that axis was often more apparent than real. There were differences in the attitudes of the two men. Moreover, for strategic reasons Major often presented himself as the victim of the two big political mastodons when the going got tough. When he talked, for example, of being the 'biggest Euro-sceptic of them all', when he described the project of Monetary Union as having 'all the quaintness and potency of a rain dance', he wished to signal a wealth of inner intentions frustrated by his senior colleagues.

John Major's appointment of Kenneth Clarke as Chancellor in 1993 proved a self-imposed burden. No change of economic policy would now be possible. The Prime Minister was happy to present himself as his Chancellor's prisoner, and he was happy to lament his condition, as he did to John Redwood on the Wednesday morning before he resigned the Party leadership in June 1995. To different audiences, he expressed varying degrees of frustration and resentment. In a *New Yorker* interview in December 1996 he anticipated a Britain that had already entered the Single European Currency and imagined himself as a Chancellor deprived of the power to set interest rates and compelled to follow the policy of a European central bank. He wished to be seen as the victim of a malign fate, fortune's fool who would do things past the power of human telling if only he could be freed of his turbulent colleagues. But the central economic strategy was that of the man himself, the First Lord of the Treasury, and it suited him to have a Chancellor whom he could blame.

It seemed strange to find a British Prime Minister envisaging himself as Chancellor and lamenting a loss of power against which he could already have set himself. Perhaps it was the result of a lifetime's adaptability derived from playing so many roles that led him to think naturally in this way. None the less, the intention was clear. Here, late in the day, was a man Euro-sceptics could do business with. The reality, however, was that he always found them infuriating and interpreted their hostility as personal offence. Indeed, so it became with time and particularly under the influence of Sir George Gardiner, the Prince Yusupov of the No Turning Back Group, a band of of MPs mired in the Thatcherite certainties of the 1980s, the 'golden age that never was', in Major's words.

Major never regarded EMU as a political and constitutional matter for serious Europeans and Euro-sceptics alike. He thought of it as an issue that could be settled on a technical cost-benefit analysis. On the issue of the survival of the British pound he offered an unconvincing agnosticism. His was the implausible middle way – the *via media* of Archbishop Cranmer – and, like the Archbishop, he found himself stranded on the high seas of doctrine. On the one hand there was John Redwood with a belief in the 'real presence' of the pound. On the other was Ted Heath with his doctrine of the 'real absence' of the pound. For Major, the balance of advantage and of disadvantage might vary according to Britain's position on the economic cycle, but the analysis would always be reduced to benefits to imports and exports rather than Britain's political independence.

Major laboured consciously in the shadow of a mighty predecessor. He soon moved out of the Prime Minister's study in Number 10, a room too closely associated with memories of Margaret Thatcher, and used the Cabinet Room for meetings with individual Ministers. These he avoided as much as he could, and, when compelled to hold them, he invariably evaded the frank discussion of political differences. He was also nervous when Cabinet colleagues attracted publicity of any kind.

Both the central Government machine at Number 10 and Conservative Central Office were there to serve the Prime Minister, but also to ensure that no other ministerial speeches should dim the effulgence of that star. Drafts of speeches circulated endlessly between Number 10 and ministerial Private Offices, with instructions to make the language less vivid. This was a Government that had become frightened of its own shadow.

Major's immediate circle of friends and allies contained few Cabinet Ministers. Norman Lamont had organized his leadership campaign in 1990 but the gloss on that friendship was peeling away very quickly in the winter of 1992–93. The Prime Minister was not an intimate of Kenneth Clarke, and he only became close to Michael Heseltine once he bound that tempestuous figure to him with hoops of steel in 1995. As Leader of the Lords and benign fixer of Government business, John Wakeham proved to be a Third Eleven version of William Whitelaw. Michael Howard's leadership ambitions made Major wary, but he was useful as a link to the right wing, a role that earned him the resentment of Portillo and Lilley and, later, of Redwood too. Relations with John MacGregor and Malcolm Rifkind, and also with John Gummer – the inexplicable survivor – were correct rather than warm. David Hunt's effusive tone sounded insincere; he had, after all, voted for Michael Heseltine in 1990. In Cabinet his solicitous warmth displayed itself by congratulating Major on his recent statements. These, he suggested, should be circulated in all their limpid purity and political vigour to Cabinet Ministers. Then, 'Prime Minister, we can all use your words and refer to them.' Discreet scoffing seemed in order.

While never close, relations with John Patten, at Education, deteriorated rapidly between 1992 and his sacking in 1994. William Waldegrave was thought to be self-consciously superior and was demoted from Health to be Chancellor of the Duchy of Lancaster with responsibility for the Citizen's Charter. Patrick Mayhew and Douglas Hurd were of an older generation and, though not threats, were not cronies either. Tony Newton's greyness rivalled that of Major himself, and his effective chairmanship of Cabinet Committees earned him the Prime Minister's approval. Number 10 increasingly smiled on Ian Lang as Scottish Secretary and on Virginia Bottomley, who was no political threat to Major and displayed an ostentatious and gushing loyalty to the last. Gillian Shephard started as an East Anglian ally but evolved into a Major-sceptic as the Parliament progressed.

David Mellor was a genuine Major crony, but in September 1992 was forced out of the Department of National Heritage, the office created for him, following allegations that a Palestinian friend had paid travel expenses. It was the first of many such ministerial indignities. However, Mellor continued to be publicly identified with the Government. He would not go quietly into the political night and his re-emergence at critical times in support of the Government on television and radio proved to be an embarrassment. Richard Ryder, the Chief Whip, professed himself to be in the job he wanted to do more than any other. He was part of Major's inner circle, but the Prime Minister's desire to be his own Chief Whip led to a cooling of relations. Norman Fowler, recalled to the colours as Party Chairman, became one of the most loathed of Party figures as he justified the unjustifiable on a daily basis.

Compared with some early Thatcher Cabinets, this was not a Cabinet of any great intellectual capacity. The low mental voltage did not improve in the Government's middle ranks, where some vigorous Major loyalists were to be found. Graham Bright, whose bulky frame belied his chairmanship of a dietary foods company, was a representative figure as the Prime Minister's PPS. Robert Atkins, a former Rank Xerox salesman, was Minister of State at the Northern Ireland office. Baroness Blatch proved to be an important ally as

Minister of State at Education when the Prime Minister detached his support
from John Patten. But perhaps the Prime Minister's closest ally was the
teetotal and chain-smoking Tristan Garel-Jones.

Garel-Jones, Thatcher's Deputy Chief Whip and Major's Minister of State
for Europe at the Foreign Office and, later, shadowy backbench informer,
amused some with the lowness of mind of a politician's politician and a
Machiavellianism that was too obvious to carry conviction. He was the most
important Welsh politician of his generation, and he enjoyed eavesdropping
on Welsh Labour MPs conversing in their native tongue in ignorance of the
extent of his understanding. When he discovered someone who came from his
area of Carmarthenshire, his English mask would drop as he leant forward
threateningly and asked the classic question of the village politician: *'Beth
ydyw enw bedydd dy fam?'* ('What is your mother's maiden name?').

Garel-Jones lacked uplift and thought most political preaching was cant.
Politics was about jobs, about who was in and who was out. He would never
be a Redwood ally. Indeed, he had been a sworn enemy ever since the two had
quarrelled in the tea-room of the House of Commons on the question of losses
at Lloyd's. Redwood thought that anyone who signed up to unlimited liability
was a fool and advertised his own wisdom in these matters. Garel-Jones, who
had lost substantial amounts as a Lloyd's Name, told him that he was being
self-righteous. As a Welshman and ex-Whip he disliked Redwood's
appointment in 1993 as Secretary of State, and dubbed him JV – 'Just
Visiting'. His scowl would assume an extra twist when he had to walk past the
Redwood-occupied Gwydyr House, the eighteenth-century building that
served as the London headquarters of the Welsh Office.

Garel-Jones shared with Bruce Anderson, Major's vigorous apologist and
biographer, a Stalky and Co. view of political life. Anderson's journalism
lovingly sentimentalized the Whips Office as a re-creation of the male
camaraderie of the officers' mess and the boys' dormitory. Belonging was
important and survival was all in a view of life that kept loneliness at bay and
justified hatred of the outsider. Anderson particularly admired the methods
used by Michael Cocks, the Labour Chief Whip from 1976 to 1979. Cocks'
tales of his methods of dealing with the rebellious involved, in Anderson's
telling, a repetition of f...s well into double figures in less than five minutes.
Redwood once found himself the enforced listener to these tales when he
stopped his car and gave Anderson a lift up Whitehall. The Scotch-Irish
thinker seized the opportunity to explain how the Prime Minister should deal
with rebellious Euro-sceptic MPs – threatening to expose the sexual
indiscretions of some of them would soon bring them to their senses. 'It
wasn't even as if it was after lunch,' said a visibly shaken Redwood
afterwards.

The early Major years were the high noon of Garel-Jones' influence. As a
new MP (both were first elected in 1979), he had detected the origins of
greatness in Major when Major had come to him and said that all his cleverer
contemporaries, William Waldegrave, John Patten and Chris Patten, were

writing pamphlets and articles. What should he do? Garel-Jones's advice was
to remain silent, to write and say nothing that might incriminate him, to
remain free of interesting thoughts so that he could rise David Frost-like
without a trace. Now, having risen, Major needed a European policy,
confronted as he was by ultras on both sides, by a soggy mass who did not
know what to think but were used to a Prime Minister who told them how to
use their brain cells, and by an American President who, in so far as he gave
a damn, thought a European Federation was a good idea.

In Number 10, Major's closest ally was Sarah Hogg, the former *Times* and
Independent economics journalist whom he appointed as head of the Policy
Unit in 1990. (The Unit was the successor to Ted Heath's Central Policy
Review Staff, and its members were normally appointed from outside the
Civil Service.) Sarah Hogg proved to be the most important defender of the
ERM in Government circles and shored up Major's faith in it. Sceptics now
rejoiced in the revenge of the markets on that flawed mechanism and pointed
out that the saga of the Single Currency should be seen as a plot that had
started with Britain's enforced entry into the ERM. Conventional opinion, led
by the CBI, big business, the Foreign Office and the Treasury, had all been in
favour. Like so much conventional opinion, it was refuted by the logic of
events. Redwood was fortunate that he was not a Cabinet member in autumn
1992 – he did not have to defend the policy and account for the Government's
continuance in office despite its collapse.

There were, moreover, other objections to Hogg. She deflected the Policy
Unit from its long-term strategic function. Together with other members of the
Unit, she briefed the press and intervened in day-to-day administration. She
was an incorrigible meddler and sought to manage news when she should
have been raising her sights to the policy peaks.

As a speechwriter in the Policy Unit, Nick True, a former Byzantine
scholar, struggled and failed to find a resonant voice and a persuasive rhetoric
for the Prime Minister. Major embarked on his British heritage trail at the
Carlton Club on the 3rd of February 1993. The Britain he now praised was a
land of Rotary Clubs and meals on wheels. His politics, he claimed, had an
ear for history and an eye for place. On the 22nd of April came his invocation
of the country of long shadows on county grounds, warm beer, invincible
green suburbs, dog-lovers and pools-fillers. The rhetoric failed because it was
implausible. The political background was not one of Baldwinesque old
maids cycling to Holy Communion. What the public saw in the winter of
1992–93, as the full political implications of the ERM's collapse developed,
were cross Ministers, a public spending borrowing requirement ballooning to
a projected £50 billion, and a return of parliamentary aggression on Europe.

What they did not see was the true range of Cabinet enmities. Shephard
was still agitated by Heseltine, whose precipitate announcement of pit
closures had cut across her brief as Employment Secretary. She became still
more enraged when the Prime Minister, without consulting her, publicly
encouraged workfare projects in which the unemployed would have to work

for their benefits. The Tomlinson Report on London's hospitals advocated the closure of Barts Hospital, and the closure of Rosyth and Devonport dockyards was announced. The Government was attacking the institutional loyalties of some of its most important core supporters.

The Prime Minister's own mind was increasingly opaque. On the 4th of March the *Independent* ran an interview in which he said that in the 1980s he had opposed the emphasis on service-sector industries at the expense of manufacturing. In the House of Commons he denied having said any such thing and accused Andrew Marr, the paper's virtuous political correspondent, of lying.

Norman Lamont's Budget, delivered on the 16th of March, was a deadly blow to the coalition of interests represented by Margaret Thatcher. He introduced higher National Insurance contributions, restricted mortgage tax relief, and introduced VAT on domestic fuel at 8 per cent from April 1994 and 17.5 per cent from 1995. It was the first time that the British public could accuse John Major of lying, for during the general election campaign he had said that he had no plans, nor was there any need, to extend VAT. The Thatcher coalition was outraged.

Margaret Thatcher had taught the Tories that politics must be about interests, their cultivation and appeasement. Labour's interest group, the trades unions, had destroyed the 1974–79 Government. The Tories under Thatcher cultivated other interest groups: home-owners, and especially first-time buyers; pensioners; small businessmen, entrepreneurs and the self-employed. The Tories basked in the glow of their approbation. A new coalition had been formed to underpin a hegemony. Astute Tories have always known that there is a natural British majority against them, formed out of the Welsh, the Scots, the poor who are assumed not to vote, the public-sector middle classes, residual socialists and Liberal Democrats. They have had to survive by the politics of guile. Thatcher gave the Tories a new coalition and a new justification for office.

The Conservative political dominance of the twentieth century is illusory. It has in truth been the social democratic century. From the mid-1890s onwards, the new Liberalism prepared the ground for the Liberal victory of 1905–06 in a way that strikingly anticipated New Labour in the mid-1990s. The Liberal-dominated wartime coalition continued the work of state expansion and bureaucratic extension. In the inter-war years Baldwin's Tory Party stood for appeasement with organized labour. Where Thatcher's new coalition refused to accept the lines of engagement and wished to evangelize the old working-class vote, Baldwin's Tories accepted the demarcation zone and parleyed on the basis of a conceded battleground. From 1940 onwards Churchill's wartime coalition brought about a massive extension of Government control over individual lives and a systematic economic organi-zation that prepared the British people for the Labour victory of 1945 and the nationalization of assets. Subsequently Rab Butler and Harold Macmillan in the 1950s, and Edward Heath in the 1960s and 1970s, maintained the Tories' dominant strand of liberal democracy.

Thatcher's new coalition was a long time arriving. The 1979–83 Parliament was a barren period characterized by wet–dry divisions and by the ultimately successful reforms of the trades unions. The victory of 1987 was dissipated almost as soon as it arrived, as the European issue loomed ever larger and the recession deepened. Thatcher found herself in a minority of two in her own Cabinet, and then of one after Nicholas Ridley's resignation in 1990. Against this background the high summer of 1983–87 seems exceptional or eccentric. Until 1995 it was a finely balanced question whether history would judge Margaret Thatcher or Edward Heath as the more influential Conservative Prime Minister, the one whose work would last longer. By 1998 there was little doubt that it was Heath, the European integrationist and free-market sceptic, who had the closest grasp of reality and the more prophetic understanding of Britain's future role.

Norman Lamont's and Kenneth Clarke's budgets in 1993 and 1994 outraged every element of the Thatcher coalition. Coming relatively early in the administration, it was hoped that the medicine would be swallowed quickly and forgotten, but the first major recession to hit London and the south-east was remembered and attributed to inept economic management. The Tories may not ever have been loved or liked, but they were thought to be good guardians of tills. That reputation was lost on the hearths of thousands of neo-Georgian housing estates. The Tories had forsaken their constituency.

The Tories' Maastricht agony seemed endless in the spring of 1993. The Committee Stage that followed the Second Reading lasted from the 13th of January until the 22nd of April. A defeat on the 8th of March on the methods of electing the Committee of the Regions made an additional stage, the Report, necessary so that the Government could have the defeat reversed by the Commons as a whole. The Government was also forced to concede a debate on two Labour amendments relating to the Social Chapter. This debate would now take place after the completion of the Bill.

The Third Reading took place on the 20th of May, following the Danes' eventual 'yes' vote four days earlier. The Government won by 292 to 112 votes, with forty-six Tory MPs rebelling. In the House of Lords Thatcher claimed that she would never have signed the Maastricht Treaty. On the 22nd of July came the vote on the first Labour amendment preventing the Treaty being ratified without the Social Chapter. The result was a tie, with 317 votes for and against. Following constitutional tradition, the Speaker voted with the Government. However, the second amendment, simply approving the opt-out from the Social Chapter, was lost by 324 votes to 316, with twenty-six Tories voting against their Government. So great was their hatred of the European legislation that they were prepared to vote tactically with Labour on the incorporation of the Social Chapter, in which they did not believe. When the Prime Minister called a confidence vote the following day, the Government won by a comfortable majority of forty.

John Major had broken his party. The humiliations and the tactics required

to push the Maastricht Bill through the House of Commons caused
Conservative self-disgust. The Bill went against the grain of Conservative
convictions and was only imposed by bullying and threats.

How to deal with the consequences of Maastricht was a key Tory problem
in 1993 and 1994. The Major/Anderson/Garel-Jones view was that the rebels
simply enjoyed rebellion. They were the excluded, those who had been sacked
from ministerial jobs or never had hope of the means of grace by holding
office. On this view, a scorched-earth policy was the only one possible.
Redwood's solution, outlined to Major, was not to whip the Maastricht
legislation through the House of Commons. A show-trial of Party loyalty for
a cause that was anathema to most of the Parliamentary Party would only
undermine the Government's authority. The European Union would have to
accept the sovereignty of Parliament. The Government would present
legislation to Parliament but, since it offered a free vote, it would not have to
resign if there was a majority against. Such a tactic might also expose Labour
divisions.

Major disagreed. The problem with Redwood's solution was that it failed
to take into account the Prime Minister's pride in what was regarded as his
negotiating success at Maastricht. He was the man, declared the Tories, who
had produced the opt-out clauses for Britain on the Social Chapter and the
Single Currency. The reality was that Chancellor Kohl's offer to allow the opt-
out had come late in the day and was solely Kohl's initiative. It was not the
product of tenacious negotiation, and it was designed as a *pourboire* to help a
British Prime Minister in his domestic difficulties. The story of a brave,
Dunkirk-like rearguard success having been produced, however, it quickly
became part of the mythology of Major's Government. The Prime Minister's
credibility as a skilful negotiator in Britain's interests had to be defended.
Redwood's scepticism about the value of the opt-out clauses only deepened
the mutual mistrust between the Prime Minister and the newly appointed
Welsh Secretary.

In the Whips' Office the ambitious David Davis and the deceptively mild-
mannered David Heathcoat-Amory performed as accredited Euro-sceptics
who could work on the recalcitrant Tories. The tarnished reputation they
gained was never lost, although Heathcoat-Amory's resignation from the
Government in 1996, once he realized that he was not going to become a
Cabinet Minister, was an attempt to display former convictions.

Now the electoral consequences were beginning to accumulate. On the 6th
of May, the Newbury by-election was lost to the Liberal Democrats with a
28.4 per cent swing. On the same day the Conservatives lost 500 seats in the
local council elections.

On the 27th of May, the Major–Lamont security pact was broken. The
public view of the Chancellor of the Exchequer was that he was both
incredible and risible. By offering a move to the Department of the
Environment, the Prime Minister effectively sacked Lamont; earlier he had
warned Cabinet colleagues not to use Lamont as an air-raid shelter. No longer

could Lamont while away the hours at Dorneywood, the Chancellor's country residence, doing his celebrated owl imitations. He departed, protesting that his intention to concentrate on spending reductions in the November budget would have corrected the public view of him as the tax-raising Chancellor. But he would learn, with W.H. Auden, that history, although it can say alas to the defeated, can neither help nor pardon. Widely seen as a Chancellor who had been shabbily treated by a cowardly Prime Minister, Lamont joined the Euro-rebellious backbenchers. For a Prime Minister for whom endurance was all, his sacking was a price worth paying.

On the evening of the confidence vote on the 23rd of July Michael Brunson of Independent Television News interviewed the Prime Minister. When the interview was over and the cameras were turned off the two had what they believed to be a private conversation. Perhaps, suggested Brunson, Major could easily replace Portillo, Lilley and Redwood were they to resign from the Government on the European issue? Major replied:

> I could bring in other people. But where do you think most of this poison is coming from? From the dispossessed and the never-possessed. You can think of ex-Ministers who are going around causing all sorts of trouble. We don't want another three more of the bastards out there.

One of the microphones on the set was still switched on, and when the recording was leaked the political theory of bastardy was born. As the Prime Minister's political condition degenerated, so did his language. When it was not blue, it was simply flat. On the 14th of May he had replied with leaden jollity to his critics in a speech to the Scottish Conservative Conference, 'Give up? Give over!'

In the Cabinet reshuffle on the 27th of May, Major had appointed Kenneth Clarke Chancellor of the Exchequer. By that single act, just five days after the Third Reading of the Maastricht Bill, he showed contempt for the chasm that now existed between the Government and the Tories' Euro-sceptic backbenchers. He advanced the Cabinet's most Euro-phile member to the office of state where he could most enrage them. Clarke's appointment was the culmination of a campaign he had waged throughout the winter and spring as he saw Lamont's position weakening. Being Home Secretary had had its moments. 'Come for a ride in my tank,' he had said to a friend on the day of his appointment, and the two drove around Central London in the armour-plated chariot deemed suitable for a Home Secretary's security. However, other delights now beckoned beyond the bullet-proof windows. He had played the press well. The high point was a profile by John Grigg – 'Primed Minister' – in *The Times*. Over many years Clarke had constructed a magnificently bloke-ish carapace that engaged public sympathies but concealed a sharp intellect and an elitist view of life.

Clarke had no political or constitutional objections to the single currency – or, indeed, to the wider European project as an exercise in political integration. The lazy ease with which he rejected the sceptics' arguments

enraged them. He paraded as a Falstaff with brains who knew and understood
the materialist under-belly of middle England. He thought his compatriots did
not mind whether they had pounds or ecus in their pockets as long as they had
plenty of them. Clarke might have been as tough on public-sector attitudes as
any Tory when he was Health, and then Education, Secretary, but he provided
the flash-point at which Euro-scepticism joined forces with the calls of the
right for a return to past certainties in economic policy. Redwood blamed him
for the failure to jettison VAT on fuel and return to tax-cutting at a time when
economic growth would have allowed the Government to do so. Euro-sceptics
blamed him, unfairly, for the withdrawal of the Whip from the MPs who had
voted against the Maastricht Bill.

The same reshuffle that transferred Clarke to the Treasury brought
Redwood to the Welsh Office. It was an appointment that owed more to
Marcus Fox's intervention than it did to any Whip. The Chairman of the 1922
Committee had told the Prime Minister that he needed more right-wingers in
his Cabinet, and that Redwood should be raised to the purple. Perhaps it was
the recollection of this advice that lay behind Major's decision to exclude Fox
from his dissolution Honours List in 1997. Major thus brought together
around the Cabinet table two men whose personalities were to come into
conflict with increasing acrimony during the next two years. Clarke's
geniality was not a pose and he was no hater. But there was no question that
Redwood became a colleague whom he actively disliked and one whose
interventions in Cabinet discussions riled him.

Clarke believed that the British middle classes had arrived at an accommodation with welfarism. They paid as much tax as they wanted, were not avid
for tax-reductions, and were happy with their lot as long as they could rely on
a decent level of provision (a very Major word) in health, education and social
services. He accepted the nostrums of mid-twentieth-century political
orthodoxy and inspected the ultras of his own party and Newt Gingrich across
the Atlantic with a wry acceptance of what he considered to be unhappy
Conservative epiphenomena. In these beliefs, he was the most representative
Englishman in Major's Cabinet.

Heseltine shared a similar assumption of European inevitability. It was the
secular version of the Marxist faith in progress that had spluttered to a halt in
1989. The world of big business, of those cosily corporatist connections with
Government that Heseltine incarnated, wanted European integration – so it
had to happen.

Although highly representative figures of their time and their country,
Heseltine and Clarke were not at home in the Tory Party. They belonged to a
political type which, while privately despising Tories for their poverty of
imagination and lack of humanity, none the less chose the Party as an
appropriate vehicle for their ambition in a mass-democratic, post-Whiggish
age. That had also been the choice of Harold Macmillan and R.A. Butler, two
liberal intellectuals on the run in the 1920s when the Liberal Party was
faltering and the Labour Party offered class politics. For Clarke and Heseltine

in the 1950s, Europe and the Tories went together as liberal alternatives to post-war drabness. Redwood, by contrast, was entirely of his Party. 'I know my Party extremely well,' he once said, and it was no idle boast. He was of the Tory masses in his opinions quite as much, ironically, as John Major. It was not surprising that Redwood belonged to the select if anachronistic group of those who joined the Young Conservatives in the 1970s.

With its undefined sense of a larger *imperium*, Europe also satisfied Heseltine's restless search for a larger stage, for the grand design, for a sense of destiny. He shared a high romantic sense of political adventure with David Lloyd George, his political hero and fellow-Welshman, a picture of whom hung in his office.

Along with romanticism there went materialism. Holding on to office was, for Heseltine, the supreme point of politics. It was a principle he shared with Michael Portillo, a politician with whose sense of bravura and aversion to detail he felt considerable affinity. Heseltine had come to regret greatly his departure from the Cabinet in 1986, and, unlike Clarke, he eventually showed himself capable of adjusting his European rhetoric to Tory reality.

Redwood and Heseltine shared a similar aloofness and exuded a sense of walking alone with the god of their ambition. Out of Cabinet between 1986 and 1990, Heseltine cultivated the Tory constituencies assiduously, but he did not bother too much with the Parliamentary Party. Both men found the task of hanging around in the House of Commons for hours on end a very great bore. Yet it was there, in the gratification and massaging of the excluded, the talentless and the resentful, that leadership votes were to be found. It might be easier to hold court and receive adulation in the suburbs and shires – but it was ultimately profitless.

Heseltine remained stubbornly stuck in a 1980s view of electoral motivation. He believed in bribery by tax cuts and in stuffing the electorate's mouth with gold – people inevitably voted according to their economic interests. It was a brand of Tory Marxism that had served the Party well in the 1980s. In the 1990s Heseltine's rhetoric merely grated. The old connection between prosperity and the inevitable Tory vote was broken in the 1992 general election. In a major recession a Tory Government was returned to power when, by the law of electoral materialism, it should have been defeated. The electorate may have failed to vote Labour, but they regarded the Tories as being on an unusually short leash. Having seen electoral pledges broken, they were not now ready to resume service as normal when prosperity and growth returned. Indeed, they were tempted to see prosperity as the fruits of their own labour. They had done it on their own and owed Government nothing. Had not successive Conservative Governments told them that that was how successful countries operated? Yet Heseltine continued to talk as if the electorate either owed the Conservatives a debt of honour or were the blindly determined objects of economic forces beyond their control. The more he continued in this vein, the more counter-suggestible the electorate became.

Heseltine made overtures to Redwood. It was a sign of favour when he attended Welsh Office receptions for St David's Day at Redwood's invitation. But Redwood remained aloof and sceptical. As a cautious politician, he detected a reckless strand in Heseltine that he found dangerous and distasteful. Redwood had already dismissed Heseltine as part of the Tory future. He did so too soon. David Evans, who had voted for Heseltine in the 1990 leadership contest, proved to be an important intermediary in the summer of 1995.

Clarke and Heseltine underestimated the intellectual importance of Euro-scepticism. They were right when they saw it as the cause embraced by a new media-class of commentators. They were wrong when they saw that as a mere Pavlovian response to the newspaper proprietors' global economic interests.

However, Euro-sceptics themselves over-estimated the electoral appeal of their cause. Britain is a country where the quiet virtues matter, where the noise of ideology alienates and where right-wing is a label to be avoided. Euro-sceptics in and outside Parliament were noisy, colourful and abrasive. They sounded ideological because they seemed to have a coherent world-view of what they were opposing. They talked of the dangers of 'corporatism', but few could have defined what they meant by it. Their standard hand-me-down cliché was the need for a Gaullist *Europe des patries*, but they had no answer when it was pointed out to them that such a Europe was not on offer. Indeed, the leaders of the European Union saw such a Europe as a cause of war, not the consequence of peace.

The Euro-sceptics had no mainstream European allies. The most significant anti-Maastricht forces on the Continent were often on the far right, among racist groups such as Jean-Marie Le Pen's Front National. British Euro-sceptics had to avoid being tarred with the same brush. Above all, pragmatic England, a country whose identity is so profound that it does not need the consolations of obtrusive nationalism, was doubtful when Euro-sceptics asserted national identity so vigorously and vulgarly. In a country where respectability matters and where the writ of the suburban privet hedge runs far and wide, Euro-sceptics committed the sin of being outrageous. They seemed irrelevant to the deeper and wider currents of British life. As much as Redwood and Major, they were both the creations and the victims of Britain's media-class. In vain might they protest that they were the opponents of a new, veiled form of European ideological politics. They were the ideologists now, and the defiling touch of their pitch eventually damaged Redwood.

Euro-scepticism was a complicated beast. Its virulent power in 1992–95 arose out of the confluence of two streams. The high, constitutional objection to Europe on the grounds of the sovereignty of the Queen-in-Parliament was twenty-five years old, and associated most powerfully with Enoch Powell. In the hands of his numerous *epigoni* the argument appeared to be merely a defence of the rights and prerogatives of the House of Commons. The other elements of the classically balanced British constitution – the Sovereign, the Church, the House of Lords, the judiciary – were ignored. It was a sad truth that the defence of the House of Commons acquired most force at a time when the reputation of its members stood at its lowest in the financial and sexual quagmire of the 1992–97 Parliament.

It was at this point that the argument about sovereignty evolved into an argument about democracy and the representative rights of British subjects. The right of free-born Englishmen to live lives untrammelled by foreign intrusion began to rear its demagogic head.

Another argument against Europe was pragmatic. It portrayed the institutions and laws of the European Union as a barrier to business and showed how the Single European Act had created new regulations rather than new opportunities. This second argument had little to do with the prerogatives of the High Court of Parliament and everything to do with small business frustration and the need to make a decent living in a difficult world. The arguments appealed to two different kinds of people who suddenly found a community of interest as the European project accelerated. The two positions merged and became formidable.

Many of the Euro-sceptics with whom Redwood, Portillo and Lilley associated were free-market libertarians. They found 'Europe' both too large and too small. It was unwieldy as a unit of government and insular as an economic unit. They had an uncomplicated belief in freedom rather than a complex set of constitutional objections. The natural habitat of MPs such as Eric Forth, Michael Brown and Alan Duncan was Michael Portillo's circle. Social exuberance was more likely to be encountered there than in John Redwood's company. The high constitutionalist doctrine was best represented among MPs by Richard Shepherd, John Wilkinson and Sir Teddy Taylor – men of intense, solitary, intelligence. Most Tories mixed an increasingly powerful cocktail compounded of both elements.

That summer, shortly after Redwood arrived in Cabinet, I was appointed to be the Special Adviser to the Secretary of State for Wales. I had a historian's concern with government and politics. But, outgrowing the faded charms of court, quad and cloister, I wanted to live, at least for a while, in the world of events. For the moment I had had enough of writing about the decisions of others, of pondering how to measure failure and success, of playing the game of causes and consequences. The narrowness of a life measured in seasons, lived in terms, and calculated in the Senior Common Room had begun to stifle. Real life, I decided, might be elsewhere, and so I substituted one neo-Gothic architectural environment for another with its own forms of enclosure.

My journalistic interests were developing strongly, and, with the predominant temperament of an observer, I would always eventually return to the world of commentary. Having stood as a parliamentary candidate, I knew that I had too developed a taste for irony to be a politician. I could not suppress a sense of the ridiculous at the sight of the journeyman politician's scramble for office and the self-deluding search for an always elusive 'power'. The public man's innate desire to pontificate and control left me cold. However, a political appointment as a Cabinet adviser meant that I would learn the tradecraft of British administration at the highest of levels. That form of existence in power's winding alleyways appealed, and Redwood had the kind of wide-ranging mind that I found interesting. He had breadth without superficiality.

So in the autumn of 1993 I found myself in office, and with some influence, in an eighteenth-century house in Whitehall surrounded by my compatriots for the first time since my schooldays. It seemed to me, a son of the Welsh professional middle classes, that I had taken both one step back in time and two ambiguous steps forward as I pondered the likely vicissitudes of the Conservative Government's future and the need for some subtle management of Wales' new Secretary of State. We had first met earlier in the year at a country house party in North Wales. As the peacocks strutted on the lawns, guests were served early-evening drinks, made inconsequential conversation, and admired the views. In that assured world, there was a touchingly uncertain quality about Redwood's angularity. He needed, I thought, an intellectual and social cicerone with instincts more worldly than his own.

The post of adviser to Cabinet Ministers was invented by the 1974–79 Labour Government. The appointments are political, and the adviser becomes a senior civil servant whose loyalty primarily is to the Cabinet Minister who appointed him. Most members of Major's Cabinet had one adviser, although Clarke, Hurd and Howard each employed two on account of their seniority. The adviser's task is to be alive to the political dimensions of the work of his Minister and to make sure that officialdom does not overwhelm him. He can range widely among his boss's responsibilities and oversee the implementation of his political agenda. Some edginess in the relationship with permanent officials is inevitable and healthy. The adviser is, after all, the official who is invariably at the Secretary of State's side, and at court access to the means of grace and the hope of glory is everything. But, to be effective, an adviser needs to cajole and oil the wheels of government rather than be adversarial. The successful adviser should possess both charm and a steely intelligence.

Originally John Redwood had not been keen on having an adviser at all. He wished to be his own boss and feared the loss of total control if he appointed an adviser. However, his Minister of State, Sir Wyn Roberts, had forced my appointment on him. Roberts (now Lord Roberts of Conwy), the Talleyrand of Welsh politics, had served as a Welsh Office Minister since 1979, and provided a fig-leaf of cultured respectability for Welsh Torydom. His elusive core was shrouded in layers of caution as he watched the passing parade of English Secretaries of State. It was important that Roberts should approve of Redwood, and Redwood did not wish to offend Roberts. 'Does Wyn think it's important?' was always Major's first question when he was consulted on internal Welsh affairs. Redwood feared that I was being appointed to spy on him and to report back to the Prime Minister. Although I had been a parliamentary candidate, there was nothing in my background or views to suggest an attachment to the kind of conservatism he espoused. He was highly suspicious but, lumbered with me, felt he had to convert rather than offend. A preliminary overture was the invitation I received to dine with him in the House of Commons on the 21st of October.

Redwood's original suspicion of my role partly resulted from temperament and partly stemmed from the Cabinet drama in which he had become involved after delivering his controversial speech on single mothers in Cardiff on the 2nd of July. The speech had been calculated to detonate a controlled explosion. Redwood highlighted the abandonment of young mothers by feckless young males, the low expectations of their children and the explosion in the benefits paid to single mothers over the previous ten years. He noted that there was a 'trend in some places for young women to have babies with no apparent intention of even trying a marriage or stable relationship'. Visiting a Cardiff housing estate, he had been told that more than half the families were single-parent families. 'I was told, "There aren't many fathers around here." In that community people have begun to accept that babies just happen, and there is no presumption in favour of two adults creating a loving family background for their children. It is that which we have to change.'

Redwood's disingenuous claim was that he was merely defending the commonsense proposition that all children need two parents. But his aim was broader and the furore justified. He had long since believed that social issues would dominate the politics of the 1990s just as economics had governed those of the 1980s. However, he saw no connection between the economic liberalism of the period and its social discontents. For Redwood, choice and free markets operated solely in an economic dimension of trade, goods and services – you could choose your dishwasher but not your values. The free market need not challenge institutions and certainly could not be held responsible for social decay. It was hysterical to think that the abundant fruits of capitalism were a solvent leading inevitably to the detachment of people from their roots and the institutions that made sense of social life. Indeed, the more hectic the global economic dance, the more important it became to complement it with traditional institutions that would mould and earth otherwise rootless individuals. Cakes were available and they could be eaten.

Less optimistic commentators thought that this was too sanguine a view. Perhaps the Conservatives had let the genie of radical individualism out of the bottle and could not put it back again. The dynamism of the 1980s had led to a questioning of social structures such as the family and of British institutions such as the Royal Family. Could liberal economics really be the bedfellow of social conservatism?

The Prime Minister thought that the Cardiff speech was the first act in a pageant of disloyalty. He wished to direct the crusade he would shortly launch – Back to Basics – towards the big social issues in health and education. A year previously he had advertised himself as the education Prime Minister. Just as Redwood thought that he could disentangle markets from their social consequences, so Major believed that there were no unpleasant and tricky ethical associations about Back to Basics. Both were wrong. Major thought that Redwood's speech was a public demonstration of how and why the Prime Minister was wrong. Redwood thought that he could push at the boundaries of permissible behaviour for a Cabinet Minister.

The immediate consequence was that Redwood was accused of preaching a moral revolution of repentance and reform by a press that scented Government blood on ministerial carpets. Commentators seized on ambiguities. Were the objections to single mothers moral, financial or a confused mixture of the two? The staff of Major's Policy Unit hated the speech. They thought that it exposed the Government on a flank whose defence they had not formulated. Worse, it made Tories look like moral zealots. Henceforth, there would be an inescapable element of Savonarola about Redwood's public utterances. He had chosen, so it seemed, to be defined in that way by the press. It was not to be a happy association.

On that October evening in the Members Dining Room of the House of Commons, suspicion and beleaguerement predominated. Redwood complained about the 'cold, unfriendly' staff in his Private Office and explained how he wished to build a core team around myself and his Principal Private Secretary. Documents that he had asked to be sent to me had failed to arrive, and he suspected obstruction rather than incompetence. He feared further revelations of corruption in Welsh public bodies to rival those already publicized in the Welsh Development Agency, with its record of employing convicted criminals and discovering that Cardiff hotel bedrooms were the ideal location to interview female candidates for jobs. He thought that the priority of Michael Scholar, his new Permanent Secretary, was to ensure that he himself would have a clean pair of hands in any ensuing publicity. It was Redwood *contra mundum* with a few select praetorian guards. The moral self-dramatization in his portrayal of his plight suited his sense of mission.

In these circumstances, he said, he could not be seen to be talking to the press lest he be accused of leaking stories. David Hunt, his predecessor, was 'a better politician than I am because he looks after the press and releases stories to them'. His own preference, he claimed, was to let a story run its course rather than to intervene. That had certainly been his rule when he had run the Number 10 Policy Unit for Margaret Thatcher between 1983 and 1985. He forbade the staff to speak to the press, although this had not prevented some freer spirits doing so. As a non-Cabinet Minister between 1989 and 1993 (first at Trade, then at Environment), he had felt freer and had often guided journalists in a deft way. His present heightened sensitivity was a measure of his isolation.

In Cabinet that autumn, as later, he found himself bereft of friendship and support. That autumn he spoke more warmly of Peter Lilley than he would on later occasions. Lilley's great merit, he thought, was a systematic scepticism about governmental activity of any kind. He had to be persuaded very hard to do anything at a governmental level – even if the cause were reform on the basis of Conservative doctrine. But Lilley's quietist conservatism had little appeal for Redwood's activist view of government, which emphasized that the system was capable of reform and that the role of government could be diminished, given the right degree of Napoleonic will.

His later views of Lilley were more sardonic. This, after all, was the Cabinet Minister who, as Redwood's boss at the Department of Trade and Industry, had summoned him to his office during the last days of the Thatcher *Sturm und Drang* in November 1990, and told him that 'it's all over for Thatcher', that he was no longer supporting her and that, if Redwood had any sense, neither would he. Yet in many respects Lilley was rather like Thatcher, in that he lacked a cultural base. As a Cambridge natural scientist, he had no broad literary, historical, humanistic frame of reference. The house in Normandy, the coat-trailing banality of the frequently invoked admiration of Charles de Gaulle, the portrait of the General in his office, were too obviously attempts to camouflage a more fundamental poverty of taste and knowledge.

Redwood's understanding of Cabinet politics at this time was that the orthodox left–right divisions had broken down, even though the conventional theses of political journalism were concentrating on the conflict between John Major and the three 'bastards' on 'the right'. Unsurprisingly, Redwood was given no guidance by the Downing Street press office when he asked for the correct response in dealing with his new ascription just a few weeks into his new job.

Major had engineered a synthetic unity. Redwood was ambivalent about Lilley. Lilley, who had never been close, grew increasingly distant from Redwood. Lilley was close to Portillo. Redwood's scepticism about Portillo was profound. Portillo lacked curiosity about Redwood's frame of mind and motivation. As Redwood interpreted it, Cabinet politics in the autumn of 1993 was dense and prismatic. He continued, despite increasing tension, to maintain his loyalty to Major, in contrast with Portillo, who would happily crack Spitting Image jokes about Major's appetite for peas. In Cabinet, a debate was raging about whether VAT should be imposed on newspapers. It was the left-wing David Hunt who argued that the press should be punished because of their new-found zeal in persecuting the Tories, while the right-wing Redwood opposed the measure on the grounds that it would only alienate the press even further.

That autumn the economy was showing signs of a strong recovery. Redwood's view was that initially the Chancellor had been kept in thrall to Treasury orthodoxy but that the recovery was now strong enough for him to break free. This was the view that he ascribed to Clarke himself. After the autumn budget, and as 1993 turned into 1994, Redwood revised this optimistic view of the Chancellor and his scepticism hardened into contempt.

Within his own Welsh fiefdom Redwood saw an opportunity to make his mark. He had greatly admired the activist vigour of Peter Walker, who as Secretary of State from 1987 to 1990 had largely ignored the Civil Service and had used his own business contacts to regenerate the Principality's ageing, heavily industrialized late-capitalist economy. Within the 1993 Welsh Office

Redwood saw a blockage of talent and an over-promoted mediocrity. Senior officials had been appointed in the late 1970s when devolution seemed inevitable. They now wasted their time running the myriad Welsh Office divisions – health, education, transport, local government – and refusing him access to their brighter, younger, frustrated colleagues whom he wished to encourage.

There was much myth-making in this view of a galaxy of talent awaiting, Cinderella-like, for the political enchanter's kiss to breathe it into life and administrative creativity. As an explanation for dismaying torpor and an excuse for sudden rage, Redwood deployed this view in many ways over the next two years. The Redwood world-view was impatient with hierarchy in institutions, distrustful of those who gloried in bureaucratic over-reach, and respectful of the original and quirky solution. Few senior politicians knew the Civil Service better or were more suspicious of its self-interested ambitions. Relations between Redwood and Michael Scholar, who subsequently became Permanent Secretary at the Department of Trade and Industry, deteriorated continuously from 1993 to 1995. Ten years previously Redwood had known Scholar, formerly a Cambridge philosophy don, in Downing Street as Thatcher's Private Secretary, and had admired him. Now he regarded Scholar as an administrative wreck, frightened of taking responsibility and incapable of original solutions. When Redwood wished staff reductions to be implemented, advertising and consultancy costs to be pruned, and lazily oligarchic quangos to be reformed, he encountered a courteously fainéant Cambridge Wittgensteinian who, it seemed, had succumbed to the Whitehall form of life.

His greatest objection to Scholar was that the Permanent Secretary was a paradigm of what he saw as the Civil Service's obsession with avoiding responsibility. The Service always wanted the Minister to take the rap. He once demonstrated this cruelly but effectively at a meeting with officials when the Permanent Secretary wished him to say in the House of Commons that no more problems would be discovered in the Welsh quangos. Redwood refused to do so, and invited his Permanent Secretary to make the same claim before the House's Public Accounts Committee, which scrutinizes Whitehall's expenditure of public money. Scholar demurred in some embarrassment. His weekly meetings with Redwood became a civil servant's nightmare as Redwood put him through the hoops.

The reality was that Michael Scholar was closer to Robin Butler, Cabinet Secretary and Head of the Home Civil Service, than he was to John Redwood. To be Permanent Secretary at the Welsh Office was to be an important person in a small country, an unusually public and political role for a civil servant. Scholar, a self-effacing man, shrank from the publicity and was made increasingly uneasy by the dramas, the noise and the fury of Redwoodian initiatives that pushed him into the front line. His hopes for advancement to a more senior department lay with Sir Robin. It was inevitable that he should be drawn into a web of concern, woven by Number 10 and the Cabinet Office, that sought to control Redwood's hauteur and energy.

If Redwood had grounds for paranoia that autumn, he also had reasons for optimism. He was delighted with his own success, as a Department of Environment Minister, in promoting the new Council Tax during the previous winter. Michael Howard, then the Secretary of State for the Environment, had been a distressing boss. He was incapable of delegating except when the issue was calculated to harm his Junior Ministers. Howard was obsessive, secretive and prone to vulgar and noisy fits of bad temper. There were few colleagues for whom Redwood felt a greater contempt. Redwood's success in replacing the hated poll tax had been a great achievement in adverse ministerial circumstances.

Now Redwood was emboldened to see in Wales fertile ground for a distinctive set of policies whose pursuit would be an implicit commentary on the wider fortunes of Conservatism. The conventional view would eventually claim that he was pursuing a 'right-wing' agenda in Wales – a kind of Thatcherism in one country. But there was a subtlety and a complexity about his operation.

That evening, he explained how he thought the Conservative Government had become too governmental in spirit. The important thing about Thatcher was that even as Prime Minister she had behaved as if in Opposition.

> I went in to see her one morning and she was in a rage. 'Have you seen what they're doing, John?' I realized, after a while, that she was talking about a Government policy with which I disagreed as well.
>
> 'Yes, Prime Minister – it's now official policy.'
>
> 'It's outrageous that they should do this.'

John Major never thought of the Government he headed as 'they'. He was grateful to be there and lacked temperamental scepticism about administrative wiles. The kind of Prime Minister with whom John Redwood could do business needed that scepticism.

In Wales, Redwood saw a decadent Party weaned on, and therefore weakened by, governmental largesse. Conservatives were quango-crazy. Unelected to public office, either at Westminster or on local councils, they sated their political ambition in the hunt for a quango. Desperate to be placed on quango boards, they spent their time ingratiating themselves with a Secretary of State who despised such sycophancy. This misplaced energy, he thought, lost the Party votes in Wales. Individual Conservatives did not go out into the highways and byways to proselytize invitingly. They would have to learn the rigours of opposition in a Labour-dominated world and stop being afraid. Conservatives' individuality had been stifled within a culture of accommodating, consensual corporatism.

This was a decisive break with his predecessor, Dai 'Delightful' Hunt, who endlessly recycled his rhetoric of partnership in a dozen press releases a day. The reality of Redwood was that he was energetically co-operative with Labour councils as long as they were prepared to work. Labour councillors

praised him for his directness and decisiveness in contrast with an equivo-
cating predecessor whom they might have liked more as a person but found
frustrating as a man of business. Redwood proposed greater candour. His
political rhetoric eschewed the lazy velleity of one-nation Conservatism that
had turned Wales into a fantasy land of Keynes-by-Sea. As a Secretary of
State whose most important job was to get on with local councils, he would
show them how global capitalism could penetrate the valleys and the hills.

Redwood's strictures on Welsh Conservatives showed that he was thinking
ahead to a time when Conservatives in Britain as a whole would be in
Opposition. The governmental spirit had undermined the Party and had ill
prepared it for the probability of defeat and its consequences. One reason, he
said, he was pursuing the social theme was that there was an audience for it
in conservative, Labour Wales: 'There's an agenda out there with good
political results for the Tories.' He hoped to detach Labour votes because of
his social views, his opposition to lowering the age of consent for
homosexuals, his support for capital punishment and his strictures on the
single-parent family and its consequences.

If, in the past, another kind of Tory had been happy to propagate the view
of Wales as different, he was prepared to play the same card for different
purposes. That autumn the Cabinet was debating John Patten's proposed
initiative for a 'Mums' Army', a volunteer force of previously unqualified
teachers who could be drafted into primary schools. Their role would be to
dilute the impact of the teacher training colleges. Redwood was sceptical.
John Patten's position in Cabinet was becoming increasingly weak, and there
was little to be gained by supporting such a measure. In any event, he enjoyed
considerable administrative autonomy in education: 'Why not divide Wales
from England and say that we won't have the policy here, or say that for the
moment we simply observe the English experiment – as the English and
Welsh did with the introduction of the poll tax into Scotland?' After all, the
army of unqualified teachers would still have to go to teacher training colleges
for short-course qualifications – they would not be immune to ideological
infection.

At the time of our conversation, the most important issue on his desk was
the reform of local government – an administrative revolution that seems to
be required every generation, costs millions, and changes very little. Redwood
had disagreed with David Hunt's zeal for the measure, and was sceptical about
the rhetoric of restoring the old county units of late medieval Wales as a
natural focus of loyalty. The measure, he thought, would provoke more
conflict about boundaries instead of building on local loyalties and generating
Conservative popularity. In its capacity to create political problems, the
measure was rather like the Welsh Language Bill that was passing through the
House of Commons at the time. Having been presented by David Hunt to the
Government as an uncontentious matter, it had opened up a Welsh Pandora's
box of problems as Government lawyers grappled with the question of
whether Welsh could be defined as an official language in Wales when English

had never been so defined in either England or Wales.

The conversation had shown how subtle and cautious a figure he was in a very traditional conservative vein. The global and popular capitalist was, after all, a conservative of a recognizably English type. There was none of the ranting with which he was now associated in the public mind. He saw himself as a direct person who responded well to being told things to his face: 'I do not respond to being dealt with behind my back in the usual Welsh way of being charming to your face and then being stabbed in the back.'

Margaret Thatcher remained a brooding off-stage presence in Conservative politics in 1993, her simplicities intact and her position as a single-issue anti-European politician strengthening. Her relations with Redwood had always been poor although, once he was in Parliament, she had made an exception and had not required him to serve in the distant domains of her empire as a PPS before he could become a Minister. He was not a natural courtier and she found his angularity charmless. He rebuffed her on more than one occasion between 1993 and 1995. For instance, when invited to meet, in her presence, Sir James Goldsmith, the international and socially exotic billionaire hostile to a bureaucratic Europe, at a social reception, he refused to attend. He maintained that 'the whole Thatcher thing is dead, it's over and done with.'

Redwood always claimed that it was he who had given her privatization between 1983 and 1985 and thereby paved the way for one of the key elements in the success of the 1983–87 Government. He had pioneered privatization since the 1970s, encountered Thatcher's initial resistance, and won her over after a six-month campaign on the need to liberate telecommunications. Until 1982 the Conservatives had not expected to win the 1983 general election. The unlooked-for victory issued in an empty programme for government. Redwood seized the moment as an opportunity to influence the Prime Minister.

Yet Thatcher's memoirs contained only one reference to him, couched in a bland generality. It was a public snub that he resented greatly. In private conversations with confidants such as Sir Michael Richardson, the sleek Old Harrovian financier, she maintained that Redwood would make a fine Chancellor but no more. When cornered by David Evans, the assiduous upholder of the Redwood sacred flame, she conceded that he might make a fine leader. But that was an admission wrenched out of her in the back of a car with little chance of immediate escape. Her true view was that he lacked the King-becoming graces. As head of her Policy Unit he had, after all, disagreed with her about the poll tax, and had explained to her how and why it would be politically disastrous. When she refused to change her mind, he asked to be taken off the case and passed it on to officials who did believe in that doomed enterprise. So it was hardly surprising that she was tardy in expressing support for him in the first leadership election in 1995. Subsequently, relations became even stickier.

Within a month of our first dinner, Redwood ran into difficulties with another female Conservative politician. He had been writing about the National Health Service since the late 1980s, and had long since felt that Clarke's centralizing reforms were badly off course and costly, and were enriching a venal administrative class at the expense of patients, doctors and nurses. It was also politically useful to present himself as the defender of the NHS – it confused those who saw him simply as a devotee of capitalism.

At the Welsh Office, Redwood started his campaign by making life difficult for his health officials by asking simple questions. The outmoded Barnett formula, named after the Chief Secretary to the Treasury from 1974 to 1979, allocated £7 billion annually to the Welsh Office. The Secretary of State could then distribute the money among different divisions according to his own priorities. Redwood took particular delight in the annual Public Expenditure Settlement – a series of meetings at which he would interview heads of divisions on what they took to be their needs for the following year. Seated behind the long dining table in the Secretary of State's elegant room in Gwydyr House, he followed a successful formula – to ask the devastatingly obvious questions that did not normally get asked. How many more teachers would be employed if a 5 per cent budget increase went through? Why were officials of the Countryside Council for Wales spending so much money polluting the environment with their petrol bills? What did the Health Promotion Authority actually do? Most deadly of all, in the Settlement discussions in November 1993 he asked two questions that nobody could answer. How many more doctors and nurses would be employed if he approved an extra £100 million? How many patients was the Health Service in Wales treating? A large number of middle-aged male bottoms squirmed awkwardly on the padded leather of the dining chairs. The failure to know was culpable. Within months, the NHS's Director for Wales had left for a post in New South Wales, and I was beginning to look at the possibility of privatizing the Welsh Health Common Services Authority, the organization that stored and delivered medical supplies for the NHS.

Redwood's speech on 'The future of the NHS in Wales', delivered in Cardiff on the 15th of November 1993, grew out of these preoccupations. He justified the furore by claiming that he was talking about an area of his responsibilities. In truth, the 'in Wales' of the title was, as usual, little more than a parenthesis. He noted that:

> There has been a growing readiness to challenge the quality of service by a minority of unhappy patients. There are worries about access to treatment with criticism of long waiting times and long waiting lists. People are left with the impression of a service with too little money or the wrong priorities.

On the ground he had found

> a restlessness among some of the medical staff about the number of men in grey suits, about some of the directions coming from far-away offices and about the balance of expenditure between administration and health care.

Some might think his view simple-minded, but for them he had an answer:

> If I and the general public cannot understand what they are saying or doing, then that indicates to me that they have made it too complicated to the point where the basics might be neglected. I still think of hospitals as hospitals, not as provider units.

If John Redwood saw himself as the well-informed layman using ordinary language, Virginia Bottomley, the Health Secretary, regarded him as a pest. She resented his characteristic combination of intellectual hauteur with disarming simplicity. Besides which, she pointed out, in Wales Redwood was only running the equivalent of one English Area Health Authority. He did not understand how complicated the bigger picture was. For Redwood, Bottomley had the ill-educated mind's characteristic respect for experts and their authority.

Assurances that he was in line with Bottomley's policy became increasingly threadbare as he worked on the speech, with timorous officials pointing out how controversial it was. When it was first issued as an official press release, the speech failed to get any publicity. Either the Welsh Office's press office had been sleepy, or else it had sought to smother it at birth. He and I therefore decided to invite a small group of journalists to Gwydyr House where we could brief them in detail on the speech and pretend that it had not yet been delivered. I included Alastair Campbell of *Today* and the late Gordon Greig of the *Daily Mail* because health was a campaigning issue for both newspapers. Campbell ran out into Whitehall as quickly as he could after we had finished. The fuse had been lit and the result was the next day's front-page sensation.

'It's strange', remarked Redwood afterwards, 'how you can plug away at an issue for months and get no coverage. Then something dramatic happens.' The truth was that this was not a random event but an exercise in hype and a raid on Bottomley's fiefdom. Redwood was too young in the Cabinet to be sacked, and he knew that after his 'bastard' remarks Major was in any event too vulnerable to do so. There was *diablerie* as well as calculation behind the raid. The same *diablerie* led him to laugh in the car as he sped away from the Welsh Office in Cardiff and thought of how relieved his officials must be behind their net curtains when they saw him leave for London.

None the less, he had not expected the reaction to be as intense as it was. I had calculated that the balloon would go up, but his face was grey when he arrived in the office and saw the reporting on his speech. Bottomley, aflame, was waxing with righteous, and self-righteous, wrath, and my role was to produce honeyed words of assurance for her adviser. Redwood, with characteristic distaste for meeting the objects of his criticism personally, spoke to Bottomley on the phone. Afterwards she claimed that he had apologized. He maintained that he had not. Throughout the episode he stuck to what he had written, blamed the press for misinterpreting his intentions, and claimed that

Bottomley stood for what he stood for. Her view was that he had been a disloyal colleague, and she used Keith Mans, her PPS, to brief parliamentary colleagues and the lobby against him. Her porcelain-white skin flushed, and the flawless cheek-bones acquired an extra edge. 'My lady is unhappy,' her Private Secretary remarked.

Redwood was fortunate in his new opponent. Bottomley was unpopular in the Parliamentary Party. She was the kind of assured, attractive and bossy woman whom a certain type of English professional male wants to harm physically. Hatred of her operated at a visceral and inarticulate level. The public nature of the row strengthened Bottomley's position in her Department of Health bunker and her recourse to officialdom became ever blinder and more bland. Her idea of a good way to resolve a problem, she claimed, was to get all her Area Health Authority Chairmen around the table. She would also telephone these fortunate individuals on a Sunday night. Redwood, mistrustful of most management chiefs, preferred to visit the local hospital threatened with closure. He did so against official advice, and usually found insensitive administrators heedless of local sentiment pursuing will-of-the-wisp administrative savings while commissioning new, expensive, centralizing hospitals.

Bottomley was now an enemy, and her closeness to the Prime Minister made her enmity a serious affair. The outrage of her husband and political liege-man, Peter, now a backbench MP, meant that the fires of anger were regularly fed.

Between 1993 and 1995, however, the predominant problem was the relationship between Redwood and the Prime Minister. Temperamentally, the two had too many qualities in common for either to be at ease in each other's company. They shared an English edginess about class. Redwood had advanced into technocratic classlessness by forgetting his origins. His public view was that it was old-fashioned to talk about where people came from. He self-consciously distanced himself from the comforting cocoons of English malehood – the talk of the school, the club, the university was not for him. His fastidiousness rejected those props. The only institution he really valued was his immediate family. It was a very modern kind of English loneliness, and one that came to inhibit him as a politician.

On political tours, Redwood failed to massage the Prime Minister's almost feminine and fragile sense of his identity. The two were thrown together, for example, while campaigning during the 1994 elections to the European Parliament. Major arrived for a private lunch on Deeside attended by Redwood and the inevitable local businessmen. As so often, he was in a state about the day's newspapers – and especially about the *Daily Telegraph*: 'I can tell you that there are at least five political stories in that paper today which have not a shred of truth.'

He turned without enthusiasm to business subjects: 'Tell me, what proportion of your budget do you spend on research and development?'

Conversation limped along, crushingly banal, until Redwood decided to take charge. There was an unconvincingly effusive compliment to Major: 'Everyone knows, Prime Minister, what a dedicated constituency MP you are.' But once he embarked on a detailed discussion of the business cycle, competitiveness and labour costs with the wide-eyed sons of local manufacturing and services, it was as if Major were no longer there.

In October 1994, Major joined us again for a two-day tour of South Wales. This time he was accompanied by John Ward, his aged and improbable PPS. Redwood was bursting to be asked about the latest economic developments and their impact on the political scene, but the Prime Minister refused to play ball. He was happiest chatting about the weather, cricket and his travel arrangements over the next few days – once the ritual lament over rebellious MPs was over. 'It won't be Mr Nice Guy from now on. Oh no.' One of Major's Private Secretaries sat opposite me dressed entirely in black and, bristling with ill-concealed aggression, tried to convince me that her surname, Reynolds, was one of Huguenot antiquity.

As an increasingly febrile Redwood sat opposite Major on the Cardiff train, the tension between them rose. Major always excelled in avoiding seriousness – it was an important part of his conservative appeal. As the train approached the station, conversation centred on whether he was wearing the right tie, and whether the knot was correctly tied, with Ward on hand to complete the final arranging of the trousseau.

Redwood's contempt for this kind of anxiety was uncontainable. 'Why should I need notes in a television studio?' he once said savagely to a startled interviewer. 'People might think that I don't know my own mind.' At the end of Major's two days, the Prime Minister and Redwood did a joint television interview. 'Did you see how embarrassing it was?' Redwood said afterwards. 'I had to take over and do most of the talking.' Major responded by ceasing to include any reference to Redwood and his work when he delivered political speeches in Wales, an insult Redwood felt keenly. Major and he communicated in a no-man's land created by the one's morbid excess of sensitivity and the other's equally pronounced lack of it. Throughout his period in Cabinet, letters from Number 10 to Redwood insisted on decorating him with an MBE, a modest honour accorded his predecessor David Hunt, but one that Redwood would have regarded as below the salt. After all, former Heads of the Policy Unit usually become Life Peers. His Private Office corrected the Prime Minister's Office repeatedly – but to no avail. The carelessness seemed symptomatic.

Major was a master of the direct appeal. At the end of one meeting, after Redwood had had to leave early, he took me aside. He placed my hand between his two vast palms in the two-handed handshake that he had made his trademark and which appalled as many as it delighted. 'You will look after John, won't you, Hywel?' he said, in the beseeching tone of one who is worried about a wayward child. But, as the summer of 1995 was to show, John Redwood was going to be John Major's uncontrollable problem.

Major had always disturbed Redwood. He had attended a Downing Street reception in 1989 when Major was Foreign Secretary, and observed how he worked the roomful of MPs like an undeclared candidate for the premiership. Redwood had sought out Norma Major, who was standing miserably on one side, hating the occasion, and kept her company. When Major was elected Party leader, Redwood's first thought was, 'We have a Prime Minister about whom we know next to nothing.' Eventually he formed the conviction that Major's sole political ambition and interest was to rival Margaret Thatcher's record for remaining in office as Prime Minister.

While Cabinet Ministers pursued their ambitions and their quarrels, their advisers advanced their interests. The Old Cabinet Room in the Cabinet Office is one of the great rooms of Whitehall, dominated by the Hanoverian throne and the square table around which Walpole's Cabinet sat. It was here, in part, that I learnt how to be a Cabinet Minister's special adviser. All the advisers met here every Wednesday lunchtime to discuss the week's business. There was an invariable contrast between the sublimity of the setting and the banality of the business transacted.

Advisers are there to challenge orthodoxies, especially those of Party headquarters, to develop policies, to write vividly and to guide the press in a coherent, interesting and authoritative manner. They stand in a tradition that started when Lloyd George brought Thomas Jones, an economics don, to Whitehall as an outside political appointment to serve as Deputy Secretary to the Cabinet. Labour's Cabinet advisers during the 1970s included such distinguished figures as Bernard Donoughue (now Lord Donoughue) and Jack Straw (now Home Secretary). During the 1980s, Sir Adam Ridley at the Treasury and Sir John Hoskyns as head of the Policy Unit infused Whitehall with intellectual energy and the spirit of administrative reform. Oliver Letwin had a distinguished innings, first at the Department of Education under Keith Joseph and then in the Policy Unit. They had no worthy successors, and the intellectual degeneracy of Whitehall advisers was one of the many factors that led to the electoral collapse of the 1st of May 1997.

Like dogs, Whitehall special advisers can acquire their masters' characteristics. 'Your man', as they referred to each other's commandants in the vaguely distressing argot of the trade, loomed intimately in their lives. Many of them enjoyed a less fractious time than was typical of the Welsh Office under Redwood. Peter Barnes echoed Peter Lilley's dry and evasive sense of the possible, the interest in administration for its own sake, as well as satisfaction at being thought useful by Number 10 on account of good behaviour against the odds. The observation that 'We do seem to be liked by the Prime Minister' was a frequent cause for purring pleasure. David Ruffley shared Kenneth Clarke's panache and verbal arabesques but had a wider, more cultured range than most of his colleagues, and consequently stood detached from them. His colleague Tessa Keswick was enjoying her current Treasury incarnation as an advertised Euro-sceptic in the service of a Euro-phile. She shared Clarke's survival instincts and his hostility to obtrusive political doctrine. Maurice Fraser, a French-educated cosmopolitan with the Levant in his blood, complemented Douglas Hurd's Anglican prayer-book Toryism.

The hostility of Elisabeth Cockerell to right-wing educationalists mirrored that of her mistress, Gillian Shephard. Virginia Bottomley's adviser, Richard Marsh, looked permanently exhausted, the black rims under his eyes a daily stigmata and a reminder to all of his Secretary of State's habit of ringing him up at dawn with requests for trivial information.

Patrick Rock had grown old in the service of Michael Howard, having had the misfortune to lose a safe Tory seat in the otherwise happy circumstances of the 1987 general election. Having produced green shoots of recovery for Norman Lamont's speeches – though not for his political reputation – David Cameron was now engaged in shoring up the reputation of Michael Howard. Crispin Blunt's vulpine appearance, like that of Malcolm Rifkind at the Ministry of Defence, concealed an absence of edge. They were both as dogs that failed to bark in the night. The permanently startled appearance of John Gummer's adviser, Keith Adams, recalled the quixotic capacity of the Secretary of State for the Environment for silliness. It took a John Gummer to propose that a permanently peripatetic United Kingdom Parliament meeting in Edinburgh, Cardiff, Belfast and the English provinces might take the sting out of the devolutionary threat.

James Gray's services to Sir George Young, who would become possibly the dullest member of any Major Cabinet, were not onerous. They enabled him to develop an Edwardian persona as an Anglo-Scottish gentlemen, perhaps seen at its best when, choosing a cigar after dinner, he murmured aloud, 'I think I'll have one of these little fellows.' Brian Mawhinney's adviser shared the Wolf of Ulster's faith in the uncomplicated transmission of Party belief; Michael Simmonds was one of that widely advertised category of right-wing individuals who claim to be martyred even as they embrace the hair-shirt of Party discipline in the hope of gaining office. Jonathan Aitken offered briefly the upwardly mobile spectacle of John Bercow. The future Member for Buckingham seized the chance to rehearse his vowels and massage his Napoleonic ego as he pursued both the Labour Party and a parliamentary seat. Eileen Strathnaver radiated the benign charm reminiscent of a 'Gainsborough lady', and, as Michael Heseltine's political intentions ebbed and flowed, so her thoughts became more opaque.

Michael McManus' Wykehamical distemper observed the scene with gloomy relish. He offered a necessary antidote to David Hunt's unwonted excess of joy at the latest employment figures. David Rutley, a former executive with Pepsi-Cola, was employed to impart fizz to the languid detachment of William Waldegrave.

Most advisers were employed to sell their man to the press, to extol his virtues and guard his back. Some worked solely to these ends. Others – Barnes, Ruffley, Fraser and myself for example – also worked on the details of high policy. Few advisers were loyal to the Government as a whole.

It was the task of the wan and ineffectual Jonathan Hill, the Prime

Minister's Political Secretary, to produce cohesion, and he failed to do so in spectacularly impossible circumstances. The white hairs framing his delicate and anguished face became more evident as 1993 faded into 1994. His querulous chairing of meetings mirrored the Prime Minister's own limpness. The advisers' discussions ignored the mounting tide of political disasters, and their policy divisions mirrored the discontents simmering around the Cabinet table that Major sought to conceal. It was safer to confine ourselves to the minutiae of universally ignored press notices.

The advisers served a Government that, like Churchill's pudding, lacked a theme. John Major ran his Cabinet as a series of shifting alliances. Dorrell, Lang, Clarke and Chris Patten were all carefully advertised at different times as the possible successor. Similarly, there was no attempt to evolve a common unity of purpose among the advisers. We were as Balkanized a rabble as our chiefs. It was hardly surprising that Sophie McEwen, a Roman Catholic amalgam of the aristocratic politics of Austria and Scotland and Lord Cranborne's adviser for the politics of the House of Lords, and I would meet for reviving glasses of champagne before crossing Whitehall for the grim ordeal of the weekly meetings. It was a sign of the times that many took to attending more and more infrequently.

If the advisers were meant to be an intellectual officer-class, the nearest military equivalent was Earl Haig and the General Staff of 1915 and 1916. During 1993 and 1994, a time of economic recovery and political disaster, the Back to Basics crusade was launched and promptly foundered in a flurry of Tory personal misdeeds, misfortunes and miscalculation. The incoherence of the policy reflected the intellectual failures of Whitehall's political advisers.

Of far greater consequence were the weekly meetings of the Permanent Secretaries of Whitehall departments. As the Government's problems became more acute, so these meetings became more political, so much so that briefing from them began to appear in the press as the Permanent Secretaries prepared for a Labour Government. Sir Robin Butler acquired an authority that he would not have enjoyed under a stronger Prime Minister. It was after one such meeting that Michael Scholar urged that I should disassociate myself from John Redwood, whose behaviour was seen as giving much offence within Number 10 and to the Prime Minister.

Personal tragedies came to loom large in the winter of 1993/94 when Back to Basics was born and boomeranged. An administration that could not handle ideas big or small went in search of a very big idea, a theme that could identify the Government's place in the *Zeitgeist*. It was not the Government's fault, nor John Major's, that individual Conservative MPs had mistresses and enjoyed exotic sexual practices. But only a Government that lacked self-belief and leadership could have been undermined by such revelations, while the defensive tone it adopted only served to maximize their impact. Back to Basics tried to respond to the social fears of the 1990s and the decay of community, as well as the need to reform public services in health and education. But the formulation was too vacuous to mean anything. Commentators filled the gaps and proclaimed a new Puritanism run by hypocrites whose private lives, sexual practices and financial stratagems disqualified them from governing. It was the beginning of Labour's sleaze campaign, the most brilliantly sustained onslaught by an Opposition on a Government in British political history.

John Major first outlined the Back to Basics campaign to the 1922 Committee on the 22nd of July as a campaign on economic issues, law and order and education. It was very much a political message inspired by the Prime Minister himself, his Policy Unit and the staff of his Political Office.

Howard played his role, announcing a twenty-seven-point programme on crime prevention at the Party conference at Blackpool that year. His proposals erred characteristically towards centralizing power. Lilley, an increasingly reliable figure for Major, produced his 'little list' of welfare scroungers who 'never would be missed'. In November, each Minister was asked to produce Back to Basics policies.

But in the world of real politics the picture was now unnervingly gloomy. Thatcher published her memoirs, *The Downing Street Years*, immediately after the Blackpool conference, but excerpts were extensively trailed during the conference week. Her description of the Prime Minister as 'intellectually drifting with the tide' mirrored the public's perception. On the 27th of October the Progressive Conservatives were reduced to just two MPs in the Canadian general election. The possibility of Conservative electoral disaster on a previously unimaginable scale was now being actively considered.

Most seriously of all, Kenneth Clarke's October Budget outraged Tory sensibilities. Clarke wanted to push spending below the £253.6 billion control figure. He insisted that Malcolm Rifkind at Defence should impose cuts of £1 billion a year for three years in a move that was widely seen as a sign that the Chancellor and the Government considered Britain's defence needs to be those of a middle-ranking European power. Interest rates were cut from 6 to 5.5 per cent, but the price was expenditure cuts of £10 billion a year over three years in order to reduce the deficit. Additional tax revenues of £5 billion would be raised in 1995–96. Fifteen million pensioners received compensation for VAT on fuel, but education and the roads programme were hard hit. The value of mortgage tax relief was reduced and new taxes were imposed on insurance premiums and air travel. Overall, Clarke presented the largest percentage annual tax increase in British history.

On the 1st of November the Maastricht Treaty came into force. Britain was now a member of the European Union, not the European Community, and all subjects of the Queen were citizens of that Union. It seemed appropriate that Britain was now developing into a high-tax European state.

The Queen's Speech on the 18th of November revealed that the privatization of the Royal Mail had been put on hold, while the Deregulation Bill lacked general privatization powers applicable to any industry or business. Thatcher's legacy had never looked so threadbare. But Clarke was seen to have a grip. At the European Council in Brussels he ridiculed the job-creation programmes of Jacques Delors, the formidable rationalizer of the European Union, who as President of the Commission had been a Tory hate-figure.

Meanwhile education, so fundamental to the Back to Basics scheme, was falling apart at the seams and becoming an important battle-ground. Major's conflicting signals were the reason. The 'Education Prime Minister' told John Patten on his appointment as Education Secretary in 1992 that he would back him to the hilt in a campaign to spread grant-maintained schools throughout the country. If most schools voted to 'opt out' of local authority control and became grant-maintained, the stranglehold of local education authorities would be decisively broken. Patten encountered opposition from a large number of Conservative councillors who enjoyed the job of running schools within their domains. Much political capital was unwisely spent on the idea that the popular will, expressed in ballots of parents held in individual schools, would favour greater self-governance. When that support became equivocal and a number of ballots were lost, the Prime Minister's support for Patten began to wane. Patten had also insisted on removing the Permanent Secretary he had inherited, and a failure to get on with the mandarinate was always a bad mark in Major's books.

After the prolonged and cruel agony of Patten's sacking in summer 1994, Gillian Shephard inaugurated a period of tender-heartedness towards teachers at the Department for Education. 'Mrs Municipal – that's what I call her,' snarled Angela Rumbold, a cross former Education Minister.

Shephard had found Agriculture, her previous Department, a difficult brief and had herself fallen foul of her Permanent Secretary. The Agricultural Development Advisory Service was a relic of the 1945–51 Labour Government that dispensed free advice to farmers. The Chairman, with a steely, fiscal glint in her eyes, urged its privatization. Commercially that made sense, but a Permanent Secretary, bent on retaining control over his budget, resisted. Shephard, floundering, sought advice and help from Redwood with whom she shared certain responsibilities, since he was also Wales' agriculture minister.

Redwood's stock was therefore high with Shephard. For his part, her readiness to sink in the warm embrace and approbation of the soggy liberalism endemic in the Education Department soon disillusioned him. The former local authority schools inspector was in her element as she backtracked on Patten's agenda, made soothing noises to the teachers' unions, and revelled in the domain of the educational acronym where the one-eyed administrator is king.

In the Policy Unit, however, were officials who believed in more rigorous approaches, including the accelerated testing of seven- and eleven-year-olds and the publication of the results of those tests, a renewed emphasis on the fundamentals of literacy and numeracy, hostility to inter-curricular mish-mash, and the protection of A-level specialist teaching. On all these subjects Number 10 thought that Shephard had gone native and that Redwood was sound. He and I were therefore urged by Nicholas True, the Unit's Deputy Director, to pursue in Wales policies that were presumed to be closer to the Prime Minister's true views. This would also be a good way of bringing pressure to bear on Shephard.

Along with Major, Mawhinney and Gummer, the Education Secretary was a member of the Cabinet's East Anglian mafia – 'a boring part of the country for boring people', according to Redwood. But it did her little good. Relations with Major deteriorated. The Prime Minister had created institutional conflict, and signals from Number 10 undermined Shephard's authority. The Department of Education obeyed the Secretary of State. The Chief Inspector of Schools, from his own independent vantage-point, quarrelled with Shephard because he was a realist and a rigorist who was supported by the Prime Minister.

In Wales, Redwood's speeches and articles demonstrated that the education crisis was a failure of leadership and not of money. He was interested in the question of whether schools were doing their job or not; he did not exercise himself greatly about the administrative details of whether they were, or should be, grant-maintained. Schools receiving the same amount of money in similar areas, he pointed out, produced widely differing results simply because of varying patterns of expectation. Redwood wished to distinguish clearly between vocational and academic education. Nothing was to be gained from pseudo-academic mish-mash. It was a nice irony that one of the last remaining planks of Back to Basics as originally conceived by John Major should survive in Redwood's Wales. At a practical, administrative level, Redwood's Popular Schools Initiative gave such schools extra money so they could expand. Shephard, meanwhile, committed the cardinal sin of re-opening in public the debate on the Budget settlement for education in the autumn of 1994. She panicked when local authorities in the Tory Home Counties claimed that they would have to sack teachers unless they got more money. She accepted their arguments – and got her way, to the resentment of other Ministers.

The saga of Major's education policy showed how deep his instinct was for dividing and ruling in preference to the long-term, consistent development of a policy. What his real views were remained an enigma.

If 1994 was bad for the Government, it was also the time when Michael Portillo's bandwagon gathered momentum. A series of speeches attracted public attention, although they also raised questions of political judgement which, as the months passed, became deafening. In January 1994 he spoke of the self-destructive sickness of national cynicism. As the son, like Michael Howard, of an immigrant, he had strong views about the glories of British institutions. Foreigners, he suggested, had to buy their degrees; Britons worked for theirs. In April he was talking in Nixonian terms about the still small voice of Britain's quiet majority. The speeches were crude, with a thin veneer of sophistication and the faint echo of a north London twang overlaying the reality of saloon-bar banter. Crass simplicities masqueraded as eternal verities. This GCSE version of Enoch Powell ignored the truth that there really was a crisis in British institutions, one that was caused by the Government's own conduct, not by metropolitan liberal sneering. The Tories were confronted by a decline in the established order – all of whose elements suddenly seemed to have stopped working. Parliament was thought to be oligarchic and self-interested. The Church of England was quarrelsome, introspective and anguished.

Scandal plagued the House of Windsor, and Sir Robert Fellowes, the Queen's Private Secretary, considered measures to shore up its reputation as the waves of disaffection broke against the Palace walls. Perhaps, he suggested privately, the monarchy could do a deal and consent to reform of the House of Lords? After all, other European royal families had survived the disappearance of a hereditary element in their upper houses quite happily. The proposal showed the old Windsor ruthlessness and willingness to jettison what it took to be excess baggage in the cause of self-preservation. Others remembered James I's dictum, 'No Bishop, No King', and wondered how long it would be before the realization, 'No Peer, No Queen', struck home in a court lightly brushed with formal education.

By the beginning of 1994, basic-instinct Tories, protagonists in a latter-day Dunciad, were smothering Back to Basics. The fleshly Tim Yeo had to resign as an Environment Minister in January because he had fathered an illegitimate child and concealed that fact. Alan Duncan, a pert backbencher, had to resign as a PPS because he had bought a Westminster council house worth £500,000 in an arrangement that was exposed to unforgiving public scrutiny. David Ashby, a Leicestershire MP, promoted holiday economy by sharing a bed with another man in an act that seemed to combine opportunism and meanness. The unhappy wife of Lord Caithness, a Minister in the House of Lords, committed suicide. The Pergau Dam affair was revealed, and the public learned that Ministers, including the irreproachable Douglas Hurd, were accused of linking aid to Malaysia with a British arms deal. On the 17th of January John Major appeared before the Scott Inquiry. On the 7th of February Stephen Milligan MP died in bizarre circumstances, a victim of sexual practices involving oranges and paper bags. Soon afterwards, Hartley Booth, Thatcher's successor in her Finchley constituency, resigned as a PPS, having written poems to a female researcher. His lyric gifts, like his political career, seemed nugatory. In March William Waldegrave told the Civil Service Select Committee that Ministers lied in exceptional circumstances. It seemed a far cry from the White Paper on open government published in 1993.

As Chancellor of the Duchy of Lancaster from 1992 to 1995, William Waldegrave was responsible for governmental and administrative issues. These issues also concerned David Hunt in his role as Cabinet co-ordinator of information and news presentation from 1994 to 1995. On quango reform, little could be expected from Hunt, who had spent much of his Welsh time in quangoland and who had exploited the system for all it was worth, since

Wales returned only six Conservative MPs. Redwood was not surprised by Waldegrave's inability to subvert the Whitehall Mandarinate. He remembered him as a Fellow of All Souls who had held a political appointment in the Cabinet Office during Heath's premiership and had subsequently served in the Political Office at Number 10 and in the Leader of the Opposition's office before Thatcher's election in 1975. Waldegrave's relaxed charm and quiet intellect cut no ice with Redwood, who saw him as a creature of the administrative system. While Waldegrave was in charge, no Redwoodian rigour would descend on the Civil Service and on what Redwood regarded as its ethic of avoiding responsibility. Redwood was also suspicious of the alliance between Waldegrave and Sir Robin Butler – a suspicion that increased when he saw them lunching together. Would they, he wondered, be embarrassed to be seen by him? If Shakespeare's Duke Senior in *As You Like It* could find sermons in stones, John Redwood could see conspiracies in cutlery. His view was that Waldegrave had survived in Cabinet because of his usefulness to Major. He had been badly winged in the arms to Iraq affair as a result of his involvement as a Foreign Office Minister. He now depended solely on Major's patronage, and the Prime Minister could therefore count on his uncritical support.

The Prime Minister had no doubt where the fault lay for all his misfortunes. 'I am going to f...ing crucify the right for what they have done,' he said to his confidant, Michael Brunson, at Gus O'Donnell's farewell dinner as Major's press secretary in June 1994. His own alienation techniques had created a hard oppositional bloc. The beam was in his own eye.

In terms of his relations with the Parliamentary Party, however, John Major's greatest European disaster still lay ahead of him. Officials at the Foreign and Commonwealth Office had for long been debating the question of qualified majority voting. The European Union was about to expand. Should the veto threshold be kept at twenty-three votes, thereby making it easier for Britain to block legislation it did not like? Or should the threshold be increased to twenty-seven, as urged by those who wanted a more cohesive Union? A Cabinet bruised by the Maastricht legislation urged Major to retain the lower figure. On the 17th of March, as always at difficult moments, the Prime Minister got the whole Cabinet to commit themselves to this view as a safeguard against later revisionist tendencies. When the foreign ministers of the European Union met in Ioannina on the 26th and 27th, Douglas Hurd could not carry the day. The Ioannina compromise said that if a state had gathered between twenty-three and twenty-six votes against a measure, the Council would try to reach an acceptable solution. It was a defeat. Major had been foolish in committing himself to a Palmerstonian posture in the House of Commons on the 22nd. He had accused John Smith, the Labour leader, of being 'Monsieur Oui, the poodle of Brussels'. Now the Prime Minister had to appear, a neutered tom, and explain his defeat to the House. In Cabinet, Howard, supported by Portillo, Lilley and Redwood, had opposed accepting a compromise. But Hurd was adamant that no better deal was available. Redwood, door-stepped by the BBC the next day, expressed only very hesitant support.

On the 5th of May, local elections were held for district councils across England, for twelve Scottish councils and for the thirty-two London boroughs. The Conservatives received 27 per cent of the vote and lost 429 seats. In the twenty months since Black Wednesday they had remained becalmed in the polls. Now, all waited for the European elections on the 9th of June and the grim inevitability of further evidence of the electorate's contempt.

During the council elections Michael Portillo had enjoyed a mischievous campaign. In an interview broadcast on the 1st of May, he said that Britain would never sign up to a Single Currency. Clarke rebuked him for breaching collective Cabinet decision-making. This did not stop Michael Heseltine saying how excellent a Minister he thought Portillo was and how he had always enjoyed working with him.

Between 1993 and 1995 Michael Portillo's subversion took the form of hanging around the House of Commons, canvassing support. He presented an imperious *hidalgo* facade to the political world's slings and arrows. The cruelly fastidious, fleshy lips combined with Castilian hauteur to attract and repel in equal measure. He had none of Redwood's populist predilections. He did, however, have a cupboard full of beautifully made suits to flatter the figure, in contrast with Redwood's off-the-peg garments, many of which looked like Man at C & A. It seemed of a piece that whereas Redwood entertained his Private Office staff in the cavernous Victorian recesses of the Horseguards Hotel in Whitehall ('Always so quiet here,' he would muse), Portillo took his to the Ritz.

Portillo stood for an intellectually simplistic view of the virtues of free markets and capitalism. He had a wider social circle than Redwood and enjoyed the backing of David Hart, a millionaire property-dealer. Hart had retrospectively over-played his role as an adviser to Thatcher during the 1984 miners' strike. In reality, Redwood had determinedly frustrated Hart's regular attempts to gain access to the Prime Minister during that period. Hart was squat, bald, subversive and rich. For many Portillo's closeness to Hart represented an early failure of judgement. Portillo's circle was social, not intellectual. He showed no inclination to debate policy and ideas at a high level, and he did not surround himself with those who might urge him to such a debate. His evenings, he told his officials, had to be free; work on his ministerial red boxes would have to be done in the early morning, between 6.00 and 8.00 a.m., before his arrival in Whitehall.

Redwood, who had worked in banking and commerce, knew that free-market nostrums were simplistic and that the global capitalism he understood so well required an ethical and cultural framework. This would be so even if the Conservative Party and Britain were not going through a crisis of insecurity about its identity and its institutions. But Portillo remained strangely blind to these profounder currents of the time.

The differences were as much temperamental as doctrinal. When Portillo invited Redwood to his flat in Ashley Gardens, close to Westminster

Cathedral, to dine with his guest, José Maria Aznar, leader of the Partido Popular in Spain, Redwood was indifferent and unimpressed. Aznar might declare himself to be the leader of Spain's democratic, Euro-sceptic future, but in Redwood's eyes both he and his host were arrogant, youngish men with a weak grasp of reality. Aznar's subsequent *volte face* when he led Spain into greater European integration as Prime Minister justified this suspicion.

Peter Lilley was the Albert Speer of Major's Government – an administrator whose loyalty could always be relied on and who in return was kept gainfully employed designing social security models. Michael Portillo was a different proposition. This powerfully fruity figure was seen by many as the artfully tempting Eve in a fast-decaying earthly paradise. His enchantments were great – so much so, indeed, that in 1993 John Redwood had offered him his support when the time came for Portillo to run for the leadership of the Tory Party. Lilley and Redwood were sedulous Ministers at ease with the machinery of Whitehall administration. Portillo was a politician who scorned such laborious hours and spent his time in the House of Commons cultivating MPs with a powerful charm. Resentment was never far from the surface. While John Redwood might labour manfully over a powerfully argued, wide-ranging pamphlet (*Views from Wales*) that earned little publicity, Michael Portillo scored heavily with a thin work (*Clear Blue Water*), light on learning and empty of policy but adorned with a fetching photograph of the hero of the hour, an ample right thigh displayed to the photographer's lens.

Treasury officials apply a test – the Annex Test – to judge the excellence of a Minister. It is based on the extent to which a Minister masters the arguments and details, not just of the main body of a submission but also the annexes which, in the Civil Service way, contain the heart of the matter. Of the Conservative Chief Secretaries to the Treasury since 1985, only John MacGregor and John Major passed the test. Mellor, Lamont, Aitken and Waldegrave all failed. Portillo was a borderline pass. He was not alone in his administrative detachment, besides which, he regarded himself as having more substantial fish to fry.

In vain might Redwoodians lament intellectual crudity and cry that the climate of the age had changed, that the electorate did not want the simple-minded economic nostrums of the Chicago School. They might argue that John Redwood was the politician with the surer understanding, the complexity and subtlety of mind to understand the age of anxiety. Like Margaret Thatcher, Michael Portillo was never a hero of the British public, but his restless individualism and touch of the louche – Raffles dressed by Aquascutum and transposed to the Home Counties – made him a local Tory hero. His was the triumph of personality over policy. As Secretary of State for Employment, he might have been expected to take a dim view of the Training and Enterprise Councils, those bureaucratic and corporatist drags on the labour market invented by Lord Young, the quango king of the 1980s. Yet he showed no interest when proposals for their reform were put before him. He was a remote figure in Cabinet discussions, contributing little, as if recognizing as early as 1993 that the game was up. He certainly played little part in discussions on public spending and reducing taxation between 1994 and 1995. Perhaps he understood the futility of the enterprise more fully and more cynically than John Redwood, whose faith in ideas and reasoning remained undimmed.

'So, God's a Tory after all,' said one crass Tory backbencher on hearing the news of John Smith's death on the 12th of May 1994. If so, he was one with a distinctly mordant sense of humour. Smith might have been difficult for the Tories to beat, but his successor was an even graver proposition. Smith, with all his respectable Scottish solidity, belonged to an old Labour establishment. Blair, and the act of parthenogenesis that issued in New Labour, fashioned a new respectability that was bourgeois, Christian and responsible. The Tories never grasped the challenge. Indeed, their leader told them not to for many months. Major instructed his Cabinet to restrain themselves in attacking the Opposition for the first few months after Smith's funeral. In the summer and autumn of 1994, Blair gained a heady lead that he never lost.

Smith died on the eve of a Welsh Conservative rally in Cardiff. Redwood's jibes at his expense were already in the prepared text of his speech. The entire speech had to be rewritten overnight, but even the blander version with its generalized attacks on Labour failed to pass the Downing Street test. The now familiar tussle between myself and the Political Office ensued. We arrived at an accommodation, but it was another black mark for Redwood that he should have proved so unamenable. Downing Street was no longer the friendly place it had been in the 1980s where the audacious backbencher could get *sotto voce* permission from the Political Office to float an idea that was not Government policy but deserved to be tested in public.

As Peter Lilley remarked, Cabinet was not a forum that discussed anything serious. Raising the issue of the Government's unpopularity on a Thursday morning would certainly be thought unhelpful. Cabinet now had to be scripted and controlled. This was why on Wednesday afternoon a call would come from Number 10 asking icily whether there was 'any issue that your Secretary of State wishes to raise at Cabinet tomorrow'. Tory thinkers were superfluous men.

In preparing for the European elections, Major found it politic to graft some Euro-sceptic phrases on to his developing body of Baldwinesque metaphors. On the 23rd of May there was talk about how depressed he felt whenever he left Britain. His heart always lifted when he returned to his country with its 'Parliament and universities formed over seven hundred years ago, [and] a language with its roots in the mists of time'. Hostility to foreign travel was not at the heart of the objections voiced by critics of Major's European policy. It was characteristic that, in trying to appease, he ended by parodying, so profound was his lack of understanding. But bad history could not save him from the electoral consequences of his policies. The Tories saved only eighteen of the thirty-two European seats they were defending.

Defending Eastleigh in a Parliamentary by-election on the same day, they gained just 25 per cent of the vote.

Euro-virility was planned to be on display again at the European Union summit between the 24th and 26th of June, when Major vetoed the appointment of Jean-Luc Dehaene as President of the Commission in succession to Jacques Delors. Dehaene, fat, unprepossessing and Belgian, was easily pilloried, and became the victim of a star witness in a show trial to demonstrate Major's awakened scepticism. But, once Dehaene had been thrown to the wolves as a federalist collaborator, Major had no objection to the appointment of Jacques Santer, fat, unprepossessing and Luxembourgeois. Dehaene's views did not differ from Santer's, but the Prime Minister, having created a scrap in which he was the victor, no longer cared. He thought that his Euro-sceptic critics would be easily pacified by the sight of a fomented European quarrel. In reducing European issues to the level of a bad-tempered pantomime, he simultaneously showed contempt for sceptic views and created further problems for himself on the continent.

By autumn 1994 it was clear that the Conservatives could use one of two tactics against Blair. He could be a socialist wolf, red in tooth and claw but dressed in Bambi designer-chic, or he could be an opportunistic closet Tory who was stealing Tory policies. But he could not be both. Having chosen one version, the Tories would have to stick to it, day in, day out for three years. But in endless political Cabinets Major was irresolute, wavering between the attractions of each thesis. His uncertainty infected every other Minister; the confusion about the Tory view of Blair was never resolved.

This was a Government that was timorous when it should have been bold, but was heedless of creating unnecessary foes among its own supporters. Its White Paper on the BBC in July 1994 was barely worth publishing since it left the Corporation's Charter largely intact and closed its eyes to the transformation taking place in communications. In the same month, a second White Paper, *Front Line First*, continued the Government's preoccupation with the deep defence cuts necessary for an average European power.

The reshuffle on the 20th of July resulted in a new Cabinet organized according to the principle that, if enough people in differing camps are given jobs, their disagreements will cancel each other. Major always believed in an office-holder's charter. As Party Chairman, Jeremy Hanley was given the task of spreading sweetness and light after the departure of Norman Fowler. Brian Mawhinney as Transport Secretary filled Fowler's previous role as the Tories' Mr Angry. Jonathan Aitken and Stephen Dorrell arrived at the Cabinet table, the one from the non-Thatcherite right, the other from the managerial centre-left inspired by Peter Walker. Careerism, orthodox and non-threatening Euro-scepticism, plus a liberal application of rigid centrism when it really mattered, explained the elevation of David Davis and William Hague to positions just below the Cabinet table. Inexplicably, the septuagenarian John Ward became the Prime Minister's PPS. Robert Cranborne, propelled by a writ of acceleration that enabled him to sit in the House of Lords while his father, the

Marquess of Salisbury, was still alive, became Leader of that House. He became an important as well as a self-important figure over the next three years, and Major encouraged the widespread delusion that he was in awe of Cranborne. In reality he was adept at playing on Cranborne's pleasure at the survival of the House of Cecil in a Conservative Cabinet. During the next year Cranborne sought, with increasing frustration, to define his role as that of the Cabinet's constitutional spokesman. But defending the Union was considered to be an attractive role, one keenly contested in a political undergrowth populated by Howard and Gummer, Redwood and Lang.

Redwood's own position was unaffected in the reshuffle. *The Times*, in a leader on the 1st of February 1994, had described him as an 'obvious candidate' for removal, since he 'seems to pride himself in making life difficult both for the Prime Minister and his colleagues'. 'Mr Major should sack Mr Redwood *pour encourager les autres.*' Redwood dismissed the speculation. 'They know', he said of the Government, 'that I would be more trouble for them on the backbenches.' Besides which, he benefited personally from Major's policy of a Balkanized Cabinet. In one sense, the last thing the Prime Minister wanted was a united Cabinet which might pluck the mystery out of Major. Redwood was convinced that plots and the rumours of plots against the leadership would continue. He was also convinced that 'nothing will happen' as a result of such activity. Major and his Government would simply stagger on with that infinite postponement of leadership that they had made uniquely their own. He apologized for the rocky Tory horror show in which we found ourselves. Life as an adviser 'under Margaret' had been so different. But now suspicion, not boldness, had to be the order of the day in civil affairs.

Major continued to play with the idea of a 'multi-track', 'multi-speed', 'multi-layered', and confusingly metaphored Europe. His speech in Leiden on the 31st of May was intended to be a statement with canonic authority that would inaugurate a new period in Tory Euro-rhetoric. 'Leiden' opposed the creation of a hard core of European States that could go ahead with their own centralizing schemes while leaving other member States in a semi-detached condition. From now on, all Cabinet Ministers were meant to quote reverentially from the Leiden speech. The problem was that the game of 'as the Prime Minister has said...' could be played in so many different ways.

Michael Portillo played the game to strident effect at the Party Conference that autumn when he promised to 'stop the rot from Brussels' and protect British jobs. That week Major's own voice was more muted. He told his Party that he offered it 'no windy rhetoric, no facile phrases, no pious cliche, no shallow simplification' that could 'conceal the infinite complexity of Government'. It was the speech of a strangely self-absorbed politician mired within the administrative ethos and in awe of its own complexities. It was a moment at which the more astute realized that the Prime Minister was incapable of change.

The Party to which he spoke was elderly and denuded of members – a fact that was attracting increasing attention. If the Government was bankrupt of ideas, the Party's problem was that it had no money and that the average age of its members was sixty-two. The managerial and professional classes had deserted the ranks of Tory membership in droves. Those that remained, some with authoritarian tendencies, enjoyed Michael Howard's conference speech, which promised identity cards as a way of combating crime. But the spectacle they presented to the rest of the country was of an organization with at best a semi-detached relationship to modern Britain. Polls showed that the Government should be responding to a new age of anxiety, and that worries about housing and job security loomed large. Conservative voices, strident or muted, failed to capture this mood.

In their weird new political world of perpetual rancour, how the Tories handled policies became more important than their policies themselves. When Michael Heseltine launched a Green Paper on the privatization of the Post Office on the 19th of May, it was seen as his bid to build bridges with the right. When the proposal was shelved after a Cabinet debate on the 23rd of November, Heseltine's defeat was rightly seen as a classic example of Majorism in action. The Prime Minister had allowed Heseltine to commit himself publicly and damagingly. He had then used Hunt and Ryder to subvert the idea before full Cabinet discussion, when he had declared his hand. Major had never advocated privatization – this, after all, was the Lambeth councillor who, according to Frank Dobson, the senior London Labour politician, had written to council tenants rebuking them for painting their doors without first seeking council permission. Now he used the excuse of a small majority to withdraw a proposal to which he was indifferent. However, when the issue was a European one in which his own *amour propre* was involved, the smallness of the majority made no difference to his thinking.

The passage of the European Community (Finance) Bill provided another vivid illustration of this trait. After its announcement in the Queen's Speech on the 16th of November 1994, it was clear that the Bill, which proposed to increase the British contribution to the running costs of the European Union, would be a contentious matter. When the inner Cabinet – Clarke, Hurd, Heseltine and Howard – met Major for dinner on the 13th of November, Ryder and Rifkind joined them. All agreed that the vote on the Bill should be treated as a vote of confidence in the Government. Were the Bill to fail, Major would resign and request the dissolution of Parliament.

Later, Clarke was blamed when the strategy backfired, but there is no doubt that Major's tactical sense inspired it. However, Clarke did raise the stakes by briefing the lobby that every Cabinet Minister had agreed that none of them would take over in the event of Major resigning. Redwood was particularly insistent on the lobby being counter-briefed that no such undertaking had been given by the whole Cabinet, and certainly not by him. Like Portillo and Lilley, he regarded the episode as a breach of trust. All three felt that they were being press-ganged into a decision of which they disapproved, and

Redwood was contemptuous of Howard's role as the inner Cabinet member delegated to square him. The situation foreshadowed the secretive and conspiratorial mechanisms used to call a leadership election the following year. Sir Robin Butler might say until he was blue in the face that this was an issue of international treaty obligation and that no choice was involved. Euro-sceptic Ministers thought he simply gave the advice Major wanted to hear. Their most vivid memory of these matters was Thatcher renegotiating Britain's contributions to the European budget, and of how she got her rebate.

For the moment, the line was held after a Cabinet meeting on the 24th of November ended in general agreement on the proposed strategy. But legitimate doubts were expressed at the time about the propriety of Major's scheme. Could a Government simply declare that a particular vote was to be treated as a vote of confidence? Moreover, if it lost, why should there be a dissolution? The Sovereign might ask another Minister to form a Cabinet.

Whatever the constitutional doubts, Major achieved his end. The Bill passed with a majority of twenty-seven. But the price he had to pay was the highest yet in his Parliamentary career. Eight MPs – Nick Budgen, Michael Cartiss, Christopher Gill, Teresa Gorman, Tony Marlow, Richard Shepherd, Sir Teddy Taylor and John Wilkinson – abstained. Though full of reservations, Richard Ryder was instructed to remove the Whip from them – they were no longer members of the Parliamentary Conservative Party.

For the Euro-sceptics, the whipless eight were martyrs whose authority grew daily. Soon Richard Body, the temperamental and profoundly sceptical MP for Holland and Boston since 1966, decided to join their number. Major's tactics meant that each of the whipless was more important a national figure than most Cabinet Ministers. To the fixedness of principle was now added the adrenalin of the camera and the allure of the lens. The whipless might be playing to the gallery, but the gallery enjoyed the spectacle of Valiants-for-Truth, however self-advertising.

In these months the personal conduct of Tory MPs was again the subject of public debate. On the 11th of July, Graham Riddick and David Tredinnick were suspended from their unpaid posts as Parliamentary Private Secretaries after the *Sunday Times* trapped them into accepting money to ask Parliamentary Questions. On the 25th of October, Ryder and Heseltine forced Neil Hamilton to resign as a DTI Minister. Revelations about his involvement with a lobbyist, Ian Greer, had made his position untenable. Characteristically, Major could not bear to see him face-to-face and sack him personally. A Gallup poll in October showed that two-thirds of the British people thought that the Tories appeared sleazy and disreputable. The whipless at least demonstrated that there was another, principled, side of the Parliamentary Party. Major's appointment of Lord Nolan to head a committee enquiring into standards of conduct in public life was designed to lance the boil of public cynicism about Parliamentarians. Characteristically, it enabled Major to shelve considering the question and avoid taking decisions for a few more months. It was a step that would have unhappy personal consequences for him.

The economic recovery was now well established, and Redwood ran a campaign to persuade Clarke that, as Government revenues were increasing, there was no need to proceed with the doubling of VAT on fuel. By now relations between the two were very bad, and Redwood's advocacy did not improve matters. Clarke's proposed £100 million compensation package for pensioners failed to prevent a Parliamentary rebellion. Indifferent to public opinion at its most shriekingly obvious, the Government seemed ready to prove its authority by penalizing the elderly. When the Government lost the vote by 319 to 311, the Chancellor increased duties on alcohol, tobacco and petrol in order to recoup the lost revenue. The drinking and smoking Tory on a modest income took a dim view of the Chancellor.

By the end of 1994, Major had probably inflicted as much damage on his Party in the name of his European policy as it was capable of sustaining without collapsing completely. He was also harming Britain's European interests, having created, by his own methods, a Government and a Party that took a relentlessly carping attitude towards those interests. Judged on his actions and their consequences, Major should be seen as the most pro-European Prime Minister the Tories ever produced with the exception of Ted Heath. But for Major Europe was an issue to be used as a tool in domestic and Party politics.

On the 22nd of January 1995, Clarke said in an interview that he supported the principle of the single currency. On the 9th of February, in a speech to the European Movement, he denied that monetary union entailed political union – an article of faith to all Euro-sceptics and many dispassionate observers. The predictable row with Number 10 followed, but it soon blew itself out – as the Chancellor knew it would. If he thought about the issues at all, Major agreed with Clarke. What annoyed him was the flouting of his authority. At the time he was strengthening some Euro-sceptic elements as a way of checking an over-mighty Chancellor with an unflinching world-view. Redwood, Portillo and Lilley found themselves on the Cabinet Committee, OPD (E), considering European policy. On the 22nd of January Major acquiesced when his Cabinet rejected Hurd's paper on possible negotiating positions at the forthcoming Inter-Governmental Conference. Hurd and the Foreign Office had to redraft the paper to take account of the sceptics' position. The resignation of Charles Wardle, the Home Office Minister in charge of immigration policy, had raised other European worries. Wardle, who was known as a man of liberal views, said that he doubted whether the United Kingdom could retain her current immigration policy as the European Union moved towards abolishing internal border controls. Wardle's unhappiness at working with Michael Howard did much to clarify what was otherwise an obscure episode, in which the pretext failed to justify the resignation.

Major promised that he would no longer use the inner Cabinet and would consult more widely. Labour's honeymoon period was over, and long-term thinking was now his goal. His personal dislike of Blair certainly increased from now on. He resented Blair in the role of a man after his own job – but, as he would eventually put it all too characteristically, 'Sorry, Tony, job's taken.' It was his job, he liked doing it, and nobody was going to take it away from him. Apart from a greater degree of personal animus towards Blair, Major changed neither his own style nor that of his Government.

By the autumn of 1994, political advisers were enjoying the process of briefing and counter-briefing against their bosses' Cabinet colleagues. It was hoped that the arrival of Howell James as Major's Political Secretary in November 1994 would herald a Tory *glasnost*, but while the brisk and dapper James brought a lighter touch to the job, he achieved no greater a degree of success.

James had been an adviser himself, to Lord Young at the Department of Trade and Industry between 1987 and 1989. David Young was famously praised by Thatcher for bringing her solutions not problems, but Redwood had long-standing reservations. As a Whitehall adviser in the early and mid-1980s, Young had been bent on creating, and doing, the job of Chief of Staff at Number 10. The result would have been to marginalize Redwood's position in the Policy Unit and to intensify Young's closeness to Thatcher. Redwood decided that flattery was the best way to deal with the situation. He agreed with Thatcher about Young's consummate skills, told Young that he was far too talented a figure to be confined to Number 10, and advised Thatcher that Young should be made a Minister with a seat in the House of Lords. Thatcher agreed, Young became a Minister without Portfolio and subsequently Secretary of State for Employment, and Redwood was left in peace. Even from his own point of view, it was an ambiguous legacy, and at Employment Young proceeded to re-create the quango-State with the Training and Enterprise Councils. He was a corporatist lover of big business and the quango beasts that came to haunt the Tories in the 1990s.

Redwood hoped that James would share some of the better values of 1980s Whitehall. 'Isn't it interesting', he remarked, 'how the old Thatcherites are now coming back?' This was a sentimental illusion. James had no politics – other than the survival of John Major. His interest was in package and process, not in content and policy. He was the perfect Majorite Political Secretary. Glib and assured, he was, like Evelyn Waugh's Trimmer, a man of his hollow times.

James' appointment also betokened a shift in the power base at Number 10. The Political Secretary and the Head of the Policy Unit have to work together closely, but one must be more powerful than the other. Redwood had ensured that he had the upper hand over David Wolfson, who ran the Political Office for Thatcher from 1979 to 1985. Sarah Hogg had smiled on the appointment of Jonathan Hill. Now, however, Norman Blackwell, Hogg's successor, retreated into the shadows to develop the great themes that would guide the Party in the run-up to the general election. Blinking nervously behind his owlish glasses, Blackwell embarked on the historic task of bringing the full deadweight of McKinsey management consultancy to the heart of Government, and disappeared from daily sight.

If Thomas Aquinas had his five ways of demonstrating the existence of God, Norman Blackwell had five themes to justify the re-election of a Conservative Government: 'Enterprise and Prosperity', 'Opportunity and Ownership', 'Law and Order', 'Public Services', and 'Nationhood'. They had an unnerving tendency to slide into each other. Having been unveiled at the Party's Central Council in Birmingham at the end of March 1995, they were intended to inform a lengthy process of consultation. This was now a listening Government. Party members were encouraged to express their views in a series of meetings held during the summer and autumn.

Filtered through Central Office, the consultative process was a sham. Collective Conservative *aperçus* informed the writing of the manifesto in only the most general way. Observers soon pointed out that the Government had only resorted to 'listening' because it had nothing left in its head. Major's description of the Government as 'still fizzing with ideas' was cruelly wide of the mark, given that he had slaughtered so many policies at birth.

For instance, the Government hardly touched broadcasting and multi-media issues. They were very dear to the heart of John Redwood, who saw them as the next leaps forward towards a global, popular capitalism that would liberate the laity and break down the power of professional hierarchies. He thought that technology was developing so rapidly that it was outstripping the capacity of any government to intervene and regulate. That, indeed, was part of its charm for Redwood – it was an inherently subversive development. In describing the new world, he could combine technology and Arthur Bryant-style romanticism about the island race – England might have lost an empire but its language and values were sweeping the air waves.

Redwood found the Government's response low-spirited and unimaginative. The subject demanded both imaginative sweep and technical command of the detail. Michael Heseltine, whose departmental brief covered the subject, had the former but not the latter. In 1994 Stephen Dorrell entered the Cabinet as a resentful Secretary of State for National Heritage who lacked interest in the arts and sport and was unprepared to develop the broadcasting issue. His decision to hang a portrait of Oliver Cromwell in his office seemed an austere omen. His favourite subject was his own background in a family manufacturing firm in the Midlands. From this he broadened into global capitalist themes. But, where Redwood saw opportunity and change, Dorrell saw teeming Asiatic masses whose superior productivity and low wages would undercut the West's standard of living. He was the economist's version of Dickens' Fat Boy in *The Pickwick Papers*, who wanted to make his audience's flesh creep. Nevertheless he displayed considerable territorial possessiveness when Redwood started to make public pronouncements on the future of the multi-media world.

Redwood's interest in the debate contained an important political dimension. He had been close to News International ever since he had negotiated a deal in Brussels as a DTI Minister that protected the organization's technological and business interests in the face of European technology. He thought that the Government's rift with Murdoch was politically disastrous; it was certainly to his own advantage to remain on good terms with the organization. Hence his self-conscious and unconvincing populist praise for the *Sun*. Hence also his defence of the widest free markets in broadcasting with no restrictions on ownership.

In the spring of 1995 Redwood negotiated a deal whereby every school in Wales would be offered free access to Sky television channels. The deal was closely watched by Tony Blair, who later announced a similar agreement with British Telecom extending the offer to hospitals as well as to schools. Redwood was delighted to be asked to deliver a lecture on the future of broadcasting sponsored by News International when the Party's Central Council met in Birmingham in April 1995. The prospect, eventually unfulfilled, of a Murdoch attendance stirred his political loins. It also stirred Stephen Dorrell's jealousy.

Dorrell objected to as much of Redwood's draft text as he could. When Redwood refused to budge on certain key sections, Dorrell appealed to the Prime Minister, whose officials then asked Redwood to withdraw the offending passages. Redwood persisted in claiming that he had a prior agreement with Dorrell to deliver the lecture on his own terms. Dorrell objected strenuously to this interpretation of his conversation with Redwood. Agitated debate on the text continued between them by mobile phone as Redwood's train approached Birmingham New Street station, with Dorrell vigorously continuing to maintain his territorial rights from his Midlands home.

Eventually Redwood had to back down. The episode showed his capacity to annoy and his colleagues' resentment at his interpretation of his brief as giving him the right to intervene in any mainline department of state.

It was perhaps with a measure of smugness that the Department of the Environment and the Foreign Office combined to intervene in Welsh affairs and to queer Redwood's pitch in 1994. Mostyn docks in north-east Wales had long since been derelict in an area of high unemployment. Now a Canadian company, Hamilton Oil, had discovered oil in the Irish Sea, and proposed to develop the docks as a base for its operation. Redwood proposed that the local authority, keen to create local jobs, should itself approve the planning application rather than referring it to the Secretary of State. It was at this moment that the Whitehall machine swung into action to undermine him. The docks were in an area designated as of 'special scientific interest'. If the Secretary of State did not involve his own planning officers, he would fall foul of European law and be arraigned before the European Court. If, however, he called in the case for a decision by his own planners, the process would take at least a year and Hamilton Oil would go elsewhere. Eventually Redwood yielded, though to be defeated by the massed forces of Gummer, central planners and European-minded environmentalists was a cruel blow.

The experience only encouraged him in the belief that he should undermine the authority and powers of the Countryside Council for Wales

(CCW). Gummer was in the middle of creating the Environment Agency, the quango with the largest staff and the biggest budget, whose powers would cover both England and Wales. Redwood could have little impact on that Leviathan. However, the CCW would continue to enjoy a separate existence within his vice-regal ambit. In the Council Redwood saw a prime example of the self-serving bureaucratic mind. He wished to reduce its budget and transfer many of its planning responsibilities to democratically elected local authorities. A powerful alliance of two otherwise opposed forces, men in tweeds and men in beards, worked to undermine him.

Redwood had a fine democratic contempt for oligarchies, whether national or local, as an episode in the spring of 1995 showed. I had established contact with residents in the Brecon Beacons National Park, who thought that they were being denied their democratic rights when applying for planning permission to extend their properties or to build on their own land. Often they would be rebuffed by the Park authorities in cases that affected their livelihoods. Suspicion was widespread that in a small, enclosed world of rural oligarchies arbitrary likes and dislikes masqueraded as objective decisions. Moreover, those who were denied permission had no right of appeal to the democratically elected powers of the local authority. The Park's board was judge and jury in its own cause.

Redwood and I travelled to meet the individuals affected in a secret meeting on the Welsh Borders. There we discovered how the modern State's quangocracy had re-created neo-feudal relationships of obligation and hierarchy. Redwood was frustrated by his own impotence to intervene, but smiled on the public attention I brought to bear on the iniquities that flourished beneath the smilingly bucolic surface of National Park life.

As the spring of 1995 moved into early summer, the Government's self-absorbed aimlessness acquired extra dimensions. The return of the whipless to the Parliamentary Party on the 24th of April was bungled. Michael Spicer, the MP for Worcestershire South and a former Minister of State for Housing, continued to perform the role of a Majorite double-agent who could deal with the Tory *maquis*. He reported the insurgents' willingness to acquiesce, but Ryder's peremptory note goaded them to a triumphalist press conference at which they boasted that they had not had to recant their views. There they sat in moral pride; they could do no other.

When the Government decided to spend £12 million of lottery money on buying the Churchill papers, the decision was seen as Conservatives enriching a Conservative MP, Churchill's grandson. In May, the Government had a majority of only twelve in a debate on the future of London hospitals, with a beleaguered Virginia Bottomley not waving but drowning at the dispatch box. Peter Brooke, MP for Westminster and the embodiment of a sadly antediluvian Tory rectitude, refused to support the Government.

Lord Nolan's report on Parliamentary standards, published on the 11th of May, reflected public contempt for the House of Commons, and the

Conservative Party in particular. He proposed stringent new guidelines on MPs' outside earnings and consultancies, and wished to ban them from working for lobbying firms with more than one client. A new Parliamentary Commissioner would oversee Ministers' appointments to quangos.

A newly formed committee of MPs now considered the report. It was a dangerous moment for Major and he knew it. His was now a Parliamentary Party of office-holders formed in his own image. Nolan's report had reinforced the universally low opinion of MPs, while MPs blamed the Government for setting in train a process that would end their self-regulation. Many a Tory MP saw his income in free fall. The Parliamentary Party began to think that a Major premiership did more than just threaten their jobs. They now knew that even if they did survive the fast-approaching electoral storm they would be poorer afterwards. Some came to the conclusion that Major's survival techniques conflicted with their own desire to survive.

That summer was the fiftieth anniversary of the Allied victory in Europe, and Lord Cranborne put on a good show. But the most potent political image was of Blair walking down the Mall acclaimed by the cheering crowds. On the 4th of May his Party had abandoned its commitment, as enshrined in Clause Four of the Party's constitution, to a geriatric socialism. Only a sclerotic Conservatism now stood between Labour and power. In the May council elections, the Tories gained their now customary and insulting 25 per cent share of the vote. They defended 4000 seats and lost 2042 of them, while Labour gained 1799 overall and the Liberal Democrats 495. The sea-change was becoming a tempest.

When Major met the Euro-sceptic Fresh Start group of MPs in the House of Commons on the 13th of June, they were openly contemptuous of him, and he resented having to waste time on them. At his most irritable, he told them to stop making a fuss about the single currency. The British people did not care about Europe, and his Parliamentary Party should be more helpful. It seemed the moment at which the Tories' ring-master had run out of options. But he was more resourceful than they anticipated.

From 1992 to 1995, Euro-sceptics tended to be as dismayed by the Clarke–Heseltine axis in domestic policy as they were infuriated by it in European policy. The connection between the right's agenda in economic policy – tax cuts, fiscal orthodoxy, and tightly controlled public spending – and a general hostility to European integration had not always been as rigid and inevitable as it seemed in the 1990s Tory Party. For example, in the 1970s Nicholas Ridley had enthusiastically advocated British membership of the European Community. The original Conservative enthusiasm was for a Europe that seemed to have made the world safe for liberal capitalism at a time when Britain was experimenting with a socialist siege economy. Only fragments of that edifice of belief remained. There were still some Tories who saw the Single European Currency as a sound-money project in accordance with Thatcherite principle. Quentin Davies was an intellectually formidable advocate of this view on the Tory backbenches. His originality and qualities as a member of the professional 'awkward squad' earned Redwood's respect if not his agreement. For the rest, anti-European obsession had narrowed all distinctions and subtleties to a terrifying simplicity.

By the mid-1990s, the vacillations and enmities of British Tories had led to the sidelining of Britain in Europe. British foreign policy had traditionally played the balance of power game, seeking to play France and Germany against each other on the understanding that it would never be in Britain's interests to allow a Franco–German alliance to dominate the Continent. Yet Britain's failure to assume her true role in the affairs of the European Union guaranteed this result.

Euro-sceptics had succumbed to the illusion that the Union was a monolith, a power bloc with a single mind. In reality, it was simply a new arena for the old European diplomatic game of the pursuit of competitive advantage and disadvantage among states. Except that the sting of war had been removed, the game was no different from that familiar to Talleyrand and Castlereagh, to Canning, Palmerston and Metternich. John Redwood's own recollections of negotiating on trade policy as a DTI Minister bore that out. He had constructed new alliances among European States in order to isolate the French and support the British position.

The more contemptuously they were treated by Ministers, the more furiously the Euro-sceptics propounded their historical myths, and showed that a semi-intellectual hatred is the worst. They opposed a 'sturdy English individualism' to continental corporatism. They asserted that the British parliamentary tradition of representing a locality was wholly distinct from the continental tradition of representing a party on a list system. Some of this was fanciful history. It was also possible to argue that, in the absence of an English Revolution, English society remained a web of distinctly corporatist *ancien régime* institutions, and that individual liberalism characterized Continental society. The list system of nominating Parliamentarians to seats did give parties more power in European politics. But it was a fantasy to suppose that the deputy in the Var was any less conscious of representing his locality than the Hampshire MP. The more ferocious the myth-making became, the more difficult it was to persuade a sceptic to emerge from his fortified position.

The spread of such attitudes was a sign that the Tories were increasingly detached from reality, an ideologized rump party with no Whiggish sense of adaptability and evolution. In poll after poll, the electorate refused to accord the European issue the importance that many Tories felt it deserved. In part, Europe became an important issue for the Tories because they chose that option. In a new age when Labour was colonizing the common ground secured by Tories in past battles, they were searching for a defining issue to distinguish themselves. If Labour could be portrayed as federalist, then they would be anti-federalist. But for a government to define itself negatively is never a good idea. The attempt to persuade the British in the 1989 European

elections that Labour would feed them a diet of 'Brussels sprouts' had been
an inane failure. But that decisive defeat did not cause a change of strategy.
The Conservative Party and the Government continued to reflect a fifty-year-
old strategic failure on the part of Britain's governing and administrative class
to define the nature of its European interests. The frustration and ambiguity
became so great that at one stage Redwood said that it would be preferable for
the Party to opt for European integration than to maintain the present debilitating condition in which it could not tell a hawk from a handsaw.

The polls insisted that the electorate wanted answers to the big domestic
issues. They worried about their jobs, schools, hospitals and children. Europe
featured as an issue that showed how rudderless, fractious and unpleasant the
Tories were. Just as the Health Service was the issue that defined Labour, so
Europe defined the Tories and their introspective domestic conflicts as a
family at war.

Britain's new, large middle-class felt abandoned. Their importance and
predominance in a new England had first been identified by George Orwell in
the post-recessionary late 1930s. Power had moved from the industrialized
north to the suburbs served by the new arterial roads of the south-east and the
Midlands. In the millions of new detached and semi-detached houses that
sprang up across Britain, new and stable patterns of life had been forged as
the cinema had replaced the chapel in the 1930s, and was then in turn
supplanted by the 1950s television set. The inter-war light engineering factory
had displaced the mill and the mine, and became the motor of post-war
prosperity. The 1980s neo-Georgian housing estates were only the
culmination of a fifty-year development. When Redwood looked at them, he
saw the march of Everyman to increasing prosperity, dignity and
independence.

The decision of the new, post-industrial middle class to stick with the
Tories had seemed to herald the end of Labour. Much deterministic ink was
spilt on the belief that the death of the old working class meant that Labour
would never again form a government. The Tories were lulled into a false
historical determinism, and they behaved as if they had a freehold on
government.

If Heseltine had his own version of this belief in Tory invincibility, so did
the Prime Minister. After all, Major's background and upbringing had
qualified him to be a member of the old South London Labour ascendancy.
Major saw his own rise to power as emblematic, proof positive of the rise of
a new Tory ascendancy. That was why he harked back to his origins so much.
The ascendancy was new but also highly traditional in its belief that it could
get away with defining conservatism as simply what the Conservative Party
happened to think at any given time. Oligarchic and anti-intellectual, the
ascendancy was soon precarious and vulnerable.

But oligarchies suited Michael Howard and John Gummer. In the spring
of 1995, at a policy group meeting convened to prepare the manifesto,
advisers told them how unpopular quangos were; they were undemocratic,

unaccountable and inimical to good government. 'But', said Howard with a characteristic zeal for total control, 'we can't give up our control over these bodies. It's very important that we continue to get our people on to these boards.' At the same time Gummer was pushing on with his plans to create the biggest quango of all, the Environment Agency.

Talk of 'our people' was, indeed, a recurring feature of the Government. The phrase had started its Tory life as Thatcher-speak for the members of her coalition of interest groups. But the phrase really belonged to the Labour Party, and its use by Thatcher showed that she had inherited the old Labour traditions of aggression towards the wider world combined with a self-serving defence of interest groups. She was, after all, a very natural successor to that other monetarist Prime Minister, James Callaghan. The phrase underwent a further degradation under Major's Ministers. 'Our people' now meant those to whom we give jobs, rather than the kind of people who vote for us. There was an historical neatness about the final reappropriation of 'people' in Blairite talk of a People's Britain.

By the spring and summer of 1995, the Government had lost all authority and Major all credibility. At a Government reception in May that year, Michael Portillo, in his wife's absence, clung to John and Gail Redwood. He discussed the political situation, and concluded that 'the trouble with you two is that you are just intellectuals.' Soon a contest would begin to test who had thought hardest and, also, who could act on their thoughts.

The Government had created a situation in which Teresa Gorman and Bill Cash, the Jesuit-educated Staffordshire MP and informal parliamentary leader of the sceptics, were seen as more important than any individual Cabinet Minister. Britain's authority as a middle-ranking European power was waning. As Foreign Secretary, Douglas Hurd had allowed British troops to become involved in the European Union's attempt to evolve a foreign policy in Bosnia. Chancellor Kohl was the most important politician in Europe, and the drive towards a European federal organization made a mockery of Hurd's claim that Europe was coming our way. If it did so, it was with the force of a bulldozer over which British foreign policy exercised no influence. Within Cabinet, Michael Howard as Home Secretary was opposing proposals for the repatriation of powers from European institutions and was hostile to limiting the powers of the European Court of Justice. Both Howard and Gummer were opposing measures to curtail the spread of bureaucratic government and the powers of the quangos. Michael Heseltine was producing Government initiatives on competitiveness and deregulation that required the publication of ever-more expensive brochures and the formation of ever-more numerous task forces. The Citizen's Charter was ridiculed. The Government had capitulated to a terrifying 1990s world of rule and advice from management consultants, the new secular priesthood whose bills grew as the circles and arrows on their charts came to mean less and less. The Tories had lost their scepticism about government and its work.

By June 1995 a contest that autumn for the leadership of the Conservative

Party seemed inevitable. In 1994 and early 1995 John Redwood had believed that John Major would stay in his half-embittered, half-impassioned conviction that he should be Prime Minister. This, after all, was the First Lord of the Treasury who was so pleased to be there that he wrote his Number 10 address in full, including the postcode, when signing an official visitors' book in the Middle East shortly after his arrival in Downing Street. He would not be driven out by events or by individuals. Events and individuals were about to assume an unfamiliar guise.

SUMMER LIGHTNING

22nd of June to 4th of July 1995

O N THURSDAY the 22nd of June 1995 John Major founded the myth of his own political courage. He resigned as leader of the Conservative Party and gambled that bastards would be cowards. A genuinely brave Prime Minister would have released his Cabinet colleagues from the bonds of loyalty to him and thrown the contest wide open. Major presumed, instead, on their acquiescence in his plot. He wanted a phoney war that he would easily win – not a real battle against a serious candidate.

The *coup de théâtre* masked a dereliction of duty. Twenty-one years previously another Prime Minister had resigned and asked the question, 'Who rules?' The British people had replied that since their Prime Minister, with sixteen months of his mandate left to run, did not know, they would oblige him with an answer – which was not to his liking. At least Edward Heath had taken a genuine risk, resigned as Prime Minister, and called a general election. Major's ploy, by contrast, was contrived. It was another exercise in lack of leadership and yet another way in which he could pass on to others the responsibility for his Government's shortcomings. Major's feint almost failed. John Redwood's decision to resign from the Cabinet and stand for the leadership of the Conservative Party was not on Major's timetable. It nearly did for him.

Major had a shrewd understanding of his Party's mass psychology. Publicly, he paraded his own impotence in the face of what he portrayed as a feckless and divided Party. As so often, he knew that his strength lay in his weakness. Now he relied on the traditional Tory sycophancy towards the leader. The strategy was desperate but calculated. If it worked, the independence of the Parliamentary Party would be further weakened and his own authority strengthened.

In the spring of 1995 Redwood had been expecting to be moved to another Cabinet post in a summer ministerial reshuffle. We had discussed his possible move to the Department of the Environment, his preferred option. However, he recognized that this was unlikely. He was already well known in that Department and would be seen as a threat to its established practices as a paradise of central planners. Like so many, he expected a challenge to the Prime Minister in a November leadership contest. The challenger would probably be Norman Lamont, in a contest that John Major would win easily, although experiencing a further attrition of his authority.

The third week of June started with some characteristic manoeuvring by

Major. On Monday the 19th his Euro-phile views were on display with the publication of a pamphlet by Ray Whitney, an MP whose European credentials were well established. Whitney accused the sceptics in his Party of lacking the courage of their convictions – what they really wanted was Britain's withdrawal from the European Union. Major wrote a foreword to the pamphlet commending it as a valuable contribution to the debate.

Kenneth Clarke did not offer the threat to Major's leadership that he had done in 1992–94, but, for familiar tactical reasons, it suited the Number 10 briefing-machine to present him in that light. The housing market was still in the doldrums. The word from Number 10 was that the Prime Minister and the Policy Unit wanted action to stimulate it, but that Clarke was resisting and frustrating the Prime Ministerial will.

Meanwhile, a respectable Euro-sceptic group was emerging, pledged to stick to nurse Major for fear of something worse – Michael Heseltine. James Cran was reported to be the group's co-ordinator acting in association with Sir Nicholas Bonsor and Sir Archie Hamilton. All three lacked the rough edges of the Euro-sceptic ultras and, while dislike of Heseltine might have been their pretext, their real preference was for a quiet and stable political life. Cran had been an unofficial whip for the Maastricht rebels, but had not enjoyed the experience. He had now detached himself from them, and they in return shunned him as an equivocator and defector. Personally unpopular in his Beverley constituency as a Scotsman on the make, by 1995 he had re-established himself in the Government's good books, and was now Parliamentary Private Secretary to Sir Patrick Mayhew, the Secretary of State for Northern Ireland. In that lowly office he vented a number of strongly Unionist views. Hamilton and Bonsor were confident, large-boned, loose-limbed and empty-headed Old Etonians. Both saw themselves as William Whitelaws in waiting. Hamilton had served as a PPS to Margaret Thatcher when she was Prime Minister and would be elected Chairman of the Executive of the 1922 Committee in 1997. Bonsor, an MP since 1979, had been ignored in the Thatcher years, but became a Minister of State in the Foreign and Commonwealth Office from 1995 to 1997, as a reward for keeping on the right side of scepticism. All three were hungry for patronage.

During that week Heseltine's position was strengthened by the leaks from the Scott Inquiry. Scott was reported to conclude that Ministers had failed to inform Parliament that the guidelines on arms sales to Iraq had been relaxed. William Waldegrave looked unusually pale as these reports reached the press, while Jonathan Aitken's involvement as a non-executive director of BMARC, one of the companies involved in the arms sales, was rapidly making his position untenable. Heseltine, who had been out of Government at the time, was happy to reveal that he had asked his Department to investigate BMARC before the Opposition's questions made the affair public, and when questioned in the House offered only a very tepid defence of Aitken.

Not surprisingly, speculation about the leadership that week centred on Heseltine and on Portillo as his running-mate. A glowing *Panorama* profile of

Portillo on the Monday concluded that he would win back disaffected Tories. On the same day a disturbed Portillo, fearful of the disloyalty tag, was telling the party that it had to 'pull its socks up and back the Prime Minister'.

The week was a hot one, and in the Commons Chamber the Tories perspired. The Prime Minister let it be known that the Cabinet reshuffle would be postponed until July. On the Wednesday the 21st, the massed ranks of the Euro-sceptics were on display. At Foreign Office Questions Nick Budgen, Tony Marlow and John Wilkinson, three of the eight Maastricht rebels, and five other prominent sceptics – Bill Cash, Sir Ivan Lawrence, John Sykes, Sir Peter Tapsell and Bernard Jenkin – all ambushed Douglas Hurd and harangued him on the issue of European Union payments to poorer member countries. In default of prime ministerial leadership, they established the predominant tone of the Parliamentary Party, and with John Redwood would hold the centre-stage during the next two weeks.

Those who asked Parliamentary questions that afternoon were a good representative sample of sceptic opinion in its strength, its weakness and its internal variety. Bill Cash had been MP for Stafford since 1984. Although he eventually voted for the Maastricht legislation, he had spent his time since 1990 actively pursuing the European issue, and had established himself in the informal role of the sceptics' leader. He had an obsessive mind, a lawyer's eye for the details of parliamentary drafting, a hectoring manner, a large number of suits with obvious and hectic stripes as well as a private income from Cash's name tapes. He had enjoyed his emergence as a politically important figure on account of his predominance in a ragged band of misanthropes, and he found his displacement by John Redwood a difficult process. A friend of Sir James Goldsmith, he was the Conservative MP most Conservative MPs enjoyed disliking the most.

Nick Budgen was heir to Enoch Powell's Wolverhampton South West seat as well as to many of his views. He was short, clever and oppositional in temperament. He had developed his own English historical myth, which held that sturdy yeomen had been replaced by quirky, questioning and independent-minded workers and manufacturers during the Industrial Revolution. The electorate of his own Black Country seat had, he thought, been framed by this inheritance. For Budgen, Englishry meant a radical scepticism as well as a suspicion of most forms of authority and of all forms of government. The European Union was a threat to his view of a Protestant and a peculiar people.

Tony Marlow had been the first Conservative MP to call publicly in the House of Commons for John Major's resignation as Prime Minister. A pro-Palestinian, he had a serious interest in and knowledge of Middle East politics, but this was obscured by a hectic, desperate and noisy political style. He had been MP for Northampton North since 1979, was easily ridiculed, and was disliked by other Euro-sceptics who knew that his support was fatal to any serious project.

John Wilkinson was methodical, courteous, precise and unyielding. The son of an Eton housemaster, he had already enjoyed a long Parliamentary career, as MP for Bradford West from 1970 to 1974 and for Ruislip-Northwood since 1979. He eschewed the love of drama that consumed other sceptics and guarded his conscience even as he developed a wide range of interests in the defence industry.

Sir Ivan Lawrence's coarseness of tone had won him few friends in a long parliamentary career. He had the hectoring manner characteristic of a barrister practising at the criminal bar. A member of the Board of Deputies of British Jews, he was the only Jew among the inner circle of Tory Euro-sceptics. Having been an MP for Burton since 1974, he was increasingly happy to use law and order issues in order to bring himself to public attention. His consolation prize for not being made a Minister in 1992 was the chairmanship of the Select Committee on Home Affairs. He viewed his exclusion from Government as inexplicable and was increasingly happy to flirt with Euro-scepticism.

Sykes, Tapsell and Jenkin were representatives of a soft crypto-sceptic underbelly. John Sykes, a large and blustering Yorkshireman who had been MP for Scarborough for just three years, soon found that his formal espousal of sceptic language got him into difficulties with which he was ill-equipped to deal. He was easily bullied by forces loyal to the Prime Minister, and would be seen in a state of advanced distress on the day of the ballot as appeasing convention struggled mightily to gain the upper hand over recessive conviction.

In 1995 Sir Peter Tapsell was sixty-five, and could remember another Tory world. He had been an MP since 1959, except between 1964 and 1966, and his political pedigree went back further still, for during the 1955 general election he had been a personal assistant to Sir Anthony Eden. He had a First in Modern History from Oxford, and had enriched himself during the long years on the backbenches as a stockbroker. Unable to give full value to the letter R, he enjoyed referring to Helmut Kohl as 'the German Chancellor' in a Churchillian manner reminiscent of earlier antagonisms. Uniquely among the Euro-sceptics, he retained an attachment to high-spending welfarism as a way of maintaining social stability.

Bernard Jenkin was the son of Patrick Jenkin, a Conservative Cabinet Minister under Margaret Thatcher, and had a pleasing singing voice that had eventually gained him a choral award to Corpus Christi College, Cambridge. In the increasingly *macho* world of sceptic politics, he acquired a reputation for crumbling under pressure.

Whether virile or appeasing, however, all those who claimed the sceptic label would be tested in the next two weeks. In the process unleashed by the Prime Minister, John Redwood would force all Conservative MPs to look into that increasingly beleaguered inner space they called their conscience. They would now be judged according to the canons of Tory belief. John Major and the Cabinet had created a situation in which it now seemed plausible to separate those canons from the cause of preserving a Conservative Government.

* * *

In deciding on his tactic Major had reverted to the 'inner Cabinet' method of consultation that had so enraged Lilley, Portillo and Redwood at the time of the debate on qualified majority voting. Major consulted Hurd, Clarke and Howard, and then Michael Heseltine. It was important to stop the possibility of a challenge by Heseltine at an early stage. Major's deal with Heseltine was the fruit of these earlier discussions rather than of the last-minute meeting between the two on the afternoon of the leadership ballot. Major's acute psychology recognized the appeal to Heseltine of the title First Secretary of State and Deputy Prime Minister, with a variety of responsibilities whose grandeur of appearance belied their Gilbert and Sullivan reality. Michael Heseltine had been bought off with a title that appealed to his vanity in a job that had no substantial Whitehall power-base behind it in the form of a significant spending department. He would now be a meddler in other departments' affairs, a Mandelson before his time, with all the powers of irritation that implied.

By the time Major returned from the G7 conference in Nova Scotia early on Sunday morning, the 18th of June, he had formulated his plan with Clarke and Hurd, who had accompanied him to Canada. Lang, Newton and Howard were told at the beginning of the week, Cranborne and Ryder were informed on Wednesday, and Cranborne was then asked to be Major's campaign manager. Newton, Lang, Ryder and Hunt, organized by Cranborne, were then meant to spread the information to other Cabinet Ministers. Major saw Heseltine himself. The Prime Minister said nothing about his plans when his Cabinet met that Thursday morning. The one person they needed to square more than anyone else was told last.

John Redwood was first informed of the Prime Minister's decision by Michael Howard as they stood and talked behind the Speaker's chair in the House of Commons after Prime Minister's Questions on the Thursday afternoon. It was the last possible moment at which he could have been told, with less than ninety minutes to go before Major started his press conference. The choice of intermediary was also foolish, given Redwood's distaste for Howard's obsessiveness and secrecy. Howard told Redwood that 'we' thought Major's decision a good idea, so reinforcing the impression of an inner circle excluding the wider Cabinet. Redwood told Howard, 'I think you are all mad,' and that it was a disastrous decision for the Party and for the Government. The conversation took no more than a couple of minutes. Prime Minister's Questions finished at 3.30 p.m., and by 3.35 p.m. Redwood had joined me in the car waiting to leave the Commons.

Some commentators thought later that Redwood disagreed with the decision because he thought that it would lead ultimately to Michael Heseltine's election as leader. But tactical judgements of this kind were not uppermost in his mind that afternoon. Resentment was.

In the previous weeks I had been increasingly concerned about his detachment from Number 10 and from the Prime Minister. I had urged him to talk directly to Major, and I had arranged with Number 10 for the two

to meet on the Wednesday afternoon, the 21st of June. Redwood agreed
only very reluctantly, and on Monday and Tuesday he was getting cold feet.
None the less, after further cajoling, he agreed to stick to the scheduled
meeting.

He talked to Major about the memos he had sent him, about how to get
more private sector investment into the London Underground, and about
reforming the privatized monopolies, including the water companies, which
had caused widespread offence in recent months. Lacking the impulse of
competition and abusing their monopoly, many of the companies charged high
prices for a service that included substantial leakages from underground
carrier-pipes as well as the crowning irony of water-restrictions in the summer
months when their product was at peak demand. They were a striking instance
of unpopular capitalism, an offence to the Apostle of privatization, and an
illustration of how monopolies, deprived of a competitive spur to subvert their
laziness, could dig their own grave. However, when Redwood produced
proposals to deal with the European issue, 'Major just said to me, "I can't do
this because of Ken and I can't do that because of Douglas."' Redwood left
with the impression that Major always wished to convey – that of a
checkmated Prime Minister. It had been the obvious time for Major to tell
Redwood his decision, and, when he learnt of it, Redwood was offended by
the evident lack of trust.

Thursday was another hot afternoon as Redwood and I drove to a
television studio. We could not speak about the drama that was about to start
because we were not alone – the ministerial chauffeur was driving. As we left
the House of Commons, the press was beginning to gather in the rose garden
at Number 10 for the Prime Minister's statement. After Redwood's interview,
I returned to my office in Whitehall and Redwood was driven home to
Wokingham. As the car sped along the M4 the implausible tributes began to
be broadcast. For Clarke, it was a sensible and courageous decision. Michael
Portillo hoped that the moment of glory in the rose garden would 'bring to an
end a damaging period of uncertainty'. Hurd thought it was 'a brave step by
a brave man'. As if on cue, Hanley thought it was 'a very courageous act by
a very courageous man'. Thatcher thought that 'it is a good thing that he did
this' because, bafflingly, 'it shows that he cares. It is a bold move and it will
clear the air. I believe the Prime Minister will be re-elected and by this move
he will have strengthened his authority.' This was a response to a candidature
that had no manifesto. Major's statement gave no reason why his Party should
re-elect him other than the sullen and oligarchic assumption that the
leadership was his by right.

However, the tone of Major's statement riled Redwood. Its tone riled
Redwood. He regarded the decision itself as an abdication of leadership. Now,
the inelegant injunction to 'put up or shut up' seemed designed to end the
conventional courtesies of Cabinet Government. Were nobody of significance
to stand, Major could effectively close down any future Cabinet discussion
and dismiss opposing views. It would be an uncritical mandate for his state of

permanent stasis. He would have the Cabinet and the Party in the political equivalent of a half-Nelson.

Peter Lilley did not join Portillo in the first wave of public declarations from the Cabinet. He spent most of what remained of Thursday and Friday trying to get hold of John Redwood, who had now gone to ground and would not answer the telephone. Lilley disagreed with Major's decision, saw it in the same light as Redwood, and was contemplating resigning and standing as a candidate for the leadership. When I spoke to him on the phone, I said that I thought the Prime Minister's action was one of desertion. In the absence of Redwood to stiffen his nerve, Lilley collapsed when Major's men got to him by Friday. He had always wanted to be Chancellor, and the possibility of fulfilling that ambition in the next two years remained real to him – if not to Major. He agreed with an increasingly nervous Major campaign team that he would appear on television and declare his support. When interviewed by the BBC, he said that the Prime Minister had lanced the boil and that he would support him.

The statement had been extracted from Lilley just in time to stop speculation about his position. Lamont was the only significant politician to break cover immediately. In an article published in Friday's *Times*, he refused to endorse Major and he broke the consensus on Major's Maastricht negotiations. 'The only time he intervened in the negotiations was when he wished to make Britain's membership of the ERM a legally binding obligation. I refused to go along with that.' This damaging revelation was Lamont's first salvo.

On Thursday evening, Barry Field, the amply girthed Member for the Isle of Wight who had been enriched by the sale of his family's undertaking business, announced that he had been approached to stand. Field formed a Flanagan and Allen partnership with David Evans, whose millions came from contract cleaning in Hertfordshire. Evans was Redwood's closest Parliamentary friend, and it was only with great difficulty that the Whips had persuaded him to resign as Redwood's PPS when he was elected to the 1922 Executive in 1993. On the Friday, the 23rd of June, Redwood was due to spend the day with Evans at Lord's watching cricket. It was only late on Thursday evening that journalists began to notice that John Redwood had not yet issued a statement of support for the Prime Minister.

Redwood's stylish silence flummoxed everyone. Here was the political dog that refused to bark in the night. He had tried, unsuccessfully, to speak to Jonathan Aitken on Thursday afternoon when he phoned Aitken's Private Office. The rest was silence. Redwood's Private Office collapsed in chaos as an avalanche of telephone calls began. When the pressure became intolerable on Friday afternoon, I issued a statement through the Press Association saying that 'The Secretary of State for Wales has always been a supporter of the Prime Minister. He voted for him in the leadership election of 1990 and he continues to be a supporter.' This ambiguous phrasing did nothing to lessen the crescendo of speculation. I sat in the Secretary of State's room and tried to impose order on the largely female Private Office staff, most of whom, as usual, seemed to be 'women on the verge of a nervous breakdown'. When I spoke to Redwood on a mobile phone at Lord's, I told him of the form of words I had issued, and we agreed to speak on a secure land line during the weekend.

That Friday and Saturday, negotiations began to ensure not only that Norman Lamont would not stand himself, but also that he would support John Redwood. This was no easy matter. Lamont had been looking forward to the autumnal glory of a scrap with Major. In yielding to Redwood, he would implicitly be conceding that Redwood was now the more significant politician. Redwood had also been a stringent critic of Lamont's tax increases, and the former Chancellor had responded in kind with a low view of Redwood's political gifts. By the end of the weekend, Lamont had recognized the reality of his diminished powers of irritation, and he would be rewarded with the role of honour in the subsequent Redwood campaign with all the publicity that would entail. Lamont had described himself as singing in the bath after Britain's enforced exit from the ERM. Perhaps he recalled how Enoch Powell had sung a celebratory *Te Deum* while shaving on the morning of Edward Heath's defeat in the first 1974 general election. Powell's principle, however, contrasted with Lamont's opportunism. After he left the Government he had courted the Euro-sceptics. Some welcomed him. But many still viewed him with suspicion. Now he relied on the counsel of his louche adviser, Rupert Darwall, an investment analyst, and of Edward Leigh, the MP for Gainsborough and Horncastle.

Though a vigorous sceptic, Leigh had a chequered history. Orthodox sceptics were suspicious of his support for Michael Heseltine in the 1990 leadership contest and many thought that his virulent views reflected his disappointment at being sacked as a Minister in 1993. Once he had left the Government, he implausibly compared his tribulations with the sufferings for conscience's sake of his co-confessional, Sir Thomas More. He had four children and little money. David Evans took a dim view of his scruffy appearance and his failure to clean and polish his shoes. Indeed, Evans always took a high view on footwear. He admired the immaculate Heseltine but thought that Clarke let himself down. 'You can't trust a bank manager, let alone a Chancellor, who wears suede shoes.' However, Evans and Leigh did collaborate in securing Lamont's withdrawal. By next Tuesday Lamont was writing pointedly in *The Times* that 'John Redwood will provide magnificent support for his Chancellor in the ceaseless fight to hold back the public sector.' Later that summer Redwood repaid his debt by trying to persuade Rothschilds to keep Lamont on their books as a non-executive director.

Major had the mechanics of his campaign in place. He might not have the message, but he had men and safe houses. His campaign headquarters were established under Cranborne's direction at 13 Cowley Street, a house owned by Sir Neil Thorne, a former Tory MP. His senior campaign managers also met in Alastair Goodlad's house in Lord North Street. A battalion of imperilled office-holders joined the colours. They included David Davis, the grim survivor who kept being assured by Bruce Anderson that he was about to be appointed to the Cabinet, and the colourless Michael Jack, the Minister of State at Agriculture.

A large number of special advisers also joined the campaign, much to Robin Butler's discontent. As Cabinet Secretary, he took the proper constitutional line that they were not paid by Her Majesty's Treasury to engage in such directly political work. Those who wished to work on Major's campaign were therefore told by Butler that they had to resign. David Ruffley, Clarke's Treasury adviser, refused Majorite blandishments, but most advisers remained *en poste* and contented themselves with working in their spare time in the evenings and early mornings – an equivocation that increasingly encroached into office hours.

Central Office was also now springing into action to work for Major. This too was constitutionally improper. During the previous leadership election Kenneth Baker, as Party Chairman, had issued a memorandum to all staff reminding them that, after Margaret Thatcher's resignation, there was a vacancy in the office of leader and stating that it was therefore inappropriate for Central Office facilities to be used by any leadership candidate or for staff to support any candidate in their official capacity. Jeremy Hanley, who was still – just – Party Chairman, enforced no such rules, though he was genial towards Redwood personally and Redwood had, indeed, supported him in Cabinet as Hanley's position became increasingly precarious during the first half of 1995. Such acceptance of rule-breaking and of economy with the truth was a further sign of the Conservative Party's internal decadence. Tolerance of lying and subterfuge had entered deep into the collective Tory soul. As John Redwood liked to say, 'It's John Major's party now. He has taught Tories to think that it's all right to lie.'

Tim Collins, the Party's Director of Communications based at Central Office, briefed vigorously on behalf of the Prime Minister. A mechanical and effective apparatchik, he directed a vitriolic character assassination of Redwood and his Parliamentary colleagues.

On Saturday the 24th of June, Major addressed 160 Conservative Constituency Chairmen at Central Office and talked with characteristic felicity about the dangers of 'Euro-crap' and how he would fight it. As Redwood contemplated his position that weekend, he had no men and no safe houses, apart from his own increasingly besieged suburban home, where cameramen and photographers gathered, turning on their lights as dusk fell on Saturday evening. He had no men because, unlike Michael Portillo, he had not conducted an unofficial leadership campaign for the previous two years. David Evennett, his sorely inadequate PPS who had succeeded Evans at the end of 1993, had organized early-evening drinks parties for a few backbenchers to meet Redwood in the winter of 1994/95, but he had never enjoyed Redwood's confidence. Such was Evenett's grim dependence on the hope of office that he continued as a PPS until 1997, despite noisy protestations of imminent resignation.

What Redwood did have was a message. Ideologically he was better prepared than any other possible candidate to take on Major. Alone of all his political tribe, Redwood had a synoptic view of the nature of government. His desire and pursuit of the whole set him apart from his colleagues.

Over the previous two years, John Redwood had embarked on the most wide-ranging and independent critique of Government policy ever attempted by a serving Cabinet Minister. He had seized the opportunity offered by the wide responsibility of the Welsh Office portfolio to pursue policies on education, health and economic regeneration that he took to be fundamental to Tory recovery. Among his last private initiatives to Cabinet were proposals to privatize the underground, reform the water companies and reduce public expenditure. They were only the latest in a series of proposals he submitted for Major's consideration. The documents (see pages 263–72) illustrate Redwood's frustrated pragmatism and were the means whereby the full scale of the Tory cataclysm could have been averted. However, he always encountered a wall of silence and hostility. In Cabinet he had few allies, and his portrayal as a junior member of a triumvirate consisting of Portillo, Lilley and himself was an annoyance of which he was free only after June 1995.

In their different ways, both Portillo and Redwood showed how politics is the interaction of personality and policy. No politician can afford to be an island of policy prescriptions. John Redwood was the most intellectually inquisitive as well as the furthest-sighted member of the Major Cabinet. He earthed his policies in his canvassing sessions in his Wokingham constituency, and he was unusual among his colleagues in the importance that he attached to such chores. Out of the mundane and the suburban and the small-town he wrested insights denied his more management-minded colleagues. During the Council elections of 1994 and 1995 hardly any Cabinet members bothered to take part in national campaigns that were important judgements on the Government's performance. In contrast, Redwood's dynamism on long forced marches in the search for Welsh Tories was the stuff of legend.

Redwood's complaint was that 'the still, quiet voices of the man and woman in the street should be neither ignored nor patronised.' In becoming professionals, politicians shared the common failure of professionals to listen to the layman. 'They should seek a common language, one which connects.' 'Language can conceal rather than clarify, alienate rather than bring together.' He understood that in language, as in government, less could be more significant.

In issuing these *obiter dicta* Redwood saw himself as a populist who was also demonstrating in subtle fashion the problems of Major's over-governed Britain. He certainly said populist things. But his populism was always too careful an intellectual construction. The praise of the *Sun* as the incarnation of manly British commonsense was too effusive to carry conviction. The overall impression was that of a clever politician who used popular convictions for well-crafted purposes.

Although an ardent Shakespearian, he shared none of Shakespeare's mistrust of the populace, of the ease with which the crowd, 'throwing their sweaty caps in the air', can withdraw and transfer their allegiance. Like Lord Randolph Churchill a century earlier, he believed in trusting the people who, in turn, would recognize his integrity. It was a disarmingly uncomplicated belief, and its naivety ill-prepared him for the dramas ahead.

'I'm not going to do something just because it plays well in Wokingham,' John Major once said bad-temperedly. It was an unwise attitude. Wokingham's electorate, with their housing estates, carefully preserved greenery, shopping malls and happily hedonistic consumerism, were the people who had to keep on voting Tory nationally if there was going to be another Conservative Government. Redwood knew how fragile their support was. He mirrored their concerns with immediacy and passion. What was good for Wokingham was good for Britain – or so it sometimes seemed. But, in the fastest growing town in Britain, the new economically enfranchised bourgeoisie were not happy. The electorate might, Redwood speculated, be more indulgent towards personal lapses than the press thought. But they did have very strong views about governments that broke their promises – especially on taxation. His electorate's discontent bothered him from the autumn of 1992 onwards. As he observed of the British people more generally, 'There's a lot of jealousy out there on the streets.'

In his self-imposed isolation Redwood proceeded, from the autumn of 1993, to build a tightly loyalist and inward-looking group in his Private Office. He removed an amiable diary secretary and replaced him with an enjoyably quirky virago from the Department of the Environment who threw a ring of steel around his engagements. He made sure that the Principal Private Secretary he had inherited from David Hunt, a Treasury official with a penchant for reading nineteenth-century novels on long train journeys to Wales, was replaced by Kate Jennings, his previous Private Secretary. He elevated her from her previous post, and her loyalty to him reflected that act of patronage. After his abrupt departure, she left for the private sector, an effect which, he was happy to note, a period in his office often seemed to have on higher civil servants. He also kept his previous official driver, Ian, a droll black Glaswegian who had become a confidant. He also insisted on keeping the same official car, a Jaguar that had been threatened with replacement by a more mundane model. Soon supine journalists accepted and relayed as established truth the engaging fiction that territorial Secretaries of State were uniquely blessed in their Jaguars.

The arrival of Ffion Jenkins (now, as Mrs William Hague, metamorphosed into the Eva Perón of British Conservative politics) as an Assistant Private Secretary in 1994 threw a spanner in these cosy works. He took against the grim neophyte, finding her clumsy and unaccommodating. Arrangements were made for her to accompany him on trips to Wales in the hope that closer acquaintance would improve matters. Prolonged intimacy aggravated the situation. When Jenkins went with him to Aberystwyth, where they were surrounded by demonstrators, he suspected her of involvement because she had been at the University there and knew some of the miscreants. David Evans shared the general scepticism. 'I expect this is a big promotion for you, love, isn't it?' he remarked archly on being presented to the arrival from Cardiff.

Scepticism about the Government might be widespread, but Redwood's self-belief was invincible. He had the politician's knack of deciding that the world should conform to his own expectations of it. He would deftly sidestep unwanted or contentious official advice by scrawling 'no' at the head of delicately drafted submissions and thereby throw them back into the Civil Service cauldron. He found this an useful way of separating the wheat from the chaff. If a matter were really important, officials would have to come and explain to him why he had to approve a proposal. Otherwise, the submissions would die a natural death of administrative inertia. He was not interested in the doubts, complexities and self-imposed ambiguities of the administrative life. He was interested in questioning it at every turn. Every day offered an opportunity, eagerly seized, to subvert a musty mandarinate hiding behind the files in the Office of Circumlocution. 'I will know that I've lost it,' he said, 'the moment I feel glad to enter a Government building in the morning.'

As a matter of public profession, Redwood was scrupulously loyal, but the disadvantage of a face that registered every flicker of scepticism meant that he was not believed. The more he tried to control his features, the more Aztec-like the mask appeared. It only compounded a difficulty both observed and created by the journalist Matthew Parris when he first described Redwood as a Vulcan in a *Times* sketch in 1989. Parris actively developed Vulcanology as an important political science – the study of a half-human, half-alien politician. It became the most important single element in the public picture of John Redwood and was immensely damaging. Redwood found that he lent himself all too easily to caricature in an age when the media class found politicians irresistibly easy targets. He never found a way of deflecting the jibes. The more wooden he became in defence of a Government in which he did not believe, the worse the situation became. Later, when he tried to laugh at the ascription, his proud sensitivity made an unconvincing show of it all.

Intellectual confidence developed in Euro-sceptic circles even as the Tories' electoral fortunes looked increasingly dire. The American Republicans' victory in the mid-term Congressional elections in 1994 generated waves of Tory excitement. A grey establishmentarian, George Bush, succeeding a clear-sighted leader, Ronald Reagan, had led his Party to defeat. He had broken an election pledge not to raise taxes, and his replacement by vigorously conservative true believers had led to electoral success.

The analogy was not a happy one. The techno-nerd qualities of Newt Gingrich, the *de facto* Republican leader as a newly elected Speaker of the House of Representatives, would become more obvious with time. His dependence on pollsters, and his shallow view of technology and communi-cations as a panacea, placed him in an American tradition of fraudulence represented by William Jennings Bryan and E. Ron Hubbard, the founder of

Scientology. Besides which, the British electorate did not enjoy the consolations of America's mid-term elections. In Britain it was winner take all, and Major's replacement, it seemed, could only appear after an electoral defeat.

Gingrich based his appeal on the promise of a contract with the American people – a contract that would have to be fulfilled in order to restore the people's faith in government and its works. Contracts had been part of America's political language since the eighteenth century. For Americans, it was natural to think in terms of a covenant between subjects and rulers. Britain had no history of such a language. It simply had a very large number of disenchanted Tories who were attracted by Labour. For these reasons Redwood thought that the contract had little relevance to Britain and to British Conservatives.

Redwood's initial reaction to Gingrich and his revolution was welcoming. Indeed, he had to be restrained by Number 10 and the Foreign Office from writing an article praising the new Republicans. Douglas Hurd's officials explained agitatedly that it would be folly for a British Cabinet Minister to criticize an incumbent American President either implicitly or explicitly. Redwood complied. Besides which, he respected Hurd. Hurd might be more of a diplomat than a politician, but Redwood had first known Hurd twenty years previously when he was an Oxfordshire County Councillor and Hurd was a local MP. The Foreign Secretary was the only member of the Cabinet whom he could be certain was not briefing against him behind his back in the whispering corridors of power

Portillo and Redwood adopted different forms of subversion. Portillo used personal charm and the House of Commons as a power base. He wrote warm, welcoming letters to each new Conservative MP elected in 1992. Redwood concentrated his unfriendly fire on the administrative order. At Oxford he had rejected the advice of the historian Hugh Trevor-Roper that he should master the French, German and Italian sources in order to write about the Enlightenment. He only wanted to study the Enlightenment in England, and foreigners didn't matter. Now he showed the same grim sense of inner direction in order to make sense of the world in which he found himself.

When, for example, Jean Gueginou, the French Ambassador, proposed to make an official tour of industrial South Wales, he had to be rebuffed: 'We don't want the French finding out why we're so successful at getting inward investment.' Reservations about the Tories' materialistic image received short shrift: 'There's nothing wrong with money and with wanting lots of it.' He eagerly accepted the BBC's request to make the Welsh Office the subject of one of its tediously realistic fly-on-the-wall documentaries. It was another opportunity to reveal his Department's administrative sloth and his own heroic mastery of difficulty. The cameras accordingly filmed a meeting between himself and his officials in Cardiff as he prepared for House of Commons Questions. The fact that it was conducted by video-conference while he stayed in London made it easier to trip up his officials on details.

Europe and Europeanism provided Redwood with some of his best Welsh battles, and in one instance brought him into direct conflict with the Chief Whip. Voting on the Maastricht legislation had been so tight that the Government did a deal with Plaid Cymru to secure that Party's four votes. The plot involved David Hunt, still Welsh Secretary, Tristan Garel-Jones and Richard Ryder. The Maastricht negotiations had resulted in a commitment to establish a Committee of the Regions. Representatives of each European region would sit on a Committee that would meet in Brussels and make recommendations to the Council of Ministers and the Commission. For Euro-sceptics the proposal was part of an imperial, centralizing ploy, a pincer movement that would accelerate the internal disintegration of the nation state and encourage a common dependence upon the institutions of the European Union. This was bad enough, but Plaid Cymru wanted more. It urged the establishment of a reporting-back mechanism. The Secretary of State, Welsh Office Ministers, Welsh MPs and councillors would meet as a constitutionally approved body, debate European issues and receive the good news brought from Brussels to Cardiff. Ministers would be obliged to attend and answer questions. Hunt agreed, and a deal was done. Plaid Cymru voted for the legislation. A document, signed by all parties and recording the terms of the agreement, was said to exist in the Whips' Office. Redwood was horrified by his predecessor's action and saw the innocuously named 'reporting-back' mechanism as a Welsh Assembly in all but name. He refused to implement the agreement, saying that it should be a matter for local councils if they wished to establish such a body. He would not be involved, and neither would his Ministers. He was prepared to embarrass the Whips Office and he stood his ground, much to Ryder's annoyance.

Other European issues had a more symbolic importance. Each year, on the Catalan national day, the 23rd of April, President Pujol of Catalonia, an ambitious and wily politician who was the key to the survival of the Spanish Government's coalition, sent a red rose, the Catalan national emblem, to the Welsh Office. A volume of Catalan poetry accompanied the rose. Hunt had signed various trade and friendship agreements with the regional governments of Rhône-Alpes, Lombardy, Baden-Württemberg and Catalonia. The Welsh link with the 'four motor regions of Europe' was then acclaimed with a typical Hunt flourish. For Redwood, of course, this was further evidence of a desire to destabilize. The day came when President Pujol wished to pay his respects in person to one whom he saw as a fellow provincial premier. Pujol left the Welsh Office in no doubt about the coolness of the object of his constitutional affections.

Redwood spent much his time during his last few months in office trying to remove the signs on Welsh roadworks stating that the European Union was responsible for the grants that paid for the work. Every time Redwood spotted the twelve stars he detected a propaganda coup masking the reality that the lion's share of the cost came from the British taxpayer. Hours of meetings and several yards of frayed official nerves later yielded the conclusion that the triumphalist signs had to stay.

Redwood wished to see the press as his allies in an anti-government crusade inspired by Parkinson's Law – probably his most important intellectual influence. His own official press office was inadequate to the task. It was too slow-witted, too provincial and too much part of the Whitehall machine. A morning spent reading the *Western Mail* meant that his information officers could not respond quickly enough to events. They had become used to David Hunt's regime, in which a series of press releases recorded the Secretary of State's mounting and implausible delight at the success of his initiatives. Public credulity had become strained. Redwood decided on an open-door policy to put his messages across. He would be assiduous and subtle in his dealings with the press. Out of office, Redwood thought that William Hague, his successor, had succumbed to bad old administrative habits. He was run by the Civil Service and journalists found it difficult to get to him.

Iconoclastic daring, together with doctrinal raids on his colleagues, was now a well-established Redwood characteristic. So, also, was his isolation as a cat that liked to walk by itself. He attributed much of the ensuing period's vulcanology to the Downing Street briefing-machine.

> They found that there was no scandal that could be attached to my name. There were no financial problems and I wasn't having affairs. So they decided that I wasn't human and that that was the way to brief against me. Bruce Anderson took me out to dinner once and tried to get me to talk about sex so he could report back to the Prime Minister and they would then get a hold over me.

Redwood blamed Anderson and Tristan Garel-Jones for the foul language, the coarse tone and the brutality that surrounded Major and his circle.

Other possible avenues of co-operation with Downing Street proved equally sterile. Ministerial prayers are a weekly meeting at which a Cabinet Minister gathers his political staff around him and discusses in confidence the political issues of the day. No permanent civil servants are allowed to attend. Redwood's prayers took place on Thursdays after Cabinet. But few issues of importance were discussed because of Redwood's suspicion of most of those present. Damian Green, the Policy Unit official with responsibility for Welsh affairs, he regarded as a Major spy. The Welsh area Whip, David Lightbown, the 20-stone MP for Staffordshire South East, would deliver homiletic addresses on the need for Party discipline with a strong undercurrent of malice and suspicion about MPs' private lives. A pimply presence from Central Office would offer bland lines to take on the issues of the day. The rump of Welsh Tory MPs would cower while Redwood commanded the show.

The more Redwood's reputation grew in the vacuum created by Major's Government, the hungrier he became for publicity. He became addicted to the 'hit', and the cry, 'When am I going to get my next hit?' became familiar. When he wanted to issue a contentious press release or make a controversial speech, both of us became adept at exploiting the ambiguities between the Political Office and the Civil Service side of Number 10 about who was really in charge and who could authorize the final draft. There were plenty of flapping left hands who were ignorant of right hands. Leaks at the Welsh Office were often to his advantage when the story showed that the political agenda on health or education needed to be moved on. When, on these occasions, he was confronted by an outraged Permanent Secretary calling querulously for the adviser's head, he displayed an admirable *sang froid*. Nelsonian attitudes were useful on all sides when the furthest boundaries between confidential discussion and public knowledge were being explored.

Redwood had always been happy to see himself as an anti-institutional figure, an articulate Dave Spart of the Right, and the experience of being a Cabinet Minister only served to accentuate these tendencies. When the explosion of summer 1995 eventually detonated, he was well prepared for the experience personally and mentally. It was a lean, angry and canny David who stepped from the shadows of the Welsh Office to confront a flabby Goliath and the rest of his tribe of Cabinet Philistines. He was better prepared than they knew.

Rather like Ronald Reagan, whom he admired greatly, John Redwood believed in politics rather than economics. Reagan may have left a record deficit in Government borrowing, but he is remembered politically as the American President who created the largest number of jobs in the peace-time history of the United States. Similarly, although Redwood could, and did, produce economic arguments against a Single European Currency, it was the emotional and political aspects that stirred him most. In his case reason was a clarification of what his emotions had already told him. He understood very well the truth of Burke's dictum that 'we should clothe ourselves in our prejudices. They keep us warm.' This made sense for a practising politician with a romantic-historical imagination. Economics might have its suspect pretensions to scientific status, but that delusion could be left to the PPE mind. The historian knew that the job of the dismal science was to serve his vision of England.

When it paraded itself in economic jargon, Treasury orthodoxy had to be questioned, not respected. Its passive acceptance by the Government, to its own political cost, infuriated Redwood. Nobody knew better than he the Treasury *Red Book*, the official document that sets out the Government's patterns of current and projected expenditure and revenue. He was adept at exploiting the information it contained because hardly any other politician could be bothered to read it. Nobody could fault his figures when he showed in a speech delivered at Winchester on the 6th of January 1995 that Government expenditure was rising at double the current rate of inflation. His official object was to show how false were the Opposition parties' claims of 'cutting public expenditure'. 'Our critics debauch the language to talk of cuts.' 'There has only been growth.' In the real world of the press, the story became one of high public debt and of a Cabinet Minister who thought that 'the Government is at the limit of what the nation is prepared to pay.'

Redwood's rhetoric about global capitalism was an attempt to move forward and to give Tories a new political language suited to the English at the end of the twentieth century. He talked about the need to explore wider horizons than the European, and prayed in aid the Elizabethan values of the sixteenth-century explorers rather than Thatcher's Victorian verities. Given the Elizabethans' frequently exotic private lives, this had the added advantage that transgressing Tory politicians who preached the values of the society of Essex and Southampton, of Bacon and Ralegh, of Drake and Hawkins, need not be accused of hypocrisy.

Despite his puritanical reputation, Redwood always professed the folly and pointlessness of building windows into men's souls. He was enough of a *politique* to understand that he was dealing with a Parliament and a Party of ambitious adulterers, many of whom had shady business backgrounds. 'Very few of my colleagues', he once said sorrowfully, 'lead lives that bear very close examination.'

He grasped the surface detail of a man intuitively and immediately. For Redwood, the appearance of Kenneth Clarke mattered because it represented what he took to be the chaos of his mental furniture. Indeed, the general slovenliness of his Parliamentary colleagues appalled his genteel fastidiousness. They had reasonable salaries and they should look the part – a point New Labour had long since grasped. When Alan Clark was filmed on his estate wearing venerable garments that would not have disgraced Lord Emsworth, he was appalled. 'You judge people by the company they keep,' his wife, Gail, once said dismissively of Major's circle. It was no superficial part of Redwood's critique of the Government in which he served that the inner circle of cronies – Major, Mellor, Garel-Jones, Robert Atkins and, initially, Lamont – all looked so shabby and low-minded.

As a newly appointed Education Secretary, John Patten launched the Tories' ethical debate with an ambitious article on 'Hell' in the *Spectator* in 1992. Belief in Hell, he maintained, had its uses for a morality based on prudence and obligation. Redwood, a more secular and low-key Anglican figure, was careful not to stray into such theological territory. He grasped that Britain was a secular country with residual Christian cultural values. His early book on the seventeenth-century conflicts of belief, *Reason, Ridicule and Religion* (1976), had been noticeably cool and detached about Christianity as a way of life and pattern of belief. The book observed the waning of Christianity and religious passion with polite, but resigned, regret. Each age had its own 'superstition' and its own form of 'reason'; one century's 'reason' might be the 'superstition' of the next.

On Christmas Eve 1994 he issued a press release criticizing the spread of comparative religious education in Welsh primary schools. It roused the conventional ire of Anglican liberalism. But he had been careful to stress that his concern was with the existing pattern of Christianity as a culture and set of values rather than as a system of belief. Teaching five- to eleven-year-olds about Festivals of Light simply confused them when they had no practical experience of such religious exoticism.

Redwood's own moral passion was for truth-telling. For a politician, he was unusually distressed when he encountered a liar. Officials who evaded problems or tried to put an unreasonably optimistic gloss on a situation were found wanting before a Tribunal of Truth and never trusted again. This could create panic and neurosis. When the unfortunate Chairman of a Health Authority failed to live up to her optimistic, Redwood-inspired, projections of what she could deliver in administrative savings, the consequence was an emotional accusation that she had lied. As for the Prime Minister, Redwood thought that Major lied habitually. On the other hand, Thatcher's consistency he took to be an important element in her political success.

The strength of his European convictions came from a similar moral conviction that the British people had been lied to. They might be slow to wake up but, confronted with a national crisis as in 1940, they knew what to do. The time when Britain could resolve its European difficulties peaceably, by negotiation, was coming to an end. Before long, perhaps by the end of the century, the situation would be irreversible. The European Union's institutions would by then be part of the warp and the woof of Britain's own institutions and constitution. In such a future, Britain could only extricate herself from the European Union through the use, or the threat, of force. By then diplomatic options would be not so much exhausted as irrelevant.

In a Westminster and Whitehall world of suspicion, treachery and evasion, Redwood knew that words were the only reliable weapons at his disposal. He refused to meet lobbyists, partly because he had a democratic hatred of oligarchies and partly because he knew that the lobbyist always lands the Minister in the soup sooner or later once the fact of a meeting has been established. The purity of Redwood's words had to be safeguarded. They were the key to his reputation for integrity.

Similar reasoning lay behind his decision not to sign official letters and documents that had been translated into Welsh. The logic was impeccable. The words were not his. He did not understand them. How could he lend his name to them? But in the real world of politics and Welsh sensitivities, the decision seemed mere prissy donnishness. The impression was that of an insensitive English Tory giving needless offence. 'A Passage to India', I said to him, 'is the best book to read on the Welsh relationship with the English.' A subjugated race wished to please and, in over-egging the pudding, succeeded both in annoying the conquerors and in exacerbating its own latent self-disgust. He grasped the point but was also convinced that 'the moment a majority of the Welsh population speaks Welsh is the moment at which Wales leaves the Union with England.' He understood how national loyalty is defined by language, but remained attached to the crass neo-colonial cliché that the Welsh speak Welsh in order to deceive the English. As he put it in his book The Global Marketplace, published in 1993: 'Special language betrays special thoughts. If an Englishman enters a shop in Welsh-speaking parts of Wales, the locals are likely to switch promptly to speaking Welsh. Thus the Englishman cannot be sure whether they are talking about him.'

His most successful visits to Wales took place in the anglicized and commercial south-east. Elsewhere he was ill at ease, notably on one occasion when Hollywood came to town. In the spring of 1994, he visited the set of *First Knight*, an Arthurian fantasy being filmed on the coast of Meirionethshire. After a shaky flight in a light aircraft, we arrived on a vast muddy plain populated by Babylonian hordes of extras. Redwood's conversations with a handful over lunch convinced him that most came from Islington. Despite this congenital disadvantage, they were deemed to have shown a spirit of enterprise lacking in the indigenous Welsh. When we were received by Richard Gere, the film's star, in his caravan, it soon became obvious that Redwood did not know who Gere was, apart from being an American with dirty hair. Gere laboured under a similar ignorance about Redwood. Gere and I maintained a conversation about the merits of each other's ties, while a bored and miserable Redwood looked out of the caravan window at the rain descending on the hills. Wyn Roberts, his Minister of State, had been urging him to write speeches that showed that he actually enjoyed being in Wales and was fond of Welsh company. But the expression of emotion, even in politically sanitized forms, was not his detached way. Perhaps, as the wind howled around the caravan and Gere's conversation explored new extremes of shallowness, he recalled his mordant remark that Patagonia was the only Welsh success story. In any event, he had not long to wait to effect his escape.

During the first week-end of the leadership contest, Major's men became increasingly worried. The failure to consult Redwood had been, first, Major's and, second, Robert Cranborne's. On the Saturday afternoon, before I had spoken to Redwood, Bruce Anderson, as Cranborne's intermediary, asked me whether Redwood would stand. Knowing Redwood's cautious temperament, I was still sceptical. There followed much talk of 'how we know John and understand him. We know what he's like, how he needs to be looked after and handled carefully.' This was the unconvincing and shallow bluster of men who knew that they had made a terrible blunder and who now wished to smother with the unconvincing tenderness of a Medea.

Afterwards Major's team claimed that they were making desperate attempts to contact Redwood so that the Prime Minister could speak to him on the telephone. Redwood was, indeed, frustratingly elusive throughout the weekend, as Portillo and Lilley also found. Redwood later justified his behaviour by saying that they should all have tried harder if they really wanted to speak to him. A British Prime Minister, in particular, could get hold of anyone he wanted, all the more so if he was just forty-five minutes' drive away from central London. Undoubtedly Redwood was beginning to enjoy the situation and the sensation of boots on other feet.

On the Saturday afternoon he played cricket in what looked like a photocall but was a long-arranged game. On the other side of England, a disconsolate Peter Lilley was spending the weekend at Castle Rising, the

Norfolk home of Greville Howard, the rich, reclusive and politically austere Tory. Howard had been Enoch Powell's private secretary in the 1960s, and a friend of Lord Lucan and of Sir James Goldsmith as well as a supporter of Euro-sceptic causes. Being neither sociable nor smart, Redwood had never met Howard, but he was a friend of both Lilley and Portillo. When Portillo rang Castle Rising that weekend to talk to Howard, he found that Peter Lilley was answering the phone. In the absence of a Redwood encyclical, they talked. Portillo was coming under pressure from David Hart to stand himself, but his position was impossible because he had already publicly declared his support for Major. The next best step would be to make plans to enter at the second ballot, which he now confidently expected to take place and which would result in Major's withdrawal. (The rules allowed new candidates to enter for the second ballot, and excluded no first-ballot candidate from continuing in the race.) Portillo would need a campaign headquarters. Howard was the philanthropic owner of a large house in Lord North Street in Westminster, and arrangements were made for the furniture to be removed in readiness for a campaign.

By Sunday afternoon, when Redwood and I spoke for the first time since Friday, his mind was made up, and a steely calm had descended upon him. We agreed to meet at 9.00 a.m. on Monday morning in his office in the House of Commons. A meeting of his Parliamentary supporters would then take place an hour later in the same room, a cavernous and gloomy affair reserved for the use of the Secretary of State for Wales.

Redwood spoke briefly to Major on the phone as the car drove him into central London on Monday morning and informed him of his intention to resign. He did not expect to win, but he thought he would be the catalyst who could force changes on the Conservative Party and Government – and, most importantly, secure the removal of Major.

He was unusually short of breath as he walked in. We discussed the timing of the resignation and the calling of an afternoon press conference. I told him that I intended to resign with him and would be prepared to arrange the press and extra-parliamentary side of the campaign. He had not expected such a gesture. After all, neither of us thought he would win, and I would have been a catch for Major whose camp would have made much of my defection. But it was the moment of what Americans term the 'judgement call', and Redwood's face recorded intense emotion.

We agreed on the text of his letter of resignation. Redwood pointedly reminded Major that he had never allowed his supporters to place unhelpful speculation about the leadership in the press. He claimed to be 'devastated' that 'another Minister' had informed him of Major's plans and that Major himself had not told him at their Wednesday meeting. An early draft reminded Major that

> I opposed extra VAT on fuel and was unhappy with the way we pushed through
> additional budget contributions to the EC. These and other matters I accepted

as part of the swings and roundabouts of collective agreement. On Thursday I was again in a minority of one with my proposals for reducing wasteful spending and taxes to tackle the problems of the housing market.

In his early draft, he had been 'dismayed to hear you say after you resigned the leadership that there would be no changes in policy. I cannot in all conscience state that I support this.' In his final text he wrote that he had 'decided to offer my resignation from the Government as I do not support your decision to resign'. The Party needed 'firm but understanding leadership', and Major's decision 'leaves our party in limbo'. Late that day, his room in the Welsh Office would be stripped of his belongings, and, eschewing sentiment at a time already unusually full of drama and emotion, Redwood slipped away, avoiding what he would have seen as the sham and formal obsequies of the Private Office farewell. He had been a Cabinet Minister for just two years and one day short of one month.

After the text of the letter had been finalized and sent to the Prime Minister, he left the room to talk to Michael Portillo, who was working in his room a few doors down the ministerial corridor. This was the meeting whose consequences dogged Portillo both throughout the campaign and subsequently. Redwood told him that he had now resigned, but had not yet declared his candidature for the leadership. If Portillo wished to take the lead it was still open for him to do so. Redwood was amenable to an accommodation. Years previously, he had offered to support Portillo when the time came for him to stand for the leadership. He could see that Portillo wanted the crown in a way that he did not. He rationalized it to himself by saying that he still had children at school and that it would be easier for the childless Portillo to cope with the domestic upheaval. For a few more moments the possibility of a Portillo challenge remained.

Portillo replied that he would not resign now but that he would be a candidate in the second ballot, on the implicit understanding that Redwood would withdraw at that stage. Redwood might not think that he was going to win outright, but he was certainly not going to allow Portillo to be the beneficiary of his resignation. 'You do realize,' he said, 'that if I do well in the first ballot I'm not going to withdraw so you can take over after I've done all the hard work?' It was the start of the collision between Redwood's moral pride and Portillo's resentment. Redwood returned to his room where we now awaited his parliamentary supporters.

It was immediately clear that the quality of those supporters would be a major problem. Sir Tom Arnold had gravitas as a past Vice-Chairman of the Party who had been in charge of the selection of candidates. He represented a marginal seat in suburban Manchester which he was fated to lose if the present situation continued. As the owner of musical copyrights under the will of Ivor Novello, he brought a rare touch of the light and graceful to the proceedings. However, the core team consisted of Cash, Field, Evans and Wilkinson from the sceptic heartlands. The melancholic figures of Barry Legg and David

Martin were also prominent within the inner circle.

Legg, a lugubrious accountant sedulous in the avoidance of charm, had been elected for the marginal seat of Milton Keynes South West in 1992. Soon after his election, he was investigated as part of the District Auditor's enquiry into the Westminster City Council scandal of the late 1980s. Conservative councillors were accused of allocating housing stock in a way calculated to increase Conservative support in marginal wards. The former Chief Whip of the Conservative group, Legg was eventually acquitted of involvement, but in June 1995 that decision still lay in the future. It was therefore important that he was not associated too publicly with the irreproachable Redwood. David Martin looked at his 242 majority in Portsmouth South in the grim conviction that he would be defeated at the next general election. The Hawks Club tie that he wore round his neck was a memory of Cambridge sporting glories, but his future held little consolation. The sober mien of Legg and Martin contrasted with the exuberance of Julian Brazier, the Member for Canterbury. His keen mind had been trained in philosophy and mathematics, and his Catholic integrity allied with a remorseless bonhomie fused the boy scout with the boffin. No one had greater conviction. Only Redwood looked more alarming on television.

Other founder-Redwoodians included Christopher Gill, the brusque Member for Ludlow whose family's ancestral glories included ownership of a chain of butchers' shops in the Midlands. He had some serious ministerial ambitions and was the only member of Redwood's team who asked him what job he could expect to have in a Redwood administration. Roger Knapman, who represented Stroud, quietly chain-smoked his way through the campaign, while Andrew Hargreaves, the breezily Blyton-esque member for marginal Birmingham Hall Green, emerged as a visible supporter and campaigner at a later stage.

Iain Duncan Smith, Norman Tebbit's successor at Chingford, joined Redwood's campaign half-way through. A former Army officer, he claimed – inexplicably – to have been educated at the University of Perugia, an institution best known in English-speaking circles as a language school where British youths could enjoy romantic summer escapades. He had gained the easy reputation of a thinker in undemanding Euro-sceptic circles, and his pretensions increasingly grated on Redwood.

With the exception of David Evans, who combined the exotic with the earthy, and the bubbly Brazier, Redwood's campaign team erred on the side of greyness. 'We'll need someone to mother us while this is going on,' said Redwood to them, thinking of his parliamentary team's need for domestic comforts in the long days ahead. 'Can someone get hold of Christine Hamilton?' The prospect of the termagant wife of the Member for Tatton taking charge of their 'rest and recuperation' tinged the cabal's collective face with an ashen hue. The moment was allowed to pass.

These were tired, not especially clever, middle-aged men who despaired of a Tory victory and, in many cases, of their own electoral survival. But that was not the impression created by Redwood's first press conference in the Jubilee Room of the House of Commons that afternoon. As Redwood and I walked across Westminster Hall, we realized that we would not be able to make our way through the melee of journalists, photographers and camera crews. Redwood's resignation had become an international news event. We changed tack and arrived through the back entrance where a handful of Euro-rebels had congregated. Now they gathered around Redwood, Lamont and myself as we sat down for the press conference at which Redwood formally declared his candidature for the leadership.

Although she was dominated by a strong excess of joy, Billericay's Teresa Gorman, the Boadicea of the sceptics, had not intended to highjack the event. Redwood was strong, witty and confident in a performance that surprised many. But, with Gorman and Marlow standing behind him, the image for the cameras was that of a candidate who was in the pocket of Mrs Gorman's hectic green dress and encased in Marlow's Old Wellingtonian summer blazer. The impression was that of a coup launched by a group of dissident Latin-American lieutenant-colonels who had just taken over the local airport and cancelled all flights.

It was ideal copy for Tim Collins, who immediately started briefing on Redwood's madness and that of his supporters. The idea of an unhinged Redwood had started the previous Friday, when the BBC had unearthed footage of Redwood displaying an antic disposition while trying to mouth the words of the Welsh National Anthem at a Welsh Conservative Conference two years previously. He had been trying to conceal his ignorance in his first week as Welsh Secretary and ended up looking foolish. Endlessly re-played subsequently by the BBC, the footage did great harm to his reputation. However, his supporters were more inane than insane. They were either terrified of the press or inept at dealing with it. As Parliamentary males they under-estimated Teresa Gorman's appeal as a clever and vigorous woman. After the photographs of the first press conference appeared, they ran scared and alienated her rather than managed her.

By that afternoon we had decided on a pattern of daily press conferences, preceded by a meeting of the Parliamentary team at 9.00 a.m. in the House of Commons to decide the text of the daily press release. Major had no message other than that of the grand principle of immutability. We would set the agenda with a different theme each day.

Until later that Monday, the 26th of June, the campaign had no headquarters. Earlier that day I went to see Sir Michael Richardson, whose merchant bank, Hambro Magan, had premises at 32, Queen Anne's Gate in Westminster. We discussed using the large basement of the building as a campaign base, but the bank panicked at the thought of a large number of over-excited Tory Parliamentarians taking over part of their premises and the consequent threat to the security and confidentiality of that building. Later that day, the somewhat inter-war figure of Sir Benjamin Slade emerged. Slade, a catering and container millionaire, had a dandyish Dornford Yates streak and

a dim stream-of-consciousnesss conversational style that made him a Fourth
Eleven version of Virginia Woolf. However, he liked to be thought of as well-
connected and had a flat at his disposal in Ashley Gardens, close to
Westminster Cathedral. This, on Tuesday, became the Redwood caravansarai.

Redwood's eruption suddenly made the whole of Major's Cabinet, and the
uses of his political world, look weary, stale, flat and unprofitable. Margaret
Thatcher, furthermore, was beginning to sound uneasy. In Washington on
Monday, she said how excited she was about the Gingrich-fuelled revival
among the Republicans: 'I suppose something similar is about to happen in
my own country. We must have the true Conservative policies I pursued –
policies of lower taxes, keeping our national Parliamentary sovereignty, and
the independence of the pound sterling.' The words matched Redwood's at his
Monday press conference.

Major's team began the campaign by briefing that the Prime Minister
would only be in trouble if one hundred abstentions were recorded. Now they
panicked and started saying that a majority of one would be enough. On this
view, all Major needed was 165 votes from the 329-strong parliamentary
force. An Independent Television News poll of 229 MPs conducted on the
Saturday before Redwood declared showed that only 156 would definitely
vote for the Prime Minister; as many as sixty-eight refused to answer. Major
was at Cannes for an EU summit at the start of the week in circumstances
eerily reminiscent of Thatcher's visit to Versailles in November 1990 – once
again it was a bad time for a Conservative Prime Minister to be out of the
country.

In something of a funk, the Cabinet decided to try the hypocrisy line.
Major complained that Redwood had 'sat there, accepting our policies. Just a
fortnight ago he was part of a policy-making Cabinet.' For many, including
Redwood, it was the first time that they had heard Major talk of his Cabinet
as a policy forum rather than as a cast of competitive egos to be artfully
manipulated. More cautiously, Hurd said, 'I have seen him sit around the table
very recently when the policies which he may be about to criticize were
endorsed by everybody.' Brashly and rashly, Kenneth Clarke committed
himself to the view that the Conservatives would never be elected in a
thousand years on the basis of a Redwood programme. Peter Riddell in *The
Times* agreed: Redwood would find it difficult to separate himself from
collective Cabinet decisions and was heading for a policy cul-de-sac away
from the grand certainties of the middle ground.

Redwood avoided the charge of inconsistency simply by being consistent.
His suspicious mind knew that his enemies were always ready to ambush him,
and so he never committed to paper thoughts that he could not defend later. If
words, spoken or written, were to be his only secure allies, then he had to be
sure that they were his and no one else's. He always knew that at some stage
spies in the Whitehall jungle would ransack his correspondence in order to
find incriminating evidence. They would be frustrated in the next few days.

Redwood intended to use the campaign as an opportunity to push the Government on to his agenda, but he was not about to repudiate great areas of what that Government said it stood for. Indeed, he hardly needed to do so. The problem was rarely what the Government said it was doing. Rather it was the gap between rhetoric and reality that had created difficulties. Besides, when in doubt, it would always be possible to insert the catch-all phrase 'as the Prime Minister has said' in front of most policy prescriptions.

Redwood was clear that the campaign had to be about ideas, policies and the Tory future. He refused to offer jobs for votes and to haggle over ministerial posts as a patron-in-waiting. He also did not want the campaign to be about John Major, his personality and the absence of policy. He would adhere to that position however much time Major's team might spend on character assassination. This went against the grain for Lamont. Once Redwood could no longer use his Secretary of State's room, our morning strategy meetings were held in the small office shared by Evans and Field. Seated in the only armchair available, and with all the authority of a quondam Chancellor, Lamont's litany was constant: 'You've got to go for Major. You've got to go for Major – and I can show you how to do it.'

Our meetings soon degenerated into a babel of conflicting voices and discordant egos. Bill Cash thought that he was not on television often enough: 'I'm really very good and very experienced.' Excluded from the meetings, Marlow would parade up and down the corridor outside hoping for crumbs from the table. Bill Walker, the MP for Tayside North, raised the importance of the Scottish dimension with wearisome regularity. Legg looked increasingly glum as Brazier became very excitable. Evans' costermonger roar would bawl for order. Lines of communication between Ashley Gardens and the House of Commons were exiguous. When MPs were given bleepers, they refused to use them, and some were thrown away and found in wastepaper baskets. Not surprisingly, Redwood and I decided that the only way to proceed was for us to meet at increasingly early hours of the morning in order to decide the text of the press release. We would then present the text to the 9.00 a.m. meeting.

On the morning of Tuesday the 27th of June, the day after he had declared, Redwood held his first press conference devoted to policy questions, in the Queen Elizabeth II Conference Centre across the road from Westminster Abbey. The main hall was packed. Booking the Centre was the main expense of the campaign; Evans and Cash had promised to pay the bills between them. Cash was specially keen to spend money, and explained to me that he had access to very substantial sums held abroad. I assumed that these were Goldsmith bank accounts, but did not enquire too closely. It would have been disastrous had it been believed that Redwood's campaign expenses were being met, however indirectly, from such a source. In any event, bills were only paid very slowly – parliamentary promises were cheaper than the bills incurred as a result of those promises. Alas, Redwood's parliamentary supporters shared in the general decadence of Major's Tories.

Redwood's message was that 'the Conservative Party is the party of low taxation or it is nothing.' The Government's £303 billion budget could be pruned by reducing overhead costs. Redwoodian populism was catered for with a defence of small local hospitals and their staff, with opposition to 'abolishing the pound', with warnings about the powers of the European Court, and with measures designed to increase crime detection and to stop defence cuts. At our meeting that morning, Barry Field, as an Isle of Wight man, had raised the issue of the decommissioning of the Royal Yacht *Britannia*. The final text of the press release therefore included the famous sentence, 'Tories keep Royal Yachts, not scrap them.'

The general effect was of a shopping list that covered too many areas and gave hostages to fortune by combining an unconvincing populism with unspecified savings as a result of mere administrative economies. It was not even as if the cause of *Britannia* were popular, given the current dissatisfaction with the Royal Family. Redwood would have to produce more detailed budgetary solutions at the next morning's conference.

After the initial drama of Monday's declaration and Tuesday's press conference, it was obvious that Redwood had changed the terms of the Tory debate. By Monday, Peter Lilley had become convinced that Redwood had done the right thing in resigning, and told him that he too would resign by the middle of the week. Some Cabinet Ministers were now saying that Major's campaign team was wrong when it briefed that a mere majority of one in the Parliamentary Party would be enough to secure the Prime Minister's survival. Speculation increasingly centred on the possibility of a Heseltine–Portillo pact. 'Senior MPs close to Heseltine' (usually Michael Mates) were saying that Heseltine knew that he would now have to concede to the right on Europe. They were unaware of how far Heseltine was implicated in Major's plot. Commentators also consistently over-estimated the strength of Heseltine's parliamentary army. When it came to the crunch he could call on the loyalty of no more than twenty to thirty MPs. The untested assumption that up to one third of the Parliamentary Party would follow Heseltine was a legacy of the late 1980s and early 1990s. Time and association with Major had dimmed that once formidable lustre.

From Tuesday onwards, Michael Portillo's supporters began to recover their nerve as relations between them and the Redwoodians deteriorated. The latter claimed the high moral ground – always a dangerous territory in political life. The former masked their irritation by talking of the dangers of a split on the right. Redwoodians, and Redwood himself, thought that the only split was caused by Portillo's failure to resign and support him, or at the least agree on a joint ticket. In order to cover their resentment, Portillo supporters such as Alan Duncan, Bernard Jenkin and John Whittingdale, Thatcher's former Political Secretary, talked up the dangers of a Heseltine succession. In part, being ignorant of the machinations of Cabinet politics, perhaps they genuinely believed in such a danger. But it also provided a good excuse for not supporting Redwood.

At the same time the respectable right, such as James Cran and Michael Spicer, were sticking to their line. Major had to be supported in order to stop Heseltine. It was not the least of Major's achievements that not only did he split the Conservative Party, he also split the right-leaning part of it into warring factions. The legacy of these days was that the 'right' ended up loathing each other more than the 'left'. Truly, the Tories had become the nasty party.

On Wednesday, Redwood set out a modest proposal for a 1.67 per cent reduction in public spending, amounting to £5 billion. The Conservative party had to be a tax-cutting party. Modern Government had to wake up to the reality of British business, which had made enormous administrative savings during the recession. Now the Government had to contract out more services, sell its empty houses, office blocks and land, and stop recruiting administrators and managers.

> There are far too many layers of management, far too many consultants doing jobs that could be done by civil servants, and expensive buying when different rules could produce a better and cheaper answer. We can raise more money by private finance and sell more under-used assets.

The culture of commentary was unimpressed. They had expected better of a man with an appetite for global explanation. Redwood suddenly looked intellectually timid. But he was trying to tread a narrow dividing line between two groups of protagonists. On the one hand, there were those who said that every penny of the £303 billion of Government spending was sacrosanct: touch it in any way and nurses would be reduced to begging on the streets while new-born babes would be thrown from Westminster Bridge. Kenneth Clarke added his criticisms. Redwood, he complained, was plucking figures out of the air and Treasury figures had already assumed efficiency savings of 2 to 3 per cent. Another group maintained that there was no point in anything other than deep and immediate cuts – these were the only 'intellectually honest' responses. That answer was also one that led to imaginings of Calcutta-like scenes on the streets of London and the major cities. Redwood found both sets of attitudes extreme and silly. Both groups of attitudinizers had a common interest in ridiculing his cautious ambitions that suited the assumptions of neither left nor right. Many others found Redwood's plan disappointingly timid and simplistic, given the depth of understanding attributed to him in these matters. None the less, Redwood thought that the first step on the journey was the most important one to take. His critics' demand for an exhaustive plan to be mapped out before they even began the venture seemed to him unreasonable.

It was at this stage, in the middle of the week, that Lilley decided that he would not resign after all. Redwood's campaign was beginning to stall, and Major's men were starting to brief that a group of MPs would resign the whip were Redwood or Portillo to become leader. George Walden and Alan Howarth both delivered themselves of this threat. It was characteristic of Major to invoke at this stage the spectre of a general election rather than commit himself to action through policy. When the Prime Minister returned from Cannes he was forced into his single manifesto proposal of the election – a vague commitment to abolish inheritance tax.

At Thursday's press conference, Redwood returned to Europe and the delusion, widespread in the Conservative Party, that the Tories could win on the basis of clear hostility to the Single Currency. A single market, he pointed out, 'does not need a monopoly currency. Firms and people can trade in the currency of their choice.' Moreover, if it is to work a single currency area requires a common political allegiance to work.

> Once you are in a Single Currency area, you must accept the need to send extra
> tax receipts to the poorer parts of the Union. Southern England sends money
> to Liverpool as part of our national pattern, the accepted price of a Single
> Currency and of shared history and sense of identity.

But southern England was not yet ready to send its pence to Sicily, Greece and Portugal. He proposed, blandly, 'A Europe of free peoples where trade grows ever greater, regulations are reduced, diversity flourishes. We are not against more Europe; we are against more government.' Cross-breeding could not harmonize the dachshund and the English bulldog. The Government's opposition to devolution within the UK had to march hand in hand with this new European agenda.

The problem with this back to ideological basics strategy was that Labour was the most effective pro-European party in British politics and its lead in the opinion polls remained massive. In the previous few days, the Conservatives had indeed increased their standing in the polls – by seven points from a lamentable twenty-two to a not quite so derisory twenty-nine – for the first time since September 1992. The shaky renaissance was due to the impression of a Party and a Government that had suddenly once again become interesting. But this was not because of the appeal of Euro-scepticism, which, if anything, was seen as old Tory rather than as part of some putative new Tory agenda. The contest was developing a *Blitzkrieg* intensity compared with the trench warfare of the 1997 campaign; unlike that contest, it was turning into a one-sided battle of ideas as well as a clash of wills. It showed that the Tory Party could still be a vital force, and the polls recorded that impression. There was still just enough life left in its political body to fight the virus of decay.

Norman Tebbit, guardian of the collective Euro-sceptic conscience and Margaret Thatcher's Party Chairman from 1985 to 1987, declared for Redwood on Tuesday, following his magisterial performance the day before. Thereafter, however, Redwood's campaign struggled to get a single major Tory to declare for their man. Outside Parliament, hopes were raised that Lord Hanson, one of the great capitalist figures of the Thatcher era, would support Redwood. However, in an early example of the indifference of the Thatcher-establishment to Redwood, Hanson refused to intervene. Approaches were made to the disaffected Kenneth Baker, who had been dismissed as Home

Secretary after the 1992 general election. But he had his eye on a peerage in Major's dissolution honours list. John Patten proved to be a magnificent tease and much afflicted by a lightness of political being. He enjoyed being canvassed and insisted on Redwood talking to him very publicly in the Committee Corridor, 'so everybody can see I am talking to you'. But he was a disenchanted and detached being whose future lay in the City. He would not declare.

On Friday, Redwood returned to the question of how the Conservatives could win elections. This was a broader and more promising issue than the European one since it raised questions of reliability, truth-telling and competence. On Wednesday, he had been blown off course badly by the *Independent*, which had highlighted his response to the question of how he would select members of his Cabinet. Light-heartedly, Redwood had used an unfortunate phrase, when he said that he would 'ask my colleagues to confess their sins'. The sins he had in mind were strictly financial and departmental. How much money was left hidden in their departmental budgets at the end of the year, and where were the inefficiencies? But the cue was a maladroit one, and led back to the back-to-basics débâcle.

When asked to amplify his initial remarks, Redwood explained that he would have a chat with aspirant Ministers, in the course of which he would spell out the risks and pressures of the proposed job as well as the standards he wanted to be upheld. 'I would explain to the potential Minister that there would be a lot of intrusion.' He would ask, 'were they happy that their financial affairs and their love life and all the rest of it were in good working order?' His justification was an old one: 'I think there is a danger that if someone cheats financially or on their wife, they might cheat in other ways.'

Redwood's direct moral code saw nothing wrong with saying that he would ask his future colleagues whether there was anything in their past or present lives about which they felt uneasy. It took a politician with a rare simplicity of view and a high regard for truth, as well as one with a private life devoid of late twentieth-century ambiguity, to think that this would be an effective screening process for crooks and adulterers. So long as they claimed that the land was bright as they looked westward, all would be well. Otherwise, the presumption was that anguished introspection would overwhelm the candidate, who would subsequently withdraw in recognition of the public opprobrium that might be his lot if he persisted. It was a striking instance of Redwood's naive rationalism when dealing with human nature, especially in its political form.

The press reaction was immediate. Redwood was described as a political leader intent on leading a government of saints, and the story undoubtedly reduced the number of votes eventually cast for him. There was also a moral majoritarian element among some of his supporters, which was alien to his spirit but which was undoubtedly happy to support the impression of a campaign run by scribes and pharisees. Duncan Smith, for example, was much given to inveighing against those whom he called, in his semi-intellectual way, the libertines. Many of these were to be found in Portillo's circle, where they found a more relaxed attitude to personal and sexual morality than was current among Redwood's supporters.

Generally the press was generous to Redwood because they wanted a proper campaign and he had delivered them a real contest. The *Daily Mail*, especially, championed him as Middle England's family-values man, and decided that it was time to ditch the captain, although evenhandedly the *Mail on Sunday* endorsed Major. Simon Heffer prevailed on Max Hastings to throw the *Daily Telegraph*'s weight behind Redwood's world view, despite Hastings' reservations. Heffer and I organized a meeting between Conrad Black and Redwood in Black's Chester Square home on the 28th of June. There, surrounded by Napoleonic memorabilia, Black quizzed Redwood on his prospects. Redwood told him that he was running to win. Black was not convinced, but he did think that subverting Major was a good idea. The *Telegraph* declared that it was time for Mr Major to go, although it also said, sniffily, that Redwood would have to improve his credibility on tax-cuts in the campaign for the second ballot.

The *Sun* enjoyed Redwood views and values, although it found his populist embrace chaste, chilly and unconvincing. It enjoyed teasing him as a gawky scholarship boy, but otherwise Redwood versus Deadwood summed up its views. This, after all, was the paper that believed that Major could not lead a cinema queue. *The Times* gave Redwood a fair wind and said that, 'If MPs want a change, they must vote for Mr Redwood whether they like him or not. Good Conservatives should vote against Mr Major'. William Rees-Mogg thought that he had discovered another world-historical figure with whom he could leave his visiting card. It was agreeable to find a Tory who might talk about Augustan, rather than Victorian, values.

David Hunt was sent to the Welsh Office as acting Secretary of State on Monday the 26th of June in order to dig up as much discreditable information as possible on Redwood's record in office. It was thought that, as a former Welsh Secretary, he would know where the bodies were buried. His only coup was to discover that Redwood had refused to distribute certain European monies to Welsh farmers – never a favourite occupational group with the former Secretary of State. The information was passed on to Keith Raffan, a left-leaning former Welsh Conservative MP who now worked as a journalist. Raffan raised the question at a press conference, but the issue died a political death.

At the final weekend, Redwood presented himself to the Party and the press as a Conservative who could win elections. On Wednesday the 28th he had written to Major proposing a debate. Major replied on the following day:

> I recall when I was a Tory candidate fighting a hopeless seat with no chance of winning, I was advised to challenge the incumbent MP to a debate. The gist of his reply was, 'nice try, but no'. You may wish to know he went on to win a handsome victory.

The smug indifference was characteristic. However, Major was eventually prevailed upon to address, with Redwood, a meeting of the 92 Group of Tory intransigents at an eve-of-poll meeting the following Monday night.

On Friday Redwood clarified the central question for the Conservatives: 'How can our party lift the electoral curse that has descended upon us?' We had agreed that the only question that mattered to Tory MPs was 'Who gives me the best chance of keeping my job?' Redwood therefore asked a simple question: 'Do you really believe that we can win again if nothing changes?' He presented his truisms about education and families, about self-discipline and communities, about housing and crime. But the real point was the proclaimed need for a new, unabashed Conservatism that would create 'a new dash, an excitement, a passion for what we are doing'. New Labour, it seemed, needed new Conservatism.

By this stage Peter Lilley had reverted to his earlier posture. He now thought that John Redwood had been right to resign. He wished he had done so as well, but he was locked in and Major had thrown away the key. Teasingly, Evans heightened expectations of Lilley's early release, and remarked to the press: 'I haven't seen Peter Lilley with a grin on his face like that for years.' But now Lilley had to remain confined to quarters.

During his campaign, Redwood told his followers that they should see themselves as Tory cavaliers bringing back vivacity and colour to a grey and tired Party. Legg looked at him mournfully, Duncan Smith pondered the allusion, Brazier looked all set to be Prince Rupert of the Rhine. Now, Redwood wished the whole party to be rescued from brutes in suits: 'Labour are trying to occupy our ground, as Tony Blair raises money from the politically correct to pay for opinion research to show how unpopular political correctness is.' Conservatives had to awake, 'set out our beliefs, and get back the habit of winning'.

Redwood's press campaign was extraordinarily successful. It met a need in British politics and fulfilled all the demands of the media-class. On the Friday afternoon before the ballot I made sure that Redwood spoke, in turn, to the *Sunday Times*, the *Sunday Telegraph* and the *Mail on Sunday* in the calm surroundings of Belgravia, well away from the heat and dust of Westminster. The *Sunday Telegraph* was the only national newspaper to endorse him on his own merits as leader of the Conservative Party, but the other titles blessed his campaign as a means to an end and a force for change.

The one failure arose following a commission from the *Spectator* for an article setting out his personal credo. Robin Harris, who had briefly served as head of Margaret Thatcher's Policy Unit in 1990 and was still on her staff, volunteered to ghost-write the article, and Redwood agreed that he should submit a draft. What emerged was a complete article that had to be rejected because the tone was crass and confrontational. Harris eventually transferred his loyalties to Michael Howard, another aggressive Tory, at a later stage in the Conservative drama. The loss of an article was no very great matter, although it would have been better to please the *Spectator*, whose readership remained influential. But to offend the considerable *amour propre* of Thatcher's chief political intimate, who had ghosted much of her memoirs, was a different matter, and a very great mistake. The moment marked the further cooling of the already tepid relationship between Redwood and Thatcher.

At a personal level, Redwood was now at ease with journalists as he never had been before. When I first persuaded him to improve his acquaintance with Simon Heffer, Major's Grand Inquisitor, earlier in 1995, he did so very nervously. When he learnt that Matthew d'Ancona, then of *The Times* and latterly of the *Sunday Telegraph*, was not only a friend of Michael Portillo but had also written a celebrated story on the basis of a leaked version of the draft Ulster Peace Agreement, he became alarmed and cancelled lunch with him. Now, however, he was a liberated man who had confronted his political demons, discovered that they were baseless, and laid them to rest.

It went with the grain of Redwood's nature and mine that we should do well in the battle of the written media. We both spent less time on the artifices of television and, on the day of the ballot, this omission proved to have important consequences. Redwood remained tense and awkward on camera, although once he started winning and relaxing, as he did against Brian Mawhinney in a *Panorama* debate on the eve of poll, his performance could improve.

During the second half of the week, the flat in Ashley Gardens became increasingly fraught. A seemingly inexhaustible army of pustular young Conservative males had to be turned away each day, although some managed to infiltrate the building and join the campaign. The atmosphere became foetid. Neighbours, who supported Major, complained that the campaign, which surely qualified as a business of sorts, broke the terms of a lease designed for domestic existence. With the weariness of crusaders on the way to a very distant Jerusalem, the Redwoodian campaigners moved to offices in Buckingham Gate on the Thursday, claiming that these were additional premises needed for their burgeoning activities.

In the House of Commons, a quarrel raged all week between David Evans and Marcus Fox. Evans was rightly suspicious of the neutrality of the 1922 Executive Committee and of Fox as its Chairman. Memories were still vivid of the inept conduct of Cranley Onslow, Fox's predecessor, during the 1990 leadership contest. At the close of poll, Onslow had picked up the ballot box, and promptly dropped it, perhaps because of the emotion of the occasion. The ballot papers cascaded on to the floor, and the Chairman of the 1922 Executive Committee could be seen stuffing them back in. Many feared a repetition of such bungling in a managed electoral process.

The first request was that the Electoral Reform Society should be brought in as neutral outsiders to run the election. Fox stood by the rules. Only the 1922 Executive could invigilate. Next, Evans proposed a secret ballot, in which each MP would vote in private. Fox agreed that screens should be erected in a corner of the Committee Room in which voting was to take place. If MPs wished to vote in secret, they could do so behind the screens. Equally, if they wished to vote more publicly by marking their ballot paper on the desk behind which the scrutineers sat, they could do so.

Evans was unimpressed. The scrutineers would be the eighteen members of the 1922 Executive, who would take turns to invigilate for one-hour shifts. Only four – Rhodes Boyson, James Pawsey, John Townend and Evans himself – had refused to sign the Prime Minister's nomination papers. Overwhelmingly, the 1922 Executive were Major's men. Those who voted behind the screens would be assumed to have voted for Redwood. Brave Tory MPs were not so thick on the ground, and effectively every vote for Redwood would be declared. Those who wished to curry favour would seize the opportunity to vote publicly for Major. Evans threatened to take the matter to court and seek an injunction. By this stage, however, Tory rancour was so profound that nothing would have been gained from the accusation of curmudgeonly behaviour. None the less, when the day came, Evans' suspicions were justified. Many an MP voted publicly and, to demonstrate loyalty, showed their ballot paper to the scrutineers before placing it in the box. For example, Peter Luff, the MP for Worcester, bragged to journalists of how he had shown his Majorite vote to Fox.

However, Redwood's followers were delighted and astonished by the behaviour of the Whips Office which, when not neutral, was actively friendly. Neutrality was officially enjoined upon them during any period when the Parliamentary Party was without a leader. None the less, Major had been a Whip, he was one of them, and often visited the Whips Office when he was Prime Minister. An official requirement of neutrality was not preventing Central Office behaving in a partisan way. The contrast was instructive. Major had made the Whips' job needlessly difficult during the previous three years as he used them to force the Parliamentary Party to vote against its wishes and convictions. Many of them saw in Redwood's candidature, and in what might issue from it, an alternative and less stressful way of conducting Government business in the House of Commons, with more free votes being offered. Richard Ryder was now tired and disillusioned with Major's methods. Andrew MacKay, his deputy and a former Birmingham car-dealer with a persuasive manner, was angling to be his successor, and as a fellow Berkshire MP had always been friendly with Redwood. Other Whips were also friendly. Derek Conway was decent and uncomplicated, although resentful at being kept in his post for so long. David Willetts, a former Redwood *protégé* at the Policy Unit, was openly hesitant about voting for Major. The Prime Minister's own original power base had become shaky.

In other areas, Major's authority remained unshaken. During the last weekend before the election, Sir Basil Feldman, the Chairman of the National Union of Conservative Associations, popped up, looking more than ever like a character in a Whitehall farce. In a surreal intervention worthy of a 1930s Stalinist Communist Party Congress, Feldman opined that a survey of the

Party's activists, by now a severely metaphorical concept, showed that 90 per cent supported John Major. It seemed that the grass-roots wanted more weed-killer.

Once he had returned from Cannes, Major knew that he had a real fight on his hands. On Wednesday evening he had dinner in the Commons with two Parliamentary henchmen, Archie Hamilton and Eric Pickles, a bulky stage Yorkshireman out of the pages of an early Priestley novel. They realized that they had to respond to the élan of the early Redwood campaign. Fear would be their handmaiden. Now Major would talk of the abyss that threatened the Party. Under a new leader, the party might split asunder. There would certainly be demands for an immediate general election in order to validate the mandate of a new Prime Minister with a radically different set of policies. Who could doubt, they would point out to waverers, the result of a 1995 election? These were bad arguments. Macmillan in 1957 and Callaghan in 1976 had both taken over from incumbent Prime Ministers; Macmillan had waited for nearly three years, and Callaghan for three, before calling a general election. But Major's supporters knew their men, the constituency of the craven and the confused on whom such a ploy might work.

On Europe, Major decided to develop an argument to which he adhered with increasing implausibility over the next two years. He would not rule out joining a Single Currency because Britain's interests would be harmed were she not to be represented at the negotiating table. He addressed the Tories' Positive European Group along these lines on Thursday evening, the 29th, and was supported by all twelve MPs who spoke. Again the argument was foolish. The conditions for joining a single currency had already been established at Maastricht and no more negotiations would be undertaken on that front. As a member of the European Union, Britain could not be excluded from discussing the only remaining issue: who would be allowed to join the new currency club? But repeated often enough, the mantra of losing influence acquired a persuasive, if unexamined, force.

Major's team also played a clever and complex game in teasing the press and the Parliamentary Party over predictions of the result. They had the field to themselves, since Redwood and his team decided that their only safe option was not to predict any numbers at all.

The complex rules of the ballot meant that to win outright Major not only had to achieve a simple majority of those voting, he also had to be ahead of his rival by 15 per cent of those entitled to vote. The total electorate was 329, since one seat was vacant and Sir Richard Body was continuing to refuse the Conservative Whip. Thus Major had to be clear of his rival by fifty votes. Much therefore depended on the number of abstentions, and it was thought that these would mostly come from supporters of Heseltine and of Portillo, willing to wound but afraid to strike in the first round.

By Thursday, Major's team had moved on from the first weekend's happy confidence that a majority of one would be enough. The Prime Minister needed a convincing win. The game was to define what 'convincing' meant.

Majorettes were happy to read press reports that day estimating Redwood's support at between eighty-five and ninety-five and their own at 165 to 195, while the number of abstentions and 'undecideds' fluctuated between forty and eighty. Their tactic was to inflate the Heseltine threat, in reality a paper dragon, in order to frighten rightish MPs into their camp. If such MPs also supported Portillo, the high level of support for Redwood was an additional argument to deploy to drag them into the Major camp – at least initially. Portillo's men, never as numerous as commentators thought, wanted Redwood to do well, but not so well as to assume a commanding lead at the first ballot.

It was important for the Major camp to establish what would count as a significant anti-Major vote, i.e. the vote for Redwood plus the abstentions. By the middle of the first week, too many commentators for Major's liking were writing that a combined vote against him of ninety would be very serious, and that with a hundred he would have to go. It was always the case that the Prime Minister would survive a total vote against him of eighty or fewer. Any more votes against the Prime Minister would require Redwood to persuade a significant number of the pay-roll vote (all Ministers and Parliamentary Private Secretaries) to vote for him or at least to abstain. The pay-roll consisted of almost half the total number of Conservative MPs and the presumption was that they would vote for Major. Redwood needed to make some inroads on their numbers in order to gain a convincing first-ballot result. He could not rely on the backbench vote alone.

By Friday, Major's team had managed to shift the ground and to establish in the press that the situation would become seriously damaging at a total of a hundred anti-Major votes. In raising this possibility, they were overtly telling Portillo's supporters that Redwood was now threatening to consolidate his position and a that a vote for Major, rather than mere abstention, was the best way of avoiding that prospect.

The first, misleading, indication of a Heseltine deal came on Friday with reports from right-wing sources that Heseltine's supporters would vote for Redwood in order to boost the anti-Major vote. Towards the end of the campaign, Evans met Keith Hampson, the Member for Leeds North West, one of the diminished band of Heseltine corporals who had aged in the expectation of their master's call to arms. But if Heseltine's men talked of sending Blücher-like reinforcements it would only have been in ignorance of Heseltine's true intentions or out of a desire to dupe Redwood's team into excessive confidence. It was always going to be helpful for Major's team to encourage expectations of a high Redwood poll. Anything below eighty to ninety could be represented as a defeat for Redwood, and they did not expect him to do as well as that.

While MPs left Westminster for the weekend, the campaign teams continued in their headquarters. Redwood's pallid young men perspired into their take-out pizzas. That Saturday the temperature at the Centre Court at Wimbledon hit 110 degrees Fahrenheit. Majorettes continued the game of inflating Redwood's expectations. They claimed to be expecting ghastly headlines at the weekend with possible Redwood endorsements from Kenneth Baker and John Patten. Both were visibly busted flushes by that stage, and the endorsement by John Townend, the austere Yorkshire accountant and MP for Bridlington, suffered by comparison. When Sir George Gardiner endorsed Redwood on the final Monday, he made it clear that he did so only in order to open the way for the second ballot.

The shape of things to come began to emerge with reports on Monday the 3rd of July that Heseltine's supporters were now preparing to vote for the Prime Minister rather than abstain. The same supporters also said that they had been approached by Redwood's supporters asking them to vote for Redwood rather than abstain. As 'right-wingers', and not just the core Redwood supporters, began to get wind of the danger they were in, they started to use scare tactics on right-wingers who were refusing to vote for Redwood lest his high vote in the first ballot lead to ultimate victory for Heseltine.

On the eve of poll, Major's men continued their calculated gamble. Well-placed sources now said that the Prime Minister might have as many as 120 against him, and that he needed between 220 and 230 votes in order to survive. Between 210 and 220 supporters would leave him in dangerous territory. Matthew Parris reflected the new urgency among Major's supporters, and wrote a *Times* article that could have gained him a First in Counter-Factual Studies. He urged those who would be shopping in Oxford Street five to six months hence to give thanks to John Major for their deliverance from Christmas bombing. The Prime Minister's involvement in the Irish 'peace process' would keep them alive.

'If you want a new leader,' wrote John Redwood to Tory MPs on Monday, 'you have to vote for me on this ballot. There will be no second chance. This is the only leadership ballot before the general election.' Events conspired to prove him right. But, as the temperatures soared beneath a sweltering Westminster sky, Conservative MPs disappeared from view in a fog of calculation and counter-calculation, finding, like Milton's fallen angels, 'no end in wandering mazes lost'.

If Major's campaign recovered in the last few days before the ballot, Portillo's unofficial campaign lurched into absurdity. Wednesday brought the revelation of the full scale of the preparations at 11, Lord North Street. A platoon of British Telecom engineers had been at work over the previous three days installing an estimated forty telephone lines, and three floors had been stripped of their furnishings. Interviewed on Thursday in Luxembourg, where he was attending a meeting of EU Social Affairs Ministers, Portillo expressed sympathy for BT engineers being harassed by the press. Back in England on Sunday, he appeared at a cricket match between the Department of Employment and industrial journalists – as an observer. The comparison between Redwood's cricket match a week previously and Portillo's non-playing status proved a gift to commentators. An enthused Maurice Cowling said breathlessly that his old pupil had 'courage, charm, subtlety, intelligence, youth and conviction'. Others thought that, on his own chosen ground of manoeuvring in the thickets of high politics, Portillo needed guidance from his old teacher.

Redwood's ten days in the sun had given focus and energy to the causes of Tory discontent. Previously, discontent had congregated around the ragged and rebellious army of Euro-sceptics. Now the European issue had been placed in the context of wider concerns about nationhood and identity, about the health service, education, crime and taxation. Redwood had had to do this, because Euro-fury remained a minority pursuit. A MORI poll published in *The Times* on Thursday the 29th of June suggested that only 26 per cent of the population ranked Europe as among the most important issues facing Britain. By contrast, approximately double that number defined employment, health, education, and law and order as important issues. However, Europe mattered disproportionately to Tories, 45 per cent of whom ranked it as important. In the wake of Major's divisive strategies, the Tories needed a realistic European settlement before they could start getting anything else right.

Redwood had avoided direct criticism of the Prime Minister. He simply said that he stood for a new style of politics, for an Elizabethan verve and excitement. 'Everything', he complained, 'is so drab.' But his own personality had failed to ignite the public. A further MORI poll published the next day showed that a Redwood-led Conservative Party would suffer a further 2.5 per cent swing against it, whereas with Heseltine as leader there would be a marginal 2.5 per cent swing in its favour in the continuing shadow of Labour's mountainous lead. As the dog days of July approached, Redwood's merit was that for a few days he had taken the political battle out of the nerveless hands of the professional political class. It was no idle boast, as well as a clever riposte, for Redwood to respond to one question at a press conference that his chief intellectual influence was the British people. Portillo, by contrast, was the consummate professional politician bred within the bone of his Party's political machine. That accounted both for his appeal within his party and for a wider public suspicion. Redwood might not be the alternative, but he had shown that the British public found its political class arrogant, second-rate and stuffy – especially in its Conservative form.

Redwood had been very apprehensive when Christopher Gill issued, without authorization, a poster enjoining MPs to vote for Redwood because 'No Change Equals No Chance'. Whatever the provocation from Major's circle, it was important not to personalize the contest. Their tone was well caught in the remark by Anthony Seldon, Major's licensed biographer, that Redwood was a 'joke figure' lacking in 'political acumen or charm' and in Archie Hamilton's belief that he 'sounded like a joke'. The success of Gill's poster, and its crisp encapsulation of his message, made Redwood bold. When, at his last press conference, he criticized 'the Cowley Street style – uncertainty based on indecision', it was a direct dig at Major. 'There has been no consistency, only the shifting sand of unattributable briefing responding to the challenging headlines.'

Perhaps Major's most significant endorsement came from Tony Blair, who gave him a relaxed time at Prime Minister's Questions on Thursday and allowed him to shine. On Friday he endorsed Major's leadership and wrote in *The Times* that only Major could unite the Conservative Party. The Blairite project presupposed Major's continuance in office.

On Tuesday the 4th of July, the day of the ballot, the usual eerie calm of an election day fell on Westminster. The Parliamentarians of what Canning had called 'the stupid old Conservative Party' trooped into Committee Room 12 to vote. Redwood and I sat with Lamont and a few others in Evans' and Field's office in the late afternoon. With his usual precise election manager's touch, Lamont forecast that Redwood had won between eighty and ninety votes. We settled down to wait for five o'clock, the hour when the voting stopped and the counting began.

Marcus Fox had arranged to telephone the result to Major and Redwood immediately after the vote was counted and before the formal announcement was made in Committee Room 14. When the phone rang just before 5.15, Redwood picked it up and wrote the results down on a sheet of paper. He repeated the figures to those of us in the room, and then phoned his wife to tell her that he had done well, but not well enough to force a second ballot.

Eighty-nine MPs voted for Redwood, 218 for Major, and twenty-two either abstained or spoilt their ballot papers. Just over one third of the Parliamentary Party – 111 MPs in all – had refused to support the Prime Minister, who was in the upper reaches of territory previously regarded as ambiguous. The truth was that Major had done badly. Had a few more *dévots* of Michael Portillo been less tenderhearted about their leader's sensibilities and less inclined to hide their heads in the sands of self-regarding, and ultimately futile, second-ballot calculation, Major would have gone by the evening of the 4th of July, Independence Day. The moment at which Redwood's vote approached three figures, or the total number of anti-Major votes reached 120, was the moment at which, on its own admission, the Major campaign would have had to capitulate and allow the Party leader more time to fulfil his ambition of building a second pond in his Huntingdon garden. Nevertheless, however narrow the margin, Redwood knew that it was politically important for him to concede immediately and graciously – all the more so since Robin Oakley and other television journalists could already be seen on the office TV screen acclaiming a decisive victory for Major.

The Major team had understood the importance of a first strike in establishing the significance of the result. Their supporters were outside the House of Commons ready to acclaim the good news and preach it in simple, clear terms to the television cameras. Major had won the largest percentage share of the vote any Conservative leadership candidate had ever received in any seriously contested election. It was vital that the message that Major had won, and won well, should lead the early-evening ITV and BBC news. Once that had happened, the message would become established fact.

No journalist had been able to predict the contest, so scant and unreliable was the evidence from the most evasive electorate known to man. Having downgraded their expectations, Major's team now acclaimed as a decisive victory a result that only a few days previously would have been seen as destabilizing. Preached at authoritatively and given a clear lead on a story – a rare event in the Major premiership – journalists responded meekly, at least for the first few hours. No one immediately recalled the recent reportage that the Prime Minister would be in grave difficulties if between 100 and 110 MPs voted against him. Decisive briefing in an otherwise uncertain cause, television journalists' willingness to accept a clarification for their immediate consumption of what would otherwise appear murky and confused, Redwood's own willingess to acquiesce lest further damage be done to Tory authority: all played their part in Major's 'victory'.

Redwood knew that the Parliamentary Party had to be lifted off the rack and that the contest had to be closed down. Nothing would be gained from pointing out today what would become very obvious tomorrow, that this had been a very good result for him, an uncertain one for Major, but a bad defeat for the Tory right. The surprisingly low number of abstentions meant that the handful of Portillo's supporters had swallowed Majorite logic and voted for the Prime Minister. Rumours began to circulate that Heseltine had met Major for two hours at lunchtime and that a number of his supporters had voted *en bloc* later that afternoon. The notion of a last-minute deal to save the Prime Ministerial skin made a dramatic appeal to Westminster's fevered imagining. But Heseltine had been bought as a job lot earlier on, and the afternoon's events were merely the culmination of two weeks' planning. Heseltine's supporters now joined Portillo's in sufficiently large numbers to ensure that Major's votes were lifted just far enough above the 200–210 barrier to justify his supporters' acclamations on Palace Green.

The Tories' torrid two weeks in June and July were a neat instance of Wellington's sorry remark that next to a battle lost the greatest misery is a battle gained. Major's summer contest had institutionalized conflict in the Party. It was the only way he had known how to win. Several reputations lay in tatters, and Portillo's and Redwood's mutual coolness congealed into dislike and acrimony between them and many of their respective followers. Portillo said that he was 'very relieved that it has worked out so well', while an empty house in Lord North Street cast the long shadow of a summer's night over his ambition and reputation. With an insider's glee, Major gave thanks that the contest had been decided at Westminster and not by 'commentators outside Westminster with their own particular views'. He and his circle indulged in a brief triumphalist recrudescence of the spirit of April 1992. Eventually it had suited them that the media class should accept their briefing that the contest would be a close-run thing, even though they resented keenly the commentators' premature delight at Major's demise. They had then redefined what would count as victory so that, although unconvincing, the result was seen to endorse the Prime Minister. It was the mechanics of party politics at its most professional, but it was also debilitating in its avoidance of the heart of the matter. As the *Daily Telegraph* pointed out: 'In a few months – or even weeks – all the problems of the Government are likely to assert themselves.' The *Sun* put it more brutally: 'Chickens hand it to Blair.' In setting their faces so clearly against the power of the Fourth Estate, Tory MPs had provided that power with more reasons for disenchantment and contempt.

As Redwood made his statement outside the St Stephen's entrance to the House of Commons, I returned to the campaign headquarters to prepare for Redwood's visit when he would thank the campaign team. After his hero's reception we had a private meeting with a small number of supporters. I said that the result was a very great victory for Redwood, who was now 'the prince of the right', and that the task ahead was to develop and consolidate his position. I might be detached about the Conservative Party, but I could recognize courage and grace when I saw it. I escorted him through a crowd of well-wishers, cameras and photographers to the car which then disappeared into the dusk of London in high summer.

We met again the next morning for a final act of disengagement. We were allowed to return to the Secretary of State's room in the House of Commons while accommodation arrangements were still in flux during the reshuffle. We were both apprehensive lest Major should invite Redwood back into the Cabinet. Many, including both friend and foe, were urging this course of action on Major. A politically astute Prime Minister would have done so, and the truisms of Party loyalty would have obliged Redwood to accept.

As Chief Secretary to the Treasury, the post for which he was being canvassed, Redwood would have had to undertake the expenditure reductions he had proposed during the leadership contest and for which he had been criticized so heavily. It would have been easy for the Prime Minister to frustrate his proposals and undermine his reputation. Trapped within a Cabinet from which he could not resign a second time, and briefed against by the Prime Minister's political office, he would have been in an unenviable position.

Redwood hoped and gambled that Major's vindictiveness would overwhelm his political judgement. If offered the Chief Secretaryship, he would say that while he was delighted to accept he could not do so while Clarke remained Chancellor, so profound and widely ventilated were their differences of views on Europe and the Single Currency. It was not the best answer, but it would have to do. Number 10 would brief against him as disloyal and ungrateful to the last in the face of the Prime Minister's magnanimity. As we sat in his room and lunchtime moved into early afternoon without a call from Number 10, he began to breathe more easily. No dilemma would be posed. There was a world elsewhere.

Major's reconstruction of the Government was widely held to be a victory for the Tory left at the expense of the right. But such labels had ceased to have much meaning in the doctrinal mêlée and entrenched factionalism of Tory politics. The most important result of the contest was that it confirmed the impotence and lethargy of the Conservative Parliamentary Party. It had shown itself to be dependent on the Prime Minister's manipulative will. Major's dominance over it was no different in substance from that of Margaret Thatcher. Both had created a dependency culture among Conservative MPs. Now Redwood was being drawn ineluctably into the inner machinations of a Parliamentary Party that he had kept at arm's length until the 22nd of June. The chicanery, banality and fraudulence of Conservative MPs were boring and repellent, but a measure of defilement by pitch was necessary to achieve the Party leadership in the next contest. The inevitability of that contest, and of Redwood's candidature, was the common assumption as the House of Commons rose at the end of July.

In late July Douglas Hurd spoke for the first time in the House of Commons since his return to the backbenches after his resignation as Foreign Secretary. The political actors, he said, might delude themselves as they declaimed on the stage, but their audience, the British people, were leaving the theatre. Thoughtful Tories knew that they were now eking out their days in a theatre of the absurd. They were locked inside the sham mediaevalism of a Palace of Westminster whose powers drifted daily to Brussels, the television studio and the editor's chair. A familiar assembly of the lonely, the perfidious, the adulterous, the lazy, the disorganized and the self-important, they lived lives on the margin of events. Their fall was inevitable. All actions now conspired to that greater end.

BLANK MISGIVINGS

1995 to 1997

'I$_T$'S LIKE France in 1945', said one Member, looking at the Tory MPs assembled in Westminster after the leadership election. 'Everyone was in the Resistance.' Much mordant amusement could be extracted from the Tories' mounting recognition that the Rubicon they had crossed now looked like the Reichenbach Falls.

If any had illusions to shed, they prepared to shed them when John Major formed his new Cabinet on Wednesday the 5th of July. Major's instinctive Machiavellianism followed the Florentine's precept that the ruler should distance himself from those who had made his victory possible. He could not afford to be indebted to them lest they presume. This meant that Peter Lilley, Michael Howard and Robert Cranborne, the 'loyal right' who had made his victory possible, received no advancement. David Davis was left scrambling below the Cabinet table and James Cran was rebuffed, although eventually even he got the message and resigned as a PPS to Sir Patrick Mayhew in 1997. An irate Cranborne left for the country to avoid Major's victory celebrations. In a calculated move, Michael Portillo was moved to Defence, where he would have to balance the virtues of fiscal prudence against the temptations of post Cold War sabre-rattling. Surely, reasoned Major, no matter which alternative he chose he would end up offending some part of his natural constituency.

Rather as Kenneth Clarke had started to campaign in the winter of 1993 for the Chancellorship while he was still Home Secretary, Rifkind had launched his successful campaign to become Foreign Secretary while he was still at Defence. In a series of speeches in 1994 and 1995 he discussed the need for a new Atlanticist dimension to British foreign policy and proposed an Atlantic Assembly composed of legislators from North America and the United Kingdom. These engagingly proleptic thoughts now achieved fruition. In the months ahead at the Foreign Office, he would propound the peculiarly Foreign Office doctrine that Britain's 'interests' and her 'influence' were separable. There were moments when she would sacrifice her influence in order to protect her interests. The sophistries of King Charles Street were designed to justify Britain's possible withdrawal from some areas of European Union policy-making – most notably the Single Currency. They convinced few but a nimble-witted Scots advocate who knew how to handle a brief left on the desk. The problem was that Rifkind never conveyed a sense of believing in anything very much at all, and the suspicion that he was giving a passable imitation of an actor playing the role of Foreign Secretary in a 1930s drawing-room comedy grew with time.

Alastair Goodlad rewarded a fine piece of casting in the role of a droll and lugubrious Chief Whip with the melancholy air of the headmaster of a declining second-division public school about to receive a grim official inspection. 'I've got something very important to say to you,' he told an avid journalist one day at lunch. His host lent forward in imminent expectation of a first helping of spilled Whips' Office beans. 'I have to say that . . . this is really quite excellent claret.' Stephen Dorrell was released from Heritage and sent to tame the National Health Service manager. Virginia Bottomley, who had once defended the decision to close Barts Hospital by saying that the National Health Service was not the Department of National Heritage, now became the Tory *châtelaine* of Heritage. Michael Forsyth, the angular Scottish face of Margaret Thatcher while an unpopular Scottish Party Chairman and subsequently Minister of State at Employment, was rewarded with custody of his native heath. He had been an eager telephoner of John Redwood on the Prime Minister's behalf during Redwood's weekend in suburban purdah. Now he tried to make emollience his bride as he shed the skin of Thatcherism, and was soon drawn into the cabalistic hotbed of Celtic Toryism. Major let it be known that he was sending William Hague to the Welsh Office in order to mend the fences blown down in the hurricane of the Redwood years. Ian Lang would be a rare beacon of urbanity as President of the Board of Trade.

Redwoodians and Portillistas agreed that these arrangements ignored their world view, and then fell out among each other in apportioning blame. Commentators decided that this was a 'left-wing' Cabinet imposed on a 'right-wing' Parliamentary Party. John Major himself enjoyed playing with these infantile categories, but his was a mind innocent of coherent doctrinal intention. He was simply rewarding those whom he needed to reward without destabilizing the circus ring too much. This meant that Kenneth Clarke got a Chancellor-friendly Treasury team. William Waldegrave became an agreeable Chief Secretary, and Angela Knight, as Economic Secretary, proved to be untroubled by any views of any kind.

Two weeks previously, Major had discussed the range of a wider Heseltine *imperium* when telling him of his decision to resign as Party leader. While Heseltine was negotiating the full scope of his remit with the Prime Minister, he asked to see his proposed new office. The magnificent set of eighteenth-century rooms in the Cabinet Office, designed by Sir William Chambers in his classical style at its most refined, clinched the deal. The classical orders were the delicious icing on a cake that was less than the sum of its parts. There was a late Austro-Hungarian flavour to the amplitude of Heseltine's titles. Not only was he Deputy Prime Minister, the office invented by a cynical Harold Macmillan for the trumped Rab Butler, he was also First Secretary of State, a title originally used in the seventeenth century. He chaired Cabinet Committees on the environment, local government, industrial affairs and

regeneration as well as the Economic Committee, EDC. He retained his
competitiveness and deregulation portfolios from his time at the Board of
Trade. The efficiency unit, the machinery of government groups and the
Citizen's Charter were his ultimate responsibility through Roger Freeman,
who was a discreet batman as Chancellor of the Duchy of Lancaster. Heseltine
could attend any Cabinet Committee of his choosing, and chaired EDCP, the
Cabinet Committee on the co-ordination and presentation of Government
policy. The only elements lacking in this glorious plumage were a special
court dress to be worn solely by the Deputy Prime Minister and a book of
etiquette describing the ceremonies to be performed at his court. He also
needed a major-domo, approached David Evans in the hope of appointing him
his PPS, and was rewarded with a series of remarks offering tribute to, and
thanksgiving for, Redwood's masculine organs while observing the Deputy
Prime Minister's absence from the field of recent battles.

Major had become Prime Minister because he knew and understood men's
weaknesses. The position pandered to Heseltine's romanticism and bravura.
In his neutered state, he never troubled Major. His EDCP Committee declined
into the enfeebled state of its predecessor, the No. 12 Committee, and
succumbed to elephantiasis. For the Prime Minister, that was a small price to
pay, since he had achieved a grand objective, a Heseltine lion in a gilded cage.

At Conservative Central Office the reign of Brian Mawhinney as Party
Chairman seemed ill adapted to the politics of the television age. The rolling of
his shirtsleeves seemed all too likely to reveal a Belfast tattoo. The Mawhinney
forearms were much in evidence during the heat of July and August as the
reconstructed Cabinet went about its business and congratulated itself. The fear
that Redwood might 'do a Tebbit' and disrupt the 1995 Blackpool Conference,
as Tebbit's speech from the floor had done in 1992, was very great. The Prime
Minister sent Cranborne, Goodlad and Mawhinney as emissaries to seek clarification of Redwood's intentions. The deft and sinuous Redwood, enjoying the
experience, played it long. When he saw Mawhinney it was in a bleak
Chairman's office in Smith Square devoid of furnishings. There were some
strained initial pleasantries as Mawhinney assured Redwood that he did not
regard him as just an ordinary backbencher. Redwood registered neither gratification nor surprise. As he warmed to the business in hand, Mawhinney leant
forward and asked in tones as close to silky as he could manage whether
Redwood was experiencing any problems with his constituency. These were
matters he could arrange, and he would be happy to intervene. Interpreting this
as a coded threat to disrupt his Association, Redwood responded that he had
indeed had problems. An eager Chairman leant forward. Once they knew that
Redwood would not be Prime Minister and leader of his party, he explained
smoothly, it had been very difficult to control the ardour of his followers. A
baffled and frustrated Mawhinney withdrew.

Mawhinney was, indeed, the incarnation of the principle of central control
as he and Alan Duncan, his PPS, toured the country. In his Peterborough
constituency, Mawhinney's agent defined her job as 'guarding Brian's back

when he is away in London'. A suspicious tone was typical of the final two Major years. Loyalty was the Prime Minister's last public weapon as he bound a battered Party to his own self-interest and tried to persuade it to 'spit in the eye of malign fate', as he described his father doing in that autumn's Conference speech.

It was also important to silence Thatcher ahead of the Conference. Major had always known how to flatter that mighty ego. Her seventieth birthday fell on the 13th of October, during the Conference, and he therefore arranged a birthday dinner, which was duly held in Number 10 on the 26th of September. Having hijacked her celebrations, Major calculated that she would cease to be a thorn in the Government's side. 'But John's always so nice when he comes to see me,' she said in self-justification, when criticized for falling in with his plans.

As it tightened the internal screws, the Government also tried to solve the external problem of its self-definition. What was the Government for? To preach the virtues of loyalism noisily was a sign of failure. The louder the protestations, the more threadbare the substance of its appeal. There had to be other answers. One possibility was to trumpet the idea that Britain was 'the enterprise centre of Europe', and in his Conference speech Major told Tories that Britain was 'unrivalled' in this regard. Unsurprisingly, hearts and minds refused to be stirred.

Alternative strategies were the responsibility of Daniel Finkelstein who became director of the research department at Conservative Central Office in September. Previously he had served as director of the desperately centrist Social Market Foundation and, before that, in his SDP days, as a political adviser to David Owen. A political scientist *manqué*, he emphasized global themes, the dangers of European centralism, the threat of constitutional reform and the challenge of the new Asian economies. But the dance of these bloodless categories was a lumbering affair. They were abstractions and lacked Tory suasion. There was no particular reason why they should lead to Tory rather than to Labour votes. For the moment, he advanced what became known, portentously, as the Finkelstein doctrine: that Labour was not 'new' and that Tories should never concede that ground – Labour was old, dangerous, and red in tooth and claw. Finkelstein and his friend David Willetts, who as Paymaster-General enjoyed responsibility for presentation, would have to think harder.

In the absence of any grand strategy, the Major Government was soon drawn back to its condition of frippery and insensitivity. The Prime Minister's first initiative after his re-election was to produce a policy paper on sport. *Raising the Game* proposed to create a new British academy of sport and to increase the number of schoolhours spent on sport to six per week. The effect was less Drake in his hammock than Nero in his palace. The old brashness reappeared with the Chancellor's decision, subsequently rescinded, to tax share options. The storm-troopers of popular capitalism, the middling sort, who had bought shares in the 1980s had been declining steadily from eleven to seven million. Now the Government proposed to turn its fire on those share-owners that remained – the check-out girl and the BT engineer. Here was the Bourbon of modern government who had forgotten nothing and learnt nothing. Only a Chancellor indifferent to the mood of the time could even have contemplated such a measure.

The reduction of the Government's majority to nine after the loss of the Littleborough and Saddleworth by-election in late July seemed just dessert for so minatory a gesture. As Charlie Whelan, Gordon Brown's press secretary, said laughingly: 'We love Ken because he is always off message.' The truth was that after the leadership election Clarke knew that defeat was inevitable and that it was only a question of limiting the damage. He had a sanguine response to Heseltine's prognostications of electoral abundance on the back of economic prosperity: 'Michael only says those things in order to make us feel better.' Because Clarke felt certain that it was closing time in the Tories' municipal garden, he could express himself more freely – hence his appointment of the openly federalist Anthony Teasdale as his political adviser in 1996.

If the Prime Minister was hoping to raise his game, Tony Blair was also upping his. On holiday in the south of France, Major disported himself in the dispiriting company of Lord Harris of Peckham (the carpeting millionaire also known as Lord Phil of Carpet), Sir Nicholas Lloyd of the *Daily Express* and the *pasticheur* Andrew Lloyd Webber. They were a representative trio from Major's Britain. Tony Blair had more important fish to fry. On the 16th of July he addressed the executives of Rupert Murdoch's News Corporation at Haymond Island, Queensland, and told them how he admired Margaret Thatcher, who was 'a radical, not a Tory'. The admiration was long-standing. In the 1980s he had often shared the train journey home to the north-east with another local MP, a Tory, who recalled that even then Blair was obsessed with the phenomenon of Thatcher as a leader who drew strength from a party that had become a mass popular movement. Blair's Thatcherist *esprit d'escalier* was consciously designed for the powerful tentacles of Murdoch's corporation. It was not the least of New Labour's ironies that it should be founded on so backward-looking a mythology. Thatcher herself repaid the compliment when, on the very eve of the May 1997 general election, she remarked privately that 'Tony won't let Britain down.'

The emergence in New Labour's counsels of Irwin Stelzer was an important sign of Murdoch's favour. Stelzer, a consummate ironist, was Murdoch's political intermediary, with homes in London, Aspen and Washington. Like Loge, Wagner's messenger from the Gods, Stelzer conveyed messages, arranged meetings, and dispensed favours from above. He had been an university professor in the United States and then founded an economic consultancy in Washington specializing in anti-trust legislation. Once established in bored early retirement in Aspen, Colorado, he found that Rupert Murdoch was a neighbour. Soon it became established practice for him to travel the world in Murdoch's company and 'kick ass' wherever the corporate body of News International offered that inviting prospect. He spoke to Murdoch on most days to relay his political intelligence. In London he spent mutually gratifying interludes with Blair. But he also kept his eye on the Tory succession stakes and on John Redwood, whom he found personally difficult but strategically interesting. As the election loomed larger, so his role would inflate.

Much attention was now directed to 'Our Nation's Future', a compendious questionnaire sent to all Conservative Constituency Associations as part of 'the most wide-ranging consultative exercise in the Conservative Party's history', in Central Office's words. As they met in groups that increasingly looked like cells, Conservative Associations pored over their answers to such questions as, 'How do we encourage more people to become active citizens?' and 'How can we make the most of our national culture?' This catechism stirred Redwood's irony, and he sent a set of sample answers to every Association to help them in their grave deliberations. The cynicism was justified. The exercise took eight months, and when the responses were finally published at a meeting of the Party's Central Council on the 30th of March 1996 they were largely ignored, few of the proposals influencing the eventual manifesto. The effect was of a Government so denuded of imagination and reasoning that it required a mass bureaucratic machine to ascertain a few home truths. Having subjected the Party to this platitudinous process, it turned its back on the exercise, so revealing its self-obsessed condition.

A lacklustre domestic scene required a transatlantic corrective, and the remainder of Redwood's summer was spent preparing for a political tour of New York and Washington. He and I had also decided to establish a policy unit to provide him with a social and administrative base. As an escape clause, however, in case anything went wrong, he would not hold formal office in the Conservative 2000 Foundation, but would simply work there every day. The first port of call for money for the Foundation was Margaret Thatcher, who pleaded poverty. Over the years she made many such excuses to Redwood as, increasingly resembling the Silas Marner of Belgravia, she sat in Chesham Street obsessively counting the gold amassed from her American lecture tours. 'Because of the years we have devoted to public service, Denis and I have never been able to make any money.' However, she did arrange for Redwood to meet Sir James Goldsmith in her office that summer. Along with Alderman Roberts and President Reagan, Goldsmith was one of the three men whom she most admired in her life. In his presence she fell silent as Goldsmith's eyes blazed a bright blue and the formidable flow of exposition continued. Redwood could only raise the question of money at the door on the way out as the unimpressed and imperious Goldsmith eyes gazed into his.

By a neat irony the Foundation started its life at 11, Lord North Street, where unopened boxes of telephones gathered dust in the corner as mute witnesses to the vanity of Michael Portillo's political ambitions. It was there that Malcolm Tyndall, Portillo's fractious constituency agent, arrived to declare a discontent with his imperious Member. By October the Foundation had acquired its own home in Wilfred Street, close to Westminster and the House of Commons but not so close that Parliamentarians would feel spied on when they visited.

James Roe, an urbane, tough-minded and elegantly-suited former director of Rothschilds, became its Chairman. Brian Myerson's eager, restless mind had already been the victor in many a corporate skirmish as he advanced the cause of shareholders against lazy boards that presided over decline. He would bring the zeal of his company, Active Value Advisers, to a cause which was the political equivalent of its business battles. Greville Howard contributed sardonic, amused and questioning qualities. Among more general supporters, Crispin Odey would see the point of the Foundation's intellectual work and its publications as they investigated the relationship between capitalism, its discontents and the fractured social condition of England. The architect of Odey Asset Management was the Keynes of his generation and, although a Redwood-sceptic, appreciated the originality, the importance and the daring of the enterprise.

The experiment was common in European and American politics. There, a major politician outside Government but running in the long term for office could be expected to have an entourage – a Private Office, a campaigning organization and a Chef de Cabinet. Chirac and Mitterand, Gingrich and Buchanan, could engage in such politics. Britain, with her tighter brand of Party loyalty, offered no encouraging parallels. Twenty years earlier, in the same street, the Centre for Policy Studies had been established, but it had enjoyed the official patronage of the then Opposition front bench. Could Redwood and the Foundation survive until the general election as ideological entrepreneurs? Could they be interesting and newsworthy without being obtrusively subversive? The Conservative Party was about to find out.

John O'Sullivan, a *déraciné* Irishman, had been a Thatcher speechwriter at Number 10 in the 1980s. After the fall he had reinvented himself as editor of the *National Review*, a conservative journal in the United States, and had become a person of consequence among American conservatives. He had been enthused by Portillo, but now decided that tomorrow would be Redwood's day. He worked on the details of a tour that would present Redwood to America's revivified Republicans and thereby add an element of transatlantic glamour to the hero who would appear before the bedraggled Tories at the Blackpool conference.

Major's victory had simply buried the Tories' electoral problems within the interstices of their own Party structures. For the time being they were resolved not to talk about them. Redwood's strategy was to keep on reminding them of his presence and to show how much easier life would be if he were in charge. He wooed MPs by supporting their privileges and opposing the proposals made by the Nolan Committee for the external regulation of Parliament. He continued to present himself as the public representative of the constituency of five million voters who had voted Tory in 1992 but now threatened to abandon the Party, and promised to restore mortgage tax relief, abolish VAT on fuel, and raise the tax threshold. Redwood also advocated the raising, rather than the lowering, of the married couple's tax allowance as a sign of the Government's belief in family values and also in order to lift the tax burden on low-income families, who would thereby be given an incentive to work. 'I have heard of many reasons for getting married,' jeered Clarke, 'but the married couple's allowance has never been one of them.'

Redwood indulged in wry but public pleasure when, within a month of his defeat, the Treasury reduced public spending by £1.6 billion. Lower unemployment meant that less money would be spent on social security payments and more money than expected would flow into the Treasury from privatization receipts. For one of his Manichaean mind, it was a sign of his own righteousness and of the Government's relentless capacity for evasion and trickery that these figures, which demonstrated that the argument was coming his way, should only appear after his defeat. Redwood also continued to maintain that for the Tories quangos were the problem, not the solution. They could be rash, were often insubordinate, and with their 'voracious appetites' were 'rarely grateful for largesse'. In developing these arguments, originally deployed in a Welsh context, on a wider stage, he was attacking the self-interest of the Tory office-holding classes.

Only once did Redwood put a foot wrong that summer, when he returned so obsessively to the question of single parenthood. In the heat of August, he started to attack teenage mothers. Benefits paid to single parents now amounted to an alarming £10 billion per annum, but teenage mothers represented fewer than one in twenty single parents. His suggestion that grandparents and the extended family should look after the child before the State intervened was moderate and neutral in tone. However, when he wrote that, 'if no one in the family can help, maybe the girl should consider letting a couple adopt her child', the blue touchpaper of welfarism was lit. Stephen Glover, a journalist much given to Anglican liberal musing, had described Redwood as an inhuman 'odd fish'. Redwood now appeared to reinforce that suggestion with a prescription which was alien to the anxious and introspective spirit of the 1990s.

During Parliament's summer recess, the Tory battle moved out of Westminster and into the newspapers. Martin Ivens, the intellectually forceful editor of *The Times*'s comment pages, persuaded me that the task now was to use newspapers as part of a planned political campaign, and to take advantage of the full Murdochian irreverence for the ancestral pieties of British consensual life. As collaborators, we ensured that Redwood's articles said the right things and were given generous space. William Rees-Mogg's affections were also liberally displayed. For Rees-Mogg, Blair and Redwood were representatives of the new politics. They were youngish, concerned about the twenty-first century, and imbued with moral purpose. Major's politics were 'old' and claustrophobically ensnared within traditional Party structures and patterns of thought. In his writings, Rees-Mogg presented a Redwood who was Newtonian, enlightened, Augustan – anything, in short, that Rees-Mogg's flight of fancy might dictate him to be.

It would have taken heroic lack of self-love not to be moved at finding oneself the object of such effusions. But, as the elder statesman of the media movement, Rees-Mogg was stirred by Redwood's popularity and hour in the sun. These were useful tributes when the public view remained stubbornly that of Stephen Glover. The *Evening Standard*'s commentator wrote that, while Redwood's views might be 'more sophisticated and reasonable than his critics assert', he also communicated a sense of enjoying 'some private joke that the rest of the world cannot be expected to share, much less to understand'. Would Americans get the joke in September?

The object of going to New York was to persuade conservative New World money to make a return journey to the new conservatism's base in the Old World. On our first evening in New York, Dusty Rhodes, a legendary Republican financier, gathered a collection of bankers and brains to meet Redwood and myself. Before that, we had already had our first encounter with New York's underworld as the inevitable stretch limo carrying us from the airport ground to a halt outside Brooklyn Tunnel. Alarming fumes and smoke started to envelop the back of the car. The driver, a central European immigrant of a few weeks' standing in New York, had little English and less knowledge of the New York traffic system. He left the car, and we were immediately surrounded by policemen. They were investigating a nearby car that had also stopped and that contained a large number of suspiciously low-browed individuals. It was immediately clear that they were not conservative intellectuals. With guns in their hands, the police bundled us back into the car despite our protestations that it might be about to erupt in flames. Violence was in the evening air. Redwood had arrived in New York.

The modern Babel, the city of the great European diaspora, disturbed Redwood, who was glad to escape to Washington. It was his ideal environment. 'Just think,' he said, as a more successful car journey took us from the airport to the centre, 'behind so many of those doors there's a think tank or a research institute full of people doing the kind of things we are interested in.' Indeed, Washington was the ideal Redwoodsville, a vast university campus where policy-makers moved in and out of government with consummate ease, while big money securely in the background kept the institutions in the style to which they had chosen to become accustomed. The centrepiece of his visit was a lecture to the Heritage Foundation, where he indulged in rhetorical flourishes and mock-heroic prose:

> The world needs more stable democracies to balance the scales of justice. For too long the twentieth century has seen tyranny and darkness outweigh the forces of freedom. Now the army of liberty has many more recruits. They will look to us, tried and tested in the cause. With belief and discipline there is no territory that our army of ideas cannot conquer. So – let the Stars and Stripes and the Union flag unfurl. They can both blow proudly in the breeze, for ours is a moral cause. We do not occupy countries by force of arms. We liberate them by the force of ideas.'

The main point of being in Washington was to meet Newt Gingrich, then in his second year as Speaker of the House of Representatives. No meeting had been confirmed by the time we left London. Gingrich's schedule was notoriously a last-minute affair, but a failure to meet would have been a grave snub. On our first evening we met Tony Blankley, Gingrich's press secretary, and after frantic lobbying were invited to the Speaker's office in the Capitol the following day. Neither Redwood nor I were starry-eyed about Gingrich. His simplicities were terrifying. He preached a version of global capitalism that disturbed rather than elevated, and for him the Internet was a panacea for our times, rather than a screen before which the bored, the sad and the lonely might sit. He was an authentic American revolutionary with a technocratic edge and the uncontrolled enthusiasms of a middle-ranking college professor. As long as Redwood remained in control of the analogy, however, it was useful for him to be seen as a British Gingrich – for, after the President, Gingrich was arguably the second most important man in the United States and therefore in the western world.

We arrived in the Speaker's office, where the staff's Georgian drawls reminded us that an elected representative brings half his home town with him when he arrives in Washington. The office contained a number of skeletal models of prehistoric animals – an enthusiasm of the Speaker's – and these added to a sense of the unworldly. Earnest Georgians, liberated from tenured posts in local universities and now brought to town to serve on his staff as 'friends of Newt', inspected us much in the spirit of the Brobdingnagians gazing at the captured Gulliver.

Gingrich took a very long time to arrive, and then burst through the doors surrounded by photographers and cameramen. He was in the middle of his contrived drama in which legislative disagreements with the President threatened to close government offices across the USA. Washington was hot, cross and quarrelsome. The Humid City was drowning in the sweat of late summer, and the unforgettable sweet, damp smell of the Savannah was all-pervasive. Washington encounters always showed how profound a mark the eighteenth century had left on the structures of power. Access to the Prince was the source of all influence and was controlled as rigidly as in Versailles or Sans-Souci or the Hofburg. Now, Gingrich, the Prince of the hour, had arrived with his minions in the Speaker's office.

Redwood was unimpressed by Gingrich's obsession with polling and electronic communications. For the Speaker, it seemed that the medium had overwhelmed the message. Like any other American politician, he had allowed politics to become a professional business, and he was run by campaigning organizations that made money out of candidates running for office. He was disappointingly mechanistic. The Grand Old Party Alliance Committee, which trained tyro conservative politicians, had been revived by Gay Hart Gaines, who was married to Stanley, a tall lantern-jawed millionaire with a laconic recognition of a bored wife's political imperatives. She had persuaded her husband to move to Georgetown, where she entertained, dressed whimsically in a manner irresistibly reminiscent of Bette Davis in some of the more festive moments of *Whatever Happened to Baby Jane?* She was a member of Margaret Thatcher's circle of American millionaires who ululated their adulation in her presence.

Gingrich and Redwood had a stilted conversation in front of the television cameras and a slightly less formal one after they left. Redwood stiffened perceptibly when Gingrich compared their positions with that of Keith Joseph in the 1970s – John the Baptist figures who, speechifying in the wilderness, had made straight the eventual doctrinal way. This was not part of the Englishman's vision of his future. Gingrich had no ambition to be President of the United States, he told a frankly incredulous Redwood. He was running a movement of ideas and did not wish to run a country as well. But there was enough in the fact of a meeting having taken place for Redwood to issue a statement praising Gingrich's 'phenomenal energy, enthusiasm and drive'. He also had the all-important photograph of himself with Gingrich which he needed for domestic consumption. 'That's it,' he said, 'we don't need to do anything else. We could go home tomorrow if we wanted to.'

Redwood's message from Washington was that the 'special relationship' had declined because Clinton and Major were not interested. An act of will had changed the relationship between the two countries rather than the end of the Cold War and the consequent American withdrawal from intimate involvement in European affairs. The Clinton White House's enthusiasm for a multi-cultural United States, and its consequent coolness towards Anglo-Saxon attitudes, had made matters worse. Redwood, by contrast, was prepared to give thanks for the American century and to persuade America's policy-makers that an integrated Europe would harm their country's interests. Gingrich was prepared to share these sentiments, but wherever Redwood went there was widespread indifference, even among Republicans, to his passions about the emergence of an anti-American Europe. Redwood could certainly talk more freely about capitalism in the United States than in Britain, but the American conservative revival was also based on religious conservatism, and that made Redwood, who was very cool on religious enthusiasm of any kind, instinctively cautious.

As he prepared to return to Britain, it was an open question how firmly based and how broad was the appeal of the Gingrich experiment. Redwood's campaign was based on the communication of ideas, which meant that words had to be used in a lively and creative way. An age of instant-response politics required an early-warning system fuelled by verbal vigour. Gingrich relied on gadgetry, pollsters and money. There was a gap. It seemed an all too appropriate conclusion that at the end of a briefing session at one think-tank, the only two questions the Greek-American siren Arianna Huffington could think of was whether I was married and what were the latest thoughts of Bernard Levin, her former companion, on British politics.

The lesson of these adventures was that American conservatives shared their countrymen's indifference to foreign policy. The continental complications of a diplomacy governed by the problems of borders exposed them as innocents abroad. Later that year, Redwood entertained his new friend Pete du

Pont, Governor of Delaware from 1976 to 1984 and an important figure in the new Republicanism, or the 'leave us alone coalition', as some of its storm-troopers liked to call it. The Foundation gathered a largely conservative circle of sympathizers, and du Pont started to talk about 'freedom'. He had just been to the movies, he told his audience, and been stirred by *Braveheart* and Mel Gibson's portrayal of William Wallace, the hammer of the English and defender of the Scots. The frosty reception accorded him by glassy-eyed English Tories seemed to make little impression, but the Governor's testimonial to Scottish nationalism showed that conservative hands across the ocean found it difficult to distinguish left from right.

Being a highly political diplomat, Sir John Kerr, in his second week as British Ambassador in Washington, was eager to see us. Redwood had thought him a keen ally in the days of his Brussels battles as a Trade Minister, when Kerr was Ambassador and Permanent Representative to the European Communities. There was some naivety in this view. Supporting a Minister of the Government of the day did not stop Kerr being an articulate exponent of the Foreign Office orthodoxy that European engagement and integration were in Britain's interests and that the United States viewed Britain as a close ally who should participate in these developments. In 1995, Kerr thought that the new Republicans on Capitol Hill exuded the same sense of heightened expectation that he had first experienced among the Kennedy Democrats of the early 1960s. Now, with a cigarette dangling between his fingers, he was sitting in the library of his Lutyens-designed ambassadorial residence with one who was happy to present himself as a British Gingrich.

The aim of the North American Free Trade Association (NAFTA), which issued from the negotiations of the early 1990s, was to remove tariffs on trade between Canada, the United States and Mexico. Americans were strongly hostile to supra-national bodies such as the United Nations and the World Trade Organization. Many American conservatives had reservations about the way NAFTA was creating its own central bureaucracy in order to enforce, in the dread European phraseology, a level playing-field. Redwood was therefore taking a gamble with some of his friends in the United States by stating that he approved of NAFTA and wanted it to expand to include Britain and other 'right-thinking' European nations. From his own point of view, this was a useful gambit – a way of questioning the thesis of Britain's inevitable European destiny by postulating a revived Atlanticism. He enthused about the idea to Kerr. The conversation must have made an appearance in the diplomatic telegram to the Foreign Secretary that evening, for Rifkind made it the centrepiece of his speech to the Party Conference in October.

Redwood was prone to accuse Rifkind ungenerously of stealing his ideas, and he always had a low view of him as a carpet-bagging Scot on the make – a Boswell lacking the original's libido and prose style. Yet it was Rifkind who, during his campaign for the Foreign Office, had claimed a year previously that the Atlantic community of nations needed 'a new symbolism and a new framework'. Rifkind's 'trans-Atlantic common market' also formed an

important part of Major's speech in Blackpool. Its advantage for the Tories
was that it could have been used to defuse the explosive power of the
European issue by recognizing the desire of the United States to treat with
Europe as a whole. It embraced a wider Atlantic world but in the name of a
European dimension. It might even square the circle.

In dealing with European politics, American foreign-policy makers had
always preferred the 'one telephone number' theory. For them the internecine
rivalries of European capitals and powers were part of the bellicose and dead
Old World. The Euro-sceptic view always failed to grasp the attraction of
European integrationism to American impatience and zest for the gargantuan.

The prospects for the expansion of NAFTA as a bold and reconciling
political advance looked promising that summer and autumn. Sir Leon
Brittan, Britain's senior European Commissioner, backed the expansion, as
did Germany, Ireland and Scandinavia. Economic forecasts predicted that
two-way trade between North America and Europe would be boosted by up to
30 per cent. Expansion was the obvious next step after the conclusion of
GATT (the General Agreement on Trades and Tariffs). Yet nothing happened.
The development of NAFTA joined the grammar school in every town, the
reduction of public expenditure to below 40 per cent of national income, and
the abolition of inheritance tax in the ever-lengthening queue of Prime
Ministerial announcements that then gathered dust on the shelves of the *salon
des refusés* of policy.

Redwood was audacious and relentless in propagating his new foreign
policy. He always considered Douglas Hurd's famous phrase, that Britain was
'punching above her weight', demeaning and redolent of post-imperial guilt.
Britain did not need to engage in such pugilistic acrobatics in her foreign
policy. What she needed now was 'a foreign policy which is global in reach
and human in scale'. 'Just because Britain has lost an empire, it does not mean
Britain has lost a global role.' European foreign-policy makers were
ungrateful as well as short-sighted. There was a 'churlish lack of
understanding of how it is NATO and the United States that have kept the
peace in Europe for fifty years, not the European Community'.

It was the autumn of Redwood's content, yet as the leaves fell he detected a
second thieving political magpie. Tony Blair had electrified his Party with his
messianic fervour at its Party Conference in Brighton. In an echo of
Redwood's proposed deal with Sky, the television arm of Rupert Murdoch's
UK empire, the prosaic detail of his speech included an agreement with
British Telecom to extend Internet facilities to schools and hospitals. Blair's
proposed reduction of VAT on fuel and promotion of private pensions to
supplement the state pension continued the Redwoodian themes.

The conventional categories of British politics were breaking down in
other directions that autumn. The 'left-wing' Cabinet was no more popular
than its predecessor. William Waldegrave made noises about reductions in tax
and public expenditure. The Prime Minister asked Stephen Dorrell to consult

Redwood on how to tame the NHS manager, and he duly appeared for a Redwood seminar. But the Health Secretary's managerialism of the spirit meant that there was no halt in expensive and needlessly antagonistic hospital closures. Middle managers continued to assault local sensitivities. The briefing from Number 10 was that the Government's continuing unpopularity was somehow the fault of 'the right', and the Opposition, with its talk of a 'lurch to the right', agreed. The confusion deepened when the news of the Government's next disappointment arrived – from 'the left'.

On the eve of the Party Conference, Alan Howarth, the MP for Stratford-on-Avon since 1983 and a former Education Minister, resigned the Tory Whip and crossed the floor of the House to the Labour benches. He blamed a 'left-wing' Cabinet's 'right-wing' politics. A sign of things to come, in early 1995 he had voted against the Job Seekers' Allowance Bill, and the Whips had been slow to grasp the scale of his discontent. Emma Nicholson, MP for Devon West since 1987, proclaimed similar reasons when she defected to the Liberal Democrats at the turn of the year. The Government's overall majority had now been reduced to four, and Peter Thurnham, the MP for Bolton North East, was on the point of resigning the Tory Whip. On the 11th of January, Margaret Thatcher offered her explanation of Labour's twenty-six point lead in the polls. Aspirants to the middle class 'feel they no longer have the incentives and the opportunities they expect from a Conservative Government'. For commentators, Nicholson and Howarth signalled that the Government was 'too right wing', while Thatcher thought it was 'too left wing'. The labels were being eviscerated of any meaning they might once have had.

Thatcher's most deadly coded criticism of Major came in a passage whose significance she may not have fully realized as she read out Robin Harris' prose. 'For a politician,' she said 'integrity is everything.' 'In politics, integrity really lies in the conviction that it's only on the basis of truth that power should be won – or indeed can be worth winning.' One-nation conservatism, she added brashly, was 'no-nation conservatism'. The speech was received ecstatically as a reminder of times past. Yet the problem now with all her interventions was less what they said than their uncritical reception. Thatcherite sentimentality blinded the Tory right to contemporary reality and arrested its development. The former leader offered an opiate for the Tory masses that they were all too eager to swallow so as to stop thinking about the state they were in. 'This is how it was, how it could be and how it will be again,' said one Old Believer after a direct oratorical hit by Thatcher. It was a widespread delusion.

Confronted by these awkward developments, the easiest displacement of responsibility was for the Government to blame an amorphous, 'right-wing' conspiracy. Labour had now moved on to Conservative ground with its audacious talk of an appeal to one nation. This had been hallowed Tory turf since Disraeli had deployed the phrase to exploit the Tory Party's ability to reach beyond the confines of class politics and to exploit the sensations of a newly invented imperialism and royalism – the Tory bread and circuses of the late nineteenth century. In the mid-twentieth century, it acquired a secondary meaning, providing a justification for the Tory accommodation with the new forces of the welfare state and the planned economy. Tories recognized that capitalism was the only way to run an economy, but they also saw that it had unhappy social consequences. Capitalism was safe in their hands because they were prepared to acknowledge its ambiguous side, prevent it becoming unpopular, and spend money on repairing the fences that the market winds had previously blown down.

Conventional wisdom has it that the recognition of social needs explained the Whiggish mantle of mid-twentieth-century conservatism. It was the revival of an old tradition in English political thought. Property, Protestantism, progress, ordered liberty and humane scepticism about doctrinal cravings defined the Whigs who created eighteenth- and nineteenth-century England. Those worldly, tolerant instincts, absorbed within an accommodating twentieth-century Conservative Party, now urged a *rapprochement* with the forces of the age.

The beliefs of the pre-modern, seventeenth- and eighteenth-century Tory party, by contrast, had been those of a country party. Squirearchical and Anglican, it had stood for provincialism, narrowness of mind and hostility to metropolitan values. Its political judgements were grounded in abstract theology and ideas of indefeasible right. The Divine Right of Kings lived on in this old Tory world. Had these forces prevailed, the conservatism of throne and altar would have been a variant of the legitimism that infected continental conservatism in the wake of the French Revolution. Such a counter-revolutionary politics – the politics of resentment, hatred and nostalgia – would have suffered the same marginalization that was visited on it in continental Europe. A Whiggish spirit showed, some Conservatives believed, how they and their Party could still be winners.

Some Conservative writers, among them Julian Critchley, the long-serving MP for Aldershot, were suffused with nostalgia when they looked back at that benign accommodation with the forces of Whiggery. They painted a 1950s golden age that had never truly existed. There were, after all, in that Eden plenty of people like Gerald Nabarro – brash, flash and Jaguared – who were regarded as typical exemplars of the mercantile Tory virtues and vices, not as Thatcherites before their time. Such men were not out of place in the Conservative Party, but were part and parcel of the party of shop-keepers. Moreover, it was possible to argue that Whiggery did not have all the best tunes. Thatcherism had a very Whiggish belief in its own invincibility and purpose – that was part of its problem. As an alliance between nationalism and materialism, it lacked a characteristic Tory scepticism, a sense of the imperfectibility of man and the illusory nature of progress.

Whatever its origins, the Tories of the 1990s mislaid the idea that government was national rather than partisan, and representative of the great bulk of the population rather than of sectional class or economic *parti pris*. In an audacious and historic shift, John Prescott, Labour's Deputy Leader, spoke of New Labour's 'one-nation' appeal at the Brighton Conference during the first week of October 1995. Twentieth-century Conservatives had stolen collectivist clothes in order to stay in office for the century. Now, at the end of the century, New Labour stole the Conservative rhetoric used to justify that same collectivism and purged it of association with a State-run economy. Blair and New Labour had a genuinely historical sense of how the splits in the centre-left since Lloyd George's First World War coalition had given the Tories electoral dominance. The end of the century would see the *rapprochement*. In Blair's words: 'Today's Labour Party, New Labour, is a party of the centre as well as of the centre left.'

To the public these political labels mattered less than the fact that they thought the Tories were nasty, selfish, and vituperative. Michael Portillo's Conference speech provided astonishing confirmation of Tory folly. Portillo knew that he had to make up for ground lost since June. To Redwood's frustration, the force of his personality meant that he was still significant. Redwoodian policy agendas held little appeal for him. For Portillo, high politics remained a game involving posture, fun and political insider dealing. Populism had to be exercised within the constraints of that genre. It was a game of skill and chance, and some three hundred people, the members of the Conservative Parliamentary Party, were the players in the game. Electoral reforms might come and go, and the franchise might gradually extend during a century and a half, but the continuity of the internal parliamentary game was unaffected by the spread of democracy – 1997 was not that different from 1867. This was the lesson Portillo had been taught by Maurice Cowling at Peterhouse two decades previously. But in the age of mass popular journalism and television, the risk of appearing self-absorbed and insensitive to a wider public and popular world made this a dangerous path to pursue. The politician's privacy had disappeared, along with any sense of deference towards him. All Tory politicians were exposed in the process, but their own folly left some more exposed than others.

Like all Cabinet Ministers' Conference speeches, Portillo's had been sent to Number 10's political office some time in advance, and the Prime Minister himself read it shortly before its delivery. Its approval was either an act of stupidity or one of low cunning. The Secretary of State for Defence declared that no British troops would ever accept orders from Brussels: an original proposition given that NATO's headquarters were located in that city. He wished to march the Tory Conference to the beat of a military drum. His area of responsibility left him little room for the predictable anti-European rant that was the easiest path to the Tory Conference's heartbeat. Portillo therefore decided to exploit the language and tone of a braggadocio to support Tory impulses. It was offensively inappropriate for a man so much of the post-World War II generation, who had never borne arms, to engage in such an ideological hit-and-run raid. His point of departure was a recent judgement by the European Court of Human Rights condemning the killing by the SAS of suspected Irish terrorists in Gibraltar in 1988. Portillo evoked the SAS motto,

'Who Dares Wins', and concluded: 'We dare. We shall win.' This exhortation seemed particularly inept from the previous summer's political Hamlet. He described a Brussels that 'wanted to harmonize uniforms and cap badges'. British history was a 'real history of heroes and bravery, of Nelson, Wellington and Churchill'.

Portillo had indulged in a conventionalist strut, and had allowed himself to be considered as one who exploited a soldier's suffering and wallowed in the blood of the long-since dead. Those who thought he had indulged in the effete ranting of an insecure identity relished the exploding shrapnel engraved on the newspapers' front pages. The impression was of a comfortably off, youngish London-based professional who had sought to make political capital out of the rude British soldiery and of the 'freedom for which they shed their blood, the democracy for which they suffered and the sovereignty for which they died'.

On the day, Portillo's support mechanisms were in place. Young men with staring eyes from Conservative Way Forward, a group presided over by Lord Parkinson and largely sympathetic to Portillo, were positioned strategically in the audience to act as cheerleaders. Major himself applauded vigorously, standing at the side of his Defence Secretary. However, in gratifying the gut instincts of a Tory Conference, Portillo appalled a wider public. The speech was seen as lacking in taste, judgement and intelligence. The armed forces objected to being used politically, and in so vulgar a fashion. Within a few days Portillo had to apologize to the heads of the armed forces. It made for a very shaky Portillo autumn. He was also lectured by Thatcher. Did he not realize the folly of further military cutbacks? He had to defend Britain's defences in a dangerous world. 'Still,' as she said dismissively after one such encounter, displaying characteristic depth of European knowledge, 'what can you expect of an Italian?'

Major's Conference speech was not without its own lapses of taste in a now all too familiar ancestral invocation. His father 'made garden ornaments, and some people find that very funny. I don't.' But his main message was the unveiling of yet another great pledge that would gather dust on the shelves of forgotten policies. Now he wished to reduce state spending to 40 per cent of national wealth. Later, in an interview on the 28th of January with the *Sunday Telegraph*, he talked of reducing it to 36 per cent. His pledges were developing the ontological status of Billy Bunter's postal orders.

Michael Howard's *dirigisme* was much in evidence at Blackpool as he continued to gratify primaeval Tory urges for punishment. He talked of abolishing automatic early release for prisoners, and continued to outrage a judiciary that felt its independence threatened. But on returning to London the following week, he too played his role in what was emerging as the modern Tory immorality play. Ethical issues, the avoidance of responsibility and the readiness to occupy a very low moral ground now characterized the public view of the Government. The Learmont Report had concluded that there were great defects in the running of the Prison Service, one of Home Secretary's departmental responsibilities. On Monday the 16th of October Howard announced to the House of Commons that he therefore intended to sack Derek Lewis, the head of the Service. Howard declared that 'policy' was a matter for the Home Secretary, while the head of the Prison Service did something else, which was called 'operational'. The distinction was seen as the Jesuitical reasoning of an all too practised advocate. Howard survived a debate in the House of Commons, but he lost the argument and was seen as yet another Tory who refused to accept responsibility.

At the beginning of November, the consequences of his own actions were heaped on Major's head. The committee of MPs he had set up in May, in the shadow of Nolan, to consider the outside interests of MPs had delivered its judgement on the 31st of October. Tony Newton, its Chairman, gave his casting vote to reject Nolan's proposal that MPs should reveal payments received for parliamentary services. The committee's preferred alternative was a broader, more diffuse, ban on paid advocacy, and on the 1st of November Major accepted the committee's advice.

The public reaction was virulent contempt for another example of weak-kneed self-interest. Parliament's was one of anxiety and fear at the threat, however modified, of regulation. Major and Goodlad, the Chief Whip, offered a technical free vote in the debate on Monday the 6th – Major had offered his own judgement, but the Parliamentary Party could make up its own mind. No great new love of liberality underlaid the decision. Major and Goodlad knew that it would be impossible to impose an official Government Whip in support of a policy of shallow equivocation that nevertheless still threatened the financial interests of Tory MPs. However, Tory Whips were now accustomed to resolute bullying in an irresolute cause. MPs were left in no doubt that they should vote in support of the Major line. The Government's defeat by fifty-one votes resulted from twenty-three Tory MPs voting with the Opposition, with a further twenty-nine Tory abstentions. Public contempt and parliamentary resentment made for a potent brew as the winter set in.

The Queen's Speech on the 15th of November showed that it was to be Michael Howard's legislative session. Tighter asylum procedures, the enlistment of the security services in crime prevention and restrictions on the right to silence in criminal law cases were the background to an increasing number of invitations which were sent to aspiring Tory candidates in safe and safe-ish seats to attend the Home Office, where Howard briefed them on his policies. Redwood was undertaking the same exercise. Lists were drawn up of which percentage swing would ensure the election or the rejection of which candidate in which seat. An unusually large number of Tory MPs were retiring, and there were seventy new candidates in current Tory constituencies, or in new seats that would have returned a Tory on figures projected from the 1992 election. These rather battered political virgins were now wooed with invitations to lunch, dinner, drinks and tea in a gratifying display of concern for their electoral health.

Howard's imprint meant that the legislation would be presented as a

continuing 'lurch to the right'. In the absence of any other defining message
from the Government, that was certainly how Tony Blair portrayed it. In a
measure first advocated by Redwood in Cabinet in 1993, tenants of housing
association were given the right to buy their homes. Otherwise, Blackwell's
Policy Unit themes of enterprise and opportunity were barely visible in the
legislation, while the Family Law Reform Bill, with its apparent readiness to
rid the divorce courts of the concepts of blame and responsibility, merely
promised trouble ahead.

The Budget in late November displayed a characteristic Clarkeian failure
to think about tax cuts, while the political markets had already discounted the
totemic one penny off the standard rate of income tax. Much had been made
of William Waldegrave's study of Redwood's proposed tax and expenditure
savings, but these had all the relevance of a Quaker preaching at a Papal court
run by the Borgias. It was clear that the rise in the overall tax burden of the
equivalent of six to seven pence in the pound would be one of Labour's strong
suits in the ever-looming general election. But Clarke remained in a
stubbornly dualistic world devoid of fiscal subtlety. In the Clarkeian universe
there were on the one hand 'right-wingers' (otherwise simply known as the
enemies of John Major). They thought that tax cuts were the only way Tories
ever won votes, believed in scaling down the welfare state, and were 'living
in cloud cuckoo land'. On the other hand, there were the dedicated followers
of Treasury orthodoxy who insisted on the need to retain the fiscal hairshirt.
This had reduced Government borrowing to £23 billion, but yet more
reductions were needed. Clarke would protect the welfare state, but would
still make life difficult for Lilley at Social Security, Shephard at Education and
Dorrell at Health in order to hit a new public-sector targeted expenditure total
of a maximum of £263 billion. Hence the improbable sight of Peter Lilley
entering the lists as the defender of single mothers' benefits, which the
Treasury had targeted.

Clarke had a static view of taxation and expenditure as taking place within
a single allocated cake. The idea, beloved of Reaganomics, that tax reductions
stimulated growth, employment and thereby tax revenues was foreign to him.
He was also astonishingly indifferent to increases in the tax burden that might
appear small but had a real impact on the Tories' middling sort. He, by
contrast, was the Midlander who had finished paying for his house. The
Conservative-voting policeman who paid £20 to £30 more tax per month saw
that as an attack on his annual holiday and the possibility of dining out more
than once every couple of months. The idea that he was paying a worthwhile
price to secure 'high-quality public services' eluded him – especially when he
saw his local hospital closing and his children being taught in the local
comprehensive by methods dear to the progressivist heart. Conservative
statements about taxation – such as the wearisome repetition that Britain
enjoyed the best economic conditions for a generation – remained at too
theoretical a level. Just 29 per cent of those polled trusted the Government on
taxation, National Opinion Polls reported that winter. No connections were

made between the taxation policy of a Conservative Government and Conservative beliefs. That was why the need was not for cuts in the standard rate but for tax packages aimed at particular groups of people in particular circumstances – at families, businesses and pensioners. Tax was the point at which the pound in the pocket connected with the ethical resentment at broken promises.

Redwood regarded it all as a Treasury plot. Artificially induced economic misery was inflicting pain on too many people and electoral damage on the Tory Party in order to ensure that Britain met the targets for entry into European Monetary Union. Budget policy was geared to reducing the deficit below the level required by the Maastricht Treaty. The Bank of England was following an equally tough inflation policy. The Government might say that all of this made sense anyway, but for Redwood it was 'all part of the ineluctable process to prepare us for the Single Currency'. Clarke's caution, and that of the Treasury, was in line with Euro-requirements but at odds with Britain's real post-recessionary needs.

Could Tory Ministers be released back into the community without being lynched by the electorate? How could one 'sell' – or even present – a collection of individuals with such a tenuous grasp of reality? Like Jacob wrestling with a very dirty-faced angel, the Tories' presentionalists grappled with Tory dilemmas and disillusions. Maurice Saatchi, Sir Tim Bell and Peter Gummer, advertising luminaries of previous campaigns, were now enrolled in the struggle to sell the Tories. They had to find the right words quickly. Hugh Colver, the Director of Communications at Conservative Central Office, resigned in November after just six months in the job, opining that 'the Tory Party behave as if they are in office by divine right.' The *Daily Telegraph* conducted a brilliantly inverted 'fear poll', which showed that fear of the Tories remaining in office was greater than the minimal disquiet about anything the Labour Party might do in power.

The 'New Labour, New Danger' campaign was born at the beginning of 1996. It reversed the previous doctrine that the adjective 'new' should never be conceded to Labour. New was the ad man's most potent word, conjuring appealing ideas of zest, youth, openness and possibility. The Conservative Party spent millions of pounds advertising the fact that Labour was new. It then sought to counter that impression by showing that this novelty contained danger – not hope. The Party seemed to have solved one of its problems. No longer would it say that New Labour was a cunning disguise for traditional Socialist aspirations. Now it conceded that Old Labour was an old danger that had passed. Labour really had changed.

But what were the new dangers? Here the problems started. The danger was threefold. First, constitutional change in Scotland, Wales and the House of Lords, to which nobody in England much objected. Some Tory politicians might wish to raise a storm about Celts being over-represented, over-subsidized and over here, but the English silence was deafening. Nobody really cared. Second, the Social Chapter was to be presented as intrusive, European and regulatory. But polling showed that even Tories did not disapprove of a measure that could be held to improve living conditions and whose interpretation was a matter for negotiation. Opposing it was rather like jeering at virtue. Third, the minimum wage would be presented as a 'threat to jobs'. The Government had achieved some striking successes in denigrating what could be regarded as a measure to promote decency. This showed what could be done to persuade public opinion when the Government of the day had a point of view to communicate. But feeling did not run deep on the issue. Some Tories were sanguine about the minimum wage, and most knew that its introduction could be finessed at an innocuous level of pay.

If the Tories wanted to make the electorate's flesh creep, they could barely raise a shiver. Once Gordon Brown, the Shadow Chancellor, had accepted Clarke's current spending limits and stated that he did not intend to change them, there was no ground on which to raise the Tories' now very battered standard of the dangers of Labour tax increases. When, in November 1996, William Waldegrave costed Labour's election pledges at an extra £30 billion of public expenditure, nobody believed him. The figure was too obviously rounded and, besides, here was a Tory who had said that Ministers could and did lie to the House of Commons. Why, therefore, should they believe him now?

There was a further problem with 'New Labour, New Danger'. Ministers did not understand it. They frequently slipped back to bad old ways and described Labour as unreconstructed Socialists beneath the artful veneer. Heseltine and Clarke were particularly prone to backsliding in this way. Another related problem was whether Tories should concede that Labour had stolen their ideas. Were they artful, successful purloiners who, like Disraeli's Tories, had stolen the Whigs' clothes while they were bathing? If so, they might be opportunistic but harmless. 'New Labour, New Danger' seemed to exclude that presentation. But in conceding the idea that Labour had changed, the Tories also implicitly raised the question of where the novelty came from, and in a confused way the public felt that Labour's store of novelties stood on Conservative ground. That was what made it safe. With this degree of opacity in the message, it was easier to hang on to old certainties. Major attacked Labour's 'jackdaw tendency', and in doing so conceded the point that Labour had stolen good ideas from Tories. 'But you're off message, Prime Minister,' said Sheila Gunn, his husky-voiced Central Office minder, the latest in a long line of restful females with whom Major felt comfortable. 'How can I be off message,' he responded revealingly, 'when I am the message?' The Louis XIV of Worcester Park had had to supply his own line because of Central Office's failure to devise a clear and comprehensible strategy.

For the pre-election period, the press office and the Research Department were amalgamated into a single office. On the one hand were those who, however risibly, were called the creatives – advertising men whose role it was to produce the ideas and images that worked. On the other hand were the policy 'wonks' who worked on the details of policies to support and substantiate these ideas and images. Daniel Finkelstein and his close friend David Willetts, initially as Paymaster-General and then as Chairman of the Research Department, worked together closely on both areas. They were at the heart of the confusion, born of intellectual failure, that characterized the Major Government's last eighteen months of ineptitude.

In January and February 1996 all ministerial speeches were supposed to resound to grand declamations that 'Labour is all things to all men' and that 'the devil is in the detail.' The first was too literary and arcane a reference. Many thought that it was a good thing that Labour had so rich and varied a diet to offer all sorts and conditions of people. It seemed to bear out the truth of Labour's own brilliantly pithy, demotic claim that, in the manner of Athenian democracy, it stood for 'the Many, not the Few'. Moreover, the second claim – of a degree of detailed and dangerous policy prescription – stood at right angles to the first, of superficiality and breezy ubiquity of appeal. Both assertions were too opaque, and faded from view as still-born apothegms.

However, the Tories' greatest advertising mistake still lay ahead – the decision in the summer of 1996 to portray Tony Blair with a black band across his face and a pair of demon eyes imprinted on the band, such eyes representing in the Tory iconography the intrusiveness of New Labour. 'I have run the most successful advertising campaign in recent British politics,' boasted Mawhinney. The poster was the invention of a shaven-headed 'creative' called Steve Hilton with a dispensation not to wear a tie because 'it stifles my creativity.' The poster was more widely known than any other Tory advertisement. The trouble was that it was almost universally recognized as the tasteless exemplar of a low-minded Tory idiom.

In the realm of ideas, David Willetts attempted further essays in abridged history with varying success and a Lloyd-Webberian capacity for pastiche. He and other Tory apologists were attracted by the idea of English exceptionalism – the notion that the Anglo-Saxon model of free trade and limited government had set England on a long-term trajectory apart from continental models of protectionism and interventionist government. The view was as partial as any such abridgement had to be. After all, England had a very long history of protectionism. Euro-sceptics with damaged intellectual seconds to display liked to trace the long history of French protectionism since Colbert in the seventeenth century. But Colbert's measures were coterminous with the Navigation Acts of the 1660s that restricted English trade to English ships – a move that inflamed the Dutch and led to the Anglo–Dutch wars.

Similarly, nineteenth-century England had grown rich behind a wall of tariffs. There was always a characteristic Thatcher fantasy in the idea that Victorian commercial advance was fuelled by brave and brilliant individualistic entrepreneurs and inventors who stumbled on original ideas and goods while pottering around in the back yard. Mercantilism, and then protectionism, were quite as important an element in Britain's commercial story as the untrammelled energy of the unguided intelligence. Indeed, protectionism, in its latest guise as imperial free trade, remained an important element in Tory thinking until well into the 1930s, a point that Tory amnesiacs ignored. The objection to English exceptionalism was not that it was bad history written by culpably ignorant PPE graduates. It wasted mental space because it was too abstract. The Conservative Party had never won power by appealing to the thinking classes with second-rate intellectual material. It had always needed a convincing picture of human motivation and loyalties in their English guise – and this the Party now lacked.

Willetts also had a stab at communitarianism, a briefly fashionable American sociological craze. Communitarians recognized that the State was dead in its welfarist, post-World War II form, but that ties of obligation and mutuality had to survive if modern societies were not to descend into atomistic, anomie-ridden loneliness. Hence the need for 'civil society' – institutions that were autonomous, voluntary and civilizing, such as churches and schools, colleges and clubs. The problem was that the prescription was so wide as to be banal and devoid of meaning. Who would ever wish to deny such a thesis? In another sense, when narrowed down, it became the description and justification of the most intrusive forms of village life, of the twitch on the net curtain as the neighbours checked up on each other in that 'deep idiocy of rural life' bemoaned by Karl Marx. Moreover, from the Conservative Party's point of view, communitarianism could not be prayed in aid because so much of it also suited the Labour Party's new moralism and its leader's re-hashed Christian socialism.

Howarth, Nicholson and Thurnham, the defecting Tories, had all supported John Major's re-election as leader, and it was now a neat irony that it was the 'left' who blamed a 'left-wing' Cabinet for being too 'right-wing'. In January there were rumours of furtive noises off stage, with Cranborne and Archie Hamilton being prepared to ask Major to step down if the local elections in May went badly. Cranborne was recovering from his disappointment at not being made Secretary of State for Defence, but there was enough evidence for *The Times*' story of a 'Toffs' Plot' to be more than wishful thinking. The story never gained credence, and foundered on the rock of Major's adherence to office. He would have to be dragged out of Number 10 inch by painful inch until, as Paddy Ashdown said, the very key to the door would have to be wrenched out of his hand.

In February the 1922 Executive decided to suspend the provision enabling another leadership election to take place before the general election. The Chairman, Sir Marcus Fox, now ran the 1922 as a way of representing the Government's views to backbenchers, not *vice versa*. Meetings were held late on Thursday afternoons when the House was emptying of Members and he could rely on a sparse attendance. Fewer than fifty were present when the controversial amendment suspending the rules of the leadership election was pushed through. Indeed, one of the striking features of the last two Tory years was how empty the Commons was for most of the time. The Government was not keen to have its backbenchers kicking their heels in Westminster. The legislative programme was light, there was less and less to do, and increasingly less zeal with which to do it. The Government Whips found it increasingly difficult to make sure that the Government benches looked reasonably full for the benefit of the TV cameras during Prime Minister's Questions on Thursday afternoons. Even, it seemed, on those rare occasions when they were required, Tory MPs were hard to find. This was the outward and visible sign of an inner decay in both the Parliamentary party and the House of Commons itself. The vast, echoing, Gothic building, which once had seemed to contain the ark of the parliamentary covenant, was for most of the week now a place of ghosts and of tenebrous shadows. It contained marginal men and was itself marginal to the great creative forces of the age.

However, there was one parliamentary occasion that winter when the House of Commons could rage against the dying of the light. On February the 15th the Scott Report was finally published and concluded that the Government had changed its policy of not selling arms to Iraq without explaining the change to Parliament. Consequently, the Matrix Churchill case, which prosecuted British businessmen engaged in the export of arms, should never have been brought, although Scott also concluded that Ministers, confronted by the prospect of the defendants' jailing, had not passed by on the other side. With a judge's perversity, Scott had refused to issue a summary of his conclusions lest this should deflect attention from the density of his detailed report. This helped the Government to mount a vigorous defence of the indefensible. Robin Cook, the Shadow Foreign Secretary, was allowed only three hours to study the report on the day of its publication, whereas Government Ministers had had days to read it in detail. Lang's unnecessarily bullish statement to the House of Commons in support of the conclusion that there was 'no conspiracy – no cover up' lost him much credit as the acceptable face of Majorism.

The Government thought that Scott was naive about government, its ways and its pressures. But a decadent over-sophistication and a self-appraising worldliness had led to loss of judgement. Scott's concerns about the misleading of Parliament and the failure to stop the prosecution were brushed aside. The political story was that this was another example of failure to accept responsibility. Blair caught the public mood when he said that the Government stood 'knee-deep in dishonour'. Not even Major could pretend that Tory opposition to him on this issue was a right-wing conspiracy. The decision to brazen it out and to insist that the Attorney General, Sir Nicholas Lyell, should not resign made many Tories uneasy. Among Euro-sceptics, Sir Teddy Taylor, Richard Shepherd and Christopher Gill were worried, and they were joined by Rupert Allason from the mavericks, by Quentin Davies from the Euro-philes and by the broad-church John Marshall. Lang, in more emollient form for the full debate on the 26th of February, convinced Taylor, Marshall and Gill to vote with the Government. Major pulled an ancient shot out of a battered locker. If the Government were defeated, he would call a confidence vote – but after Thurnham had resigned the Whip on the 22nd of February the Government's majority had fallen to just three. With the air of dogs performing old tricks to please their huffing and puffing master, the Conservative Parliamentary Party pushed itself through the division lobbies. Shepherd was irreconcilable, and the nine Ulster Unionists voted with Labour, but Allason relented at the last minute, and the Government won by 320 votes to 319. Major had won the battle of the day and lost the war of Conservative reputation.

As the Government prepared in the spring of 1996 for the start of the European Union Inter-Governmental Conference (ICG) in Turin, European concerns returned in striking confirmation that governments that fail to make their own weather run into hurricanes. Redwood had been girding himself for battle throughout the winter. He wished to be remembered in British history as the politician who stopped Britain entering the Single European Currency. In order to do so he had to feast with panthers such as Bill Cash and the ultra-sceptics, who accepted his authority only infrequently and incompletely. Early every Wednesday evening he would meet a group of his parliamentary supporters to exchange news and plan tactics for the week ahead. He was also prepared to confront an entire Cabinet that had embraced the vacuity of a 'wait and see' policy which later, with ineffable Major logic, became one of 'negotiate and decide'.

Redwood decided that he was going to be the Winston Churchill of the 1990s. 'Churchill commanded popular opinion through the *Express* in the 1930s when he was out of office,' he said, 'and that's what I am going to do with the newspapers now.' He became the beneficiary of the continuing rift between the Tories and the press. The *Mail on Sunday* became an important platform despite its lukewarm view of Redwood during the leadership election. There were many non-European amusements to be enjoyed and bureaucratic tails to be tweaked along the way. The journalistic pulpit could be used to preach against Kenneth Clarke's Treasury puritans, and Redwood showed how tax policy could be used as an incentive to foster Tory values on families and businesses. Gillian Shephard was blocking the publication of test results for seven- and eleven-year-old primary schoolchildren. 'Don't mess with Gill,' the Prime Minister had said in one Conference speech, but Redwood was very happy to disobey that injunction. With the *Mail on Sunday*, he launched a successful campaign in January 1996 to change her mind, at least for the tests taken by eleven-year-olds. In November 1995 the *Evening Standard* was the launch-pad for his plan for London, the most important part of which was the proposal he had sent to Major earlier in the year to give a share in the tube to every Londoner and then to float London Underground on the Stock Exchange so as to bring in more private capital investment. At the same time, he opposed the controversial sale of the Royal Naval College at Greenwich, proposed by Michael Portillo, and the scheme, inspired by Kenneth Clarke, to sell parts of the Treasury building in Whitehall.

How, he asked, could it possibly be better to rent back a building that you currently owned?

In March, Redwood was using the *Mail*'s nexus of family values to record his anger at the Lord Chancellor's 'permissive and amoral' family law bill. Tory parliamentary rebellions ensued. Later that month he showed how widespread regionalism already was in Britain. Following an initiative by John Gummer, the Secretary of State for the Environment, ten regional Government offices had been established; since they distributed European Regional Development funds, they had their own representatives on the Committee of the Regions in Brussels. With these bureaucratic regimes already in operation, it would be easy for Labour, once in power, to claim that they required democratic scrutiny through a comparable network of regional assemblies. Indeed, the *Gauleiters* of the Government Office of the South East were already boasting in their literature that their area was 'a region of the European Union with Roman and Norman ties'. Redwood also revealed that the Government had extensive spare office space in central London that could be sold, and that 10,000 Statutory Instruments had come into force since the last deregulation initiative in 1992.

The lesson hammered home in this journalistic campaign was a simple one. The Government had lost sight of Conservative principle and practice. Yes, Redwood said, he did have radical ideas about taxing and spending, and they all originated in the 1992 election manifesto. This was the manifesto that had said:

> We will make further progress towards a basic income tax rate of 20p. We will reduce the share of national income taken by the public sector. We will aim to bring home ownership, share ownership and personal pensions within the reach of all families. We will raise the tax threshold for inheritance tax.

The grand certainties of 1992 had become lost in the ensuing morass.

Throughout this period of heightened activism, the golden thread was European policy and its close relative, taxation. All roads led to Brussels and to some fundamental and related questions. What kind of people were the British at the end of the twentieth century? Where did they belong? Did they still value their independent institutions?

In April Redwood had lunch with Charles Moore, the editor of the *Daily Telegraph*, and told him that when he asked his constituents what was wrong with the Government they answered 'everything'. Within a few days, on the 18th of April, appeared Moore's leader, 'Get Off Your Knees', written with Swiftian savagery and anger. Without naming him, it quoted the response of Redwood's constituents, and concluded that: 'People have no belief in the men or the measures, no expectation that they will be told the truth, no impression of competence, no faith or hope or charity.' Redwood was ecstatic, and rang Moore to congratulate him.

When he was not in a weekend world of suburban and rural adulation, Redwood now lived a life of metropolitan influence. He was entirely caught up, for it had an excitement, a daring and an influence that he had never experienced before in the world of the patiently abstracted policy 'wonk'.

Late in the evening of the 17th of April Redwood received calls from journalists accompanying the Prime Minister on his flight to Prague. John Major had been telling them that Redwood's calls for tax cuts were 'reckless and silly'. In the wake of the wearisomely disastrous Staffordshire South East by-election on the 13th of April, lost by the Conservatives on a 22 per cent swing, Redwood had reminded the Government that 'tax-cutting is a moral crusade' and that most people thought that the Government was 'destroying cherished institutions'. 'Now we've got him,' said Redwood, who had always tried hard to get evidence of Major's chronic briefing against colleagues on the record. 'He can't wriggle out of this one.' He spoke to John Ward, Major's PPS, who, being in the House of Commons, could neither confirm nor deny what the Prime Minister had said hundreds of miles away on a plane. Redwood then issued a statement in time to be reported on the 10.00 p.m. news, defending himself in aggrieved tones against the unjust imputations of his Party Leader. The next day, Norman Blackwell phoned him with the task of explaining that not only had Major not attacked him, he actually agreed with him on taxation. This could be presented as a Prime Ministerial apology to 'hurt from Wokingham'.

With events going Redwood's way, it was hardly surprising that Michael Gove, *The Times*' polished commentator, brought a Scottish enlightenment to bear, and found him 'witty, liberated and confident'. Redwood was expressing his own views in a way that tried to subvert the established orthodoxies of the left–right schematization. He had his own policy unit, a national audience and a better official car, provided by the Conservative 2000 Foundation, than the one he had had in Government. He could summon diplomats to his colloquies; Chris Woodhead, the most distinguished Chief Inspector of Schools since Matthew Arnold, would arrive for discussions about his progress. Clearly Redwood was not now going to be a remote intellectual politician, an Enoch Powell or a Keith Joseph. But might he not be Joseph Chamberlain, the vigorously practical apostle of national identity who had ended up splitting the Conservative Party?

This was a period when Redwood felt that the leadership of his Party was his by moral and indefeasible right. *Folie de grandeur* could sometimes take over. Some time after his resignation, he went, as a matter of course as a Privy Councillor, to bid farewell to the Queen in a brief formal ceremony in Buckingham Palace, which marks the convention that Cabinet Ministers are Ministers of the Crown. 'Yes,' he said largely on his return, 'I had the feeling that they wanted to keep in touch and to be kept informed. It certainly wasn't a case of just saying goodbye.' The Sovereign's decision to abrogate the deal negotiated by George V and to start paying tax was a personal blow to him after his defence of this ancestral right of extra-territoriality whose origins lay lost in Windsor mist. 'There's just no helping some people,' he said archly.

Having resigned from the Government, he took the view that he could not be blamed for the forthcoming disaster. His advice to Government was freely given, and they could take advantage of it if they wished. If not, not. While logically impeccable, the posture of detachment was emotionally false to the circumstances of the time. Like it or not, he was still treated as if he were a member of the Government. His personal fate could not be disentangled so easily from the general chaos and misery.

Forgetful of the traditional sycophancy of the Tory masses, Redwood regarded his welcoming reception at constituency meetings as a sign of a headlong rush towards him. Yet in another week's time they would accord the same welcome to a Heseltine, a Clarke or a Portillo. When the moment of truth arrived with the leadership election in June 1997 he had, as he complained bitterly, very little constituency support. He also consistently overestimated the Euro-scepticism of prospective MPs as they came to see him for ostensible policy discussions and covert lobbying. Since he lacked curiosity and patience about other minds, he attributed his own clear convictions to all too many of the confused, the timorous and the self-seeking who in most cases had only been selected because of their lack of conviction.

It suited his conception of leadership that, in April, he presented himself as the man who could do business with Sir James Goldsmith on behalf of the Tory Party. There were dangers in this approach. Goldsmith was now the leader of a party pledged to oppose Conservative candidates in the next general election. On the 14th of April he finally pressed the button and announced that he would be fielding six hundred Referendum Party candidates and spending £20 million on his campaign. In meeting Goldsmith, Redwood would be consorting with the enemy. The Prime Minister and Mawhinney had refused to do a deal with Goldsmith or even to meet him. At the very least, Redwood's actions constituted *lèse-majesté*.

Negotiations were conducted through Charles Filmer, Goldsmith's major-domo, and Patrick Robertson, his press secretary, whose eager approaches carried with them the whiff of the Levantine merchant who might at any moment urge upon a likely buyer a small silver box containing samples of raisins. It was important that neither side should claim that the other had instigated the meeting, although the truth was that it was I who first requested it. We agreed to meet on the afternoon of the 24th of April in Goldsmith's suite at the Dorchester Hotel. Redwood now presented himself as an intermediary on behalf of Conservative candidates whose prospects of electoral success the Referendum Party threatened. Goldsmith could be viewed as the chieftain seated in his bejewelled tent, magnanimous enough to receive the emissary of a foreign power. By leaked stages I made sure that the secret meeting became a very public affair, with camera crews waiting to greet Redwood as the Foundation's Jaguar finally purred to a halt outside the main entrance to the Dorchester. We had spent a quarter of an hour driving aimlessly up and down Park Lane and around Marble Arch and Hyde Park Corner because we had realized that we were too early. It would not do to appear too eager.

When we arrived in Goldsmith's suite, it was to discover that Sky Television had taken over one of the rooms to record the meeting's initial stages for the benefit of a grateful posterity. The exclusive deal, arranged by Goldsmith's team, annoyed other camera crews as well as ourselves, and once the cameras had left the meeting got off to a sticky start. Redwood could not influence Major and his Party; Goldsmith was immovable on his project. But Goldsmith did listen to Redwood and his arguments, which was more than he did for Thatcher. The two most prominent pairs of eyeballs in British politics inspected each other.

Redwood, dressed in a suit of a better cut than usual, sat in a deep sofa that seemed about to be swallowed by the deep pile of the carpet. Goldsmith, encased in an elegantly draped dark grey suit, sat apart in a Louis XV chair. Alan Walters and I looked at each other for the first time since it had become a sad and nervous necessity to de-commission his introduction to a Foundation pamphlet because of his awkward new allegiance as a Goldsmith Major-General. Goldsmith was told by Redwood that, so far as Britain was concerned, the European problem did not start with Maastricht. The principles of the original Treaty of Rome themselves had been extended and interpreted in a centralizing way. The 'ever-closer union' of the Treaty echoed the 'more perfect union' envisaged by the framers of the constitution of the USA. The notion of a United States of Europe was implicit in the Treaty of Rome. From here, it seemed, it was just a short step to saying that the whole enterprise was flawed and that Britain should leave.

However, Redwood was a canny enough politician to know that that was still regarded as an extreme position. It was now useful for him to be outflanked by politicians such as Lamont, who were beginning to talk of withdrawal – they emphasized his own moderation. He and Goldsmith also agreed that of itself a referendum would solve nothing. It must be the start of a process. A form of words for a referendum question had to be found that would encourage the right answer. Redwood suggested: 'Do you want a common market or a common government?' At all events, a simple question about whether the British people wanted to be in or out of 'Europe' had to be avoided. Withdrawal was a minority and extremist view, and confirmation of Britain's membership might therefore be taken to justify further political centralization. However, if the people assented to a common market rather than a common government, the House of Commons would have to start effecting the political will through legislation. Many thought this a fantasy. What evidence was there that British Euro-sceptic fare even appeared on the menu of the European Union? The sceptics' reply was that the IGC was already renegotiating the Treaties of Rome and Maastricht in one, centralizing direction. Why could they not be negotiated and interpreted in another?

Redwood and Goldsmith never met again, but each approved of the other's existence. They were both mavericks, agents in the dissolution of party. Pictures of the two of them making a joint statement outside the Dorchester would be too strong meat for the Conservative Party and for Redwood's

ad my lips. John Major, author of Tory woes, bering up for a BBC interview.

Margaret Thatcher in characteristic posture outside her London office in Belgravia, where successive aspirants to the Tory crown arrived seeking benediction from the keeper of the Tory grail.

November 1992: two months after the failure of the Exchange Rate Mechanism experiment, Norman Lamont retains the key to the door.

Tristan Garel-Jones, Welsh Machiavel and Major confidant, whose skills as a former Deputy Chief Whip and authority as Minister of State at the Foreign and Commonwealth Office helped the Prime Minister to impose the Maastricht legislation on the Conservative Party.

The man who could have been the Conservatives' King. John Major ponders Michael Heseltine's Churchillian gesture as, once again, Heseltine storms his way into Tory hearts at the Party Conference, Bournemouth, 1996.

High noon. After Cabinet, John Redwood crosses Whitehall and returns to the Welsh Office, where for two years he would articulate his view of the Conservative future.

Chris Patten, a Tory philosopher-king in exile as Governor of Hong Kong, is joined by his political ally, Foreign Secretary Douglas Hurd – two representatives of an English tradition of liberal thought now vanishing into insignificance in the Tory Party.

William Waldegrave, Chief Secretary to the Treasury, Malcolm Rifkind, Foreign Secretary, and Michael Portillo, Defence Secretary, celebrate John Major's re-election in 1995 and their own survival in office after Redwood's summer *Blitzkrieg*. In two years' time they would all lose their seats.

John Major looks to the future and finds Tony Blair. The details of New Labour's policies might be hazy, but the leader-in-waiting's personality was dominating the political landscape.

In the autumn of 1995, Secretary of State for Defence Michael Portillo, at the controls of a Sea Harrier, looks back on a three-year period as the Tories' Crown Prince. There would be stormy weather ahead.

Lord Harris of Peckham, a carpeting millionaire, is introduced to the House of Lords. He was Deputy Treasurer of the Conservative Party from 1993 to 1997.

In the 1997 election, Tories threatened the voters with claims that Labour had a £12 billion 'black hole' of hidden tax increases – but hardly anyone believed them. Brian Mawhinney, the Party Chairman, and Kenneth Clarke, the Chancellor of the Exchequer, join the Prime Minister in putting on a brave face.

Lord Archer, with customary flair, attempts to breathe life into Peter Lilley's campaign for the Tory succession in 1997. The Tory creator of fables came to dominate that melancholy enterprise.

Michael Howard, the resilient former Home Secretary, ran a determined campaign for the Tory leadership – but came bottom of the poll.

Stephen Dorrell, centre, leads his *Reservoir Dogs* team of backers to a news conference where he announced his intention to stand for the Party leadership.

After the collapse of his own campaign, Stephen Dorrell joined that of Kenneth Clarke, with no guarantee of a Shadow Cabinet post.

Kenneth Clarke and John Redwood celebrate their non-aggression pact for the third ballot of the leadership campaign. However, the Conservative Parliamentary Party refused to accept that the quarrel over Europe could be settled. The two most purposeful Tories were rejected, and the conflict was set to continue.

Raising the Tory spirits. Steve Bell's *Guardian* cartoon illustrates Margaret Thatcher's eventual endorsement of William Hague.

THE KISS OFF

Unveiling his management changes in September 1997, William Hague suggests why tomorrow might belong to him.

The freshness of the future is cast in doubt with the re-emergence of Cecil Parkinson as Conservative Party Chairman.

William Hague's Shadow Cabinet meets for the first time in June 1997. Having accepted the leader's invitation to be the Trade and Industry spokesman, John Redwood becomes a 'team player' once more.

A leader among men. William Hague conducts a management-consultancy-inspired bonding session at an Eastbourne hotel in October 1997. The entire Conservative Parliamentary Party was required to attend – at its own expense – and all but three (Messrs Heath, Heseltine and Soames) did so.

prospects. He stood alone to make a statement that they had agreed on many fundamental issues and that he would now act as an intermediary, making representations to the Government. They both proposed that a referendum be held on the same day as the general election so that discontented Euro-sceptic Tories could vote Tory and at the same time express their Euro-discontent, without having to vote Labour. The reality was that straight electoral switching from Conservative to Labour was already occurring, and would continue to do so for myriad reasons. On its own, a different Conservative policy on Europe would not prevent that switch happening on a massive scale.

Despite being very nervous about the plan, Redwood had got away with it, and Goldsmith enjoyed his nerve. The message was that Redwood was already the unofficial leader of the Conservative Party. But Redwood also needed to cover his back. His attacks on Tony Blair acquired a new stridence and a new violence that made him seem old rather than new Tory. He wrote that 'I loathe the insincerity which oozes from every sound bite. I can't stand the phoney grin. The lawyer's cleverness at ducking the detail while appearing to answer the question leaves me wanting to bring him down a peg or two.' Writing about Blair in this vein revealed more than a touch of class animus in the thrust of his rapier. The heir to so many putative leaders of the over-cultivated centre-left ground in British politics – to Hugh Gaitskell and Jo Grimond, Roy Jenkins and David Owen – touched on a very raw nerve indeed inside Redwood.

In writing about Blair, Redwood was often making covert criticisms of Major. 'True leaders', he wrote, 'unite their parties by understanding the common principles that led people to join. They fashion policies and speeches at a speed and in a way which the country will accept.' If it was the task of the Leader of the Opposition 'to unite his Party by the force of personality and the justice of his lead', how much more was this true of the Prime Minister? Redwood's personal complaint about Blair was that he ignored him in the House of Commons. After he relayed this complaint to Mary Ann Sieghart, a *Times* journalist who was a friend of the Blairs and therefore a reliable conduit, Blair made good the deficiency within two days, separating himself from his entourage one afternoon and enquiring anxiously after Redwood's health.

Unconvincing abuse aroused suspicions that there was an uneasy side to Redwood. Vitriol did not harm Blair, and did nothing to mend fences with the Government. The ideological differences between Government and Opposition had now been reduced to a matter of fine-tuning. On the European issue, on economic policy, on divorce legislation, on gun control, the two front benches shared a unanimity of view that was often at odds with large sections of their backbenchers. At times, indeed, it seemed that Major, like Stanley Baldwin, his admired predecessor, could lead the Conservative Party into a National Government. Blair, Redwood noted ominously, was providing ineffective parliamentary opposition because 'he seems to like the antiseptic Parliaments of some of our European partners.' But politics, and especially House of Commons politics, requires battles. If beliefs could not provide the flashpoints, personalities had to do so – hence the unnatural prominence of delineations of personality, as well as the artificial importance of character assassination, in the politics of the period. Phoney Tony, Vulcan Redwood, Portillo the Castillian, Michael 'Prison' Howard, Peter Lilley and the Lilliputians were the caricatures engendered by the conventions of the political stage army.

Redwood was on stronger ground when he attacked Labour's intellectual vacuity. At the end of 1995, Will Hutton, editor of the *Observer*, published his critique of Britain, *The State We're In*. It captured a public mood of generalized discontent with the results of market economics and the shiftlessness of modern British life. For a time Hutton became Blair's social-philosopher-in-residence until the practical implications of his proposals became more obvious. Hutton would rejoin the Exchange Rate Mechanism and attempt to manage currency rates; he would increase trades union power, and impose compulsory union representation on company boards; he would attack savers by reducing the dividends paid to pension funds and shareholders. In vain might Hutton protest that he was expressing the social democratic pieties of increased training and attacking the root causes of British companies' 'failure to invest in the long-term future'. Blair and Brown soon sidelined him as a dodgy stowaway on New Labour's upholstered charabanc as it took the road to power. Although there was room for everybody in the New Labour odyssey, some, it seemed, were less equal than others when they imperilled the 'project'.

Redwood believed that he could push the Cabinet towards an ever more vigorous rejection of the Single Currency, and his rhetoric became increasingly strident. Monetary Union, he claimed, was a plot to switch business from the City of London to Frankfurt. It was part of a project to create a single Franco-German state with more people than Japan and with German access to nuclear weapons for the first time since World War II. He was appalled at Rifkind's suggestion, on the 5th of March 1996, that the European Union needed 'a single figure to represent the foreign policy of the Union to the outside world'. This was to propose an embryonic Foreign Secretary of the embryonic European state. Clarke was criticized for presenting arguments in favour of the Single Currency outside Cabinet. Redwood's exasperation with the magnificently sanguine Chancellor was boundless. He found him sloppy, arrogant and mischievous, 'a lazy scholarship boy who thinks he doesn't need to do any homework'.

Clarke was certainly unhappy from spring 1996 onwards. He had opposed the Government's publication of a White Paper in preparation for the Inter-Governmental Conference because it would only create trouble. He also argued against even raising the question of the Single Currency as the IGC approached. The issue had been settled at Maastricht and was not an official part of the Conference's remit. A referendum on the Single Currency went against the spirit of constitutional government in Britain. It was a matter for the Government to decide – and Michael Portillo agreed with him. After all, governments used referendums as a discreditable way of evading difficulties.

Major was attracted to a referendum less because of democratic passion than because it let him off the hook. On the 7th of March he set the process in motion, remarking at Prime Minister's Questions that 'a referendum on a Single Currency could be a necessary step.' Clarke threatened resignation – he had a principled position to defend. Moreover, the Chancellor saw the issue in a wider light as the touchstone of a way of understanding the world, of a generosity and openness of spirit threatened by a tidal wave of small-mindedness. He had not come all the way from Nottingham to give in to the forces of reaction and obscurantism. He insisted that there should be no further concessions, and that the referendum would apply only to the lifetime of the next Parliament and only if the Tories won. For the moment he was willing to abide by the Cabinet statement on the 4th of April that any decision during the next Parliament to join the Single Currency would be ratified by a referendum.

'Everybody says this guy Clarke's a problem and that he's threatening to resign,' said Pat Buchanan, the Republican Presidential challenger, to Redwood when he visited London during the summer. 'So – why don't they let him resign? What's the problem?' Redwood and the sceptics always maintained that there wasn't a problem. Clarke would not resign so close to an election, and he would not wish to be held responsible for initiating the electoral calamity that now stared everyone in the face. As the Government's life limped to a close, and the prospect of a handful of votes loomed, the universal game, bred of fear, was the avoidance of blame. No one wished to be the political equivalent of Lord Dawson of Penn, the royal doctor who had helped King George V to die. Moreover, it suited Major to have Clarke in his camp. Without him, he would be a perpetual hostage to the sceptics. He needed his neighbour for late-night moans over the whisky about the horror of Teresa Gorman and Bill Cash, those major threats to the stability of his Government and to life as they knew and liked it.

The beef crisis gave the Government's European dramas an additional twist. Like Scott and Nolan, the episode was important for what it showed about the conduct of government in Britain under the Tories. The statement Stephen Dorrell made on the 20th of March as Secretary of State for Health was couched in neutral, scientific language and lacked all human sensitivity. It led to mass panic. Evidence had come to light of a link between Bovine Spongiform Encephalopathy in cattle and Creutzfeldt-Jakob Disease in humans. Infective material had been eradicated after 1989, but because the Government lacked all credibility a domestic boycott of British beef developed of its own volition. On the 25th a committee of the European Commission banned the export of British beef as well as its by-products, gelatine, semen and tallow, on a worldwide basis.

The Commission was responding to national panic in Britain. If so many in Britain felt threatened, it was difficult for Euro-sceptics to develop the theme of knavish Europeans lying in wait for the roast beef of old England. The Government tried to undo some of the damage it had caused by agreeing to ban the sale of beef from some high-risk cattle. But this failed to alleviate the Government's bovine dramas. On the 20th of May, the European Union's veterinary committee voted against lifting its ban on the export of British bovine by-products. In earlier years, the Government had had to deal with the consequences of the procreative urges of some Conservative MPs. Now it dribbled to an inconsequential close as it dealt with another form of bovine folly.

On the 21st of May, Major announced a policy of European 'non co-operation', which led to Britain exercising its veto on seventy European measures. Red-faced and deluded, Tories whooped with joy in the House of Commons at what seemed to be decisive action – the Government was holding its own, confounding the European Union, and taking up arms against a sea of troubles. But the public impression was of Government impotence and incompetence. There were no votes in anti-Europeanism for the Tories if this was what it involved. In November of the previous year, Major had tried to engage the affections of Jacques Chirac, the newly elected French President – another politician in whom commentators detected a gap between profession and reality. Major had offered British support in the teeth of Commonwealth opposition to the French nuclear testing which had taken place in October on Mururoa Atoll. Now, in Major's supposed hour of need, Chirac was invisible.

By its own actions, the Government had created a problem, and charac-teristically it sought to blame others for its own folly. Competence in dealing with European institutions was needed. It was a very typical Major calculation that the right way to be a Euro-sceptic was to cross the Channel and to be nasty to everyone in sight. However, one consolation was that he now had another wounded Cabinet Minister on his hands – he was happy to pay the price of supplying the public with another vilified Cabinet Minister. As Sarah Hogg's husband, Douglas Hogg was never going to cause trouble, but a winged Cabinet Minister could be stored away as a useful commodity for a political rainy day. Hogg survived as Minister for Agriculture until election day, and somewhat surprisingly Dorrell escaped public opprobrium on the stupefying Hogg scale.

It takes a sentimentalist, or a very credulous Tory, to see in beef wars and the wider development of the European issue examples of the Major Government's extraordinary 'bad luck'. Bad governments attract bad luck; good governments make their own good fortune. Tory European quarrels were a symptom of a deeper problem – the absence of leadership. Complaints about division and about parliamentary squabbling missed the point and mistook the symptom for the cause. The Prime Minister who 'defied Brussels' on beef was the same Prime Minister who, at Number 10 one day shortly after entering office, remarked to Jacques Attali of the European Bank for Reconstruction and Development: 'I am going to have to exorcise many of the anti-European ghosts which still haunt this room.'

*   *   *

Major had proved to be less of an exorcist than a raiser of spirits from the vasty European deep as, Jekyll-and-Hyde-like, he played one faction off against the other.

The louder the Tories preached about 'loyalty', the faster they counted the possible leadership votes. The noise of possible leaders' protestations about believing in, and working for, a general election victory joined the long queue of lies generated by the Major years. Statements about Europe became leadership bids by proxy. Until 1995, for example, Michael Howard had opposed in Cabinet any measures to reduce the powers of the European Court of Justice. Britain, he said, had to take the rough with the smooth. The Court produced judgements on trade liberalization that suited Britain's interests as well as more contentious political judgements that did not. The Government could not pick those it liked and reject the rest. Now, as he contemplated his future and a vote-delivering Euro-sceptic phalanx in the Parliamentary Party, the Home Secretary abandoned his establishment view. The Court had to be controlled and Britain's powers had to be repatriated from Brussels.

If there were political advantages for the Tories in their new stance, they were difficult to detect in the council elections on the 2nd of May 1996, the last national poll before the general election. The Tories gained 27 per cent of the vote and lost 567 seats. In normal times this would have been seen as the expulsion to an electoral *gulag*, but over four years the Tories had become immunized against electoral pain. Some commentators had predicted that the Tories might lose between 650 and 700 seats. Judged against this possibility the result was less a democratic cataclysm than an event to be discounted. Some Tories thought that this was the last moment at which John Major could have been removed from office. But this judgement ignored the reality of Major's adamantine grip on his Party. Others, seen as 'revolutionary defeatists', longed for the 600-seat barrier to be broken as a fine anticipation of the scale of the inevitable defeat. They knew that Major could not be removed from Number 10. Indeed, they wanted him to stay as an essential prelude and contributor to that purification of the Party by fire that they both predicted and sought. For them, Major had to be there to take the rap. Afterwards, the age of reconstruction could begin.

Redwood tried to persuade his colleagues to 'forget all this business about right or left'. His thesis on historical revisionism was hardly calculated to endear him to Thatcher. After all, he reminded fellow Tories, Thatcher had paid larger subsidies to the railways, had never troubled the index-linked pensions of the public sector, and had 'presided over large increases in welfare'. Moreover, 'the first time she faced a threatening miners' strike she bought them off.' But the Tories were in no mood for subtlety. They wished to be defined by Europe. Redwood despaired when Teresa Gorman insisted on introducing a Ten Minute Rule Bill in order to force a vote on a referendum on Britain's membership of the European Union. The trick was always to maximize the Euro-sceptic vote in the House of Commons. A threat of withdrawal could never do that, and would enable the Government to deride the insignificant level of support it obtained.

Euro-sceptics enjoyed the beef war because it showed that the European Union could have a rather different effect on jobs and prosperity from that proclaimed by the Euro-philes. It demonstrated, they thought, that any British government was powerless in the face of the institutions of the Union and that British Ministers had been reduced to the level of poverty-stricken supplicants. Sceptics stiffened slack ministerial backbones and opposed talk of a need for a general 'framework' rather than a timetable for lifting the ban. However, every Conservative action only reinforced the impression of a Government that had lost control of events. There were no votes in beef wars. MORI's poll at the end of May showed that support for the Government had slumped by 1 per cent to 27 points.

On the 29th of May the European Commission announced plans that would cut the British fishing fleet by 40 per cent, and Jacques Santer, the President of the Commission, described the UK's policy of non-co-operation as 'hostage-taking'. These tactics played into Euro-sceptic hands and also intensified a sense of governmental incompetence. 'Left' and 'right', 'Euro-sceptic' and 'Euro-phile' had become straightjackets for thought and action that reduced the Tories' capacity for creativity and response. Redwood might insist that he regarded himself as a European, and that he never talked of going 'to' Europe because he was placed on British soil and was therefore already there. But his own subtleties were being overtaken by events, and the political process reduced his rhetoric to no more than an impotent English nationalism.

The *Mail on Sunday* might acclaim the work of the Conservative 2000 Foundation as that of 'an administration in waiting', but the compliment would always be double-edged. While John Major was Prime Minister, John Redwood was inevitably caught in a trap of 'disloyalty'. Major, certainly, had no doubts about his intentions. One evening he was in conversation with Dame Sue Tinson, editor-in-chief of Independent Television News and one of the Circes of his acquaintance. As he escorted her to the garden door at the back of Number 10, she raised the question of the millennium celebrations. 'I think,' he said, 'that that's one for Prime Minister Portillo or Prime Minister Redwood, don't you?' Knowing, as he did, that the remark would be repeated, he showed, once again, that he knew how to play on ambitious hopes. Socially there were now no links between Major and Redwood. After the leadership election, the Majors had invited the wives of many of those MPs associated with Redwood to Chequers in order to help to re-establish relations. Gail Redwood was not invited. 'All right,' said Redwood's determined wife, 'we said, if that's the way it's going to be...'.

Mischievously, Redwood would tell Constituency Associations from Edinburgh to Exeter that their task, in effect, was to go out and work hard for another five years of John Major. Most failed to get the joke, and Redwood noted their lack of enthusiasm at the prospect of a Major Redivivus. Although it was funny, the joke was also his problem. Nobody believed that his true objective was another five years of Majorism. He had never believed, he said, that the Tories' best interests could be served by silence, but his own interventions were often contentious. Even when he did not intend to be factional the commentators ensured that he was. He provided too good copy for them. Out of office, he was certainly energetic and liberated, but also at the mercy of an indiscriminate craving for publicity. He would accept any invitation to be interviewed, even if it was the equivalent of Radio Humberside's Wednesday afternoon phone-in.

There was also the continuing problem of his relations with Michael Portillo, who still, as Redwood conceded through gritted teeth, 'looks the part'. He found it difficult to resist a dig. At lunch with the *Guardian* one day, he was asked what the differences were between them, and replied, 'I am more sympathetic than Michael is to people who are down on their luck.' However, Portillo looked unlucky himself as his summer went from bad to worse. Having been unfairly blamed for plans to sell off Admiralty Arch in Whitehall, he held a party in his ministerial office on the evening of the Beating the Retreat by the Household Division. The sound of noisy revellers strayed from the open windows on to the deathly hush on Horse Guards Parade, disturbing the onlookers at the solemn ceremony.

Portillo's plans to sell off the Army's married quarters to private developers aroused another storm. Was this not the insensitivity of market economics run riot? Was not conservatism supposed to uphold historic institutions rather than pander to accountants? Redwood voiced opposition, although Portillo's policy could be confused with his own advocacy of the sale of surplus Ministry of Defence houses in order to help to balance the Treasury's books. Perhaps hoping that circumstances could be presented as objectively altering cases, he waded into the controversy. Until now the Oxonian Redwood was supposed to be more like the supposed Cambridge intellectual – austere, idealistic and unworldly – while the Cantabrigian Portillo had the more characteristic Oxonian virtues of worldly, metropolitan, political calculation. What if the stereotypes of the two universities and their products were true after all? Perhaps Portillo did not understand the world as well as he thought he did. 'You get all this publicity,' he lamented to Redwood, 'when you're not even in the Cabinet.' It was all very puzzling – all the more so since being in the Cabinet was supposed to make a man important. 'You can tell Simon Heffer that Enoch Powell was only in the Cabinet for a year,' Portillo once said to an intermediary after the *Daily Mail*'s vestal Powellite had savaged Portillo's love of office and contrasted it with the purity of Powell's wilderness creed.

Redwood had genuine reservations about Portillo's readiness to change defence procurement policy, to develop the defence capacity of the European Union, and to set up a tripartite arms agency with Germany and France. Conservative institutions had always opposed these measures as the first steps to an European army. But personal sensitivities made it impossible for him to mount a campaign on the issue, and Redwood did not encourage his followers to denigrate Portillo. But neither did he call off the yelping sceptic terriers.

Nicholas Soames, Portillo's portly Minister of State at Defence, had no doubts: 'I know your game, Redwood. I know your game,' he bellowed at the willowy thinker in the lobbies of the House of Commons one evening.

A MORI poll confirmed Redwood's lead over Portillo in the putative leadership stakes, although a score of 9 per cent against his rival's 4 per cent was hardly the makings of a mass popular movement. As cause for the continued fermentation of bad blood, however, it could not be bettered. John Townend tried to broker peace between the two men, and arranged a meeting in his flat. When the time came, would one agree to stand down in favour of the other as the candidate of 'the right'? Redwood said yes, after a first round in which both could test their strength. But Portillo would not be drawn. He thought that in the forthcoming disaster all would be consumed, and that blame would be allocated universally – the 'right' would be whipping boys, and there would be no happy exit. Silence was the only option. That had not been Redwood's chosen course but, he conceded pensively, Portillo 'may well be right'.

Redwood found fame an enjoyable spur, waved merrily at taxi-drivers offering obeisance, he hoped, as they hooted their horns, and rode the horse of popularity hard. His posture was that of a man who wielded more influence outside Cabinet than he ever had inside. Whitehall's running costs had been squeezed by 5 per cent and, of the £5 billion of expenditure reductions derided as impossible in June 1995, £3.2 billion had been achieved. Unlike Portillo, Redwood was now seen as a creative politician who could persuade people to look at issues in a different way, who could surprise and be deft. He was Tony Blair's only real rival for the post-Thatcherite crown in British politics, respectful of her achievement but recognizing its limitations. The problem was that Blair was leading his Party in that direction while Redwood's was mired in the sentiment and the acrimony of Thatcher's double-edged legacy.

Could sceptical language about European institutions be used without appearing to be politically obscurantist? In early July, reports from the European Court of Justice indicated that in September the Court would evade the 'Major opt-out' and impose a forty-eight-hour working week on Britain as a health and safety measure rather than as an employment one. The directive would set the maximum working week, compulsory rest periods every six hours, a minimum daily rest period of eleven hours, one day off each week and four weeks' annual paid holiday. Once established, these would be difficult measures for a Government to oppose or for an Opposition to promise to rescind. Tories attempted a rearguard action by claiming that employers would have to refuse their employees the right to work more than forty-eight hours. This was contestable and left uncertain in the Court's judgement. It was also uncertain whether a judgement of the German Constitutional Court had upheld the superiority of German law over European law. However, both were politically agreeable points to make. The impotence of British law seemed to parallel that of the Conservative Government and its Ministers.

Redwood and the band of sceptics were also ready to tap into anti-German sentiment when it suited. Once again there was a German problem, he wrote on the 26th of June, 'the question which has bedevilled Europe in the twentieth century'. An approaching football fixture between England and Germany at Wembley had 'raised more than the usual hyperbole'. 'There is something special about the contest. It has stirred deep feelings.' He did not share Chancellor Kohl's fear, or threat, of a return to German expansionism. Kohl seemed 'to be saying to the Governments of western Europe that Germany may bully now that she is bigger'. The threat was otiose. 'The only answer, were Germany ever to bully us, is to stand up to it.' He alarmed his hosts at a lunch at an American Embassy lunch by enlarging on the thesis of a 'German plot'. Of course, the Germans do not want to take over Europe by force, he instructed them. 'That's the cleverness of it. They've used pacifism and the fear of war instead.' The CIA man moved very uneasily in his chair.

Standing up to Clarke on taxation and public spending continued to be one of Redwood's priorities. On Thursday the 18th of July, the Cabinet met to set the public spending targets for the year ahead. From outside, Redwood urged spending reductions of £6 billion to make room for pre-election tax cuts. He suggested halving the reserve to £2.5 billion. 'Leave it as a reserve and every Whitehall department will believe there is a crock of gold at the end of the Treasury rainbow.' Falling unemployment would reduce social security payments by £400 million. Selling the usual Redwood assemblage of empty public-sector offices and houses would bring in an additional £500 million. Housing Associations, a particular *bête noire*, should attract private investment not public money, thus saving the £300 million grant. Price and wage inflation was lower than expected, and a reduction of 0.9 per cent in the forecast would yield £2.3 billion. But the problem was that the Government was already committed to spending all the £5 billion in the reserve. Moreover, Redwood proposed savings from privatization receipts, bureaucratic cuts and surplus property. However, was it right to use one-off receipts from such asset sales to finance tax cuts that would have to be continued beyond the present year?

The anti-Clarke campaign was unrelenting. Redwood had convinced himself that the Chancellor's tax policy was an aspect of his European policy. European economies needed, he thought, an implausible degree of convergence in order to sustain a Single Currency. Redwood had convinced himself that the only real economic convergence on the horizon was the one between the Chancellor's European policy and his tax policy, and that this undermined the 1980s' virtuous economic cycle of tax cuts leading to economic growth. 'We have been warned by the European Union that we cannot afford any tax reductions because our borrowing is too high for entry into the Single Currency.' It was therefore no coincidence that 'the Chancellor has warned us not to expect tax cuts and has arranged his figures for economic growth so that he just scrapes under the Euro borrowing wire next year.' For all the Clarkean talk of economic virtue, the background to the Tories' economic legacy in the 1990s was a steep rise in public spending. In 1979 total Government expenditure stood at £74 billion. By the time Thatcher left office in 1990, it had risen to just over £200 billion. Now, it stood at a little over £300 billion, and the Chancellor was proposing an increase of £11.2 billion for 1996/97.

The Government had already increased public spending by £2.1 billion in its summer forecast, published in the second week of July. Spending on cyclical social security increased by £400 million. Family Credits and other benefits to the low paid were an unavoidable element, but the sum did not reflect unemployment statistics at a time when the number of jobless was falling. The sale of assets would bring in £500 million less than forecast. There was an extra £1000 million to service the debt interest and £200 million worth of mysterious 'accounting adjustments'. Clarke's projected increase of £11.2 billion in spending was in addition to this £2.1 billion and, at 3.6 per cent, was well above the current inflation level. Over three years Clarke had borrowed almost £100 billion, but claimed that he had reduced spending by £53 billion during the same period. Now he wanted cuts of just £3 to £5 billion in the new control total of £264 billion (which excluded, *inter alia*, cyclical Social Security expenditure. His claim was that the target for public spending was strict and amounted, in real terms, to a freeze over the three-year period from 1994/95 to 1997/98.

The urgency was palpable as the EMU timetable tightened. A British Government that decided to enter would have to make the Bank of England independent almost immediately and propose legislation in the first Queen's Speech. Were a Conservative Government to propose such legislation, it could only be carried with Opposition votes. On current form, a Conservative Government recommending entry into EMU would lose the necessary referendum. There seemed every justification for intensifying the campaign against entry, but the tightrope was getting tauter.

On the 23rd of July the front page of the *Independent* carried a picture of a mocked-up membership card for a 'Redwood party', complete with a photograph of the leader as hero. Gratifying to the vanity it might be, but it was also clear that Redwood's press exposure was now beginning to harm him. The media class was ready to devour its own.

By the end of July Redwood was back in New York and Washington, this time with a camera crew from GMTV to record the campaign for the presidential election in November. Exposure in a setting of presidential wannabes would do the British politician no harm in his ambition. He also carried an official letter from Margaret Thatcher, who gave him a lukewarm recommendation to her American friends as one who had 'helped me with the Thatcher revolution in the 1980s'. There had been previous American interludes. In January he had debated in Washington the prospects for a conservative revival with Gingrich and Preston Manning, leader of the Canadian Reform Party. Manning was an unlikely Conservative revolutionary whose conversation recalled the winning entry in a competition for the most boring headline in journalism: 'From ocean to mighty ocean, whither Canada?' As usual Gingrich was more exciting, but also late, unprepared and incoherent as he embarked on his world-historical ruminations on the communications revolution. Arianna Huffington emerged again, still a tremulous presence at Washington receptions.

Earlier in July, Pat Buchanan, the conservative Catholic revivalist, had arrived in London and asked to visit Redwood. He shared with Redwood the fear of post-Christian anarchy on the streets of the modern Wild West. Both were politicians frightened of the new Waste Land, but Redwood was torn. On the one hand was the glamour and allure of a very successful former presidential candidate; on the other the danger of being seen in public with so controversial a 'right-winger'. He agreed to meet Buchanan in secrecy in Wilfred Street, and a camera crew from GMTV filmed the interview, which was subsequently broadcast in August as part of his series on American politics. Suitably edited, it could appear as part of his filming in America. However, Buchanan had mentioned his meeting with Redwood when he arrived in London, and BBC cameras soon turned up outside the Foundation's door. Redwood panicked. He refused to appear in public with Buchanan and even contemplated cancelling the meeting. But Buchanan's bandwagon had an irresistible force and was too big to stop.

Now, in a hotel bedroom in New York in late July, Redwood was woken at dawn by an irate Chief Whip phoning from London. The front page of the *Daily Telegraph* on Monday the 29th reported that he was going to launch a rival general election manifesto in the autumn. In particular he would urge a systematic cull of the 1227 quangos and the strengthening of local government by transferring their powers to local authorities. The story was the result of the vaporous fantasies of a *Telegraph* journalist with more imagination than brain cells. Redwood would certainly publish proposals that he wanted included in the manifesto, but the idea of a separate manifesto was a fantasy. Dyspeptically, Goodlad demanded the withdrawal of the 'alternative manifesto' and a statement of retraction. Redwood's reaction, three thousand miles across the Atlantic, was wry. But once the theme had been established it ran and ran. The story in Britain was not of a powerful Redwood acclaimed as a prince over the water. Rather was he seen as over-impatient, over-confident and over there.

When Redwood spoke to the American Enterprise Institute in Washington on Wednesday the 31st of July, he made what could be viewed as a rather obvious attack on Major and Clinton, two politicians not usually put in the same category. 'There is something in the air that is unheroic,' he said. The fault lay with politicians who were ruled by 'polling, media manipulation and the daily sound bite'. 'Modern politicians', as he called them, were directionless. They had forgotten where 'they originally wanted to go – if they ever knew'. 'They end up going nowhere, making aerial surveys of congestion. The times were out of joint. The issues were momentous, and political men were not adequate. Cometh the hour, cometh, it seemed, the pollster. These were high-minded, statesman-like reflections delivered from the peak of Olympus. But in the plains of British conservatism an old charge that Redwood was a Conservative version of Tony Benn was beginning to recur. Accusations of Bennery of the right were a useful version of the Majorite case that only the Prime Minister could unite a fractious Party. Many also felt that there had been too many attacks in Redwood's collaborationist name on Michael Portillo, whose beacon remained alluring among the few new parliamentary candidates who could entertain realistic hopes of being elected.

However, these considerations seemed a long way away as New York finance, Washington summer swamp, and Texan drawls absorbed Redwood's energy. In his New York office Henry Kissinger soothed Redwood with the practised diplomat's amoral understanding of power. He told Redwood how, just over a year ago, he was unknown. Now, all Kissinger's English friends had the name of Wokingham's philosopher-king on their lips. Kissinger was interested in the question of political leadership, how it was acquired, maintained and developed. Could Redwood tell him how he had performed his great feats? An eager Redwood expatiated.

Picaresque moments abounded. While strolling down a New York sidewalk filming a trailer for his TV programmes, Redwood shouted resistibly above the traffic: 'Join me, John Redwood.' The next day we travelled to Washington, where the doors of an hotel opened to reveal the massive frame of an elderly Englishman. The summer shirt he was wearing did nothing to conceal the copious perspiration precipitated by the late July humidity. Two assistants flanked him cautiously, as if in anticipation of the tottering figure's imminent collapse. As he advanced into the lobby, Redwood recognized the former leader of his Party, Sir Edward Heath. A breezy 'Hello Ted' was reciprocated by an indifferent croak of the larynx. Heath had arrived to address a conference of those who advertised themselves as the World Federation for Families and Peace, otherwise known as the Unification Church or the Moonies, whose posters adorned the hotel walls. Redwood made a rapid departure. We walked past the White House in the evening warmth. 'Next time,' said Redwood, 'we'll go in through the front door.'

In Congress grave Senators such as McCain of Arizona and Gramm of Texas marvelled at the Redwood 'ID factor', and wondered how much money he had had to spend to gain such recognition. But the felicitations did not all flow in one direction. When he spoke publicly in Washington, Redwood was fulsome in his praise of the Republicans' Welfare Bill, which had devolved many responsibilities to individual states and thereby reduced the federal budget. After much agonizing, the President had finally decided to sign the Bill as his third, uncertain, way evolved away from the old universal welfarism of Roosevelt's New Deal and Johnson's Great Society. There was a vivid contrast with Redwood's old adversary in the Treasury and his rejection of fundamental welfare reforms. In London earlier that summer, Clarke had dismissed a leaked long-term Treasury review of public spending for the years 2000 to 2005 as the work of 'kids in the office'. Labour exploited the situation as the Government nervously distanced itself from the work of Treasury officials.

Absurdism returned in Texas where Redwood's host, Cary Maguire, had just opened a new oil well. In Dallas, the improbably lacquered wives of oil millionaires offered private inspections of newly acquired Gainsboroughs in their boudoirs. Downtown tours of a collection of bronze statues of cattle in a rodeo were obligatory in the shimmering heat as an acknowledgement of Texan glory. In the evening, at dinner, an animated Redwood explained to a small collection of wide-eyed plutocrats how 'I am going to take over the Conservative Party.' References to 'Winston' and 'Margaret' gathered in conversational clusters. Like Noel Coward in the song – if in no other respects – John Redwood 'liked America', but it was surely time to go home.

The summer to which he returned had been dominated politically by the advertising fiasco of the Blair demon-eyes poster. However, there was another campaign. The Government had never apologized for imposing the ERM on British families and companies. Even when pressed in the middle of the 1997 general election, Major still justified it on the basis of lowered inflation. 'Yes, it hurt. Yes, it worked' sought to meet these discontents halfway. The words, emblazoned in a national poster campaign, had two messages. First, the measures taken to get Britain out of the recession had been painful. Yet a wise and ultimately benign Government had seen these measures through, and prosperity was the result. In practice the message conveyed was one of arrogance. An elected Government had chosen to inflict pain on the British people in order to correct the consequences of its own mistakes. The note of triumphalist apologetics was tinged with what appeared as a gloating and sadistic pleasure in having inflicted pain so effectively. Another campaign slogan first used in the 1959 general election, 'Life's Better under the Conservatives', was now formally pensioned off. The 1950s had indeed been the great Tory decade, but the electorate no longer associated conservatism with the relaxed certainties of Anna Neagle films and men in Homburg hats driving Humbers. The Government tried to move in on the seemingly impermeable Labour lead. A fragile moment of hope was seized in the middle of September when ICM's poll showed that Labour's lead had been cut to 15 per cent and that the Conservatives now stood at 32 per cent. At the end of September, the Cabinet approved the campaign slogan, 'Opportunity for All'. It was a conscious reversion to the theme of the classless society espoused by Major when he first became Prime Minister and never subsequently developed.

To many it seemed that the most obvious Conservative opportunity was the one, eagerly seized, to lambast each other. On the 18th of September Malcolm Rifkind had said in Zürich that a single currency could be divisive within Europe – a comment that enraged the Chancellor. But the most important battle remained the war of Clarke's resolve, Redwood's pen and Major's ear.

Against the background of a self-imposed, but far from splendid, isolation Major maintained on the 25th of July that 'for us to get out of the debate now would be a dereliction of responsibility.' For Clarke, this was a green light to keep the European show on the road, and Major was happy to encourage the illusion that Clarke was still holding him to ransom. On Sunday the 22nd of September, Clarke said at the Dublin summit of EU Finance Ministers that it would be 'pathetic' for Britain to wait on the sidelines of a successful Monetary Union in Europe and then decide to join at a later stage. Six or eight European countries would, he thought, set up a common currency in 1999. If the enterprise seemed likely to be successful, Britain should join then. This was a breach of Cabinet policy, since the Government intended to stay out of the first wave of entrants.

'Kenneth Clarke', said Redwood, 'is trying to bounce the Cabinet or he has forgotten what the collective line of the Cabinet is.' Clarke had 'damaged the unity of the Government'. Reports were also now circulating that it was Clarke, as a senior member of the Tory troika, who had kept the ERM alive after Britain's withdrawal. When the possibility of abandoning the system was discussed at a meeting of European Finance Ministers, Clarke had reportedly said to his colleagues, 'You don't have the right to do this, it would be a historic defeat, a rout.' With acute timing, Redwood moved in to exploit Clarke's exposed position, and unveiled a proposal to raise the VAT threshold from £47,000 to £90,000 in order to encourage one-man businesses to take on employees. Three million people in Britain now worked for themselves, and if they took on an unemployed person they would be given a one-year National Insurance holiday as a reward for reducing the unemployment total. The words vanished into the rarefied Treasury consciousness.

Conservative canvassers now reported that people seemed to be less angry and more polite when they called. Encouragement was duly taken, but it was an ominous sign. In 1993 and 1994 it had still been worthwhile venting anger because the electorate wished to change the Government's mind. The quarrels were within the extended family of Conservative voters. By now criticism was futile. Voters could no longer be bothered to expend energy on changing Tory minds. They had divorced themselves from the Government.

In autumn conversations it was impossible to avoid Tory leadership talk. Andrew Roberts had worked puckishly on Redwood's 1995 campaign. Now he reminded Thatcher of Portillo's parlous state and laid before her the detailed catalogue of the Defence Secretary's gaffes. Simon Heffer thought strategically about how Michael Howard, then considered to be the greatest threat, could be defeated in the early stages of the next leadership campaign. Richard Littlejohn, also of the *Mail*, argued that Portillo was now 'a national joke', that Major was 'venal', and that Redwood should continue to speak out in a dignified way. John Patten feared that Redwood's problem was that he did not talk to the Parliamentary Party enough. He drew a parallel with Heath, who suddenly rediscovered the charms of backbench MPs in 1974 and 1975, when his leadership was under threat, but found that he had forgotten even their names. Heath had sent Peter Walker, then a leftish lord-in-waiting to his Prime Minister, out to the Parliamentary plains to scavenge for voters, but discovered that his colleagues were leery of both his own blandishments and those of his master. Patten agreed with Heffer that Howard's formidable powers of organization and persistence made Howard the main threat to Redwood, while the attentions of the press would make Portillo an implausible leadership candidate.

The ability to tell a good life story had become the most important weapon in the armoury of the modern politician. General Colin Powell was demonstrating that ability in American politics that autumn. But the tales British Conservatives told were shabby. MPs had left Westminster that summer having awarded themselves a 26 per cent pay rise. An independent pay review body had recommended the increase after Nolan's ruling restricted outside earnings. A wider public thought the salary increase abnormal, judged by any standard other than that of MPs' inflated view of their importance and abilities. For Norman Tebbit, the Commons was 'composed largely of Parliamentary pygmies accepting a slide towards being little more than a provincial assembly with subordinate powers to legislate over a shrinking proportion of our national affairs'. Tebbit grasped the reality of debilitating consensus between the two parties: 'So far as I can see there is not much difference between the parties in the final destination. The Government would want to get off a couple of stations before Labour.' Both parties, he wrote, instead of opposing the entry of the Trojan horse stood arguing over whether the model was a good likeness of a horse.

The common impression of a self-enclosed political class was strengthened by the way in which commentators and politicians pored over the precise meaning of certain words and phrases with all the zeal of late mediaeval scholastics in their battle over the interpretation of texts. 'Wait and see' had now become 'negotiate and decide'. What was the difference? How and why did a first wave become a second wave? What did 'when the conditions are right' mean? Dangers lurked everywhere. Every word, every phrase, every inflection of meaning and quiver of an eyelash could be interpreted, misinterpreted and over-interpreted.

On the evening of Monday the 7th of October, the very eve of the Party Conference in Bournemouth, BBC TV's *Panorama* programme broadcast an interview with Redwood during which he appeared to hesitate in declaring his support for the Conservative Party at the next general election. Excessive caution in using words had undone him. When asked whether voters should support the Referendum Party or the Conservatives, he said: 'Well, I think you have to ask me that nearer the time when we see what the manifestos are of the major parties and what the views of the different candidates are.' He wished to say that he trusted that in their manifesto the Conservatives would provide better reasons than the Referendum Party, but the damage was done –

especially when the BBC held a press conference and issued a press release to dramatize the issue. Michael Trend, the party's Vice Chairman, initiated a mobile phone conversation, very agitated on his side but detached on mine, as I drove to Bournemouth. When Redwood arrived he was surrounded by a sea of Conservative hostility which worked to Major's advantage. Virginia Bottomley grimaced ostentatiously when she saw Redwood walking towards her. Other colleagues were becoming increasingly hostile.

In that Conference week the Labour Party produced a poster contrasting Major's evasion and indecision about the Single Currency with Redwood's clarity and hostility. The heads of the two politicians dominated. Labour's own ambiguities did not matter, for the message communicated was one of governmental incompetence. Redwood's prominence was double-edged and well-judged by Labour. He was indeed as important as the Prime Minister, but his influence was being squandered in the ether of journalism. He was as likely to be blamed for the forthcoming defeat as he was to be hailed as the far-sighted chieftain. He and I decided to view the largest of the posters, a vast affair to be found at the bottom of a hill behind the conference centre. As we turned the corner and walked down we saw in the distance, at the bottom of the hill, a man in a mac. He was standing on his own and looking at the poster with some intensity. It was Peter Lilley. I got the impression that he had been there for some time. His colleagues in these latter Tory days spent a lot of their time thinking about John Redwood – the once cautious politician whose interests now seemed so concentrated on the dangerous edge of things.

Tories left their Conference with an artificial spring in their step. The Prime Minister had plundered his origins one more time: 'I didn't come from two rooms in Brixton to 10, Downing Street not to go out and fight with every fibre of my being for what I believe in.' He had tried to patronize Blair. The Opposition leader could not be Prime Minister because, 'It's too big a task for your first real job.' It was his job, and he was hanging on to it. Artificial class consciousness rounded off the performance: 'You know what they say. New Labour, old school tie.' Thatcher, looking more like a histrionic pantomime dame than a *grande dame*, turned in one of her increasingly high-camp performances, told everyone to 'get cracking', and then went dramatically 'off-message' with invective that presupposed Michael Foot's continued leadership of the Labour Party.

Major's taste for intrigue against Cabinet colleagues had contributed to the Tories' alienation of British affections. Once acquired, however, the taste was long cultivated. Gillian Shephard's Education Bill did not give schools the right to impose corporal punishment. A backbench amendment to the Bill urged a free vote to restore caning. Shephard herself, interviewed by the BBC, said she was in favour of corporal punishment. Major waxed furious. He called her on a mobile phone while she was giving a press conference and demanded that she should stop expressing a view. But he did not stop there, and his office briefed that this had been an official reprimand from the Prime Minister. The thoroughly disabused Shephard stored her resentment in her handbag and decided that the best way to wreak revenge was to feed newspaper gossip that she was a serious candidate for the leadership. Although she had no intention of standing, it was a good way of inserting the stiletto heel between the shoulder blades.

Tebbit was now warning that entry to a Single Currency would break the Tory party apart. It was a neat inversion of Hurd's claim that the force of Euroscepticism would dissolve Party loyalties. Conservatives who believed in freedom, independence and democracy would, said Tebbit, join those of other parties who shared those beliefs. Major's handling of the European issues had turned into a solvent of loyalties rather than a bridge of concord. It was against this background that the Government's last great European drama, that of the 'stability pact', was played in November 1996.

On the 2nd of December Kenneth Clarke was due to attend a meeting of European Finance Ministers (known in Euro-speak as ECOFIN). Three bulky documents relating to preparations for the Single Currency had come before the Commons Standing Committee which monitored the proposals of the European Union, or the European Government as many had started to call it. Before Clarke could claim that he had parliamentary authority to approve the documents in an European context, the Committee would have to scrutinize them. There was enough Brussels ambiguity in the drafting of the documents to justify the fear that Britain's independent economic policy might be affected even if she remained outside the Single Currency. Some 150 Conservative MPs, the maximum strength of sceptical parliamentary opinion ranging from the ultras to the tepid, signed a motion demanding a full debate on the stability pact. On the 20th of November the Committee decided by a majority of one not to 'take note' of the documents, a decision that automatically led to a debate on the floor of the House of Commons. The Government had set its face against a debate, and the Committee's Conservative members had been lobbied heavily by the Whips. John Whittingdale, also canvassed by the ultra-sceptics, rebelled. After he had capitulated in the Maastricht vote, his Euro-virility had been questioned. Now he recovered his reputation. 'You're a hero,' Redwood told him.

On Thursday the 21st of November, four days before Monday's debate, Redwood had an angry exchange with the Chancellor when he happened to see him in the House of Commons. He said that he hoped Clarke realized that he now had no authority to accept the latest preparations for the Single Currency at the ECOFIN meeting in Brussels. The documents had not been 'scrutinized' or endorsed by the House of Commons. He would have to wait for the meeting of Heads of Government on the 13th of December. An enraged Clarke dismissed Redwood's claim. He could certainly claim that scrutiny had taken place, he told Redwood, and refused to talk further.

In the debate on Monday the 25th, the Chancellor came to the House to state that no binding decision affecting Britain's economy would be taken at ECOFIN on the 2nd or at the next meeting of the European Council of

Ministers on the 13th. He undertook to return with a 'copper-bottomed' guarantee that Brussels would not interfere in British economic affairs if Britain did not join EMU. Had the Chancellor intended to deceive, or was this a sceptic storm in the Tories' cup of sorrows? Clarke's fine careless flourish with incidental details was notorious, and the wording of the crucial Recital 13 was indeed ambiguous. It stated that fines would be imposed on any State joining the Single Currency whose economy was failing to meet the strict convergence requirements. Most importantly, such States would have to continue to cut their public debt to 3 per cent of GDP after entering the Single Currency area. However, the Recital went on: 'It will also be necessary to make similar rules covering the programmes and surveillance of the other member States.' To some this was innocent, aspirational talk. EU monitoring of Britain's economic performance already occurred. There was no change here. European law, unlike British, was full of such pious generalities. Others saw sinister interests at work. It was through the interpretation of such generalities and ambiguities that the European Court of Justice had extended its powers of competence. The sceptics on Bill Cash's independently run IGC Monitoring Committee had detected the supposed lurking dangers and policed the ensuing mayhem.

Redwood added his own public contribution, questioning in the press the legality of the EMU scheme's unilateral transfers from the 'Ecu' unit of currency to the 'Euro'. The compulsory replacement of contracts in pounds, francs or marks with ones in euros could result in worldwide legal challenges. Since the regulation only had force in the fifteen member countries, many outside the EU might think that such a compulsory currency conversion would disadvantage them. The Treaty of Maastricht referred to the Ecu and was undoubtedly legal in international law. If the new currency unit were to be real, the Treaty itself would have to be amended – a contentious business that any European government, as Redwood knew, would be anxious to avoid. The British Government's policy, flying away on a wing and a prayer, had met sceptic pedantry and been worsted. But even more significant was the fact that 150 Conservative MPs did not trust the Chancellor who, without a debate and on the basis of the Committee's approval, could have claimed that the documents had been adequately scrutinized in Parliament. It was a moment at which Euro-scepticism seemed to break out from its narrow hinterland and engulf the wider Parliamentary Party.

'Just what do they think they are playing at?' said Major when he heard of the insurgency. But Redwood was now speaking for a mistrustful Parliamentary Party which thought that the Government was bent on side-lining both it and Parliament. He kept up the pressure until the very day of the ECOFIN meeting, and released the text of a letter he had sent to Clarke the previous Thursday. 'I would have preferred to raise these matters in private,' he wrote.

Last week I asked the Whips for a meeting with you but nothing happened. I also wrote to you in private but received no reply. When I tried to speak to you on the way to the vote you broke off the conversation before I could offer you a whisky to talk it over. That is why I had no choice but to raise these matters in public.

The reference to whisky was calculatedly wounding, as if the Chancellor needed an offer of alcohol in order to overwhelm the dubious charms of a Clarke–Redwood *tête-à-tête*.

He now also wrote to every backbencher setting out detailed amendments to the new currency regulations. They were invited to sign the amendments and send them directly to the Chancellor or the Chief Whip. Goodlad's tolerance level for Redwood, already low, was sinking daily. To many others as well, Redwood's attempt to humiliate Clarke seemed too rich a diet of contumely. However, his hard-core troops still had doubts when Major signed the stability pact in Dublin on the 13th. Clarke could boast of a clarification that the pact would not apply to Britain if it did not join EMU. None the less the Euro had now been legalized, and the central terms of a stability pact would be enforced, possibly by an embryonic economic government. Redwood was enraged that Major and Clarke had not used the veto to stop the legalization of the Euro. The threat to keep it a bastard currency could have been used to reform the European Court of Justice, but it would have required a Government with greater authority than Major's to respond to the profound European conflict that would have ensued.

In combining a heavy hand with unconvincing bluster, the Government had been the author of its own misfortunes in its dealings with both its backbenchers and the wider public. But the issue of the stability pact had been too arcane to excite true public interest. Parliamentarians had become agitated, and there were very many Tories behaving badly, but it seemed that the noise and fury signified not a passion for democracy but a concern with MPs' own privileges as legislators. MPs had become just another other occupational group with a grievance. The true significance of the episode was that the Conservative Party and the Government had once again shown themselves constitutionally incapable of running a consistent and competent European policy in any direction.

Major continued with 'negotiate and decide', or 'divide and rule'. Talking at the end of November to the Euro-phile Macleod Group of Tory MPs, he discussed the advantages of the Euro. 'All of the argument is about how dreadful it might be if we go in,' he said to them. But the electorate should be told, thought the Prime Minister, about 'some of the adverse consequences of staying out'. It was a time when the Chancellor was particularly keen to point out how a strong pound was making life difficult for British exporters to Europe, as their goods became correspondingly more expensive. The Government's position might be one of official agnosticism about swings and roundabouts, but, fumed Redwood, 'Clarke only talks about the disadvantages of staying out. He never talks about the advantages.' Clarke's Britain was a country that had chosen to live by Europe economically. It could not therefore exclude itself from the continent's political future. That European view might be the product of a provincial boy's 1950s dream of sun, sea, sand, sangria, and Gina Lollobrigida, but Clarke also grasped the inescapable political dynamism of the European experiment. The problem with his language was that the European venture also seemed unnerving, full of possibility and yet one whose eventual goal was uncertain. Sceptics also offered platitudes, in their case about a 'Europe of nations' stretching from the Atlantic to the Urals. But they did not indicate any strategic sense of how Britain might achieve that goal, except by having a government that might somehow 'stand up for Britain'. Rifkind's Europe for its part was less than a federal state and more than a free trade area. Many winding avenues could be detected in that large and ambiguous terrain. Rifkind's hopes merely indicated generality of aim.

The breadth of possibilities suited Major strategically. On the 2nd of December the *Daily Telegraph* reported that the Prime Minister was now convinced that it was against Britain's interests to join the Single Currency. He wished to persuade Clarke to abandon his enthusiasm. The editor had recently breakfasted with Major, and the Prime Minister had given full rein to his tendency to muse about the possibilities open to him. The Tory fabulist was at work. It was the day of the ECOFIN meeting in Brussels, and the Chancellor, already under pressure from Redwood on the stability pact, rejected the *Telegraph*'s story as preposterous. However, this was also the time when, in an interview with the *New Yorker*, Major claimed that he would hate to serve as Chancellor of the Exchequer after Britain had entered EMU – for he would be unable to defend or advocate an interest-rate policy to the House of Commons since neither he, nor the Government of the day, would have had any say in the matter. Some once again heard the sound of the rain dance being performed in the distance.

This time Major had gone too far and had uncharacteristically lost one of his options in the political future. Clarke and Heseltine left him in no doubt that it was now important to kill the story. On Tuesday at Prime Minister's Questions, Blair asked whether the Deputy Prime Minister had been right to rule out a change of policy that lunchtime. Flatly and resentfully, the Prime Minister said, 'that is the position.' Blair needed to say no more. An ocean of shortly to be unemployed Tory MPs sat forlornly behind Major. 'That's it,' said one of them, Michael Brown. 'This is the day we lost the general election.' From sceptics to tepids, the Tory Parliamentary Party had convinced itself that, in the absence of any other serious domestic policy, only Europe could win them the next election. Now their leader denied them even that possibility.

Clarke was contemptuous of Major's indiscretion. His remarks to Moore had been 'a boomerang laden with high explosives'. But he himself was indiscreet. His remarks at lunch with two journalists in a Park Lane restaurant were subsequently reported. As the lost leader, he was now a Euro-beast at bay, full of confidence and resentment. He would not be coerced into Euro-scepticism by Central Office juveniles, any more than Nigel Lawson, his predecessor, had paid attention to teenage scribblers. In another leaked remark, Clarke said to Mawhinney, 'Tell your kids to get their scooters off my lawn.' Daniel Finkelstein, a mature kid in his thirties, might enjoy success with Stephen Dorrell, whose statements were now beginning to drip with an opportunistic scepticism, but if necessary Clarke would stand alone as the Tory Euro-philes' Grace Darling.

Stephen Dorrell was the leading Euro-phile among the younger Tories, but now he started to talk of the need to renegotiate Britain's relations with the European Union. However, closer examination of his effusions in January showed that he had redefined his terms. One of the worst aspects of British politicians' uneasy reaction to European Union policies and language was that it forced them to be unusually evasive, even by political standards. All too often they stooped to deceive. In this instance, 'renegotiation' was merely Dorrell-speak for Britain's diurnal round of Brussels negotiations. As 'Redwood-lite', it was pain-free scepticism on the road to the main chance.

It was no coincidence that at the beginning of 1997 Dorrell became the latest Cabinet member to labour, all too willingly, under the albatross-like burden of being 'Major's preferred successor'. The evasive language about 'renegotiation' was indeed typically Majorite, and many thought that Dorrell was being used to fly a Major kite. There had been another signal mark of favour. Dorrell was now the Cabinet's overall spokesman on constitutional issues, a keenly, if unintelligently, contested position among Cabinet Ministers who suddenly decided that they had constitutional 'views' and that it would be both safe and interesting to advance these reflections.

Clarke's last concession to the Euro-sceptics was made on the 23rd of January, when he agreed to the Cabinet formulation of a policy that inched forward from the statement of the previous April. It was now 'very unlikely', Major told the House of Commons that day, 'but not impossible that the Single Currency can proceed safely on 1 January 1999 – but if it did proceed with unreliable convergence we would not, of course, be part of it.' The sober civil-service prose drained the statement of any political vitality. Indeed, it left the Chancellor still free to maintain, as he did eagerly, that Britain could join in 1999. The Government only needed to introduce additional enabling legislation late in 1997 – by which time he himself had ceased to expect a Conservative Government to be holding office.

The Government had long since forgotten how to be popular in an unfriendly world – if indeed it still cared. However, the Conservative Party was still convinced that the adman's arts could cast an electoral spell over an otherwise dismissive populace. For January, Saatchis recommended an expensive lion's roar. The new campaign launched on the 6th centred on the potent myth of the British lion. But, after a few initial frolics, the beast Saatchis engaged for the purpose seemed old and tired. Apparently fearful of New Labour's onslaught, the lion in the Tories' political broadcast lay down on the ground and started to cry a red tear. The public forgot the roar and saw in the lion the emblem of a despairing party. It was not only the lion that was tired. Later that month, on the 27th, after a very good lunch at Chequers, a number of Cabinet Ministers fell asleep while discussing the future campaign.

Portillo's announcement on the 24th of January of a £60 million replacement for the Royal Yacht *Britannia* showed a clumsy Tory hand at work. Britain had become cool about its Royal Family as hostility to public money being spent on the restoration of Windsor Castle after the fire had shown. *Britannia* was seen as a way of keeping Tory popularity afloat, and Portillo foolishly boasted that he had wrong-footed Labour. In its briefing the Royal Household objected to the politicization of the issue, and Labour deftly said that they would raise the money by private, not public, finance. The self-conscious pursuit of clear blue water – of making the Tories different – was shown to be self-defeating because it was too obviously soliciting votes. Now, when Tories tried to be popular, they looked like aged, leering lechers clumsily attempting to repeat the courtship rituals of their youth. Forsyth had appeared similarly gauche the previous July when he had authorized the removal of the Stone of Scone from Westminster and its return to Scotland, where it was revered as part of the coronation seat of Scottish kings. Tories had ceased to be effective and credible exponents of a union that had withered in their hands. Now they resorted to an ineffective public relations ploy and used the Stone as a prop for the decomposing corpse of Scottish Unionism.

The tenacious backbench Tory opposition to gun-control legislation following the senseless savagery of the shooting in a Dunblane school showed the dimension of modern Conservatism's problem. The legislation was overwhelmingly popular, and was the settled will and conviction of the *Sun* and the *Daily Mail*. Tory instinct prided itself on expressing such convictions, but here the popular sentiment wanted an expansion of the law and the criminalization of the plebeian pleasures of the gun club. Tomorrow, some feared, might see the statute book moving against the grouse moor and the more exclusive pleasures of the shoot. What was wrong with the more effective enforcement of existing legislation? Although shaken by the scale of the opposition, Michael Howard led the charge and won the day in the House of Commons. Legislation was passed banning certain categories of handgun. But an amendment banning all handguns was lost by 306 to 281 votes because of overwhelming Tory hostility. If the public approved of the more limited legislation that had been passed, they were still left with a picture of happily gunslinging Conservative MPs – and Labour would do nothing to alienate its growing suburban bourgeois constituency for whom gun ownership was a sign of criminal intent.

One of the bittersweet spectacles of 1996/97 was the sight of Tory MPs searching for safer seats. When the Opposition's electoral hitmen came after them, many Tory MPs went on the run. Basildon, the Essex marginal seat, had acquired huge symbolic significance. When the Tories retained the constituency, against all expectation, in 1992, it seemed to demonstrate how they had also retained the hopes and trust of the aspirational sons and daughters of the old Labour-voting working class as they moved into manage-rialism, small businesses and disposable incomes. David Amess, the victor of 1992, transferred his affections from this Tory electoral shrine to the villas of Southend, a much safer seat, and so revealed the true Tory view of his Party's prospects. Many followed his example. The Party Chairman himself, Dr Mawhinney, got on his electoral bike and left Peterborough for the safer pastures of Cambridgeshire North West. Slough was no longer fit for John Watts, and the Minister of State at the Department of Transport left his highly marginal seat for Reading East – which promptly fell to Labour on a 13.9 per cent swing on the 1st of May. Peter Lilley departed newly marginal St Albans for cosy Hitchin and happy Harpenden. Stephen Dorrell quit rugged Loughborough for dozy and rural Charnwood. Nicholas Soames abandoned light-manufacturing Crawley for lush mid-Sussex. Men were judged by their deeds, not by their words. Labour christened them the chicken-run candidates, and helped to create the public view of Conservative careerism pursued at the expense of loyalty and principle. A few Tories with low majorities and established reputations could have absconded on the night-mail from their highly marginal seat, but chose not to. Phillip Oppenheim at Amber Valley and Tom Sackville in Bolton West, David Martin in Portsmouth South and David Shaw in Dover: all stood by their constituencies, lost on the high ground, but found they could still shave in the morning.

By January 1997, the Tories had lived with the sense of an ending for a very long time. They had almost forgotten that their Party's politics could be anything other than apocalyptic in style and in tone. Major had presided over, and aided, the disintegration of the Conservative Party's political structures. Personal hatreds within the Parliamentary Party ran high, and the Government had progressively deprived the electorate of any reason for voting Conservative. The final Conservative Budget did move against under-taxed industries and fraud as it tried to deal with disappointingly low tax revenues, but it was the dampest of squibs. Reducing income tax by another penny in the pound barely registered in the public mind. After the withdrawal from the ERM, the Chancellor had presided over a devaluation-led recovery in Britain's fortunes, but his stewardship lacked creativity. He was the night-watchman Chancellor watching an economic recovery barren of votes and devoid of Tory hope.

If the Tories had collapsed, so also, in another sense, had the Labour Party. Shorn of its Socialism, denuded of its defining creeds, and guided by the pungent phrase, the social abstraction and the hope of office, Labour had become less of a party and more of a movement animated by a 'project' – the removal of the Tories from office.

The time was ripe for an experiment in political science that might test the dominance of party. The official Conservative manifesto would not go beyond the established platitudes and ambiguities about a 'Europe of nations'. Indeed, many ultra-sceptics, anticipating defeat, did not want a stronger position to be embraced officially, lest a succeeding Labour Government could say that the

British people had rejected strong sceptic meat. Herein lay an opportunity. A *Daily Telegraph* survey of 402 Conservative candidates published on the 16th of December 1996 showed that 147 would declare their opposition to a Single Currency in their election address. Of those 147, seventy-eight would oppose the Currency altogether, while sixty-nine would rule it out for the lifetime of the next Parliament. Of the 145 sitting MPs and candidates in seats currently held by the Tories, thirty-five expressed opposition in absolute terms and thirty-three ruled the currency out for the next Parliament. The survey excluded Ministers who, officially at least, would have to support the Government's line.

When approached by newspapers, candidates had been either effusively eager to communicate their views to a wider public or had retreated into a sullen and timorous silence. Their reactions were a tribute to the subversive, democratic power of those who wielded the arts of communication, first clearly expressed by Thomas Carlyle a century and a half previously. 'Invent writing', he had said, and 'democracy is inevitable.' 'Whoever can speak, speaking now to the whole nation, becomes a power, a branch of government, with inalienable weight in law-making, in all acts of authority.' Since the political no-man's-land had expanded to include the trenches of both Government and Opposition, 'Europe' seemed to be the only distinguishing issue in the general poverty of political ideas. These candidates were keener on being elected than on being impaled on the blunt sword of Major's evasive rhetoric. Could other candidates be encouraged to be bold?

Newspapers' eve-of-poll declarations of allegiance and recommendations to readers are an important feature of general election politics. But the 'Conservative press' was in a quandary. It was dismissive of Major, suspicious of Clarke, but wary of endorsing Labour. It also needed a story to enliven what would otherwise be a dull anticipation of inevitable defeats as the Tories wound their way down to Labour's May Day. Conservative newspapers also knew that their readers, the former Conservative-voting public, could not be corralled back into the Party fold. Having spent so much energy on criticizing the Tory record, most papers would find it difficult to turn round, endorse Major and lend credence to the barely credible. Perhaps, therefore, newspapers should become actors in the drama rather than observers? Britain's first coupon election had been in 1918 when Asquith, on one side of the Liberal divide, had referred contemptuously to the Government's officially approved list of Liberal candidates as having received a 'coupon'. In a 1997 'coupon' election, a newspaper could play the same role and endorse certain candidates, regardless of party, who subscribed to certain beliefs. A newspaper could then produce its own national, approved list of candidates. It would be a gratifying display of media-class power as a solvent of the ties of party.

The *Telegraph* would always have to return to the beat of an antique drum by the 1st of May. But News International was a different proposition. I discussed the idea with Irwin Stelzer. The Murdoch-owned tabloid, the *New*

York Post, had already conducted such an exercise in state elections. News International executives had been gratified at the sight of New Yorkers going into the polling booths holding copies of the *Post*'s special edition with its recommendation of whom to vote for in the confusing plethora of offices up for election. Now *The Times* decided to develop the idea for the British general election. Inevitably the issue chosen was the Single Currency. *The Times* would endorse parliamentary candidates, regardless of Party, on the basis of evidence of opposition to the EMU project supplied by election addresses. The list of recommendations would be published towards the end of the campaign. *The Times*' close interest in their views agitated many candidates who would otherwise have enjoyed a quiet election. For example, Peter Butler, Clarke's PPS, was disturbed by the refusal of *The Times* to endorse him, and rang the newspaper to complain vociferously. He saw his 14,176 lead vanish like snow in the early May sunshine, to be replaced by a Labour majority of 240.

Money also came to play a role in the coupon election. Paul Sykes, a Barnsley autodidact, had made a great fortune out of the Meadowhall development, the consumerist's paradise where the citizens of Sheffield could conclude, like the late Duchess of Windsor that if they were tired of shopping, they were going to the wrong shops. Sykes' favourite conversational topics were the Single Currency, the danger of 'on costs, lad' in the regulated European economy, and the delights of Yorkshire ('there's everything a young man could want here'). His obsessive enthusiasms extended to sitting at his dining-table with a Union Jack draped around his shoulders against the unlikely possibility that any of his guests might be unsure of the drift of his convictions. He now lived in a restored classical house near Ripon whose furnished interiors revealed startling profusion and variety. The effect was one of Mervyn Peake's Gormenghast crossed with a Yorkshire Palladio. It was an appropriate setting as Conservative politics lurched into a laboratory of the bizarre.

Sykes had started an Internet company but was still bored. Money meant that people were prepared to dance to his tunes. He had been a generous supporter of the Conservative 2000 Foundation and, in one of the less didactic moments of his London visits, I had explained the idea of a coupon election to him. We discussed the possibility of his contributing to the election expenses of candidates who opposed the Euro. In previous elections, he had donated money to the Conservatives in Yorkshire, but he was no longer prepared to give unconditional financial support to a Party whose official European thoughts were as a blank. He agonized for weeks over whether to proceed, and eventually decided to advance into new and dangerous territory. The publicity would be immense, but nothing with which his temperament could not cope.

Sykes was prepared to spend up to £750,000 sending cheques of £2000 or more – with his EMU string attached – to Conservative candidates in the 324 existing Conservative seats and to candidates in some selected marginals. His money became an important adjunct to the coupon election. It was a good bargain. Sykes's £750,000 rivalled Goldsmith's £20 million for publicity. I briefed the press about the campaign on confidential lobby terms, and helped Sykes to draft his literature. Only during the general election campaign did the full extent of my involvement become known. There was a great rush for the money, and I advised Sykes on the credibility of some of the Euro-welfare claimants. Candidates had been very explicit in their election literature. Many remembered the unhappy precedent of the Maastricht debate, when the Whips had used the argument that they had been returned to Westminster to support the Government and not to express their own point of view to force MPs through the division lobby. If they were re-elected, they now wished to be able to say that they had a direct mandate from the electorate to oppose a Single Currency and would therefore not succumb to any future bullying. The coupon election and Syksean gold were the most potent examples of how the Conservatives, deprived of leadership, had ceased to be a political party. 'Connection' of an eighteenth-century kind, using patronage and money, had re-emerged with Sykes as a plebeian Duke of Newcastle.

Confusion engulfed the final stages of the drama. In the best traditions of amateur dramatics, Tories never ceased to produce entertaining vignettes right up to the final curtain of their end-of-season show. In January Robin Hodgson, Chairman of the Executive Committee of the National Union, produced new proposals for conducting future leadership campaigns. Hodgson recommended that the Parliamentary Party should cease to have its exclusive say, and that 20 per cent of the votes should be allocated to the National Union as the representative of the voluntary wing of the Party. Sceptics and malcontents panicked. It was an astonishingly public preparation for the true battle that lay ahead. But the proposal could also strengthen John Major's position were he to stand for election after a general election defeat. Any incumbent leader would receive the automatic support of the National Union, whose role was less one of vigorous democratic representation than of oligarchic reinforcement of the *status quo ante*.

Cranborne's appointment as Chief of Staff for the period of the election confused most, including the office-holder. The relationship of his function to those of Mawhinney, Blackwell and Heseltine, who also had a presentational role as master of ceremonies, was opaque. Nobody quite knew what the scion of the House of Cecil was supposed to do. Confusion was worse confounded on February the 19th, when Malcolm Rifkind remarked that he was 'hostile' to a Single Currency, and the Chancellor commented mischievously that this was 'obviously a slip of the tongue under pressure from a very skilful interviewer'.

The cold, clear light of a disenchanted dawn in February arrived to place these paltry manoeuvrings in their true perspective. Early in the morning of Friday the 28th came the result of the by-election in comfortable, suburban Wirral South. Major had agonized for weeks over its timing. Now it was the worst of times. Any remaining resolve faltered as pink Tory cheeks turned pale. Labour won the seat on a 17.2 per cent swing, and replaced an 8168 Conservative majority with a Labour one of 7004. Repeated nationwide, the result would give the Labour party a majority of 296 seats. The Tories' night-sweats had started.

When, on the 17th of March, John Major called the general election for the 1st of May, it was with no sense of drama or élan. By now the Tory Party really could not bear very much more reality. It was the last practical date that Major could have chosen. He had long since said that he would leave Downing Street at a time of his own choosing, when people least expected him to, and in a way that would surprise everyone. That undertaking now seemed the last in a very long line of broken promises on whose shards he trod as he made his way to the front door of Number 10, there to intone his announcement. As the wife of one former Cabinet Minister said: 'He'll never do the decent thing, will he?'

EYELESS IN GAZA

17th of March to 19th of June 1997

O N THE FIRST of May 1997, a day of brilliant sunshine, the British people accomplished their determined electoral task. Afterwards, some Tories clung to the wreckage of their hopes and told themselves that this had been a verdict on the Major Government and that the electoral attachment to Conservative convictions remained as an inarticulate desire frozen in mid-expression. But this was a judgement on eighteen years of Tory rule. The British had long since decided to throw out Thatcher babies with Major bath water in a gratifyingly purgative spree. It had been no ordinary general election, and it seemed an appropriately irritating Tory act to subject the country to an unnecessarily lengthy six-week campaign when the issue had long since been resolved.

The Conservative Government fell because of its sins of omission and of commission, and it was held to account by an electorate whose desires recoiled from the devices of a degenerate Toryism. In prolonging the agony, the Government only succeeded in annoying an electorate that had ceased to equate economic well-being with voting Conservative. In the country, the Tory coalition had evaporated and individual MPs' constituents had revolted. In Parliament, John Major's quarrelsome charges had kept him *en poste* as the ostentatiously harassed nanny. In doing so, they exhausted themselves, each other and the country with their melancholy tintinnabulations.

It was not the law of a fated electoral pendulum that made the Government's fall inevitable. However long the eighteen years had become, time for an electoral change did not determine its disappearance from power. Governments fall because of what they do. Tory deeds led to Tory rejection. The scale of the defeat disposed of the last lazy and patronizing excuse. This was not an electorate saying that it was 'time for a change'. This was an electorate deciding that it was time for the imposition of a curse.

Tactical voting was the weapon the electorate used to ensure that the Tory defeat turned into a rout on the electoral killing field. The split Opposition that had ensured Conservative success in the past turned into an unforgiving pincer movement. Voters had learned the relevant lesson and applied it with a steely determination. Labour supporters voted Liberal Democrat where that was the best way of defenestrating the Conservative candidate. Liberal Democrats supported Labour where that was the best route to achieve the same, devoutly desired, consummation. The electorate's tactical voting ensured an implicit

Lib–Lab alliance, and this guaranteed the recession of the Tories from verdant suburbs and county towns. The deflation of the Liberal Democrat vote led to Labour victories in Hove and in Wimbledon, in Enfield Southgate and in Chatham and Aylesford, in Thanet South and in Norfolk North West. Similarly the Liberal Democrat victories in Lewes and in Twickenham, in Richmond Park and in Weston-super-Mare, in Winchester and in Torbay, were the result of a containment of Labour's electoral surge.

Labour's 271 seats in 1992 were transmuted into 418, and the Conservatives' 336 were reduced to 165. The Liberal Democrats more than doubled their seats from 20 to 46, their best result since 1929. Among Major's Cabinet colleagues, the heads of Ian Lang, William Waldegrave, Malcolm Rifkind, Tony Newton, Roger Freeman, Michael Forsyth and Michael Portillo rolled on to the funeral pyre. A third of all Government Ministers lost their seats. At 30.7 per cent, the Tories' share of the vote was their worst result since 1832; their vote fell from 14.1 million in 1992 to 9.6 million.

The national swing to Labour was 10.5 per cent, and its overall majority of 178 was boosted both by tactical voting and by the alchemy of Britain's first-past-the-post system. Labour's 43.2 per cent of the votes earned it 65.2 per cent of the seats. The Liberal Democrats' share of the vote declined from 17.8 per cent in 1992 to 16.8 per cent, while their increased representation only amounted to 7.2 per cent of all seats. The Tories had to chew the husks of the system they had always advocated, lived by and benefited from. Their 30.7 per cent of the overall vote gained them 25.7 of the seats in the House of Commons.

Only thirty of Sir James Goldsmith's 547 Referendum Party candidates saved their deposit. The party won 812,000 votes, 2.7 per cent of all the votes cast, an important achievement, on a day on which many people, mostly unhappy Tories, stayed at home. Only 71.5 per cent of the electorate voted in 1997, compared with 77.7 per cent in 1992. The Referendum Party's intervention was most striking in seats where the European Union's Common Fisheries Policy had hit hardest. In Falmouth and Camborne as well as in Harwich, the number of Referendum Party votes exceeded the Tories' margin of defeat. Most of the blood drawn by the Referendum Party was coloured blue. Disillusioned Conservatives formed the bulk of Goldsmith's adherents, and may have caused the loss of up to twenty seats. There is no doubt, for example, that Newton's defeat in Braintree and Freeman's in Kettering were the result of Referendum interventions. Other effects are more imponderable, since the Party drew on some non-Conservative support. It is even possible that the Conservatives retained some seats with very low majorities because the Referendum Party split the Opposition vote.

In 1997 the Conservative Party ceased to be the party of the Union. It lost all its Scottish and Welsh seats and withdrew to the south of England. Even here, there was naught for Tory comfort. Given the size of the Labour majority, it is not surprising that Labour took so many seats by low margins. In sixty-four Labour seats its majority was less than 10 per cent of the votes cast, and in sixty-one seats its majority was less than five thousand. But the Conservative hold on many seats was equally precarious. In sixty-five of their seats their majority was less than 10 per cent of the vote, and in fifty-nine seats their the majority over either Labour or the Liberal Democrats was less than five thousand.

In other words, it could have been even worse for the Tories. In the future the Lib–Lab pincer could tighten yet further. Labour's huge majority masked the fact that the 1st of May primarily represented a rejection of the Tories. At the next general election it would take only a very small additional swing to reduce the number of Tory seats still further. Labour's performance in the opinion polls continued to improve in the months after the election, showing that such a renewed catastrophe was a possibility. Indeed, of the forty-seven national polls conducted during the campaign, only three (those produced by ICM) forecast a lower swing than Labour eventually achieved. The other pollsters predicted swings of between 11 and 16.75 per cent.

So it was not the worst, but all too many Tories said that it was. Like the reprieved on death-row, the Tory elect congratulated themselves and each other on their survival, indulged in a spot of *Schadenfreude* as they discussed the fate of departed colleagues, and concluded that, to have survived such slaughter, they must have been protected by a particularly prevenient grace. Their own campaigns, they complimented themselves, were obviously partic-ularly formidable, and their personalities and records extraordinarily winning. This was as bad as it was going to get, and things, as the new Prime Minister might say, could only get better. These were foolish fragments to salvage from their ruin, and ones calculated to compound the chronic Conservative complacency.

In 1964 Harold Wilson's Labour Party won a similar percentage of the vote to Tony Blair's New Labour in 1997, and gained an overall majority of four. Within less than eighteen months, at the the 1966 general election, Wilson had increased his majority to ninety-six and Labour's share of the vote to 48.7 per cent. A further increase in the years ahead was now a possibility for the Blairite project. Wilson's majority in 1964 was small because Labour's vote was concentrated in its historic redoubts of Scotland and Wales, the North and the Midlands. Increasing the size of these majorities without making significant advances on the suburbs of the south, as happened in 1964, yielded no advantage in the number of seats. However, the 1966 election did bring just such an advance, by a Labour Party that presented itself as the spirit of modernity tamed for the suburbs.

Thirty-one years later, New Labour's New Model Army established its base camp on the same territory, and surveyed the terrain for further advances. It had learnt the lesson of the 1992 election. Its resolve to win marginal seats had been unwavering, and it was rewarded by huge percentage swings in such seats. The same exaggerated swings also turned previously safe Conservative seats into Labour marginals. This phenomenon was particularly noticeable in the London suburbs. For example, Harrow East recorded an 18.1 per cent swing from Conservative to Labour, while Harrow West inflicted one of 17.5 per cent. Hendon fell on a 16.2 per cent swing and Wimbledon on one of 17.9 per cent. Where once the Finchley Victor roamed, her successor (on new constituency boundaries) was felled on a 15.1 per cent swing, while in Upminster, on the fringes of Essex, Nicholas Bonsor, fruitiest of Tories, was struck down by a 15.4 per cent swing. At Mitcham and Morden, they decided that Dame Angela Rumbold should have more time for her early-morning swim, and ordained a 16 per cent swing. Beguiled by the electoral fruits and drowsy Necropolitan pleasures of Worthing West, Peter Bottomley, Virginia's husband, had abandoned Eltham after fourteen years. The scorned south London marginal rewarded Labour with a 13.6 per cent swing. Now, the new Conservative front line was defined by Dorset South, where the majority was 77, and by the 238, the 1,994 and the 1,035 skins of Tory teeth visible, respectively, at Lichfield, Eastbourne and Chipping Barnet.

Labour's was a bourgeois revolution. That morning, New Labour voters tripped down the drives of The Laurels, The Beeches and The Firs. Garden gates closed behind them in Cherry Grove, Laburnum Avenue and Maple Crescent. The anti-Tory coalition returned to watch the results of its handiwork on television sets snugly ensconced in Jacobethan houses with conservatories and mock-Tudor porches as well as in back-to-back terraces, in bungalows with sea views as well as in high-rise inner-city flats. Gallup's post-election survey showed that the 59 per cent of the professional and managerial classes who had voted Conservative in 1992 declined to 36 per cent in 1997 on a 22 per cent swing, while the Labour-voting proportion of the the same classes rose from 16 to 36 per cent. Among white-collar workers, the Conservative vote suffered a comparable collapse, from 50 to 31 per cent on a 19 per cent swing, while Labour's percentage rose from 27 to 46 per cent.

Tory Euro-sceptic and Tory Euro-philiac alike were at last allied – in common humiliation. Apart from the speculative and negative impact of the Referendum Party in a small number of seats, their views about 'Europe' made little difference to Tory candidates' ability to weather the common storm. In Rushcliffe, Kenneth Clarke's majority was reduced from 19,766 to 5055 on an 11.5 per cent swing; benign assurances that European evolution was coming Britain's way could not lift the curse of the national anti-Tory consensus. In Billericay, Teresa Gorman's 20,998 majority almost vanished as a 17.6 per cent swing cut it to 1356; rumours of Eurocrats under the bed could not provide her with a *cordon sanitaire*. In Old Bexley and Sidcup, the 1992 majority of 19,572 fell to 3569 as a swing of 14.1 per cent rocked Sir Edward Heath, the figure who was, for Euro-sceptics, the father of all their discontents. Defending a 9211 majority in Harrogate, on election night Norman Lamont confronted a Liberal Democrat victory by 6236 on a swing of 15.7 per cent; the threatening maw of a mighty European power cast no shadow in North Yorkshire.

Even if former Tory voters had their Euro-sceptic moments, none the less they decided to vote Labour. Many concluded that Europe could not be less safe in Labour's hands than it had been in the Tories'. What Conservatives presented as danger seemed a price worth paying. For example, a MORI poll found that 56 per cent of readers of the *Sun*, that virile and vigorously anti-European paper, voted Labour. Labour took no risks as it sedulously courted Euro-doubters, frequently wrapping its words and actions in the Union Jack and posing Peter Mandelson with a bulldog, although the creature looked less Churchillian than close cousin to a pampered pug.

The effect of newspapers' interventions on the European issue was to accentuate the cumulative collapse both of the Tories' self-respect and of the electorate's trust in their protestations. By the 18th of April *The Times* reported that no less than 247 Conservative candidates had accepted or applied for Sykes' money on the conditions he proposed. Newspapers' determination of electoral choices is necessarily imponderable, but 1997 showed how, when tested, newspapers influenced the behaviour of some candidates and could thereby be solvents in the more general dissolution of party. Their interventions and actions were not those of an external, mechanical force which could 'deliver' a victory for a cause – a foolish, manipulative myth beloved of some politicians. Rather was it the case that newspapers, if they wished to be successful and read, had to go with the democratic grain, read the signs of the times, and echo the profound currents, sometimes quiet, sometimes torrential, of Britain's public, and popular, mind.

Major eventually gained the endorsement of three daily newspapers. The *Daily Telegraph* returned to its ancestral allegiance with the formal acquiescence of a prodigal son, the *Daily Mail* offered its support through gritted teeth and continued to be critical during the election campaign, while the endorsement of the *Daily Express* was bestowed in so distant a manner that it could be mistaken for neutrality. The *Evening Standard*, much courted by the Labour Party, reflected the mood of its London readership and came out for Labour. The *Mail on Sunday*, which had played an important role in Redwood's campaign in 1995–96, made a contrite return to Major's orthodoxy in time for the 1st of May. There, within the fold, it also found the *Sunday Telegraph*, the *Sunday Times* and the *Express on Sunday*. The *News of the World* made a dash for freedom, jumped the walls of the Tory convent, and leapt into New Labour's waiting hands.

Major believed himself to be the Tories' last best hope, having persuaded himself that he had a unique hold on the British people. The Norman Wisdom of British politics was always falling down but, with a winning grin, he would pick himself up, dust himself down and start all over again – his lovable antics acclaimed by an indulgent populace. In his personal mythology, 1992 had been his victory. Until the election started to unravel before his eyes, he believed that 1997 would be his as well. There were many faces to be adopted in the process. Speaking to the Party's Central Council in Bath in March 1997, he said that he was very much 'in the tradition of one-nation conservatism', and wished, in a characteristically awkward phrase, 'to bring wealth and welfare hand in hand'. These traditions, it seemed, had always been his, or so he maintained to the *Sunday Times* on the 6th of April.

At a press conference on the 16th of April, he made one last excursion into the fantasy that negotiations on the Single Currency could still be pursued, allying the issue with his personal probity. 'Like me or loathe me,' he croaked with bogus authority, 'do not bind my hands when I am negotiating on behalf of the British nation.' Clasping his hands for the benefit of the cameras, he became an icon of Tory enfeeblement. The leader of the Conservative Party had committed himself to the view that the Single Currency was 'the most important issue that any Government has been asked to make for generations' – but had also refused to disclose his own view on that issue. Interviewed the following day, he stumbled and, without intending to, committed himself to allowing Conservative MPs a free vote if ever the issue of entry into EMU came before the House of Commons. On the 23rd of April he was due to intone in a speech at Aberdeen: 'Look in my eyes and know this. I will always deal fair and true by this great nation.' The sentence was never delivered – perhaps by that stage of the campaign there had been sufficient ocular imagery from the Conservatives.

Another image appeared on the 18th of April, when the Conservatives offered a cartoon of a puppet Tony Blair sitting on Chancellor Kohl's knee. Michael Heseltine later calculatedly revealed that the cartoon was based on a doodle of his own. The great European was also the grand opportunist.

When Europe was not an issue, sleaze was. Major was accused of proroguing Parliament early in order to prevent the imminent publication of the report by Sir Gordon Downey on the 'cash-for-questions' scandal of three years previously, when Graham Riddick and David Tredinnick were accused of being prepared to accept money in return for asking Parliamentary Questions. On the 25th of March, Tim Smith, the MP for Beaconsfield, was forced to stand down having admitted accepting £25,000 from the Egyptian grocer, Mohammed Al-Fayed. On the 26th, Beckenham's Member, Piers Merchant, embarked on a long and ultimately futile attempt to hang on to his seat. On that day, the *Sun* printed several photographs of Merchant enjoying the company of the 'pouting teenage temptress' of Fleet Street legend. Even in an area fabled for Tory innovation and 'market testing', it seemed that the Party was abandoning its capacity for originality. In attempting to deal with a Constituency Association whose suburban stalwarts decided to stand by their embarrassed standard-bearer, Central Office veered between bullying and incompetence.

Taxation and public expenditure, the Tories' standard artillery against Labour, barely featured in the campaign. Gordon Brown, the Shadow Chancellor, had announced that in its first two years a Labour Government would maintain the spending limits already set by the Tories. In shuffling off responsibility for setting future spending limits, the Opposition sought to evade responsibility for future spending decisions in Government. Yet tax receipts were bound to change with the progress of the economy, and the inflation rate would have a necessary impact on the amount of money the

Government had to spend on health, education and the social services. Brown's brag illustrated how modern politicians, rather than seeking too much power, evaded the responsibility that it brought. Yet the ploy worked. The Tory Government could not attack its own spending plans.

The Tories' big idea, the Basic Pension Plus, handed the Labour Party the political weapon of fear. Peter Lilley's plans, the densely argued, patiently researched product of finely tuned Whitehall minds, were a scandal to the voters and foolishness for the Tories. The scheme proposed the effective privatization of the state pension by the year 2040, and guaranteed a sum of money equal to the current pension. Yet it enabled Labour to claim that pensions were not safe with the Tories. After the mauling of his proposals, Lilley looked less like the second Beveridge of the welfare state than a revived Thomas Cromwell bent on its dissolution.

There were a few moments of Tory hope. Labour suddenly looked vulnerable on the 6th of April, when it had to change its mind on two issues, trades unions' rights to recognition and the privatization of air traffic control systems. On the first, Labour thought that it had gone too far in complying with the Social Chapter, while on the second it misapplied missionary zeal and sought to privatize the unprivatizable. But these were paltry matters compared with the reality of rebellious Ministers. Angela Browning, the MP for Tiverton since 1992, had risen to the post of Junior Minister at Agriculture, Fisheries and Food, where her authority as a former home economics teacher lent gravitas to her role. Astute Labour researchers now discovered that she had pledged herself to oppose the Single Currency in her election address. So too, it was reported on the 14th, had Angela Rumbold. John Horam, the MP for Orpington and Junior Minister at the Department of Public Service, was similarly unmasked the next day, while on the 16th came the revelation that James Paice, MP for Cambridgeshire South East and a Junior Education Minister, had deviated. Though not a Minister, Rumbold, as a Party Vice-Chairman who had spent the last five years encouraging Tory candidates, was considered a big enough cheese to count for the purpose of a destabilization exercise. Browning, Horam and Paice may not have realized the gravity of what they were doing, such was the common confusion about the appropriate wording.

April, cruelest of Tory months, limped to its close. The Tories' bright day was done and now they were for the dark. On the morning of the 2nd of May, John Major announced his decision to resign as leader of the Conservative Party. The decision deprived his Party of an ideological inquest. Having endured one six-week campaign, Tories now embarked on another, whose highly person-alized tone continued their trauma. In Opposition, they repeated the quarrelsome, vindictive and perfidious patterns of behaviour long since established in Government.

On the 30th of April, there were said to be twelve prospective candidates for the leadership. The events of the 1st of May disposed of Portillo, Lang,

Forsyth and Rifkind. Gillian Shephard's candidature had always been a vengeful ploy at Major's expense. Heseltine's angina attack on the 4th, followed by a swift statement issued by his wife, ended his leadership prospects – and with them a dream that had started in Oxford over forty years before. In its stead, another ambition bred in the shallows of the Oxford Union was about to be realized. The next six weeks brought none of the *Blitzkrieg* drama of June 1995, but grim, man-to-man combat in the Tory trenches.

John Redwood's campaign suffered from lack of suspense about his intentions. The May Day slaughter was also particularly bad news for him, as his supporters had been disproportionately concentrated in marginal seats. Indeed, his brand of popular capitalism grounded in the reality of Wokingham Man had been designed with such seats in mind. A few days before the 1st of May, Major was told of the inevitable loss of the Tories' most marginal seat, the Vale of Glamorgan, where the contumaciously Euro-sceptical Walter Sweeney luxuriated in a majority of nineteen. His leader happily anticipated Sweeney's demise. 'That'll be a Tory gain, then, won't it?' he said.

As he contemplated the ruins of so many careers on the 2nd of May, there were many other disadvantages about Redwood's position. Major's immediate resignation meant that he was no longer unique in enjoying freedom of political action. Had Major decided to stay indefinitely as Party leader, or had he even announced that he would quit in the autumn so as to ensure an orderly transition, Redwood would now, during the first weekend of May, be considering how to launch his leadership bid in circumstances that resembled his first coup. His Parliamentary colleagues had advised him against such an act, arguing that it would seem precipitate and 'divisive'. Far better, they counselled, to wait for another dagger-wielding contender to emerge in the Conservative Revenger's Tragedy. But Redwood was unpersuaded. The attraction of a second *Blitzkrieg*, he pointed out, would be that his former colleagues, and present leadership rivals, would almost certainly have been obliged to serve in a Major-led Shadow Cabinet. Refusal to do so would have been tantamount to a leadership declaration, and Redwood understood his colleagues well enough to know that none would risk resignation. In these circumstances he could have maintained his freedom of manoeuvre and exposed pusillanimity of others. But now Major's act had the effect of forcing all who would be contenders into the common light of day, and Redwood had to take his place among a gaggle of hopefuls, one among many in an egalitarian scramble for office.

There was yet another disadvantage. Were Major to resign, Redwood had hoped for an autumn campaign so as to benefit from a considered audit of how and why the Tories had decomposed. Surely, he mused, Tories would want something different, rather than a continuation of Majorism by other means? Hence his strategy of presenting himself as a 'clean pair of hands', as one without responsibility for the disaster. He would be the Hyperion to Major's satyr. The times were out of joint, and he really was the one born to put them right. To some, this seemed the claim of an upright man. Opponents thought it obtrusively virtuous, the hand-washing of a Pilate who had himself been part of the problem. The irony of Redwood's position was that every time he spoke he reminded too many MPs of John Major and his failures – so indissoluble was the connection between his visage and the wrecked fortunes of Majorism. The immediacy of the leadership campaign denied Redwood his alternative strategy, the opportunity to benefit from a more leisurely, and appropriately autumnal, inquest into the long-term causes of the Tory debacle. Others indicated to him the implausibility of a Party Conference held in such circumstances of debilitating uncertainty.

The emergence of William Hague as a serious candidate had been obvious to Redwood, and had much disturbed him, since the early spring. When he saw the newspaper photographs of his newly engaged successor with his former Assistant Private Secretary, he went very quiet, emerging from his reverie only to note the awkwardness of the pose as the Welsh Secretary draped his arm around his fiancée. Hague's dismantling of Redwoodian Wales had not disturbed him, since he had the ambitious politician's reluctance to revisit the recent past. He had previously enjoyed making fun of his successor. The future leader had found himself in an awkward position after an expenditure settlement had left the maw of Welsh local government with less money than it wanted. The insecure vice-regal presence refused to be interviewed, and the BBC threatened to approach his predecessor – well known both for his accessibility and for his strong views on local democracy. With huge enjoyment Redwood reported Hague's tremulous approach in the House of Commons 'looking like a very old baby', as he expressed the hope that Redwood would refuse to be interviewed. Redwood was reassuring; Wales was another country.

The more he reflected on the matter, the more clear he was that the trimming temperament shown by Hague in Wales disqualified him from leading the Conservative Party. For example, Hague had caved in to environmentalist pressure groups and agreed to issue a White Paper on the countryside in Wales, whereas Redwood had refused to match the English White Paper, seeing it only as an excuse for a further route march of the regulatory army over the countryside.

During the leadership campaign, Redwood calculated how much Government money the Welsh Development Agency (WDA) – the Mother of all Quangos – was receiving under Hague, and made sure the figures were widely circulated. The Agency, set up by Labour to oversee economic regeneration, had acquired surplus land and property. Redwood had forced it to realize its assets by selling them, and had then reduced its grant from central Government correspondingly. Under pressure from the quangocracy, Hague reversed this policy. Where Redwood had reduced central Government spending on the WDA from £69.5 to £25 million annually, Hague increased it again to £84.7 million.

In Redwood's view, all the candidates, himself included, had advantages and disadvantages, and he recognized the reality that the Parliamentary Party did not want any one of them. But Hague's case was one of unredeemable train-spotting vacuity overlaid by the gloss of management theory. This, after all, was the candidate who, as a very young man, had memorized the majorities enjoyed by the Conservative Party in its parliamentary seats. Redwood would subsequently remark, on hearing the result of the final ballot, 'They have actually chosen the worst of all the six candidates.' His view communicated itself effortlessly to his followers.

Redwood wished the Party to raise its sights. Castigating Anglican leaders at the turn of the previous year, he had observed that 'there is a crisis of leadership in many British institutions, a sense of national failure and decline that needs reversing.' He wanted a Conservative Party that would be a movement of national renewal after six and a half years of debilitating Majorism. The more he brooded on the matter, the more obvious it was that the soulless careerism Hague offered lay at the heart of the Tory disease. Redwood's followers therefore briefed vigorously in order to establish the continuity between Major and Hague. Hague was, variously 'John Major with A levels', 'John Major with a degree', or even 'John Major with a PPE degree'. Some went further with foolish consequences, as we shall see.

There was also an undeniably personal and cunning dimension to the endless relaying of stories about how Hague, sitting on his nurse-fiancée's knee, had learnt the words of the Welsh National Anthem. Hague knew that Redwood's publicly glacial insensitivity had landed him with a propaganda coup. Apparently new Celtic convictions had led the incoming Secretary of State for Wales to stay overnight, and spend weekends of arch rusticity, in carefully chosen 'bed-and-breakfast' establishments. 'Yes,' said Redwood, in defensive response to wry reportage. 'It's a very good job for a bachelor.'

Redwood was self-critical enough to know that he needed presentational reform and renewal. As his campaign developed, many a 'communicator' went, bright-eyed, into his study to counsel on the mastery of image, tone and posture. The dapper and diminutive Sir Gordon Reece had attempted the de-suburbanization of Thatcher in the 1970s. His highly polished shoes tripped eagerly up the staircase to Redwood's office and descended much more slowly. The actress Angharad Rees offered beguiling advice on speechifying and the expression of emotion through the light and shade of the spoken word. No victor's palms would adorn her golden tresses at her re-emergence. George Ward, the hero of the Grunwick Company's battles against the trades union 'closed shop' in the 1970s, offered the services of his friend Brian Walden. Didactic seed proceeded to fall very slowly on stony ground. Harvey Thomas had choreographed many a triumph of the Tory will at Party Conferences in the 1980s. He arrived with remorselessly cheerful Christian convictions and memories of Mother (Lady Thatcher) largely intact. Perhaps it was the memory of listening to Mother that distracted Redwood as his three-hour session got into its stride. But the futility of all such attempts at self-improvement soon became obvious – Redwood's 'image' would have to remain his reality.

Michael Howard's candidature was as unsurprising as Redwood's. Ensconcing his campaign headquarters in Jonathan Aitken's house in Lord North Street, he surrounded himself with a phalanx of former Ministers, chief among them David Davis and Francis Maude, united by the principle of office-seeking. There, they issued inflated projections of Howard's share of the vote, hoping to create a bandwagon effect. Hague and Howard offered amusement in the opening stages of the campaign with a pact sealed with late-night champagne on Monday the 5th of May, Howard's last day in the Home Secretary's official house in South Eaton Place, Belgravia, and disentangled at dawn on the 6th. Uncertain of his intentions, Hague had agreed to support Howard's leadership campaign on the understanding that he would be Party Chairman. Counselled by Alan Duncan, his pugnacious and *arriviste* ADC, and by an innate sense of self-worth, he withdrew, leaving behind him a furious Howard. It was a gift to Redwood's followers who, from a very high moral ground, sneered at the shotgun marriage of convenience, the fudging of the calculation and the lack of a sense of purpose. 'In all of this', said one, 'who was the bride and who was the groom?' 'Don't be vague – vote for Hague – I think,' jeered another wag.

On the morning of Saturday the 3rd of May, Peter Lilley was due to be interviewed on a radio programme with Stephen Dorrell and John Redwood. His withdrawal was taken as a sure sign that he was preparing to announce his candidature. Lilley's tactic was to present himself as the candidate of the thoughtful, respectable, right – as one who could unite the Party in a low, modulated key. It was a decision that exasperated Redwood, who proceeded to remind Margaret Thatcher of how Lilley had abandoned her in her hour of trial in November 1990. But Lilley's resentment at Redwood's bravura had curdled within the quiet man's breast over the previous two years. Now he would stoop among the Tory remains in order to conquer.

Dorrell wished to be the chameleon of the contest, and gained instead the equivocator's crown. His positioning showed how the normal rules of intelligent political subtlety could no longer be applied in the Conservative Party, so entrenched had the varying Euro-convictions become. In normal times much would have been attractive about the alliance of one-nation Toryism with Euro-scepticism. Dorrell's development was calculated accordingly. Having distanced himself in stages over the previous two years from his Euro-phile past, he prepared the ground with thoughtful, if grim-visaged, warnings of the relentless tide of global capitalism battering against the fragile walls of European protectionism. But a thoroughly ideologized Party could not handle the attempted marriage between two entrenched positions. Candidates had to be locked in boxes. Suspicious sceptics rejected Dorrell's advances, while Euro-philes thought that he had cut his extended lines of communication with his former hinterland. Later in the contest, the forty-four-year-old Dorrell attempted self-presentation as the voice of youth and also as the representative of rounded family values compared with the one-dimensional bachelor Hague. Inanity undid him.

This left the former Chancellor, who began his campaign with characteristic insouciance as he drove his own removal van back to Nottinghamshire. Kenneth Clarke's conviction that he should be leader of the Conservative Party only grew upon him in the course of the campaign. His wife, always an important ingredient in guaranteeing Clarkean resolution, was initially cool. Who, after all, would wish to lead such an unprepossessing collection of impotents as the years of Opposition stretched ahead? Besides, could Clarke escape the label of 'Maastricht man' as effectively as Rab Butler and Alec Douglas-Home had escaped the consequences of being men of Munich? One route presented itself in the fact that the Tories had not benefited from the Euro-sceptic noises they had offered at the election. Clearly, Tories could not live by Euro-scepticism alone. Perhaps they would have to look further afield.

Clarke's core support was among the Euro-philiacs, but he also had a wider constituency among warm-hearted Tory males. There was much sentiment in favour of self-proclaimed beasts of political jungles who, shod in Hush Puppies, refused to wear their intellects on their sleeves. Of all six candidates, Clarke bore the closest resemblance to a human being, and benefited from that throughout the campaign. None the less, his campaign never truly recovered from the chaos that enveloped its early stages. For example, Michael Ancram, the Member for Devizes who had been a senior and influential Northern Ireland Minister, was eager to declare for Clarke, had his calls ignored, and eventually veered towards Hague. Always generous towards the former Chancellor, commentators decided that the chaos was the sign of a great soul.

The atmosphere throughout the six-week campaign was foetid and enclosed. The defeated Party had withdrawn in upon itself, less to examine its beliefs and purpose than to engage in acrimony and rancour amid the ruins. The contest was also marked by reluctance to debate publicly. Peter Stothard, the editor of *The Times*, offered to organize a debate between all candidates in Church House. Clarke and Redwood were eager, but the other candidates raised temporizing objections. All the hopefuls appeared in turn before the Positive European Group of MPs on the 3rd of June, one week before the first ballot, and before the second ballot the three remaining candidates, Clarke, Hague and Redwood, appeared again separately for a question-and-answer session to which the whole Parliamentary Party was invited. Once more, Hague had baulked at a debate, and agreed to the revised format at the last moment. Earlier, a rare public event was organized in his Leicestershire constituency by Andrew Robathan, who invited the six contenders to appear for questioning. Three accepted and in a subsequent ballot Redwood won narrowly with forty-eight votes over Dorrell's forty-six, while Lilley trailed badly with ten.

Suspicion of the Tory world marked Redwood's campaign. His team even required a signed receipt from Archie Hamilton, the new Chairman of the 1922 Executive, to acknowledge that he had received Redwood's nomination papers for the first ballot. Like Clarke's, Redwood's campaign started awkwardly. The press was indulgent towards the 'right-wing' Redwood declaring his candidacy at the unhappily named Goring Hotel. More substantial difficulties emerged than the unappeased shade of the late Reichsmarschall. It had long been assumed that Iain Duncan Smith would be Redwood's campaign-manager, and indeed Duncan Smith had accepted the invitation at a meeting on Wednesday May the 7th. The problem was that Duncan Smith was also considering standing, after being approached by ultra-sceptics who had tired of Redwood. For the moment, he said, he would not declare his support – on which Redwood could none the less rely. He needed to consult his Association. It was a temporizing excuse that each candidate came to encounter with irritating frequency as they courted the bashful Parliamentarians. The fact that for ten days Redwood's own campaign-manager did not declare for him was an undoubted embarrassment.

Even after his declaration, Duncan Smith proved a difficult corporal, insisting on amending Redwood's written statements in a way that the candidate's mercurial spirit found lumbering, conceited and mentally third-rate. Soon Redwood came to regret having offered him the Party Chairmanship. Yet, as he observed, baffled, Duncan Smith was highly regarded among his colleagues. It all showed how shop-soiled House of Commons commodities had become. It soon became obvious that Duncan Smith's chairmanship of Redwood's campaign, competent enough once he had embarked upon it, was also a vehicle for his own ambitions.

The most effective and unswerving members of Redwood's campaign were John Wilkinson and Julian Brazier, from the 1995 campaign, together with David Wilshire, the keenly Methodistical Member for Spelthorne, and Marion Roe, the luxuriantly bouffant-haired MP for Broxbourne. Others soon joined them. Having discovered Euro-scepticism in the previous few weeks and having enjoyed the publicity, Angela Browning acquired a starring role as the Redwoodswoman whose placid figure would accompany the lean future leader as he strode towards his destiny. As Chairman of the Tories' backbench Northern Ireland Committee, and guarded by the Special Branch, Andrew Hunter's girth lent itself easily to canvassing sessions among the more stolid. Among the newly elected Tory MPs, Howard Flight was eager for a Redwood *rapprochement* with Howard. The Dives-like banker worked for Redwood, but detached himself from other members of the group, whom he may have regarded as beneath the salt. Oliver Letwin, who giggled more than most MPs, was a Redwood protégé from the 1980s Policy Unit. He had personal attachment to account for his endorsement, but may well have recognized very early on how far the odds were stacked against any success. His semi-detachment disappointed Redwood. Julian Lewis had a lethal gift for controversy, pedantry and the spread of disinformation, acquired in his days as tormentor of the Campaign for Nuclear Disarmament. Although a shared Welsh-Jewish tenacity united him with Michael Howard, Lewis was now convinced by Redwood's 'courage, clarity and consistency', in the words of the initial campaign slogan, subsequently abandoned. Lawrence Robertson had made the long journey from textiles in Bolton to a Conservative seat in Tewkesbury but, his Westminster novitiate barely begun, was not yet ready to canvass an Alan Clark or an Archie Hamilton. Over this disparate group presided Iain Duncan Smith in a manner reminiscent of Julian, Enid Blyton's self-righteous late adolescent in *The Five Find Outers*.

Lilley's campaign acquired early momentum, although it was hijacked by Jeffrey Archer, who subsequently used it for his own self-advertisement. Archer's habitually generous interpretation of the *actualité* emerged with his description of the fifty-three-year-old Lilley as 'a very nice young man'. Among 'right-wingers' who longed for respectability and found Redwood's ardour terrifying were more significant figures who lent Lilley support. David Willetts, Bernard Jenkin and John Whittingdale were natural 'Lilliputians', as Redwood termed them, as was Gillian Shephard, who became Lilley's running-mate. Within a few days of his declaration, Lilley's aide, Peter Barnes, rang me to say that, on the figures available to them, Redwood's campaign would not get off the ground – Redwood should therefore withdraw in Lilley's favour. Time would test and untangle these hopes.

Lilley also provided a natural sanctuary for those whose true prince was over the water. Portillo's men could not countenance Redwood and in their bitterness turned to Lilley as the next best candidate. For example, David Hart now emerged as a shadowy figure in Lilley's counsels. Eric Forth was much attached both to the decorative plumage contained in his wardrobe and to Michael Portillo. Bromley and Chislehurst's be-ringed and Glaswegian Member now found himself running Lilley's campaign. A native asperity belied his gaudy appearance but also limited his effectiveness as a parliamentary emollient on his candidate's behalf.

All the aspirants made similar noises about the need to learn from mistakes made. They preached humility, and counselled the ordering of sackcloth by the yard and ashes by the ton. In Lilley's words, humility entailed the recognition that 'it was the Conservative Party which lost the election, not the Labour Party which won it.' This seemed a droll redefinition, both of the virtue of humility and of a majority of 178. Unity was the Holy Grail they all sought, and they would provide it through 'firm but sympathetic' leadership. Having waded through the preliminary banalities, the candidates set to work to demonstrate that in Opposition the Tory show would continue to provide the delights of discord displayed in Government. It would be the last time that Tories could guarantee newspaper headlines. Few realized that the game was changing. Governments can command publicity; Oppositions have to work for it.

Hague's campaign was the work of overtly calculating political professionals. They were a class attracted to Hague because, in the words of Archie Norman, the icy grocer recently elected MP for Tunbridge Wells, he offered, 'a management approach to recreating a great campaigning organization'. Redwood might offer, rather bleakly, 'to rekindle a sense of fun', but Hague's stage-set, constructed overnight for his first press conference, offered tasteful purples to symbolize new light falling on the Tory blue of old. These imperial colours were also those used by Blair in the last stages of his campaign, and the emphasis on modernization of Party structures, on methods, techniques and slogans, was similarly evocative.

In the worlds of Redwood and Clarke, in their different ways, these techniques seemed no more than the echoing brass and tinkling cymbals of a Mandelsonian hollowness. Both offered answers to the question of what the Conservative Party was for. Redwood's message was increasingly that, if there was a fudge on Europe to discover, Major, of all people, had been ideally placed to discover it. But none was available, even if some pretended it could be packaged in purple. The leadership contest had to be used to decide the Party's European issue. One side had to be declared the winner in the civil war. Clarke opposed this formulation. In a new concession he offered the Parliamentary Party a free vote on major European issues. But, he argued, it no longer mattered what the Tories thought about Europe because the decisions were out of their hands. The big domestic and economic concerns would define their message. Given a lead, the Party would unite, but it would not unite of its own accord. Both Redwood and Clarke had learned the lessons of the Major years – but the central message of the one contradicted that of the other.

The launch of Michael Howard's campaign was a distinguished affair of sober mahogany in the background and ambitious suits in the foreground. His supporters spread the calumny among more credulous sceptics such as Richard Body that Redwood opposed measures to repatriate powers from European institutions. It was a feat of disinformation worthy of one who, writing as a young man in the Bow Group's *Crossbow* magazine in 1971, admired President Richard Nixon's 'skill' and 'the adroit way he deals with law and order'.

However, Howard was running into difficulties. Andrew Alexander was an influential financial commentator and warm Redwood admirer who had tried to encourage him into more effusive self-expression in order to improve his electability. In an article in the *Daily Mail* on the 9th of May, he revived the issue of Charles Wardle and the Al-Fayed brothers. He described how Wardle, the MP for Bexhill and Battle, had left his post as a Home Office Minister in 1994 after refusing Howard's request to reconsider and reverse his decision to accept the official Home Office recommendation that Ali Al-Fayed, the brother of Mohammed, be denied British citizenship. Having been transferred to the Department of Trade and Industry, Wardle found himself in the very Department that had refused to publish an official report on the Al-Fayeds' takeover of Harrods. Now it was rumoured that Wardle wished to raise the issue of the handling of the DTI report in an adjournment debate in the House of Commons.

Ann Widdecombe had reservations on another issue. The Member for Maidstone and former Prisons Minister was convinced that Howard's sacking in 1995 of Derek Lewis, the head of the Prison Service, had defied natural justice. By the 12th of May newspapers were full of conversations attributed to her, in which she had said that there was 'something of the night' about Howard who, under pressure, would 'do things that are not always sustainable'. Lewis himself had written that as a politician Howard was 'preoccupied with tactics to the exclusion of strategy'. At times Howard appeared 'to be cutting his suit to fit the cloth just a little too finely [and was] flawed by his political ambitions worn on his sleeve'. Wardle did not name Howard in his adjournment debate, although Widdecombe made a memorable statement to the House of Commons. Howard defended himself with his usual flair. His campaign team included Tim Collins, Major's spin paramedic of 1995. Soon press reports appeared claiming that Lewis had wooed a susceptible Widdecombe with flowers and chocolates. 'He flattered her vanity,' said a Howard supporter to the *Daily Mail* on the 13th of May. 'He sent her flowers and took her to dinner. I don't think she was used to that.' Some admired Howard's resolution in adversity, but these claims, and the methods used to counter them, destroyed his campaign.

Clarke's public popularity, and both Howard's and Redwood's public unpopularity, were incontestable throughout the campaign. Within the Party around the country, Hague's neutral tones about the need for better management were making converts. Redwoodsmen might jeer at the whoring after false, alien and Mandelsonian gods, but this was a Party that Major had taught to blame Conservative Members of Parliament for all their ills. Hague was the beneficiary of that Majorite self-exculpation. Moreover, he had now attracted the support of Tristan Garel-Jones, whose political charms had not been withered by retirement from the House of Commons. Some Redwoodsmen saw this as confirmation of their thesis that Hague was a cloned version of Major. Others mischievously recalled how Garel-Jones had appeared to support Hurd in 1990 while acting as a spy for Major. Surely, they mused, his true allegiance lay with Clarke, the candidate on whose behalf he now worked as a fifth columnist within the Hague camp. This was an excess of sophistication. Garel-Jones had simply spotted a winner in Majorite terms, and Clarke's team was not deft enough for such tactics.

By the middle of May Dorrell's campaign was badly undermined, and in a meeting with Clarke he proposed an implausible joint ticket with himself as leader. Not surprisingly, Clarke rejected the suggestion, and when Dorrell eventually sued for peace he was not offered a specific role in Clarke's putative Shadow team. Rebuffed, Dorrell returned to the fray. 'Friends of Dorrell', a very select company for the purposes of this exercise, then started to brief that Hague was 'not as well rounded an individual' as the happily married Cromwellian enthusiast. This was a lowering moment. By the end of the month, Dorrell was not only offering outright opposition to EMU but also threatening to withdraw the Party Whip from rebels who might support Britain's participation. By the beginning of June he had withdrawn from the contest.

Hague's difficulties were in finding an European sticking-plaster that would do something other than advertise the seepage from the Conservative wound. In so doing it was clear that he exposed almost as many raw nerve-endings in the Conservative Party as John Redwood. Simon Heffer summed up an emerging view on the 13th of May, writing in the *Daily Mail* that, like Major, Hague was a vacuous figure who had made no enemies as he ascended in a Tory Party that he saw as 'a vehicle for his own schoolboy ambition'. It was the same vacuity to which Redwood objected when he said, after talking to Hague following the second ballot, 'I've had more interesting conversations with a bathroom sponge.' Others detected a coldness in the mirthless laugh of one who, as a student politician, had secretly taped the dinner-table conversation of a Conservative Association executive member suspected of disloyalty. Many concluded that Hague offered Blairesque opportunism without any of the Prime Minister's natural charm.

In the same article, Heffer prophetically praised Clarke's 'massive political ability'. If the choice had to be made 'between a man who believes in something and a man who believes in nothing', the Euro-sceptics should opt for Clarke on grounds of character. The notion of an alliance between Redwood and Clarke was the subject of discussion as early as the middle of May, but Redwood reacted with horror to the idea of Clarke leading his Party, and Heffer was not allowed to take the issue further in his presence. If the project had been aired, so also had been the hostility to it. Many thought that Redwood was being sophistical when, at his first press conference, he had said that Clarke and he agreed 'about many aspects of a Single Currency' simply because both thought, rather self-evidently, that entry at the wrong time and on the wrong terms would, on the whole, be a bad idea.

As the campaign developed, Hague's organizational mantras were designed to deflect attention from the European wound. They were also an exercise in collective unreality. Four and a half million voters had not stopped voting Conservative because they thought that Constituency Associations were badly run. They stayed away because of what the Government had done to them and their families. However, Hague's status as the establishment candidate was enhanced by the emergence of the plans proposed by the Executive Committee of the National Union to consult the membership during the leadership contest. Paradoxically, the need to reform Party structures became the cause of the Party establishment, and Hague's early advocacy of that cause as the central plank of his manifesto only enhanced his stature as its candidate. The paradox was more apparent than real. McKinsey-ite jargon and talk of 'consultation' obscured the extent to which a Hagueite party would be centralized in administration rather than unified in doctrine. Eventually power would flow away from the Parliamentary Party to a Conservative membership that would have a closer relationship with the leader. It was an attempt to achieve the Thatcher end by McKinsey management means. The attitude towards the Party was reminiscent of Bismarck's towards democracy – 'a system of government in which you allow the nursery to rule, but, then, children will let you do anything if you play with them'. All the candidates had to move on to this ground, and, since it had already been defined as Hague's territory, it marked his ascendancy.

Dismayed scrutiny of Tory structures did, indeed, reveal a landscape which was obscure when not simply dreary. Nobody now knew how many members the Conservative Party had left, and estimates varied between 150,000 and a very optimistic 250,000. Even if the latter figure were correct, it still represented a reduction of two thirds since 1992, and informal estimates suggested that only a quarter of these were active members. The collapse under Major had been precipitous, but it followed a slow decline from the two million membership of the Macmillan years in the late 1950s. As well as a shrinking membership and a brain drain of intellectual energy, the Party now also had to face the expensive consequences of collective fantasies. The Party's 1992 overdraft of £19 million had been cleared, but once the balance had moved back into black Central Office began to shop until it dropped with the Saatchis. Of total Conservative expenditure of £28 million in the period ending on the 1st of May, M & C Saatchi claimed the lion's share with a bill of £13 million. By the summer the Party was again a pauper. It had a £3.5 million overdraft, and its bankers, the Royal Bank of Scotland, asked for the facility to be reduced to £2 million. Annual running costs for Central Office and its staff and for the regional offices were £7 million. In the spring of 1997, Lord Harris of Peckham, the Party Treasurer, had let it be known that he intended to leave a £5 million surplus after the general election to be used in the increasingly unlikely event of a second election in the autumn. By June, however, the cupboard looked bare and Central Office finances looked as precarious as those of a British nationalized industry of the 1970s.

On the 20th of May Hague, hurt by Redwood's snipings, departed from the consultant's script and delivered a speech attacking the 'constantly shifting fudge of the past few years'. His words were seen as an attack on Major, his erstwhile patron. Hague had discovered a conviction when it cost him least to declare it and earned Heffer's jibe that he was a 'cynical little careerist'. It was the act of one who enjoyed the support of Lord Harris of Peckham, and of Lord Feldman, former chairman of the National Union, and who, having been given a fair wind by Robin Hodgson, the National Union's current chairman, was visibly the candidate of the Old Ascendancy in new apparel. The speech made its mark. When Redwood said on the 23rd that Party loyalties had been stretched to breaking-point, he was seen to echo Hague's attack. But Hague's cynical careerism was insultingly transparent to many.

Hague's courtship of sceptic voters went even further. Following his speech, 'friends of Hague' started to rumour that he would not give Clarke a job in his Shadow Cabinet. This prophecy was perhaps the necessary prelude to Hague's pilgrimage to Thatcher on the 2nd of June. After the meeting, Hague's aides told the press that her benediction was now upon him. Thatcher's own aides were more guarded, and said that she was content with any 'of the four candidates of the centre-right'. Redwood's reaction was one of fury. He phoned Thatcher immediately and asked why she had agreed to see Hague: 'Oh, but they're all coming to see me,' she said plaintively. 'Do you want to come?' Taking the view that he had been a courtier long enough, Redwood rebuffed her, explaining that he had campaigning duties with sitting members of the House of Commons. An admiring circle cheered him as he stood addressing the receiver. Icy premonitions now formed in my gut. 'Now, William Hague,' she said brightly, 'is he right-wing?' Obviously the previous day's interview had left no very profound impression. In some detail, Redwood went through Hague's record of appeasing quangos in Wales and displacement of his own regimen of thorough administration. In terms reminiscent of the younger Thatcher in full, premeditated, flow, he went on to expatiate on Lilley's transgressions, Howard's evasiveness and his own claim to be her only-begotten political heir. He was always braver at the end of a telephone line. It was the last time they spoke to each other during the campaign, and in giving full rein to his long-contained resentment he had set in motion a series of events whose consequences would be profound both for himself and for his Party.

Redwood's manufacture of Euro-frenzy was a relentless feature of the campaign. John Major had raised the cry 'Who goes to Amsterdam?' at the end of his general election campaign. The electorate's answer was that Labour would go, and negotiate on Britain's behalf at the Inter-Governmental Conference. Conventional minds in the Foreign Office had sought to dismiss 'Amsterdam' as a mere five-thousand-mile service for the common European vehicle. John Redwood took a more rigorous view of the extensions of Community competence in foreign policy areas. Indeed he rousingly declared that 'if we sign the present draft of the Amsterdam Treaty we will abolish our country.' Indeed, Britain could lose her veto if she were found to be in breach of the European Convention of Human Rights. It was difficult to conceive of Britain contravening the admirable and unobjectionable generalities enshrined in the Convention, such as 'liberty, democracy, respect for human rights and fundamental freedoms, and the rule of law'. But Redwood argued that, as in the past, the interpretative powers of the European Court could be used to extend its powers and harm Britain's interests in particular cases. The Treaty might even be deployed to wield the Court's jurisdiction over Britain's remaining dependent territories. This spurt of late-imperial *Angst* showed the extent to which sceptics now regarded 'Europe' as a foreign power armed with hostile intent.

At the same time Howard was waxing furious on the Tories' need to adopt 'one British nation' politics. 'We cannot take our national inheritance for granted,' he urged, 'neither our prosperity, nor our civil peace, nor our laws, nor our Parliament, nor our monarchy, neither our tolerance of dissent, nor our indignation at injustice.' It was a finely phrased, mid-twentieth-century view of Britain as an island bastion against European totalitarianism. In the Britain of 1997 the words sounded archaic and hysterical.

At the beginning of June some Tories seized on European political developments as a resolution of their dilemmas. Chancellor Kohl was trying to revalue Germany's gold reserves as a way of enabling Germany to meet the Maastricht convergence criteria on debt. The requirements that countries entering the Single Currency should not borrow more than 3 per cent of their national income in any given year, and that the total stock of debt should not exceed 60 per cent of gross national product, were proving tough hurdles for many European Governments. In France the election of a Socialist Government raised the hope of economic relief in the teeth of those Maastricht-inspired measures that had re-created inter-war levels of unemployment. Major and Clarke both stated that these two events meant that only a fudged currency would be available in 1999, and that delay was therefore inevitable. Closer inspection showed that their statements were less an abandonment of the faded charms of 'wait and see' than an extension of 'negotiating and deciding'. Clarke was merely stating the obvious when he said, 'If EMU heads off in a direction dictated by socialists count me out.'

On the eve of poll, Lilley's position faltered. When he appeared before the 92 Group on the evening of Thursday the 5th of June, he would not answer when asked whether he would resign from a Cabinet that scrapped the pound. Howard and Redwood said they would. On the Sunday morning, interviewed by David Frost, Lilley said that he could not rule out a Single Currency completely because 'we can't bind future Parliaments.' He was doing a Dorrell, though in a different Euro-direction, but towards the same destination of nullity. The same morning Redwood said of the European issue, 'I intend to carry on because I think the Party has to make a decision.' Anyone who served in a Shadow Cabinet led by him would have to accept that the Tories would never take Britain into a Single Currency – a condition rejected by Clarke. Clarke went further and refused to commit himself to a referendum on the Currency if he became Prime Minister. That undertaking, he said, applied only to the current Parliament. Indeed, in his negotiations with Major a few months previously, Clarke had fought hard over that very proviso. At the time he had gloried in private that so few had noticed his successful stipulation restricting the referendum offer, a condition he had demanded in order to avert his resignation. 'Look,' he said happily in the spirit of one who had got away with it, 'everyone thinks it means a referendum at any time, but they're wrong.'

Talk of a deal between Howard, Lilley and Redwood was now widespread and misleading. Lilley told Frost: 'Whoever comes fourth or fifth is going to find it very difficult to imagine that they could go on to win. I would expect they would stand down and I would appeal to a very large number of their supporters to come over to me.' Howard was adamant that there were no foreseeable circumstances in which he would withdraw. His circle claimed that he was the only one of the three who could beat Clarke. Even if Lilley did marginally better, they claimed, the solution would be the Shadow Chancellorship for Lilley, who would otherwise crumble under a Clarkean onslaught. But both Lilley and Howard had forgotten Redwood. Both expected him to come bottom of the poll and neither approached him in order to arrive at an understanding. Indeed, they would have been contemptuously rebuffed had they done so, given their assumptions about his likely performance. He had, he said, no cause for withdrawal because 'I am not on the same platform as the other candidates.' Others fudged; he guarded the currency's Thermopylean Pass. *Sun* readers, Redwood reminded the Parliamentary Party, 'back me by a mile'. Fifty-two per cent of them, interestingly almost the same proportion that had voted Labour five weeks before, supported him in a telephone poll, compared with 16 per cent who wanted none of the five candidates; 14 per cent opted for Hague, 10 per cent for Clarke, 4 per cent for Lilley and 4 per cent for Howard. But this contest would not be determined in the pages of the *Sun*, which now supported the Labour Government.

Howard's backers knew that they were in a very tight corner but continued to predict inflated levels of support until the very end, so that the *Daily Telegraph* credulously reported a sudden surge of support for Howard during the final weekend. Duncan Smith joined the game with a statement that Redwood had seventeen publicly declared votes, with another thirty MPs privately poised to take the plunge. The *Guardian*'s ICM poll, published on the 10th of June, the day of the first ballot, showed 31 per cent support for Clarke among the public, with Hague and Redwood level-pegging at 9 per cent, followed by Howard on 7 per cent and Lilley at 6 per cent.

Clarke topped the poll, but did badly. As a candidate without any rivals in his natural constituency, he needed more than the forty-nine votes he obtained. Hague's forty-one votes were the triumph of opportunism over experience and a sure sign of things to come. The drama came with the announcement that Redwood had polled twenty-seven votes, beating both Lilley, on twenty-four, and Howard, with twenty-three. The margin was small but, in a minuscule constituency, the consequences were profound. Most observers had predicted that Clarke would come first, but with a larger margin over Hague, who had been equally widely expected to come a good second. Expectation was confounded at the bottom of the scale. Redwood heard the result in his new room in the House of Commons, an eyrie up to which Parliamentarians had to puff their way. Angela Browning crushed me in her bosom, safely encased in a lilac jacket, while Duncan Smith whooped unconvincingly. Redwood phoned Lilley and Howard to discover their intentions; they replied noncommittally, and he left for the television studios.

Meanwhile, Lilley's men met. Some thought he should continue because they did not wish to be coerced into Redwood's camp and Hague held no attractions for them. By 5.30 p.m., however, Lilley had already phoned Hague to arrange a meeting, and by 6.45 p.m. the former Secretary of State for Social Security was in the office of his former Minister of State discussing the terms of his withdrawal and endorsement. Howard took longer, considered backing

Lilley until Lilley announced his *démarche*, and then arrived in Hague's office by 7.00 p.m. with his endorsement. Neither considered backing Redwood. Having returned to his office, Redwood now waited on their decision. He had said on air that 'both Michael and Peter or their camps indicated that they thought the fourth- or fifth-placed candidates should drop out and support the third-placed candidate. I am appealing to both Michael and Peter to do just that.' The wording was judicious, because there had been no agreement.

The Redwoodsmen's accusations of treachery and double-dealing filled the evening air as moral simplicities collided with the reality of political complexity. Redwood had never said, nor had he anticipated, that he would withdraw if he came fourth or fifth. Neither did he have an understanding with Lilley or Howard that they would support him if, as had now happened, he beat both. Redwood had refused to parley, and so he had no agreement either with Lilley or with Howard that could now be enforced or broken. When they expected to beat him, the defeated duo had indeed presumed upon Redwood's support in the second ballot. Either would have lamented bitterly a Redwood decision to continue in those circumstances, but they could not have complained of a breach of any undertaking. Now, in these new circumstances, Redwood could lament falsified expectations, but hardly complain of broken undertakings. If Lilley's and Howard's expectations of his behaviour had been one-sided, so were his of theirs.

In this, the hour of his victory, Redwood saw the victor's garland wither in the hands that held the telephone as Lilley and Howard contacted him in quick succession to inform him of their decision. 'Why are you doing this?' Michael Portillo had said to him on the morning of Monday the 26th of June 1995. It was now the question that Redwood asked of Peter Lilley. 'I have always thought of you as an honourable man,' he said. The moral reproach was painful, but Lilley maintained that Redwood could not possibly unite the Conservative Party. For Lilley, as for others, Redwood had become the most potent symbol of the Party's trauma. He had infused moral passion into the Tory corpse, but lacked the healing arts that might resurrect that body. His clarity over the past two years had excited powerful antipathies, so exclusive and excluded had been the self-righteousness of his ardour. His conversation with Michael Howard was briefer. 'I am not surprised by Howard,' he said, 'but I did expect better of Peter Lilley.'

All his literal-mindedness, that terrifying abhorrence of the lie in all its gradations that had led his civil servants to dig deeper and deeper holes of evasion in order to escape its scrutiny, was now directed against the other two 'candidates of the right'. In the depth of his self-absorbed disappointment, their actions seemed to represent the last dying embers of Major's Government, the collection of 'chums' who had stuck together through thick and thin, reinforced each others' mediocrity and absurd self-esteem as the shadows gathered, and excluded him. Now, in what he had decided should have been the hour of his victory, they still cleaved to each other like the members of a down-at-heel club and blackballed him. A telephone call to

Julian Seymour, Margaret Thatcher's man of affairs at the Thatcher
Foundation, confirmed his now raging suspicions about her. She had no views
to express about the decision taken by Lilley and Howard. No *deus ex
machina* would intervene on his behalf from that direction. Indeed Robin
Harris, her literary amanuensis alienated from Redwood after the 1995
leadership election, had been working for Michael Howard. The depth of the
resentment added a bitter dimension to the campaign as hatred and disgrace
etched themselves on the Tory face.

Hague was clearly the candidate to beat, and Redwood would have to
demonstrate that he could command the broader level of support at the second
ballot that Lilley and Howard had hoped to attract. The unlikelihood of his
doing so was a common assumption. His unexpected success in the first ballot
had only made Hague's victory the more probable. Writing in the *Daily Mail*
the day after the first ballot, Paul Johnson raised an intriguing possibility that
was fast gaining credence among Redwood's colleagues: 'The coming
together of the Clarke and Redwood forces would seem logical. Stranger
things have happened in politics.'

As Redwood and his followers prepared for the second ballot, there was a
grim and reckless mood in the air. He felt that everything that could be thrown
at him by way of trickery, commentary and denigration had been. 'They can't
do any more to me,' he said. He had travelled alone so far and confounded
expectations. The same solitary journey would lead to further revolutions of
expectations. He would be proven wrong in all these assumptions.

This was a contest to be decided by some fifty representative members of the
Parliamentary Party who, in their wavering affections, desperate calculations
and collective insecurity, could not be assigned consistently at either the first
or the second ballot to any particular candidate's tribe. Every vote that
Redwood had gained in the first ballot had been like drawing teeth. For
example, Sir Richard Body had told him on the 8th of May that he would vote
for him. On the 23rd, Body was rumoured to be backing Howard and then
Lilley. On the 1st of June, he confirmed to Redwood that he would vote for
him. On the 5th, he declared for Howard and, on the 9th, told Redwood again
that he would vote in his favour. On the 7th of May Bill Cash was worried
about a Redwood compromise on the Single Currency, but was also contemplating standing himself. Four weeks later, on the 5th of June, he was
rumoured to be considering standing in the second round. Only on the 7th did
he finally declare for Redwood, having gained an assurance that in a Redwood
Shadow administration he would be the Minister for Europe.

On the 7th of May Christopher Gill was not the eager Redwood supporter
he had once been. His Constituency Association in Ludlow was supporting
Clarke and, while he would vote for Redwood, he would not declare that
support. Edward Leigh's association in Gainsborough had given him a
difficult time after the last contest when he had supported Redwood so
prominently and so ably. On the 9th of June he told Redwood's supporters that

he knew that 'Redwood is the right man.' For Leigh, Lilley's campaign had been marred by his association with the libertarians David Hart and Eric Forth. Richard Shepherd also remained constant in his Redwood affiliations, though also undeclared. Owen Patterson, a Shropshire tanner who was the newly elected member for the north of his county, was 'given a strong going-over' by Duncan Smith on the 2nd of June – which may not have helped matters. His concern was that the Shropshire North Association, like that of neighbouring Ludlow, was overwhelmingly Clarkean. By the 7th he thought that he would vote for Redwood but not declare his leanings. The next day Redwood thought that Patterson could vote either for Howard or for himself.

Andrew Robathan followed his Association's ballot in backing Redwood, and was said to think that Howard 'could not possibly lead the Conservative party'. John Townend would not declare before the first ballot because he was contesting the Chairmanship of the 1922 Executive, although he had decided to vote for Redwood as early as May the 7th. The temperamentally uncertain Teddy Taylor, unique among sceptics in his personal fondness for Major, only decided late on, and told Redwood on the 5th of June that he would declare for him the following day. Ann Winterton, Congleton's crusader for family values, made the same choice, but she too shared the tendency of a Nicodemus, to hide from the light, and would not declare.

Very few of the electorate were poised between Redwood and Hague. On the 6th of May Sir Peter Tapsell left Redwood with the impression on the telephone that he would vote for one of the two. The next day another telephone conversation, with Marion Roe, showed that he was undecided. By the 3rd of June Redwood was reporting that Tapsell should not be pushed, and eventually he nominated Hague. Michael Trend was thought to have voted for Redwood in 1995, but, still in Central Office as a Deputy Chairman of the Party, would not declare. His retention of that office after the 19th of June showed his true caste of mind as a crypto-Hagueite throughout the contest.

On the 1st of June Charles Wardle, the hero of opponents of Michael Howard's crepuscular forces, told Redwood that he would not declare; when Redwood spoke to him again on the 4th his view was that only Redwood or Clarke could lead the Party and that he could not back Clarke because of his European views. Many voiced the belief that that Clarke and Redwood shared attributes, if not views. For Quentin Davies, for example, Redwood was second choice only to Clarke, and he would vote for Redwood if Clarke dropped out. Similarly Sir Peter Lloyd, the MP for Fareham and a close friend of Clarke, wanted 'someone strong-minded and with principle'. That meant, he said in the tea room on the 13th of May, that he would vote for Clarke in the first round and for Redwood in the second.

Anthony Steen was a left-wing Euro-sceptic whose constituency chairman was keen on Clarke. That meant, John Wilkinson reported on the 15th of May, that he too would vote for Clarke in the first round and Redwood in the second. Steen was also thought to have the glint of a knight's spurs in his eyes. Peter Temple-Morris, with his eclectic foreign-policy interests, supported

Clarke both because he shared his views and because the Party, as he said on the 2nd of June, 'needs leadership'. He was passionately opposed to Hague's candidature. During their canvassing conversations, many of Clarke's and Redwood's teams discovered unexpected gratifications, shared temperaments and shared dislikes among their colleagues – chief among the latter was the personality of Hague and his followers, who were viewed as insubstantial, opportunistic and spivish. Sir Peter Emery, who had represented his Devon seat for thirty years, told Andrew Hunter on the 21st of May that he wanted a strong Opposition leader with pugilistic ability. That meant that he could support neither Lilley nor Hague, whom he regarded as 'a little prep-school boy'. Even Shaun Woodward's eye for the future was averted from Hague as Witney's new MP journeyed from Dorrell's cul-de-sac to Clarke's broad and sunlit pastures of apparent opportunity. His true candidate was a prince over the water, the Governor of Hong Kong, for whom he had worked as Director of Communications when Chris Patten was Party Chairman.

Nigel Waterson, Eastbourne's representative, voiced a common opinion when he remarked to David Wilshire on the 20th of May that Hague was 'more Major than Major'. Among Clarke's supporters, the cartoon Tory figure of Nicholas Soames might express the view that Redwood was 'a dreadful shit', but more general expression of that belief was kept at bay while Hague's threat loomed ever larger.

On the 7th of May David Heathcoat-Amory wanted to think. By the 12th he was veering towards Howard, although Redwood thought he was friendly when he spoke to him eight days later. On the 22nd, Julian Brazier reported that, although Heathcoat-Amory admired Redwood's character, he 'needs a job offer'. By the 4th of June the former Paymaster-General had declared his support for Hague and signed his nomination papers. In a very awkward forty-five-minute conversation, Redwood asked the offended and indignant sceptic what Hague had offered him. By the 7th it was reported that Heathcoat Amory was already unhappy with his choice, and by the autumn he wished that he had voted for Redwood.

Michael Ancram's awkward pilgrimage to Hague has already been observed. Another MP travelled to the Hague destination by a more indirect route. Julie Kirkbride had gained the Conservative nomination at Bromsgrove by calculatedly courting a group of Redwood supporters in the Association. The misguided Midlanders had believed her professions of admiration for Redwood, and proceeded to organize themselves on her behalf. On the morning of the 2nd of May Councillor Nikki Page, a vampish Redwood admirer and close friend of Kirkbride, claimed that Kirkbride was ready to declare for Redwood. Kirkbride's subsequent silence baffled Redwood's men until they discovered that she was a Hague supporter on the basis of a shared Yorkshire childhood and a lisping pledge that she would help him one day to become leader of the Conservative Party. Andrew MacKay, her lover and subsequently her husband following his divorce, was Deputy Chief Whip and kept his counsel in public, although he had been to see Redwood several months previously in pursuit of his ambition to be Chief Whip. The fleshly MacKay was close to Eric Forth, which led some to conclude that he would vote for Lilley, but Redwood reported on the 9th of June that MacKay had 'rubbished Lilley at length' in conversation with him. He would vote for Hague throughout and be rewarded accordingly with the poisoned chalice of Ulster in the Shadow Cabinet.

On the 12th of May Archie Norman remained uncommitted – and would have been even more of a Redwood-sceptic had he known of the Wokingham One's resolve to keep the ASDA chief on the backbenches for a very long time. Redwoodian jokes that 'Archie Norman' had replaced 'Gordon Bennett' to express bewilderment at conduct of baffling peculiarity may not have helped matters. But Norman's belief that 'the party needs exciting leadership' and that that leadership had to be defined by the modern management mind led him ineluctably to Hague. David Tredinnick's great concern was to rehabilitate himself after his involvement in the cash for questions scandal three years previously. By the 9th of June he had declared for Hague and decided that a vote for one who looked like the eventual winner might ease his return to respectability. Tim Yeo, the scandal-plagued Member for Suffolk South, was thought to have similar ambitions. On the 6th of May Redwood reported after a telephone conversation that Yeo had 'an open mind', and thought he was angling for a job. But both these conditions created a fertile seed-bed for Hague's nurture and by the 12th Yeo was an avowed supporter of the Yorkshireman.

Lilley's support showed him to be an extension of Hague by other means, his salon containing dispossessed admirers of Portillo and those on the 'respectable right' who feared Redwood. However, scepticism about Lilley's prospects was widespread among his supporters. Robert Syms, who had replaced John Ward, Major's PPS, in Poole, formerly supported Portillo, but had regretfully decided by the beginning of June that he would have to vote for Lilley at the first ballot, and then for Redwood if Lilley was defeated. On the 8th of June David Willetts remained with Lilley, but was very uncertain about his candidate's prospects. Nick Gibb, a balding accountant newly elected for Bognor, was an impassioned Portillo partisan. He did not believe that Lilley could win and was ready to transfer to Hague after the first ballot. Christopher Chope, whose ministerial career had been cut short when he lost his Southampton, Itchen seat in 1992, had regained Christchurch from the Liberal Democrats; in the intervening years, he had protected the first youthful blush of his Thatcherite convictions from the encroaches of a sceptical intelligence. Chope's journey started with Howard and went on to Lilley. By the eve of poll, he was said to be 'very unhappy' because of Lilley's poor performance at the hustings organized by the 92 Group.

On the 22nd of May Julian Lewis thought John Bercow, who had replaced George Walden, the *déraciné* intellectual and dissident, in Buckingham, to be first and foremost ambitious and in need of flattery. When informed that in a second ballot Lilley might benefit from some of Kenneth Clarke's current votes, Bercow's fastidious purism recoiled at the prospect of such uncongenial company. His support for Lilley wavered. Michael Colvin, the smooth and senior Parliamentarian, was thought by all to be a 'flexible' supporter of Peter Lilley's. He was a provisional supporter for the first ballot while waiting on events and listening, much like Steen, for the clink of a knight's spurs.

Philip Hammond was bursting with convictions and professed 'complete agreement with Redwood on policy', but his Runnymede constituency's disapproval of his intellectual soul-mate decided his vote for Lilley. Gerald Howarth had been wavering in Lilley's direction since early on; after Julian Critchley's retirement, Aldershot's Conservatives had decided that they wished to be represented by a different kind of Conservative, and the obvious certainties of Margaret Thatcher's former PPS had replaced the intelligently detached irony of his predecessor. On the 22nd of May John Wilkinson reported that an offer of a Shadow defence post might make a difference to Howarth, and Brazier's reminder on the 2nd of June of Lilley's abandonment of Thatcher shook the insecure roots of his Lilley convictions.

Having voted for Redwood in 1995, Michael Lord was said on the 14th of May to be 'uncommitted and flapping'. Seven days later, the Member for Suffolk Central had declared publicly for Lilley, but in conversation on the 8th of June Redwood found him to be 'very friendly indeed' and thought himself 'in with a chance'. Piers Merchant, with hormonal teenage Furies waiting in the wings, praised Redwood effusively in the last few days before the first ballot. He would not change his public support for Lilley, but Redwood thought him 'wobbly'.

Michael Howard's support during the campaign preceding the first ballot showed similar ambiguities and uncertainties. Archie Hamilton was unusual in being a consistent Howard supporter beyond the inner circle of dogged campaigners for the former hammer of the judiciary. On the 5th of June, Alan Clark was reported to be deeply opposed to Hague. On no account, he told Redwood, should he withdraw at any stage in the contest. The historian of the Barbarossa campaign and of the siege of Stalingrad wished Redwood to continue in the heat of the battle. On the 7th, Redwood reported that Clark was urging him to continue even if Lilley and Howard withdrew and Clarke combined with Hague. On election day, Clark was thought to have voted for Howard, and in the second round he supported Redwood.

James Cran's Beverley constituency supported Hague. He disliked this fact, but he had also lost faith in Michael Howard, his original candidate, long before the first ballot. Michael Fallon, whose Odyssean search for a seat had ended in Sevenoaks, offered support for Howard that was secretive, arch, lukewarm and tinged with intellectual scepticism about all human endeavour. Publicly, and in retrospect, he was happy to be considered a Lilliputian. Before the first ballot, Andrew Lansley, the new MP for Cambridge South and a former Private Secretary in the Civil Service to Norman Tebbit, was expected to be able to deliver the bulk of Howard's vote to Redwood on the second ballot. This was a sanguine expectation. The most important feature of

Lansley's position on the 4th of June was thought to be his deep unhappiness at Lilley's maladroit pensions announcement shortly before the general election was called. According to Julian Lewis, Desmond Swayne, a novice but already white-haired Member with the permanently eager manner of a junior public schoolmaster employed because of a talent for games, had told his constituency chairman in New Forest West that he would vote for Redwood. He was then rumoured to be about to decide for Lilley. By the 3rd of June he had pledged his electoral troth to Howard.

Beyond this assembly of the semi-detached was to be found, reclining on the furthest banks of the political quicksands, a group whose intentions were shrouded in a cloud of unknowing generated partly by indifference, for they liked no candidate, and partly by opportunism, for they would always wish to be the 'leader's friend'. Bowen Wells had led the life of a happily blameless backbencher advancing the interests of Hertford and Stortford until, at the age of fifty-nine in 1994, destiny struck and he was appointed an Assistant Whip. Clearly he had acquired a taste for control, since Redwood reported on the 7th of June that Wells had only one desire, to be the Party's Deputy Chairman in charge of candidates so that he could prevent the eruption of another Julian Lewis. Theresa May offered strong, if less precise, convictions about her own advancement but a thin gruel in other areas of belief. During the general election, the Maidenhead Constituency Association had forced its new Member to express stronger hostility to a Single Currency than the evasiveness she had originally intended. As MP for neighbouring Wokingham, Redwood had played his part in this enforced conversion, and May had decided that Westminster was worth a sceptic mass. In recent months she had earned a reputation as the *reductio ad absurdam* of the sound-bitten politician, a series of press releases culminating in the Tory Toytown splendour of 'Theresa meets Norwegian Vigneron in Littlewick Green'.

Sir John Stanley, whom Andrew Hunter reported on the 8th of May as 'being very grand and aloof', afforded further obscurities. On the 15th Hunter revised his view, judging Stanley to be 'completely out of it'. These judgements may have been a reflection of the impression Hunter had made on Stanley. As Chairman of the Parliamentary Nepal Group, during May Stanley was chiefly concerned with the pension rights of the Gurkhas, and he was all too happy to concern himself with these intricacies as wider currents swirled around him.

Other MPs might be less Olympian than Stanley, but were equally elusive. On the 9th of June, Dominic Grieve, the beneficiary of Tim Smith's ejection from Beaconsfield, was said by David Wilshire to be 'terrified of people discovering his choice'. Nick St Aubyn was in favour both of shooting and of Christianity, but a failure of intelligence meant that Redwoodsmen thought that Guildford's new Member shared their vigorous opposition to the Single Currency. He had, he explained, to answer to a Belgian Chairman of his Association. Redwood, unimpressed by the spectre of terrifying Belgians, proceeded to have a very unhappy meeting with the enigmatic St Aubyn.

Nicholas Hawkins was 'temperamentally inclined to agree with everyone', Redwood concluded after his meeting on the 8th of May. The Conservative Association in Blackpool South might have contested this judgement – before the election Hawkins abandoned his highly marginal seat there in order to graze on the luxuriant Tory pastures of Surrey Heath. Peter Viggers was a firmly uncommitted defence expert with a naval yard in his Gosport constituency and a fondness for travel worthy of a Miss World contestant. How these preoccupations might affect his choice in the ballot remained a mystery. Geoffrey Johnson Smith would support whoever would cheer the happily unlined survivor of 1950s broadcasting as he campaigned for the Vice Chairmanship of the 1922 Executive. Lilley's followers thought correctly that Dr Brian Mawhinney would vote for him. The Party Chairman had been genuinely undecided, but his loathing for Angela Browning and Julian Lewis meant that he could not vote for Redwood, although Redwood's own conversations with him had been preternaturally amiable.

In the last week of the first-ballot contest, Redwood directed his fire against Hague. In personal letters to colleagues and public declarations he criticized statements about the Single Currency that were either ambiguous or dishonest as Hague sought to broaden his appeal. Excerpts from Hague's BBC interview on the 1st of June, widely regarded as a *locus classicus* of the Hague genre, were widely distributed. At one moment Hague offered 'principled objections' to EMU, but he also reminded his listeners that politicians 'never use the word "never"'. Hague's current objections were to a project advanced by a Europe that, as 'a political unit', was not 'subject to democratic control'. 'If in some future decade that is no longer the case, or if there is quite a different plan for a single currency . . . we would have to look at it anew.' At best this seemed a long-term version of the 'wait and see' policy whose obsequies many thought had already been observed. Again, Redwood reminded his colleagues, Hague had proposed at various times that the Party leader be chosen by MPs, that constituency chairmen be given 15 per cent of the votes, and that a balloted special conference of Conservative supporters should take the decision.

Hague, Redwood maintained enthusiastically in the *Sunday Telegraph* on the 15th of June as the second ballot loomed, 'has adopted all sorts of positions on a Single Currency. He has changed his view on at least two occasions on how the leader should be elected – and he seems to have changed his mind on whether he wants to debate or answer questions during this campaign.' 'Ken', Redwood contrasted, 'does not change his mind as much', and was commended for having 'moved much closer to my position'.

On a personal level, Redwood had to control his Parliamentary followers, some of whom were making foolish and cruel insinuations about the 'bachelor' nature of Hague's circle. Brazier's conduct was impeccable throughout but Duncan Smith was particularly crass in talking to journalists about the 'bachelor boys' who ran Hague's campaign, and the *Independent* gave especial prominence to this anachronistic recklessness. I told Redwood that his followers' zeal was overwhelming their judgement and that he should bring his heterosexual curs to heel. After all, he had a reputation for decency to maintain, whatever his private views. He agreed to rebuke Duncan Smith, who then delivered a homily to a partly baffled group of Redwood campaigners and urged unnamed offenders to desist from their slander. Redwood had acted, although only on my prompting and through a flawed intermediary. A climate of sneer and innuendo had developed, and been tolerated, in his presence, for he had an antediluvian horror and fear of forces that went against the grain of familial securities. He fell prey to dark and ridiculous musings as he brooded on men who shared flats and houses, as Hague had once done. 'I could never do a thing like that,' he said, as if recoiling from a particularly primitive and grotesque tribal activity.

His sensitivities flared again when the Conservative Christian Fellowship published an interview conducted with him on the 22nd of May. The Fellowship's scribes had spoken to all the leadership candidates to elicit their views on moral issues. In each case the final question was whether they supported the retention of the ill-considered, and now infamous, Clause 28, which banned the 'promotion' of homosexuality in schools. Hurrying to get away, Redwood said evasively that he was 'undecided'. A subsequent letter to the *Daily Telegraph* from the questionnaire's organizers noted in passing his ambiguity, summarized the answers given by all the aspirant leaders, and concluded that Redwood's views were closest to the Fellowship's convictions.

Distress beyond measure marked Redwood's response at what he took to be his enforced emergence in the pink corner. He blamed himself for his opacity of language and his own staff for not showing him the transcript of his remarks. 'You know how strongly I feel about that kind of thing,' he moaned miserably. 'Now it's splashed all over the *Daily Telegraph*.' This seemed a wide interpretation of a glancing reference on the letters' page. A light heart might have been the best response, but the leader-in-waiting appeared ready to rend his garments as he paced the room, a red-blooded beast at bay envisaging the shocked responses on the hearths of Middle England to the emergence of Redwood the social liberal. With a politician's capacity for revisionist editing, he maintained that his true position was that he wanted a strengthening of the disputed clause by more effective forms of legislation. That was why he had been 'undecided' – but he had also seen a difficult question looming, wished to start the next meeting, ducked, and stumbled.

In preparing for the second ballot, held on the 17th of June, Redwood wished to present a forbidding combination of austere moralism with angular Euro-scepticism. In a letter drafted but not sent, he told his colleagues that: 'Conservatives are seen as dishonest and unelectable. Each of us is now in a marginal seat. Before we have a chance of rebuilding our majorities we need to get back our reputation for keeping our word.' Many had pledged their opposition to the Single Currency. 'I am the only candidate that will help you keep your word.' Hague had 'made clear that he might abolish the pound at some later date'. 'Kenneth Clarke fought in Cabinet to keep open the option of joining.'

The rules of the leadership contest did not prevent any first-ballot candidates continuing in the second round. The only stipulation was that to win the first ballot outright a candidate had to have both an absolute majority and a majority of at least 15 per cent of those entitled to vote. However, in the second ballot a candidate with an overall majority among eligible voters would win; if there were no such victor, only the top two candidates could proceed to the third round. This made Clarke's position difficult. Enough former supporters of Howard and Lilley would vote for him in the second ballot to ensure that he received more than the fifty-five votes necessary to enter the third ballot. But victory in that ballot required a vote of eighty-three, and to achieve this a very large number of former supporters of either Hague or Redwood would have to switch to him. These supporters, wrote Redwood to his colleagues, did not exist – 'so Ken cannot win.'

Redwood was fighting against the widespread and disenchanted argument that, in order to stop Clarke, it was necessary to vote unenthusiastically for Hague. Redwood argued that there was no danger of Clarke slipping through the middle, but that there was every likelihood of Hague doing so. 'In the second round', he wrote, 'you should vote for the man and policies you want.' 'In the third round you can vote to stop the candidate you do not want.' In other words, it was inevitable that Clarke would be one of the top two candidates in round two. But Clarke could always be stopped at the third hurdle if all anti-Clarke forces united behind Redwood at that stage. In the second ballot, a tactical vote cast against Clarke and for Hague solely on the basis that Hague was the only candidate to beat Clarke was therefore a wasted vote.

Redwood's stridency on the Single Currency between ballots one and two thus suited both his convictions and his strategy. It seemed the best way to expose Hague and those more general equivocations that paralysed a disturbingly protean political philosophy. As he said on the 11th of June, 'William isn't quite sure whether he wants more European government or less European government. He would like the European question to rest there, unanswered.' His boast was that his campaign had 'honesty, integrity and decency'. How, he was asked at his press conference on the same day, did that separate him from his opponents? 'I have', he replied adroitly and with the subtle divisiveness and dismissiveness that had become his hallmark, 'never said they lack decency... .' Redwood's rhetoric of Englishry had its absurdist moments as well as its divisive displays. When he boasted at an eve-of-poll tea party in the House of Commons that his was the only party to offer 'English strawberries, English tea and English sandwiches', some in his audience must have wondered from which densely foliaged Berkshire tea plantation the leaves had been gathered and which doe-eyed Home County Tory maidens had lovingly prepared them.

In a letter on June the 12th Redwood told his colleagues that the Tory civil war had to stop and that the only way to stop a war was to declare that one side was the winner. The Party, he proposed, should oppose the Treaty of Amsterdam in its entirety, proceed to renegotiate Britain's relationship with the European Community (as he insisted on calling it) in order to repatriate powers, and also offer a referendum on Britain's position in 'Europe'. Shifting sands had undermined the Conservative house. 'We must now decide where we stand.' However, it seemed less like a Restoration Settlement than a programme of continuous revolution, a Tory Maoism, that he proposed to impose on his 163 colleagues, most of whom had chiaroscuro convictions and did not wish to be justified either by European faith or by its sceptic alternative.

Meanwhile, the Conservatives' wider problem of what they would do in Opposition was being ignored. Those who maintained that 1997 was like 1975 missed the point. It was not the time for the five-year plan or the great leap forward. Twenty-two years previously there had been a world elsewhere of Tory beliefs ignored by Edward Heath. That was why Margaret Thatcher's campaign for the leadership, so unlike Redwood's, had established her as the favourite to win at an early stage in the contest. Now Blair had occupied the dilapidated Tory villa and the beliefs had not so much been mislaid as successfully purloined. Could Tories do anything other than wait for shifting foundations to appear in the house across the road? It seemed something less than a full-time job.

Questions about Hague and his qualities continued to appear, and he quivered under the scalpel of definition. Would he renegotiate the Treaties of Rome, Maastricht and Amsterdam? Did he remain as opposed as he had been to hereditary peers? Why had he changed his mind on euthanasia and why did he now oppose it? On the 13th June, however, the scalpel struck the bone. Hague would oppose EMU at the next general election, but 'I don't know in thirty or forty years' time.' Redwood was pushing Hague towards stronger and more exposed positions. Given the coalition that he was trying to build, Hague's statement that only those who shared his opposition to the Single Currency could serve in his Shadow Cabinet was a blunder. Clarkeans thought that they could benefit from these developments, and started to claim that Hague was just a bald Redwood – a claim which, puffed the distressed Haguettes, amounted to a smear.

Clarke went for the Olympian touch as battle raged between ultras and tepids on the sceptic plains. His Shadow Cabinet, he said, could vote any way they wanted on the Single Currency. A Hague leadership, he told MPs, would exclude those lacking in sceptic ardour, while Redwood was utterly wrong: 'We unite the Party if we select a leader who will begin the process on an inclusive basis. We divide the Party if we regard the leadership election as deciding key issues before the process has even started.' For Clarke, much more than Europe seemed open for debate. As he prepared for the second ballot, he revisited the constitutional issue and refused 'to say dogmatically that devolution will automatically lead to the break up of the Union or

anything like it'. No future Tory government would abolish a Scottish
Parliament, he was reported as saying in the Scotsman on the 13th of June,
and so led the Tories' withdrawal from the blank hostility of their general
election position.

The spirit of Low's 1940 cartoon, in which an embattled Britain said to
herself, 'Very well. Alone.', hovered above Redwood's head. But Redwood
was mistaken in thinking himself impervious to character attacks and that his
moral indefeasibility, tested in the crucible of the first ballot, made the press
irrelevant to his campaign. Undoubtedly he enjoyed the sensation of having
confounded expectation so far, and wished to wield the power of his suddenly
increased prominence. Unwisely, he chose to do battle with the *Sunday
Telegraph*, and rejected the paper's request for a special interview. Why
should he accept, he said to Dominic Lawson, its editor, when he had so often
tried to get stories and articles in the paper and been ignored? He had always
intended to accept the request, but wished for a suitably humble and atoning
petition. As he warmed to his theme at the end of a telephone line, he lost his
grasp of the reality of the situation, ceased to listen, and as he was speaking
found that the editor had replaced the receiver. It was a nice illustration of
where power lay in the relationship between political class and media class.
Redwood tried to travel to his Canossa. A hastily arranged interview designed
to appease was brusquely edited and obscured by the editorial conclusion the
following Sunday that Redwood 'through the effortless transmission of his
own inimitable personality became generally hated in Wales', whereas Hague
'was widely admired'.

When he addressed the Parliamentary Party at a specially convened
meeting on the evening of Monday the 16th of June, the day before the second
ballot, Hague gave a poor, prompt-carded performance. His reluctance to
appear was justified, as was Clarke's and Redwood's enthusiasm. The anticipation of a jejune Stalinism in running his Shadow Cabinet offended Euro-
phile Clarkeans as well as many neutrals, who then rushed to Clarke as the
best way to stop Hague. 'He seemed to suggest', said Ian Taylor, a disdainful
Clarke protagonist, 'some form of contract should be signed before taking up
a role in the Shadow Cabinet.' Redwood's command performance at the same
meeting impressed many Clarke supporters such as Taylor, while Duncan
Smith led the briefing that, if it came to a choice between the two, he, together
with many other Redwood supporters, would transfer to Clarke in a
judgement based on the primacy of personality over policy. Soon Taylor was
overheard to say that only Clarke and Redwood could lead the Party. Both
camps told the press that Hague had 'bombed', but Hague's crash was to
Redwood's disadvantage. The tactics Redwood had previously outlined, the
propaganda he had issued, had been directed towards the uncommitted who
wished to stop Clarke. Now a new wave of the uncommitted rushed towards
Clarke because Hague had to be stopped. In doing so they trampled on
Redwood and deflated his vote.

However, Redwood's vote undoubtedly benefited from the impression of

Hague's sails being filled by the noxious winds of Howard's and Lilley's collaboration. On the evening of the 10th, the day of the first ballot, Redwood thought that David Amess had promised him his vote because he 'hated the treachery'. By the evening of the 16th, Amess had become very dizzy about his intentions, but would eventually stick with his promise. Having eventually voted for Redwood, Patterson now made his support more public. Redwood's men also thought that Michael Lord would continue to return to his Redwood form of two years previously. Bowen Wells remained sympathetic as he embraced his avowed intent of an anti-Lewis purge, and the reins of power as Deputy Chairman in charge of candidates appeared tantalisingly close.

'Christ, John, I have been bloody stupid,' said Alan Clark to John Wilkinson on Wednesday the 11th of June. Having voted for Howard, he now wrote to Redwood offering his support. Michael Fallon was thought to be ready to make the same transfer, as was Michael Spicer, albeit very reluctantly. Among former Lilliputians, John Whittingdale decided to support Redwood in a spirit of some pessimism, while Bercow did so with a bouncing ideological intensity. Gary Streeter, the Whip with a Christian conscience, offered a spectacle more characteristic of Lilley's recent faction as he cantered down the primrose path to dally with Hague. Andrew Tyrie, the intellectually sophisticated new Member for Chichester, veered in the same direction. Whittingdale attended Redwood's campaign meeting on the morning of the 11th to share intelligence. In the miasma of Redwoodian suspicions, the fear he left in his wake was that he might be a Hague fifth columnist who would use the information gained to Redwood's disadvantage. Piers Merchant would vote for Redwood partly in order to stop Clarke and partly out of increasing admiration for Redwood. Duncan Smith's 'tough love' was shepherding the indecisive Bernard Jenkin into the Redwood pen after his first-ballot vote for Lilley, and Christopher Chope's support was increasingly probable. Nigel Waterson hovered between Redwood and Hague, although Redwood thought that the burly solicitor's 'body language was good' when he saw him on the 16th. However, Ann Widdecombe, another former Lilliputian, found that Redwood stuck in her gullet. She took a dim view of his two-year adventure as an extensive and expensive trip in 'disloyalty'. On the 11th Redwood thought he had 'cleared up' the issue in conversation with her but, in a judgement of character, she declared for Clarke. Sir Patrick Cormack, South Staffordshire's fogeyish and ecclesiastically-minded praetor, followed her down that path.

Elsewhere, uncertainties remained. Wardle was affable to Redwood when he saw him on the 12th, thought he had been impressive on the hustings on the 16th, but would still not declare. He thought that he had seen the way the wind was blowing, and would vote for Hague in the second ballot. Michael Trend said he had 'the greatest admiration' for Redwood and was struck that, although previously he had attracted negligible support in his Windsor constituency, he now enjoyed the approval of about a third of the Association. Duncan Smith may have diminished this impression by his readiness to 'take

Trend through the figures and bully him again'. In the safety of increasing numbers, Trend would stick with Hague. Francis Maude, who as Financial Secretary to the Treasury had signed the Maastricht Treaty in 1992, had returned to the Commons as MP for Horsham, having lost his North Warwickshire seat in 1992. The inscrutably cruel features of the erstwhile member of Howard's general staff gave little away when he saw Redwood on the 11th of June, other than to assure him of his hatred for Clarke. But Howard's men were primarily office-seekers and Hague seemed the increasingly obvious choice, as a *pis aller* gratification of their desires. Maude's vote for Hague also reflected the way in which his recent relations with Redwood had been, in Foreign Office parlance, 'correct' rather than cordial as he watched his near contemporary rise to a public prominence denied him within the gilded cages of Salomon Brothers and Morgan Stanley.

David Davis was a Howardian who wanted, according to Redwood on the 11th, 'no more blowing round in the wind'. None the less he remained as inscrutable as Maude and would not vote for any camp that published his name as a supporter. It must have seemed a very long time since he had walked down a Scottish hillside in the autumn of 1994 hearing the assurances of Bruce Anderson that he would join the Cabinet before too long. He would transfer to Clarke, stay with him throughout, and find his abilities excluded from Hague's Shadow Cabinet. James Cran had been one of the few Lilley supporters who had voiced private reluctance about supporting Hague in the moments after the declaration of the first ballot. His doubts about committing himself continued as the breeze claimed him as its own. As he blinked, nervously open to suggestion, behind his glasses, he would say merely, 'There is only one person I can vote for, and you know who that is.' Nobody did.

Roger Knapman, the defeated member for Stroud, was walking in St James's Park one morning, he reported on the 13th of June, when he saw in the distance the bird-like figure of Gillian Shephard. After Lilley's demise, the Norfolk sparrow had yet to declare. Reports that she would transfer to Clarke were, she said, misplaced, and so Redwood swung into a courtship that culminated in an hour-long telephone conversation as they both skirted round her desire to be Party Chairman, his unhappy previous commitment to Duncan Smith on that score, and her adventurist leanings towards Hague.

In these latter days, Redwood was being squeezed between those who would vote for Clarke in order to stop Hague and those who would vote for Hague in order to stop Clarke. By the 12th of June, Sir Paul Beresford, the New Zealand dentist who had run the Tories' flagship Wandsworth Council and who now represented Mole Valley, was saying that his only motive for supporting Clarke was the negative one of suppressing Hague's rise. Bournemouth West's John Butterfill told Brazier on the 11th of June that it was important 'to stop Hague at all costs', and on the 16th he repeated to Marion Roe his conviction that the leader should not be Hague 'at any price'. Whether he intended to vote for Redwood was uncertain, despite Wilkinson's eve-of-poll hunch that Butterfill would act out his convictions.

Patrick Nicholls, whose Devon seat had returned him to the Commons with a majority of a bare 281, was clear on the 11th, according to Lewis, that it was 'more important to stop Ken Clarke than to vote for the man you want'. He was passionate that Hague shared his own rantingly anti-European convictions, and was conventionally dubious about Redwood's electability. David Maclean was unusual in that he had enjoyed the experience of working with Michael Howard as a Home Office Minister of State. Deprived of Howard, he had told Redwood by the 14th of June that, while he agreed with all his policies, the Wokingham seer was not the man to unite the Tories.

Unusually among Howard supporters, Andrew Lansley had veered towards Clarke because he was 'a big hitter', while the Redwood team's campaigning methods had alienated Robert Key, Salisbury's MP who had spent some of the best years of his life teaching Harrovians. Philip Hammond was 'all over the place', reported Howard Flight on the 10th, and 'extremely dodgy', barked Desmond Swayne, the only Howard supporter to join the official Redwood campaign. The Territorial Army officer was not alone in his suspicions. On the 11th John Bercow reported Hammond as saying that 'the key thing is to extract right-wing signals from Hague.'

At Saturday's Trooping the Colour, Christopher Fraser, newly elected in Mid Dorset, encountered the armour-plated certainties of Beryl Goldsmith, Norman Tebbit's parliamentary aide. He thought that he would vote for Redwood, he told her, but Lewis knew that by Monday the 16th Fraser was sending signals to the camp of his ultimate disposition, that of William Hague. On the evening of the 10th, Michael Colvin still thought that Redwood was mad, although by the 12th he had been affected by Wilkinson's graphic doomsday delineation of Prime Minister Hague with his nervous finger on the nuclear button. Also, by the evening of the same day, Rayleigh's Michael Clark had applied his industrial chemical mind and was convinced that Hague's ascent was 'the only way to stop Ken Clarke'. By the 11th an optimistic Redwood found Eric Forth amiable, although in an earlier conversation with Christopher Chope Forth had described the same Redwood as a 'nutcase'. On the same day, Wilkinson accurately thought Forth 'cagey'. Portillo-power ran deep in his veins, and he would never vote for the subverter of his idol. The tragic figure of Tredinnick was now seen arranging visits to inspect Hague. Stanley remained 'prickly' on the 12th, obsessed by Gurkhas and to be handled only by Redwood. Robert Syms completed the characteristic journey from Portillo roots, through Lilley as a half-way safe house, to Hague the comforter. By now he had diverted from his proposed ultimate Redwood destination. Reigate's Crispin Blunt was offering low-profile, Hague maintenance support, while the mistress of a former senior Minister had told John Wilkinson that her lover would embrace the same solution.

As Redwood-friendly Clarkeans, Anthony Steen and Quentin Davies repeated their conviction that in a third round between Redwood and Hague they would certainly vote for Redwood. Keith Simpson, the bristlingly moustachioed former Sandhurst lecturer who had succeeded the disenchanted

Richard Ryder as MP for Mid Norfolk, was a Clarke supporter but concealed doubts about the Single Currency within his blazered breast.

Redwood's brow darkened when he learnt the result of the second ballot. He trailed a poor third with thirty-eight votes. Hague took an unsatisfying second place with sixty-two, and Clarke was in the lead with sixty-four. It was the end of two years of hope and delusion, of ceaseless travel and staccato press releases, of the trip to the studio and the acclaim in the village hall. If it is true that all political careers end in failure, then his own had been unusually compressed and the failure correspondingly intense. It had always been emotion rather than intellect that had fuelled his conviction that the Tory Party wanted a clean break with its recent past. Reason showed that after the seven lean years of Major the Party had been fashioned in the very image of the former leader, and so it was hardly surprising that such a Parliamentary Party should choose more of the same.

Redwood had offered the Conservative Party a moral critique. He had always disconcerted with a Sunday-School horror of the lie and its political consequences. Not for nothing was he a political child of Watergate. He had told the Party's high command that it was necessary to apologize for the ERM crash and the subsequent Tory syllabus of errors. But Tory penitence was barely a strand in these May and June *événements*. Redwood with his baffled virtue was seen as part of the very structure of the Tory defeat. For two years he had explained why his Party would be defeated, and so he would be punished for his clarity. To many a Tory it seemed that his own integrity had been pursued at the expense of his Party. That Party was truly Major's and infected by that illiberal, intolerant spirit. The leadership campaign had shown how the capacity for debate and the expression of dissent had been crushed. The surviving rump was vulnerable to a management consultant's takeover bid. The world of Major and Hague, of Clinton and Blair, was carrying all before it in its crushing conformity, hostility to originality and sensitivity to the placeman's needs.

'Shouldn't we be talking to Ken?' said Gail Redwood to me when she appeared for Redwood's last press conference. As we walked together by the side of Westminster Abbey, she concluded that it had been an interesting experiment to see whether 'an honest man can succeed in politics, and now we know the answer'. But an alliance with Clarke might be a way of salvaging something from the wreckage. None among Redwood's supporters had for a moment contemplated or publicly counselled a pact with Hague, so profound was the hostility towards him and his cohorts. Hague should have done better than he did in the second ballot. An extra twenty-one votes, when forty-seven were available from those who had previously supported Lilley and Howard, was unimpressive given his 'soft-right' appeal. Clarke's additional fifteen votes were correspondingly impressive, given both his broader canvass of beliefs and also the narrower audience within the Parliamentary Party to which he could appeal.

Clarke was also the clear choice of the voluntary Party. Of the Constituency Chairmen of England and Wales, 269 voted for him at the first ballot, 242 at the second. From the same electorate, 178 had voted for Hague at the first ballot, and 223 at the second. These figures dwarfed the 25 who voted for Redwood at the first ballot and the 28 who supported him at the second.

Clarke took the initiative and rang Redwood at his headquarters. He suggested that they should meet at 6.30 p.m. at the Vincent Square home of Sir Tim Sainsbury, a former Tory Minister whose son-in-law was Shaun Woodward, the Dorrell *aficionado* who had transferred to Clarke. Redwood's response was grim but accommodating. Fifteen minutes later Hague rang, and his tone changed to one of stiff hostility. They would meet later that evening on territory supplied by Redwood – the Belgravia home in Chapel Street of Barry Legg, one of the army of Redwood Myrmidons whose marginal seats had been forfeited.

The question now in the Tory faith was whether Redwood's Geneva could be reconciled with Clarke's Rome. Early prospects were inauspicious. Clarke had given the wrong address, and the Jaguar circled the square until I discovered the 1920s Art Deco house. 'Typical' muttered the Tories' defeated Dauphin, sitting sullen in the back. The door opened and Redwood, mistaking a senior domestic for the *châtelaine*, asked her how long she had lived in the house. An excited Woodward appeared, smoking a cigar as destiny's force mounted. Redwood and I were shown into the first-floor drawing-room, and we looked out over the Square and the playing fields of Westminster School, where, in the early-evening sunlight, boys practised in the nets with mingled adolescent grace and gaucherie. Clarke was late. Redwood mused: 'You give up a lot when you go into politics. I could have lived in a house like this had I stayed with Rothschilds.' His mother had always been concerned when he gave up a proper job. In his Westminster end was his Kentish beginning.

We heard the gate open and went to the window. It was the former Chancellor. 'He's with Heseltine,' Redwood said with dark detachment. 'Don't let's stand near the window. We don't want them to see us looking eager.' The door opened and Clarke walked in, followed by Heseltine. Clarke and I, who were social acquaintances, talked of friends who would delight in the union, now seemingly imminent, of two great houses. We sat together on the settee, where later we made notes on the conversation in order to draft a joint statement. Redwood sat opposite, sunk in a chair, an isolated king-maker, where his long legs crossed and uncrossed as an attempt at elegance of posture served merely to reveal his febrile tension. Heseltine exuded a combination of aloofness and bemusement. His frame was draped along an elegant high-backed sofa, interposed between Clarke and Redwood, and ankles, elegant by any sexagenarian's standards, were revealed sheathed in stockings of the finest black silk. Truly it must have passed his mind that this was the deal that he, and he alone, would have been best placed to arrive at with Redwood. He had modified his Europeanism sufficiently in recent months for an arrangement to be plausible, and Heseltine, the businessman with hauteur, understood Redwood's drive and asperity.

Conventional courtesies were brief. When Clarke said that 'poor John' was still having to fulfil duties as Party leader and wanted the business of the election concluded as soon as possible, Redwood looked stiffly saturnine and unresponsive. It was time for business. Clarke was purposeful, scenting victory in the air: 'I think that, if we can arrive at an agreement, John,' he said, 'we can say that it is extremely unlikely that William will become leader.' We set to work on our common purpose. On the 'important issues of domestic policy', they decided that 'there has always been, and continues to be, agreement between us.' As Clarke and Redwood prepared for Opposition together with such good will, it seemed churlish to recall disputes on taxation, on public expenditure, on the level of Government debt and on the NHS's administrative nightmares. After all, this was supposed to be the Tories' Glorious Revolution, a constitutional settlement meant to endure on the basis of the goodwill of the two protagonists and the exclusion of Yorkshire William.

They agreed to my formulation that conservatism's common goal was 'an alliance between the interests of free nations and of free markets'. The Europe on which they agreed was one in which enlargement did not entail centralization, with free trade, deregulation and privatization at its contentious heart. The generalities limped along. Revealingly, Clarke's notes stated that 'our approach to the European currency is the only way to create jobs.' For Redwood, it was an approach that 'allowed job creation'. No Government, in Redwood's world, 'created' jobs.

As for Monetary Union, Clarke proposed, largely, that 'The agenda is not in our hands and is fast moving.' Developments in France and Germany, added Heseltine, made Britain's participation even more unlikely. Redwood did not respond because the exercises in appeasement were too obvious. He knew that Monetary Union and its consequences could not be derailed so easily, least of all for the convenience of the leadership of a British political party. But he agreed in opposing a form of Monetary Union 'between countries with economies out of line with each other in all important respects including fiscal discipline'. The problem was that Clarke's opposition to such a Monetary Union was a statement of the obvious, and Redwood's opposition would have been constitutional even in the event of the European economies achieving genuine convergence. Were Monetary Union and British entry 'to become an active possibility', they would have further discussions. Clarke had already offered the Parliamentary Party a free vote on EMU. Now he drafted into the joint statement the pledge that 'If we could not agree, we would have a free vote respecting the principled convictions of members of the Shadow Cabinet.' Redwood carefully amended the statement to include the Parliamentary Party as a whole. However, this was a 'very hypothetical issue which', in my drafting and in Clarke's, 'should not stand in the way of our complete agreement on the bigger European issues'. For Redwood, however, there was no bigger European issue than the Single Currency, and so the final formulation referred simply to 'other' European issues.

We relaxed. 'This is, I think,' said Heseltine, 'a historic moment in the history of the Conservative Party. It is the end of years of conflict.' He understood the importance of getting the news out, and urged that the agreement should be declared and published that evening. Redwood demurred. He still had to sell the Vincent Square concordat to his followers, he said. What use would it be if he could not deliver his forces? Besides, Clarke presumably still had to sell the idea to his followers. Moreover, I had to draft the final version of the concordat in a way acceptable to all parties. We decided to meet again in Vincent Square the next morning. Discussion of Redwood's role in a Clarke-led Shadow Cabinet was deferred until then, Clarke having already raised the question of the Shadow Chancellorship or the Shadow Foreign Secretaryship.

'You know, John,' said Clarke joshingly, as the hour's discussion came to a close, 'I don't understand what it is between you, me and Margaret. After all, I did all those difficult jobs for her in the '80s in Employment and Health and never complained. You ran her Policy Unit in the '80s and gave her privatization. Yet it's blindingly obvious that she hates the two of us.' The joviality eased the tension and we all laughed, Heseltine a shade grimly. Within a few hours, she did for both Clarke and Redwood with her plan of attack. We left together, Clarke disdaining a cigar as he went: 'I have only been smoking one a day during this election.' The former Chancellor and Deputy Prime Minister got into a cab, while Redwood and I drove away in the waiting Jaguar, which had perhaps been the Foundation's service he most valued. The disparity in their condition amused him briefly. Shadows lengthened on the grass of Vincent Square. Soon it would be time to return to Redwood's Wilfred Street headquarters to consult his followers. It had been enjoyable to sit in a cool drawing-room, but Redwood's future would be disposed of in a basement dining-room that, on a hot summer's night, was already full of parliamentary males awaiting his return.

Before seeing his followers, Redwood left for the meeting with Hague, his mind already made up. After all, he had already said on the early-evening news before seeing Clarke: 'Ken Clarke got in first. I suppose you could say he was a little bit better organized than William Hague, which might be a reason to vote for him.' This time Duncan Smith accompanied him. In the rush to Vincent Square he had been left behind in the House of Commons and was unaware of the immediacy of Redwood's meeting with Clarke. It was an expensive omission on the part of Redwood and myself, and one that may have affected Duncan Smith's *amour propre*. I absented myself from what was fated to be an unproductive meeting, and returned to draft the final statement. When he returned Redwood was adamant that the idea of Hague as leader was preposterous. The apprehensive Yorkshireman had said nothing of any consequence or interest to him in the course of their brief *tête-à-tête*. Redwood had simply inspected a very black Tory hole and recoiled.

On the evidence of conversations and increasingly explicit asides over the previous week, Redwood knew that a pact with Clarke had the implicit support of many of his followers. The proposal did not spring from his head fully formed and armed; his closest associates had encouraged him to think in these terms. Now they sat around the table eating superior Greek food supplied by Brian Myerson, Redwood's Maecenas, with the zeal that only Parliamentarians and schoolboys can bring to the consumption of free food and drink. At the third ballot, the winning candidate had to gain a majority of the votes cast, rather than of those entitled to vote, as had been the case in the first and second ballots. Some of those who found Redwood a Scylla to Clarke's Charybdis might abstain, but assuming that all who were eligible to vote would do so, Clarke would win if half of Redwood's thirty-eight voters transferred to the new joint platform. This calculation supposed that both Hague's sixty-two votes and Clarke's sixty-four remained intact.

Duncan Smith chaired a rambling meeting whose mood was overwhelmingly in favour of Redwood's evident intention as he read to the company the statement I had prepared. At this stage he made the crucial addition that 'John retains his principled objections to the Single Currency.' The only stipulation his supporters made was that Redwood should be appointed either Shadow Chancellor or Shadow Foreign Secretary, preferably the former in order to provide a lock on the door of the new agreement. None among those present voiced outright opposition to what in a few hours was to be presented as the Tory equivalent of the Molotov–Ribbentrop pact of 1939, as an 'instability pact', and as, in the words of Margaret Thatcher the next day, 'an incredible alliance of opposites which can only lead to further grief'.

Nicholas Winterton, Macclesfield's consistently activist MP, who had become noisily prominent in Redwood's counsels, thought his course of action the right one. 'You are better off inside the tent pissing out, than outside pissing in,' said Patterson, relishing the platitudinous wisdom of the self-conscious insider. Letwin warned that the Conservative press would be hostile, but he would remain on board however bumpy the ride. Lewis agonized honestly and publicly. He would, he thought, abstain. Duncan Smith had become strangely quiet.

After they left, Redwood and I returned to his room and talked to Clarke on the phone. Redwood said that he thought he could deliver the necessary votes, and Clarke offered him the Shadow Chancellorship, which he accepted. Clarke approved the final wording of the statement that would be issued at tomorrow morning's press conference at Church House. I said to Redwood how enjoyable it was to deal with Clarke. 'He has every reason to be nice,' said Redwood tartly. 'We are handing him his victory.' We turned out the lights and went our separate ways home.

High politics and mixed motives had developed an inner momentum that disregarded the outside world. It was a vicious irony that Redwood, always so sensitive to a wider democracy and so alert to the political dangers of ignoring it, could now be presented as the very model of a modern calculating-machine politician. Redwood's team reconvened early the next morning. The *Daily Telegraph* had begun to rumble. It feared a Clarke bearing gifts – were Redwood to enter a Clarke-led Shadow Cabinet he would undermine his 'reputation for integrity' with a 'blatantly opportunistic' act. John Townend attended Redwood's morning meeting in order to voice his opposition to the Clarke deal, but the flinty Bridlington wine merchant was an exception in an otherwise supportive congregation. If Redwood's core supporters detected the ground beginning to shift beneath their feet, they did not speak of it to him. He told them that he had secured the position they wanted for him and that, as prospective Shadow Chancellor, he would endorse Clarke that morning. The meeting closed. The cameras were waiting outside, and Redwood made a brief statement about his intentions. I noticed how he stood alone, apart from Flight and Leigh, on the steps with most of his former supporters waiting inside, out of the glare of publicity and behind the building's specially constructed blinds.

I spoke to Norman Tebbit on the phone, and he agreed to appear on television to defend the agreement. For him, too, it was now an issue of character, of Redwood's and Clarke's against the witless blankness of Haguery. Later in the day he recalled how Clarke had approached him in 1990 to do a similar deal at the fall of Thatcher. Clarke had always been a man with whom he could do business, and he thought that Redwood would find the same. William Rees-Mogg was bleaker when we spoke a few minutes later. 'Give my regards to Lord North,' he said, recalling Burke's defection in 1783 from the Whigs, an act that helped to precipitate the end of Whig ascendancy for half a century.

Now that he had made his decision, Redwood's mood was lighter at the morning meeting with Clarke. His new principal reported that a few of his sixty-four second-ballot supporters were suspicious of the deal, but that could be handled. Woodward joined the meeting to rehearse the Central Office ritual of 'lines to take' at the now-imminent press conference, but the duo's self-confidence had never required *aide-mémoires*. They would take it on the wing and enjoy themselves. But before they left, I had to tell them both that in Belgravia a bejewelled Baronial paw had been reaching for the telephone since an early hour that morning. They should prepare themselves. Thatcher had bestirred herself, was telephoning the unconvinced among the former Redwood phalanx, and saying, 'I'm incandescent. Don't touch Ken. Remember his record.' In rare agreement with his predecessor, Major jumped ship. He had voted for Clarke at the first two ballots, but now he told colleagues that 'Ken's gone mad.' Parliamentary pygmies stirred in the undergrowth. Soon the unpalatable would embrace the unelectable.

Surrounded by a platoon of photographers and television cameras, Clarke and Redwood walked across Dean's Yard together in the midday sunshine. Their joint appearance at the press conference was meant to be a great symbolic moment. Clarke had been the overwhelming choice of the voluntary Party, and according to all available opinion polls he was the most

popular Conservative in the country. But an effective Opposition needed the
Redwood grit to do its work within the Clarke oyster. Clarke was clear. That
Wednesday evening, he explained to sceptical friends that 'It's shit or bust so
far as John and I are concerned.' They had both gambled their political lives,
and that meant, so far as the Single Currency was concerned, 'We just won't
talk about it.'

Some non-Tory commentators saw the point. Hugo Young in the *Guardian*
on the 19th of June thought that 'Here at last is an early sighting of the
Conservative Party we used to know and fear. Ideas, it turns out, matter less
than hatred, calculation and power.' The Conservative Party 'seems on the
brink of showing it is not dead'. The subtle and introspective Don Macintyre
in the *Independent* thought it 'just possible that some of the poison of Europe
is at last about to seep out of the British body politic'. The Treaty of
Amsterdam, with Blair's redrafting of the texts, had shown how Britain could
work in a pragmatic world of European agreements and deals. The age of
grand European theory was drawing to a close, and it was difficult to become
bitter, twisted and emotional about the introduction of qualified majority
voting on research and development issues or anti-fraud measures. Perhaps,
mused Macintyre, Clarke and Redwood showed the dawn of 'the sensible
world of deals'?

Redwood had made the mistake of thinking that by his actions and by his
leadership alone he could ordain the end of the civil war. If the pact was good
enough for him with his reputation for obeying the dictates of angular duty,
stern disciple of the voice of the Euro-sceptic god, then it should be good
enough for all sceptics. But the events of the 18th and 19th of June were
further proof, if such were needed, that there was no cohesive body of Euro-
scepticism that could be led and delivered in any direction – and certainly not
by him. He had lived by an European sword; both he and Clarke would be
impaled upon it. Very few of his thirty-eight voters attended the joint press
conference. One who did, Christopher Chope, told him afterwards that he had
been appalled by the sight of Clarke followers, such as Gummer and Temple-
Morris, applauding Redwood's remarks. 'But', Redwood said resignedly to
Chope, 'isn't that the point, Christopher?' In a healed Tory Party the Redwood
lion would have to lie down with the Temple-Morris lamb, otherwise there
was no future for any Tory body.

Feeling magnanimous, daring and confident, Redwood and Clarke toured
the television and radio studios, cutting a *bella figura* together. The more they
were together, the more they liked it. 'He really is a most extraordinary
character,' said Redwood of Clarke, although he took a dim view of the
organizational powers of the Clarke campaign in comparison with his own
smoothly purring machine. Redwood, Clarke reminded an interviewer tartly,
did not need to prove that he was a man of integrity. He had resigned from
Major's Cabinet of his own volition, and his actions today were of a piece
with his principles.

But, outside the studios, hysteria was in the air. Peter Tapsell spluttered that Redwood had committed 'one of the most contemptible and discreditable actions by a senior British politician I can recall during my thirty-eight years in the Commons'. A puce-featured Peter Lilley encountered Redwood on the stairs as he left the BBC's Westminster studios. 'Shame on you, John,' he mouthed. 'I was offered this poisoned chalice and I refused.' It was the cry of an eagerly anticipatory new establishment that saw its jobs threatened by the old Redwoodian audacity that, like Machiavelli's Prince, had seized fortune by the throat, wrested advantage from her in the daring of a moment's surrender, and now threatened to infuse an old establishment with new blood.

The meeting of Clarke's supporters in the Parliamentary buildings at Number 1, Parliament Street on Wednesday evening showed that old establishment at work and play. Redwood's Wilfred Street Irregulars had run an intense, febrile campaign, and lived under the volcano. These, by contrast, were large, well-suited men, broad of mind and broad of beam, working in an atmosphere that was clubby, congenial and fatally relaxed. Michael Mates, MP for Hampshire East, concert pianist and Michael Heseltine's constant supporter for over twenty years, presided with genial charm. He had much to be confident about. Redwood had run a tight and effective campaign, one that was far superior to Clarke's. Mates only needed to rely on half of Redwood's second-ballot support, and Redwoodsmen were notorious for an intense loyalty to their 'Chief of Men'. 'They're working the lobbies hard,' said a tense Dorrell as he tried to inject urgency, 'and working in pairs'. 'We've got to get out there and keep up the pressure.' 'Yes, well, off you go, then,' said Mates with the genially avuncular air of a District Commissioner dealing with a disturbingly evangelical missionary. 'Yes', he said to me as we sat and talked in the empty room afterwards, his cohorts having scattered to the Palace's four corners: 'I'm a veteran of these things, you know. Been a campaign manager on four of them, if you include this one. Record not good – of course – so far. Lost two and drew one. Still, I think this one's going to be all right. Shall we compare notes?' We discussed happily who did, and who did not, qualify for 'chateau-bottled shit' awards on the evidence of their complicity and duplicity in the course of the campaign. The next twenty-four hours would bring forth a new class of candidates in that category.

If Redwood thought he had won, in his phrase, 'peace with honour', *The Times* leader on the 19th of June thought that 'This is his Munich. He has lost the authority won by his principled stand of the past.' Rees-Mogg wrote of Redwood that 'in the twinkling of an eye he has destroyed himself.' In its leader the *Sunday Telegraph* reached the conclusion that Redwood, 'apparently an intellectual posing as a populist . . . revealed that he was in fact a careerist posing as a man of integrity.' The *Daily Telegraph* thought that, however proud Redwood was of the offer of a free vote and the consequent protection of the integrity of views on the Single Currency, this 'is something that Mr Clarke has been offering all along and it is not a concession at all'. In the world of commentary, it seemed that Redwood had bought the Crown Prince's ticket. As Eden to Clarke's Churchill he would henceforth be fated to live out his days in the shadow of the older man's Indian summer, and this threatened to be interminable, for Clarke was still only fifty-six.

Hague's weakness as a candidate had led him, eventually and unwillingly, to box himself in. An unconvincing attempt to assert his authority had led him to make opposition to the Single Currency a condition of Shadow Cabinet membership. This would exclude Clarke and his Euro-philes. Clarke's strength as a candidate had been that his open-mindedness on the Currency, although suspected by sceptics to conceal approval, stopped nobody from hoping for a Shadow Cabinet position. Now, however, soft-sceptics, tepids and neutrals had a new justification for Hague. They discovered the uses of a new moral ardour that rushed to their heads. As the culture of commentary buried Clarke and, especially, Redwood as opportunists and cynics, the army of the confused, the cautious and the calculating could start to use the integrity card, long since Redwood's property, against the erstwhile true-blue incorruptible. Hague's own equivocations could thereby be seen as less significant. When Redwood delved and Clarke span, who was then the gentleman? Many ultra-sceptics joined in the rush, badly destabilized by the damning newspaper articles sent by Hague to the newly uncommitted early on the morning of the 19th of June, the day of the third ballot. Just as in November 1990 Major had found himself the candidate best placed to beat Heseltine, so Hague had emerged as the candidate to stop Clarke. The candidate whom most MPs knew least about, and to whom they least objected, was going to win. Hague became the beneficiary of an ideologized Euro-scepticism that had recoiled from Redwood and had, because of his own actions, nowhere else to go. The irony was that Hague had never shared such scepticism, and was only pushed towards its modulated expression with extreme reluctance.

'We'll look pretty silly', said Redwood on the afternoon of the 18th, 'if, having done all this, we can't even win.' He started to telephone for one last push, but by Thursday morning it had become clear that he would be struggling to persuade even a double-digit number of his supporters to follow him. Portillo and Lamont were also telephoning, having joined the final stages of Hague's campaign in order to ensure the nemesis of Clarke and Redwood. Thatcher put on one of her embarrassing Grand Guignol performances. She stood outside the St Stephen's entrance to the House of Commons on Wednesday afternoon, endorsed Hague, and then toured the tea-room. 'I don't know how I came to earn that,' said Redwood in bitter wonderment. He had always been clear that the ideal situation was consistent Thatcher neutrality throughout the contest, since her endorsement of him would alienate as many as it persuaded. But a decision to favour someone else at his expense would be the unhappiest of all outcomes. This melancholy possibility was now reality. Having created a Party mania for 'strong leadership', Thatcher endorsed the means least likely to achieve it, because the only alternative was the loathed Clarke who in November 1990 had told her that her political mission was over. It seemed that all Tory winding ways led back to that cataclysm, even in the hour of Hague's victory. The Conservative Parliamentary Party's majority was looking, not for a hero from the North to descend upon them with the eye of an eagle and the brow of a hunter, but for a cold and bald Yorkshire MP with organizational gifts, whose comparative youth, according to Clarke, was solely a matter of his birth certificate. What had started as a Clarke and Redwood *coup de théâtre* was fast degenerating into a tragic-absurdist text.

As Redwood surveyed the wreckage, it was clear that he could rely only on Brazier, Flight, Robathan, Gorman, Wilkinson, Leigh, Roe and Wilshire. His followers' resolute recommendations of the previous day had withered on the vine. Perhaps those who had abandoned him so readily and so quickly believed, with Talleyrand, that 'treason is a question of dates.' Their convictions were celebrated on movable feast days. Redwood's pleas became increasingly desperate as he reminded his colleagues of the intensity of their widely advertised distaste for the man for whom they were about to vote. He would be defeated by the candidate at whom so many of his own supporters had sneered and whom they had to be restrained from libelling. The Conservative Party was disappearing down an abyss created by its own lack of a capacity for self-disgust.

Duncan Smith had vanished since Redwood's Wednesday morning meeting. Redwood's campaign manager was reported as saying simply that his former chief was 'in a powerful position. He has emerged as the unity candidate. Both sides need him.' He had been careful not to commit himself to the Redwood–Clarke pact at either of Redwood's meetings, and the chilly words revealed his further change of mind. He voted for Hague, refused to return Redwood's calls on Wednesday, and found himself in the Shadow Cabinet by the end of the week. Redwood only discovered him eventually while walking through Parliament Square on the way to the House of Commons on Thursday morning. The former keeper of the ark of the Redwood covenant and flyer of the Clarke-pact kite now criticized Redwood's other followers. They had been wrong to withdraw their support, having authorized Redwood to crawl to the end of a political branch. He, self-righteously, did not count himself among their number. 'Next time,' he confided to the lobby, 'I'll be running my own campaign.'

'Trust me,' Redwood said repeatedly to his electorate throughout Wednesday and until 5.00 p.m. on Thursday. But they had lost their bearings. The taste for treachery and the habit of rebellion were deeply ingrained in the Tory way. It was the first Euro-sceptic rebellion against John Redwood. At 4.00 p.m. on Thursday, it was discovered that Owen Patterson had yet to vote. For an ignominious half hour Redwood pleaded with Patterson's inarticulate uncertainties, only releasing him to vote with fifteen minutes to spare before the ballot closed.

The result was decisive. Redwood's rump boosted Clarke's sixty-four votes to seventy. Hague enjoyed his victory with ninety-two votes, his additional thirty supporters being largely drawn from those who had supported Redwood in the second round. Alan Clark and Julian Lewis, in a convergence of views unlikely even in this contest of mismatched alliances, could vote for neither final solution. Clarke's vote held up well despite the reservations of some of his core supporters and Major's defection to Hague. Charles Wardle had returned to his earlier, first-ballot instincts, abandoned Hague, and voted for the Clarke–Redwood pact.

Angela Browning and David Wilshire were the only MPs with Redwood as, grey-faced, he watched the television set. The confident tones of Archie Hamilton, the new Chairman of the 1922 Executive, resonated in celebration of the contest's apotheosis. Redwood's supporters had backed him and then sacked him. 'I don't seem to be any good at these leadership elections,' said Redwood bleakly. In the background female whimpering filled the silence. Redwood's campaign had been unusual compared with that of his rivals in attracting the efforts of a number of young and youngish women, and the mascara was now beginning to run. I enjoyed a final manly tussle with Angela Browning's bosom. Redwood reached for the phone to commiserate with Clarke who, perhaps insensitively in his sadness, said that the problem had been Redwood's inability to deliver the vote. Redwood had no words left. 'Eyeless in Gaza, At the mill with slaves,' I said to him. Like Samson, he had first gloried in his strength before his enemies had captured and tortured him. But the Tory Philistia, far from being destroyed in a general collapse, were still rejoicing a few hundred yards away in Smith Square and in the House of Commons. Redwood's ruins, by contrast, lay all around him, and it was scant consolation that his Party, by its conduct over the previous six weeks, had chosen to continue along the path of its long-term decline. The dog days, not only of July but of the long, bitter years ahead, beckoned for the Conservative Party.

Outside, the summer weather had broken, and it was raining. At Central Office's victory parade Brian Mawhinney, with the maladroit and grinning menace he had made his own, welcomed Hague and his fiancée to what would prove 'a new experience for you and William'. Redwood gathered his belongings and was driven home to Wokingham in circumstances far different from those that had attended the end of his first leadership bid two long summers ago. 'It's been a good day,' said Margaret Thatcher. The Tory bonfire of the vanities had extinguished itself in the triumph of the banal.

REQUIEM

Where Are You Dying Tonight?

'THE GREAT parties which formerly divided and agitated the kingdom are known to be in a manner entirely dissolved.' Edmund Burke's words in 1770 were no less true in 1997. New Labour, having committed patricide and buried its past, sat crowned on the grave of Old Tory. Tories objected that Labour was squatting on their territory, but no one knew any longer where a distinctively Conservative plot of earth might be found. 'What would you do if you were running the Conservative Party?' I asked Peter Mandelson. 'Find a project and stick to it,' he said. But there was no plausible Tory enterprise.

An understanding of the magnitude of the revolution that had crushed them eluded the Tories, even though voters continued to ram the message home. At the Winchester by-election held on the 20th of November a Liberal Democrat majority of just two in May was converted to one of 21,556. Gerry Malone, the defeated Conservative candidate and former MP, had refused to accept the electorate's May Day signal, challenged the result in the Courts – and paid the price for ill grace. On the same day at Beckenham, one of south London's airier suburbs, the Tory majority of 4953 bequeathed by Piers Merchant was reduced to 1227. The anti-Tory majority was still on the march. Political actors crave optimism of the will, and few can abide pessimism of the intellect. But the Tory failure to ask searching questions about what they were for in modern Britain and why they had been defeated resulted in a year of fatuity, irrelevance and continued factionalism.

The Tories showed every sign of forgetting that political parties can and do decline and die, their faded charms withering on the branches of once mighty oaks. That decline is inevitable if parties cease to perform their job of representing certain objective interests and if they fail to follow Jesse Jackson's message to the Democrats in the 1980s: 'Reform, regroup, renew and move on.' The Conservative Party at the end of the twentieth century was just over 150 years old in its modern form as the heir to Robert Peel and the politics of the commercial classes. That was no very great age, yet it was now possible to conceive of a Britain without the Tories as a major force. English institutions have always been good at inventing consoling founding myths for themselves. Rather like the Church of England, that other invention of the early and mid-Victorian period, the Party claimed to be rooted in ancient and historic glories. Revolutionized by evangelicalism on the one hand and by the Oxford Movement on the other, the Victorian Church of England had dominated national life in the nineteenth century much as the Tory Party did in the twentieth. Now, as a marginalized, late twentieth-century institution on the run, awkward, confused and ill-led, the Anglican church offered the Tories a glimpse of their own future.

Formulaic statements were issued about how 'there are lessons to be learnt', but the Tories' pattern of behaviour remained the same as in the days of Government – rooted in rancour and targeted towards the trivial. The hollow men of British politics had resumed service as normal. The Tories looked like ghosts in an underworld far removed from the political landscape they had once bestrode like Colossi. Vignettes abounded. One dark winter evening Angela Rumbold, the dispossessed Dame of Mitcham and Morden, could be seen walking down St Martin's Lane accompanied by Robin Harris, released for a few hours by Margaret Thatcher, looking for all the world like two forlorn Bourbon exiles in 1790s London, plotting and hoping for the return to Versailles that would never come. Eager young men with parliamentary hopes went to see Roger Freeman, now the party's Deputy Chairman in charge of candidates, and were asked to use their spare time as removal men in the Central Office, staff being thin on the ground. A 'listening to Britain' exercise was launched, and Shaun Woodward produced a glitteringly costed £400,000 plan, only to be told that the party had not 400 pence to spend on the enterprise. Michael Portillo decided to mark his care for the community card, and talked at the Party Conference of the need for the Tories to be 'inclusive' and to refrain from judgement about minorities whose pursuits fell outside the Tory canon. 'I read Portillo's lecture,' opined Enoch Powell as he sat by the fire in the last months of his life in South Eaton Place. 'Not distinguished.' But Portillo also went further than his Party and, in the security of his Elba, embraced opposition in principle to the Single European Currency.

That May, Stephen Churchett's play *Tom and Clem* was performed at the Aldwych Theatre, and caught the mood of Britain's spring in a portrayal of Clement Attlee and Tom Driberg brought together at the Potsdam Conference immediately after the 1945 Labour victory. When the Celia Johnson-like Wren in attendance on the Prime Minister rhapsodized on how important it had been to dispose of the party of appeasement and unemployment, the theatre erupted in prolonged applause.

Major retained his hold on the impoverished Tory imagination. One evening he was to be observed, in that high, tactile tradition he had made his own, draping his arm around Dame Janet Fookes, the departed tribune of Plymouth Drake, as they dined together in the House of Commons. On other occasions, Tory Members, new and old, were to be seen gathering around him much in the manner of *The Boyhood of Ralegh*, as he recounted deeds of daring-do on the high Tory seas of the 1990s. Even Bill Cash, now no longer a figure whose views troubled the media mind, was to be seen within the circle. 'We just talk about cricket,' he said, defensively.

Elsewhere in London the yellowing résumés of the fallen gathered dust on the desks of many a headhunter. As early as 1995 and 1996, directors of merchant banks reported that barely a month went by without a letter arriving from a Member of Parliament or a Minister, overtly on an issue of business but covertly applying for an escape route as the recipient realized when discovering a covering letter that revealed the writer's biographical details.

The new leader's appearances during these inaugural months included the lumbering demotic of baseball caps, an inane and gauche visit to the Notting Hill Carnival, a heartlessly banal response to the death of the Princess of Wales and a foolish attack on the Prime Minister who had the right words to meet that death, did the right thing, and reaped the political advantages of public approval. 'From Oxbridge to Uxbridge – William Hague's a winner,' bawled the party's *fonctionnaires* in their continuing unedifying struggle with words and meaning during the Uxbridge by-election held on the 31st of July.

In the referendums held in September, the Government's devolution proposals were approved by a narrow majority in Wales and overwhelmingly in Scotland. Meanwhile the Opposition reclined in the last ditch of a sour and charmless Unionism. By February 1998, the leadership suggested that it might accept the Scottish result in terms that recalled Thomas Carlyle's response to a female decision to accept the universe: 'Gad, she'd better.' The Opposition had no alternative, but where was the political advantage in crawling to death-bed repentance on a constitutional issue defined as New Labour's own? Hague, urged by Michael Howard, advocated a referendum on the Treaty of Amsterdam, but the public mood was one of indifference as the Government calmed the European temperature and the cadences of a benign Blairism attracted a continental hearing. Kenneth Clarke, by now ensconced behind a battery of lucrative directorships, could not resist reporting an absence of agitated passers-by coming up to him in the street and expressing concern about 'Amsterdam'. Having talked to the Parliamentary Party individually and collectively during the terrible May and June days, Clarke concluded that his colleagues had just stopped thinking. He would look abroad, and indeed Unichem, the pharmaceuticals company he now chaired, merged with Alliance Santé, the French drug giant. Tory Europeans who approached him, convinced, like Edward VIII as Prince of Wales, that 'something' had to 'be done', found him detached. Heseltine, older, crosser, and richer brooded as his distaste for the Tory rump refused to mellow. But, after an initial flurry of autumnal speculation in 1997, no one expected a coherent Tory European group to emerge and separate itself from the wreckage. The Tory 'left' were, truly, 'wet'. Tories, it seemed for the moment, would hang, and be hung, together.

The National Union conducted the ballot of party members promised by Hague during the leadership contest. The question of assent to the new leadership, with no possibility of any other candidate being nominated, was merged with that of approval of internal Party reorganization and announced at the Conference held in Blackpool that autumn. Hague would have to be accepted together with his reforms in a ploy reminiscent of Major's 'sack me or back me' tactic. In his valedictory address, the former leader showed his familiar skill in mastering Tory sentiment, suggested archly that he might bear some responsibility for the disasters that had befallen his Party, and was rewarded with a chorus of denial from his audience of captives. Deluded Party members were minded to blame and to lynch the Parliamentary Party. Former members of the Government were happy to conspire in this avoidance of blame. Major continued to refuse to apologize for the ERM, although Hague made a dash for guilt-free territory shortly after the Party Conference and distanced himself from the policy of a Cabinet of which he had not been a member.

The Blackpool Conference was the first public opportunity to see the Shadow Cabinet in action. The dark protagonists of June and July had faded and their insubstantial dreams had dissolved in the uncertain cold light of Hague's dawn. If the hope was that these brave spirits would blow the first blast of the trumpet against the monstrous regiment of Blairites, then they displayed all of the effectiveness and none of the glamour of a Polish cavalry charge in 1939. A campaign that prided itself on offering a 'fresh start' issued in an inconsequential display of melancholy familiarity. A Party once thought to be resolute, ruthless and rigorous in the understanding and pursuit of power revealed its sentimental, venal and incompetent heart. These were tatterdemalion Tories who neither looked nor sounded like the members of a governing elite and lacked both intuitive understanding of authority and flair in its exercise. The contributions of Michael Howard and of Peter Lilley, of Iain Duncan Smith and of David Heathcoat-Amory, had been recognized with the Shadow portfolios of the Foreign Office and the Chancellorship of the Exchequer, the Department of Social Security and the Chief Secretaryship to the Treasury. The cobwebs of former distinction still clinging to his frame, Lord Parkinson was dusted down and re-installed as Party Chairman to general bemusement.

Brian Mawhinney brought with him to his role as Shadow Home Secretary the smile that had sunk a thousand Tory hopes. Among Howard's men, Francis Maude was gratified with a role as cultural *Gauleiter* and tormentor-in-chief of the Dome decreed by Michael Heseltine and Peter Mandelson for the enjoyment of stately millennial pleasures. Gillian Shephard re-emerged in the twinkling of an eye as Shadow Leader of the House, regretting nothing of the past Government's record. Stephen Dorrell, disillusioned and detached, became a night-watchmen on education issues, while Andrew Mackay was a similarly Trappist Northern Ireland spokesman. Norman Fowler, in a further remembrance of times past, decided that the British people would tolerate further displays of his didactic tones and emphatic hands when he took up the reins as a shadow Environment Secretary. Michael Ancram, a Scottish Catholic and heir to the Marquess of Lothian, congratulated himself on his good fortune in endorsing Hague as he took charge of constitutional issues. John Maples had last been seen in public life attempting to sell the ERM to his former constituents in Lewisham. The former Treasury minister lost his seat in 1992, but had now returned to represent Stratford-on-Avon. By a pleasing irony, he was asked to represent the Tory case on those same health issues that he had so memorably excoriated as electorally disastrous in the 'Maples memo', which had been leaked while he was a Party deputy chairman.

Alastair Goodlad acquired another identity and third-world convictions as he jousted with Clare Short on international development. Robert Cranborne continued as Shadow Leader of the Lords and was inelegantly briefed against by the leader's office. He had, it was said, expected a suitably moving appeal from his leader designed to persuade him to stay in the difficult circumstances created by a lack of suitably distinguished alternative peers. The press reported him to have been treated brusquely, asked to serve, and despatched accordingly.

John Redwood had expected exclusion and anticipated rejection. When the call came to serve as the Shadow Trade and Industry spokesman he was reported to be elated. He retained his doubts about Hague's close and introspective circle of advisers. 'You could feel that they were everywhere,' he said afterwards, evoking the scene in the leader's office as he strode in to assume a new courtier's role. None the less, he had, he thought, been offered the chance of redemption, and seized it. It could be presented, he said chirpily on the Friday after the election result, as his assumption of Michael Heseltine's former role. 'That's the line to brief, isn't it?' It emerged in subsequent reports, leaked by Hague's office, that the price he had to pay was to cease his association with the Conservative 2000 Foundation. He was also asked to 'wind up' the policy unit, whose effectiveness had threatened Central Office's monopoly. He explained the sophistical device by which he lacked an official position in the Foundation and was consequently detached from it. He could, and would, advise as a constitutional monarch, but could do no more. This made no difference to leaked stories about the wishes of the Tories' pocket Augustus and Redwood's subservience to them. At the start of the weekend, he may have felt able to glide around the issue, but with the appearance of Sunday's press reports he felt humiliated by the story and talked of offering the first resignation from Hague's Shadow Cabinet. 'These', he said, 'are clearly very nasty people.'

By Monday, he had recovered his *sang froid*, talked to his leader, and claimed to have extracted an apology. He packed his Wilfred Street belongings in a cardboard box and, leaving the door ajar behind him, quit the building as abruptly as he had left the Welsh Office two years previously. He had been elected by Wokingham to do a job for five years, he said, and in his eyes that meant serving William Hague in a Shadow Cabinet. Were he to go on the backbenches, all would assume that he was preparing for his third leadership onslaught. The improbability of any such further attempt after his humiliation eluded him as he reduced himself to the awkwardly grinning condition of an imbecilic hostage forced to echo his leader's cold and mirthless laugh as he sat on the Opposition frontbench. Now, eating the daily bread of his humiliation in the public sweat of a new-found loyalty to Hague, he would try too hard to prove his suspect allegiance. The Foundation with which he had been associated changed its name, averted its eyes from political life, and developed other interests.

Between 1995 and 1997 there had been a sheen about the Redwood political persona. Out of the desires of the typically buried English heart there had emerged a powerful, though suppressed, romanticism about England and the English. The toys with which he played might have been the simplistic nostrums and the tawdry remains of a post-imperial imagination, but he infused them, for that brief period, with a transforming *élan* of the spirit and the mind. He had been surprised by his own joy as he chose freedom. Now his own Party had reclaimed him in a terrible recrudescence as, like Browning's Lost Leader, he broke from the freemen and 'sank to the rear and the slaves'.

The breaking of Redwood's spirit was illustrative both of the immediate reality of Party and of the longer vicissitudes of its decline. Like Lord Randolph Churchill, Joseph Chamberlain and Enoch Powell, Redwood was a romantic nationalist and, like Churchill and Powell, a Tory democrat. Like all of them, he was distrusted by his Party and sought to mould a party-political structure that would both suit his purposes and reflect his beliefs. Again, like them, he was defeated by the apparently iron necessity of Party. But the price paid for such immediate effectiveness was wider public disenchantment with the hollow unities of Party. In the leadership election a force of collective hypocrisy engineered a synthetic amalgam out of the disparate wills of Michael Howard, John Redwood and William Hague, and attributed sincerity of intention to that synthesis. That might be the necessary lie at the heart of all party politics, but an age that valued self-expression and candour did not see that force as either amiable or healthy. For the moment party politics in Britain was defined by what Tories did best: bad speeches and anger. It was full of raw emotions and rough activities, of hatred and squabbling, of shouting and vindictiveness. Hell, for these Tories, was other Tories – and the British people agreed. When parties are no longer defined in the public minds by beliefs, dyspepsia remains to fill the gap. The hard politics of party meant Brian Mawhinney, Michael Howard and Norman Fowler – public figures who, it was clear, were no longer at home in Britain. Tony Blair, at the head of his diffuse coalition, had persuaded the British people that what he did was not party politics on these terms. His Labour Party was the beneficiary of this death of politics as ideology – the Party's doctrinal vacuity at once echoing the wider emptiness and, in its leader's presidential manner, offering reassurance, balm and aversion to rancour.

Tory strategists hoped that these things would pass and that the curse of acrimony would descend upon Labour with results comparable to the Tories' disgrace. Implausibly, they therefore tried to hoist Labour on the Tory petard of corruption. Geoffrey Robinson, the Paymaster-General, was discovered to have been the beneficiary of an off-shore trust, an arrangement of which his Party's official policy disapproved. There was low-level hypocrisy but no illegality, and for most observers the greater hypocrisy was the new-found Tory virtue. Lord Simon, the former chairman of British Petroleum, was now a Minister of State at the Department of Trade and Industry. On the advice of the Civil Service, he had placed his BP shares in a blind trust rather than disposing of them. Again, Tories tried to prove conflict of interest, but the impression was one of Tory effrontery and hypocrisy. No one thought that Simon was anything other than an honest and able man who had made a financial sacrifice in order to be a Minister. Businessmen and financiers took an especially dim view of the criticisms, and the gulf grew between public unreality and commercial practicality, between the Tory Party and the City of London.

Meanwhile the new Labour Government showed every sign of awareness that it governed as a new, Whiggish coalition of interests guided at every turn by reversing the Tory etiquette book. If in doubt, New Labour thought and recalled what the Tories did in managing public opinion during past years – and decided to do the opposite. It understood the need for a dynamic relationship with the press, fed newspapers with stories, and created an unfolding sense of a Government with a purpose and an agenda for modernity. Yesterday's story was not allowed to become today's, and an anticipated tomorrow dominated the present. In its understanding of the new force of media-class power that had turned its guns on the Tories, the Government showed an appreciation of the diminished role of, and respect for, the House of Commons as a national institution. It benefited from the direct democratic power of the multi-media age's electronic technology, from satellite and cable – forms of power that could only grow with time. Tory bleating about 'ignoring the House of Commons' seemed the lament of a special-interest group and made Parliamentarians sound like 1970s trade unionists.

New Labour's vote in 1997 was 'soft' because it was defined by hatred of the Tories and determination to get rid of them. The abyss that now opened before the Tories was that their Party's condition would continue to deteriorate. Britons lived in a benign age of material advance, one in which they recognized that an index of a well-run economy was the extent to which politicians withdrew from involvement in economic management. They knew that politicians' ability to destroy economic progress was far greater than their creative capacity, and to general content they were therefore kept in their box. New Labour eagerly accepted this consensus. If predictions of continued economic growth were to be only half fulfilled in the depoliticized economies of the West by 2001/2002, the electorate could have a positive reason to vote for New Labour rather than a negative one to vote against the Tories. In that event, the Government's share of the vote would rise from its present mediocre plateau of 43 per cent and begin to rival the Conservative achievement of 48 to 50 per cent in the 1950s. A few additional percentage points would threaten to reduce the Conservative Party's Parliamentary representation to double figures.

*   *   *

In the late 1990s Conservatives should have asked themselves the question: 'Was John Major the Conservative Party's last Prime Minister?' Perhaps the 1st of May was so uniquely terrible a trauma that most Tories did not even want to think about its significance. But every sign was that the Tories were relying on the 'political cycle' to do their work for them. The next election, they reasoned, would be difficult, but the one after that verged on a probability. This was how it always had been. Fatigue with the party in government preceded disillusion and consequent Opposition recovery as the slow, sweet and steady rhythm of Britain's two-party democracy resumed its even-handed distribution of the fruits of office.

There were many inter-war Liberals who had reasoned in this way. In the 1923 general election 158 Liberal MPs were elected. These lights of liberalism still thought themselves important, some were distinguished, and many had recently been in office in the wartime coalition. The recent rift in the Party between Asquithians and Lloyd George's followers, or the 'National Liberals', had been healed under the banner of the joint cause of Free Trade. They had even increased their representation from the sixty-two Asquithians and fifty-four National Liberals elected in 1922. Their Party was one of the pillars of the British constitution, they mused, and its roots were ancient. Surely, they thought, the electoral cycle would more than hold out for them as they oversaw the introduction of Britain's first Labour Government in 1924. In the general election of that year, their numbers fell to forty, rising again to fifty-nine in Lloyd George's Indian summer of 1929. They had to wait until 1997 for an electoral recovery that returned them to even these modest numbers. And so, the unwittingly departing captains and kings of a once all-conquering Liberalism ploughed on through the 1920s and 1930s holding summer schools where earnest and rather virtuous young men in flannels, smoking pipes and holding convictions, planned for a better tomorrow. They wrote pamphlets, attracted the young Harold Wilson and the support of Maynard Keynes and of William Beveridge. They were led from 1931 to 1935 by Viscount Samuel and subsequently by Sir Archibald Sinclair, while Sir John Simon kept the Liberal afflatus on the road inside the National Government as Foreign Secretary from 1931 to 1935. These in their day were important names now best known to the connoisseur of the political footnote and appendix. Heartless history neither knew nor cared of their fate and passed them by on the other side of the road.

The Liberal parallel was a compelling one as Tories sat in the long-haul departure lounge of British politics with William Hague plotting the journey as the Tory Archibald Sinclair. A rump party ceasing to evangelize, lacking a distinctive message, and crushed by history could still be excellent at introspective management theory during weekends from hell when Members of Parliament and parliamentary candidates could bond and play.

For all their talk of 'freshness', Hague's Tories offered a regression to old party rather than an advance to new hope. The emphasis on structure, organization and control from men with thin lips, hard hearts and narrow minds was an ancient beat, albeit tapped out on a new drum. The pride in tight control achieved by the best methods known to MBA Man was unappealing to a disenchanted electorate and lacked the power of a creative imagination. The age might be one of artfully packaged management, where less was more and the future was mauve – the colour chosen for the backdrop to the 'relaunch' in February 1998 of the Conservative Party. Indeed, Hague's campaign and his victory were witness to the power of such methods within the enclosed circle of political professionals, and represented the victory of form over content, of method over substance. But these techniques had no wider democratic charms as a self-obsessed Party lay on the management consultant's couch, looked at charts and diagrams of very large circles inter-connected with arrows supposedly illustrative of a supposedly revived Party, and switched off the reality support machine.

The Liberals died as a party of government because Labour rose. Organized working-class politics was Labour's *raison d'être* and the Liberals' death knell. Tory comforters said that no such comparable, deep-seated, social and economic changes lay behind Labour's new hegemony in 1997. The Liberal victory of 1906 had reflected a decade-old vogue for collectivism and organized social action under the label of 'new Liberalism'. Labour's win in 1945 had been prepared by the wartime experience of the command economy and the solidarity of communal effort. A scientific revolution in a social laboratory dressed Labour's victors of 1964–66 in the white coats and hopes of technocracy as social change emerged through the crucible of nuclear power, comprehensive schools and high-rise flats. Surely, reasoned some blithe spirits, no such large-scale patterns of change in belief and conduct underlay the Labour victory of 1997. It was all, they maintained, explicable and recoverable. The Tories had lied, Labour had pitched camp on the Tories' traditional ground, and the electorate had, only for the moment, given them the benefit of the doubt.

Labour's victory reached further than the grasp of the Tory Panglossian mind. The extent of the Conservative intellectual collapse meant there would be no Tory equivalent of Anthony Crosland's *The Future of Socialism*, the revisionist and prophetic text which, published in the very depths of the party's Babylonian exile in 1956, showed how Labour would have to abandon the dogma of nationalization and find new means of attaining the goal of social equality. Having lived off the intellectual capital of the 1980s for so long, and been so suspicious of mind in the 1990s, the Tory cupboard was bare of doctrinal nutrients. Of course, New Labour's condition was similar – but, with a prettier cupboard, it mattered less. Why?

Part of the answer was that modern British politics, in its incapacity to deal with great issues, offered instead a novelettish preoccupation with a romantic cult of the political personality as icon in a media age. From the court at Windsor, where a minor Scottish public schoolboy might feel especially at home, to the chic of Cool Britannia, where the restaurateur, the designer and the fashionable footballer were king, the beautifully well-mannered and eirenic Blair was an effortless winner. For this was the age that valued the expression of emotion, the pursuit of authenticity and the achievement of self-realization. We were all existentialists now at a time when it was not easy to distinguish the compassionate from the charlatan. The age was sceptical about more government and it disliked high taxation, but it did want to feel good about itself and its feelings. It was ill at ease with the protocol, the suits and the stiffness of traditional institutions, but it liked the excitement of global communications, the chic of designer values and the fruits of capitalism. Style was all, language and imagery were minimalist, and the cool of charity had replaced the heat of politics. Intimacy and candour were cultivated by an epoch whose high priest was Tony Blair and whose high priestess was the Princess of Wales. Modernity had bypassed the Tories completely. They just didn't get it. There was a terrible desert behind Hague's dumbness in the face of that death.

The Conservative historian Lewis Namier once wrote that 'What matters most about political ideas is the underlying emotions, the music to which ideas are a mere libretto, often of a very inferior quality.' If Blair's depth lay in the recognition of shallowness and its political uses, he also understood the music of modern Britain. There was much dissonance in that music as a new 'condition of England' question acquired predominance. Here, too, Labour was a beneficiary, albeit an unwitting one, of the new darkness, unhappiness and insecurity that reached a crescendo during the last phase of the long Tory years. The liberation of the 1960s had brought forth monstrous statistics, with 165,000 divorces taking place each year by 1993, crimes of violence increasing from a mere 6000 in 1950 to 239,000 in 1996, and young male suicides trebling since 1970. Conservatives in the 1980s had intensified the post-war waves of increased consumerism and of rising expectation. But, in pandering to materialistic gratification of the self, Thatcher's Conservatives proved themselves indifferent to wider and richer notions of selfhood rooted in culture, society and self-examination. The result was a very despairing country, and New Labour's victory was won on a wave of Prozac. If women were now more autonomous, men were also less rooted in their families, and relations between the genders were played out on a dark and confused arena. Birthrates were falling, life expectancy rising, the population ageing, the structures of the family decaying, and job security disappearing. When, therefore, the Tory leader unveiled his organizational charts and mouthed his mantras, he simply reminded his audience of a jargonized world of work where 'delayering' was ubiquitous, 'restructuring' a constant threat, and alienation a daily diet. In these circumstances, a night out with the local Conservatives seemed to promise some grim vicissitudes.

These were diffuse, if powerful, miseries, and New Labour could not hope to be their continuing political legatee. But as the end of the century approached, Labour had shown how a party could adapt and respond to a prevailing ethos, especially when a commanding personality was able to give form to that reaction and expression. A political party, after all, is no archetype, an immutable ideal form determining reality, but an organism that can live and breathe, decay and die. Tory ascent and Labour decline, the Tory fall from grace and New Labour's ascendancy, all reflected the deep structures of individual British hopes and fears as well as the grander, more impersonal, social and economic forces. But these dramas were always played out against the backcloth provided by leaders whose style determined the form of a party's response to the challenge of the age.

Posterity shrouds those responses with an aura of inevitability, but a little reflection and counter-factual history shows us how easily a different leadership would have led to a different history. Margaret Thatcher, for example, could easily have been a successful, traditional, authoritarian Labour leader of a very recognizable kind – an Ernest Bevin, perhaps, in drag. An East Midlands, meritocratic scholarship girl on the make would have made an appropriate heir to James Callaghan. Indeed, the practical effect of her 1979 victory was to continue many of Callaghan's economic policies of retrenchment and reform, the Labour Government having long since realized that Britain's high-spending days were over. John Major, as a South London politician, came from the conformist, controlled municipal world created by Herbert Morrison, London's Labour king of the 1930s and 1940s. He could have advanced far in that new democratic order and landed the Labour Party with the plight of the Conservatives of today. Thatcher's visit to Blair in Number 10 for a foreign-policy discussion shortly after the general election showed whom she saw as her own true heir and provided the most compelling instance of how room at the top creates its own successors regardless of party.

However, the very breadth of New Labour's coalition meant that, unless nurtured, it could dissolve as an insubstantial pageant, much as the Tories' own coalition had done. Still, Labour understood the provisionality of its approval and governed accordingly with a still soliciting eye directed towards public opinion.

Ultimately, it was constitutional reform and the introduction of some form of proportional representation that gave Labour the most assured prospect of a perpetual left-of-centre coalition which would reflect the predominant strand in Britain's twentieth-century politics and entrench the Conservative Party's tangential relevance. Lord Jenkins of Hillhead, the Brahmin of British social democracy, emerged to oversee a Government commission that would report late in 1998; a recommendation of an alternative voting system could be implemented even before the next general election. His monument to social democracy would then be found in the very fabric and interstices of British political life, and the politics of the 'radical centre' would be provided with a cornerstone. The Conservatives had lost their hold on the electoral system that had allowed them for so long, and against the odds, to flourish like the green bay tree.

Tories damned the enterprise and lamented Britain's political merger with a form of continental European politics dominated by coalitions. They bewailed the death of another form of British 'exceptionalism'. But in doing so they were amnesiac or ignorant. Future commentators will be struck by the eccentric nature of Britain's two-party 'stability' in the post-war years when seen from a longer perspective. Labour's rise, the Liberals' split on home rule and free trade together with their subsequent decline, the Tories' divisions on protectionism, produced in the first half of the twentieth century a kaleidoscopic pattern of shifting alliances and interests which were no different, in essence, from the experiences of French, German and Italian politics. When, in 1997, the Liberal Democrats acquired their representation on a new Cabinet Committee chaired by the Prime Minister and formed to discuss issues of shared concern, it became clear that New Labour also meant New Whigs. An ascendancy had returned and the shades of Macaulay and Trevelyan were appeased.

Hague showed that on the European issue he had to maintain his leadership by exercising the same art that he displayed in attaining it. Peter Temple-Morris, the Tory MP whose European convictions and flirtatious duet with Blair led to the withdrawal of the Whip in autumn 1997, accurately summed up Hague's attitude on the currency as: 'Never. But never say never in politics. So let's say never for ten years.' The Shadow Cabinet declared opposition in principle for the period of two Parliaments, after which they would revisit the scene of the battle. Sceptics found the position temporizing, Euro-philes thought it an Oedipal act of self-inflicted blindness, and the European-minded David Curry resigned as the Shadow Agriculture Minister. In February 1998, Iain Duncan Smith, the new leader of the sceptics, and David Heathcoat-Amory dined privately with Margaret Thatcher and told her that the only reason they were in British politics was to stop Britain's entry into the Single Currency. Even Tony Blair's confidante was reportedly surprised by the depth of their indifference to wider concerns of Tory revival. Her guests may simply have told her what they thought she wanted to hear. None the less, the evening showed the narrow and obsessional nature of the Tory story. Nor was the discontent confined to sceptics and Euro-philiacs. By the beginning of March Archie Hamilton, as Chairman of the 1922 Executive, was beginning to voice his weariness with the in-bred shallowness and vulgarity of the circle dominating Hague in his Private Office.

On the 27th of February 1998, the euro, Europe's new currency and talisman of unity, was effectively born with the announcement that France, Germany and Italy satisfied the criteria laid down in the Maastricht Treaty for entry into the Single Currency on the 1st of January 1999. Sceptics observed the generous interpretation of the Treaty's provisions that had allowed France, for example, to use the France Télécom pension fund as a massive contribution to reducing the country's public deficit following that company's privatization. But EMU had always been a political project – the Treaty having been written by politicians for their own convenience. Maastricht had always allowed for an interpretation that demonstrated goodwill and 'progress towards' the criteria rather than a mechanical application of their significance. An act of political will underlay the decision of France's socialist Government not to fight speculation against France's entry into Monetary Union by raising interest rates. Insistent French and German hope and conviction had kept Italy's interest rates down as the country travelled the road to EMU.

Meanwhile, the provisions of the Social Chapter, as well as a minimum wage, drew ever nearer, and soon Tories would have to accept, and explain, the inevitable. Within less than a generation, the Conservatives would turn into revisionist historians of their own past. Accounts would be offered of why the lack of a a minimum wage had led to lazy employers who relied on low wages. Such employers, it would be said, had been a brake on innovation and productivity in the British economy, low demand being fed by low disposable incomes. The revisionists of the future could summon up nineteenth-century evidence, and recall how the reform of the Corn Laws had been the cry of employers who wanted cheap food so that they could pay their employees less. The episode, after all, had been part of the story of Britain's economic decline rather than a boldly free-trade and Tory-sponsored contribution to economic advance. That was why innovation and enterprise had leapt, in the middle of the nineteenth century, to the more dynamic world of railways and technology which invested, paid well, boosted disposable incomes, created demand, and advanced prosperity's cause. Tories would have to accept these conclusions of history and apply them uneasily as they sought to understand the economy of the early twenty-first century. The scale of their late-twentieth-century opposition to the Social Chapter, and their defence of low wages, would be rewritten as they struggled to find a place in the textbooks of the future.

The prospect, indeed, was one of continuous Tory retreat into a series of receding last ditches occupied by a diminished band of perplexed subalterns trying to supply rationalizations of their regretful accommodation with the age in which they found themselves. One former Conservative Member of the European Parliament, John de Courcy Ling, looking at what passed for life in the Conservative Associations, remarked: 'They're just like the local branches of the British Legion – full of old people who have fought, and continue to fight, past wars.' The analogy was a good one. England, after all, was less a state than an assemblage of autonomous corporations jealous of their liberties. The 'Conservative Party' could take its place among the MCC and the Corporation of the City of London, the National Trust and the Inns of Court, Oxford and Cambridge Colleges, and the Athenaeum Club, the Brigade of Guards and the BBC as one among many such institutions. The Single Currency alone retained its power to summon up a few remaining forces for a last divisive stand in occupation of the few sods of suburban Home Counties soil the Tories could still regard as their own turf.

Fantasy had sustained and misled the Conservatives in Government and continued to do so in Opposition. Fantasy about the essentially Conservative-voting nature of England and how a Labour Party, lacking the experience of governing after eighteen years, would fall apart, a prey to Civil Service wiles. Fantasy about the exaggeratedly Conservative propensity of the acquisitive impulse and about how Hague and Major would 'win through in the end', and against all the available evidence of public opinion. Fantasy about their own unique abilities in economic management and how Britain's political destiny could be considered apart from that of her European neighbours. Fantasy about the existence of a 'Tory Philosophy' rather than a bundle of sensations, intuitions and attitudes. Perhaps the most expensive fantasy of all was the one about the 'Thatcher Revolution' which would never die. It was etched deep on the foolishly grinning faces of her acolytes as they gathered around the Tory Medea who arrived to endorse Hague outside the House of Commons on the 18th of June 1997.

By 1998 Thatcherism was, like Marxism, not so much untrue as irrelevant. Its gods of the copybook headings had been demythologized and had become part of a general consensus. Its detritus, a late-romantic cult of leadership, was appropriated by a Labour Prime Minister who, in his public indebtedness, gratified the sad cravings of the cult's foundress for posterity's knock on the door.

On the 8th of February 1998 there died the Tory Romantic who, more than any other politician alive, had gloried in the blessed English continuities and celebrated the instincts of those who 'felt no country but this to be their own'. Enoch Powell's mannered cadences had celebrated on behalf of the English, 'a palace near the great City which the Romans built at a ford of the River Thames, to which men resorted out of all England to speak on behalf of their fellows, a thing called "Parliament"'. A few atavistic loins could still stir at the sound of that bugle-call across the sad shires, but Powell's death coincided with the effective end of a quarter century of intermittent debate about Britain and her 'European destiny'. European institutions had been so indelibly grafted upon the old British stock that paradoxically the anti-European cry of keeping Britain's institutions 'sovereign and independent' appeared to be a revolutionary one – and England is not a land fit for revolutionaries. Powell's elegies, 'felt in the blood and felt along the heart', struck few chords among the millennial English as they acquiesced in the seeping away of their Parliament's powers. New forms of that power were emerging on the horizon in anticipated English assemblies, in the Edinburgh Parliament and the Cardiff Assembly, and in the reach of the European institutions. In this process, the House of Commons emerged as just another rather disappointing and overrated English establishment.

The Tories had bought a myth, not just of continuity, but of permanence. The irony was that, in so doing, their roots in the soil of democratic England had withered and could not sustain them in the face of the descending storm. The Tories had become an alien anachronism, and the English turned on them with the unforgiving hatred they have historically reserved for foreigners. Through the sacred grove of Toryism a great gale had blown. The rest was desecrated silence.

THE GUILTY

THERE WERE many 'guilty men', for the Conservative decline and fall that culminated in the defeat of the 1st of May 1997 was long drawn out. The day was one of historical importance and, like all such events, it illustrated both the froth of the immediate and the currents of the deep. By their actions and their beliefs, the twenty whose guilt was most profound caused and illuminated that fatal confluence. Although happily extant at the time of writing, these political actors will undoubtedly exercise the talents of future obituarists. Here follow portraits which seek to explain for posterity the dramatic functions performed by 'the guilty'.

Blackwell, Norman Roy (Lord Blackwell)

Norman Blackwell was born in 1952 and educated at Latymer Upper School, an academic boys' day school in West London, Trinity College, Cambridge and the Wharton School of Business at the University of Pennsylvania. He was married with five children. From 1978 to 1995 he worked for McKinsey and Co., and was elected a partner in 1984. In 1986 and 1987 he took leave of absence to work in the Prime Minister's Policy Unit at Number 10. He returned to Downing Street to head that Unit at the beginning of 1995 and remained there until the 1997 general election. On leaving Government service, he became Director of Group Development with NatWest. He was made a life peer on Major's recommendation in 1997. He was a member of the Royal Automobile Club and a good musician.

In his slight physical presence, Blackwell appeared to personify the Conservative intellectual collapse. His was a recessive presence, and at the beginning of meetings he would offer eager handshakes in the two-handed manner associated with his master, John Major, with whom he shared a second Christian name. Political staff at Number 10 claimed that he had been Major's fifth choice to run the Policy Unit; so dark were the Tories' days that other approaches to take up this high office were rebuffed. Blackwell's great legacy to the Conservative Party was his five themes, which provided the framework both for the constituency consultation of 1995/96 and for the general election manifesto. Blackwell was a high priest within the well-trodden cloisters of management consultancy. His characteristic *modus operandi* was therefore to concentrate on method and process – once a problem had been categorized, he thought that it had been solved. But Conservative policy required a force that was both more intellectually formidable and better attuned to democratic opinion. As the first, disastrous election results were announced on the late evening of the 1st of May, Blackwell admitted that the Conservatives had never been able to touch the Labour Party during the campaign.

John Major enjoyed working with Blackwell. Like the Prime Minister, Blackwell had little feel for the English language, and his prose was flat. He could neither express in speech nor communicate in writing the urgency he must often have felt as election day approached. At least in theory, he was the equal of Whitehall's Permanent Secretaries, but he lacked authority, and could not exert political will over a diffuse system. This mattered during the two years before an election, when the Government was seeking policies that would create a mounting sense of political immediacy and interest. He failed to engage the attention of Permanent Secretaries, who devoted their energies to preparing their Departments for the arrival of new, Labour, masters. Blackwell was an unpolitical and essentially timorous figure, whose period at Number 10 equipped him for his inevitable return, at an exalted level, to the corporate arts that were his true métier.

Bottomley, Rt Hon Virginia Hilda Brunette Maxwell

Virginia Bottomley was born in 1948, the daughter of John Garnett, a liberal-minded Old Rugbeian Anglican who promoted the merits of industrial co-operation and the removal of class conflict. He ran the Industrial Society and was a member of the Court of Inquiry that advised the Heath Government in its conflict with the National Union of Mineworkers in 1972. She was educated at Putney High School, an independent girls' day school, the University of Essex and the London School of Economics. From 1973 to 1984 she was a psychiatric social worker in south London. In 1967 she married Peter Bottomley, who was elected to Parliament in 1975 and, after she was elected MP for Surrey South West in 1984, became her most spirited defender in all her travails. They had three children.

Bottomley's advance was continuous. In 1988 she became a Junior Environment Minister, and then served as Minister of State at Health from 1989 to 1992. In 1992 she joined the Cabinet as Secretary of State in the same department, and acquired the reputation for liberal fanaticism that plagued her until her removal from that office in 1995. Bottomley's paternal aunt (herself a London County Councillor and prominent Fabian) was the first wife of Douglas Jay (later Lord Jay of Battersea), a rebarbative and astringently Wykehamical presence in the early Wilson Cabinets as President of the Board of Trade from 1964 to 1967. Belief in the rule of experts and in the guiding hand of the Whitehall committee was thus in the genes and led Bottomley to display a benevolent intolerance in the face of public opinion. Expensive and unnecessary changes to London's hospitals, the product of a credulous approach to modern management theory, resulted in closures and central-ization. Bottomley worked hard and worried about the absence of staff at weekends from Richmond House, her Whitehall fiefdom. 'What would you do about weekends?' she asked her Junior Minister, Tom Sackville, a figure who lacked her zealotry. 'Have one,' he replied. Bottomley was Thatcher-like in her quick-fire deployment of facts and statistics but lost the argument as the Tories' custodian of the National Health Service. From 1995 to 1997 she receded from public view as Secretary of State for National Heritage, and presided over the nationalization of gambling through the creation of the National Lottery – an appropriate anti-climax for the career of a Tory Fabian.

Burns, Sir Terence ('Terry')

Terrence Burns was born in 1944 and educated at Houghton-Le-Spring Grammar School, County Durham, and the University of Manchester. His early career was as a 'business' economist, and he rose to become a Professor of Economics at the London Business School. In 1980 he was appointed Chief Economic Adviser to the Treasury and Head of the Government Economic Service. He was knighted in 1983. In 1991 he became Permanent Secretary to the Treasury. He was married with three children, and belonged to the Reform Club and also to Ealing Golf Club.

Burns' appointment to high office from outside the ranks of the Treasury and the Civil Service was one of the early signs of Thatcher's resolve to break free of the mandarinate. It seemed to betoken a response to the imagined needs of 'British business' and was effectively a political appointment. Her appointee played a full role in the ten-year cycle of preparation for Britain's entry to the European Single Currency, which started with Chancellor Lawson's decision to allow the pound to shadow the Deutschmark in the late 1980s. The economic forecaster's dismal science failed to predict the effects of the 'Lawson boom' as well as the depth and extent of Britain's recession in the early 1990s. As one of the architects of Britain's entry into the ERM, Burns offered advice that led directly to the closure of British companies and businesses and to negative equity, whereby mortgages outstripped the value of the properties concerned. The first major recession to hit south-east England supplied the smouldering backdrop to the Tory disasters of the 1990s. In Whitehall's more demotic corridors, Sir Terry was known as 'Teflon Tel', on account of his capacity to survive as an adviser successive economic catastrophes. Still Permanent Secretary to Her Majesty's Treasury in 1998, Sir Terence continued to offer his advice to Whitehall's new masters.

Clarke, Rt Hon Kenneth ('Ken')

Kenneth Clarke was born in 1940, the son of an electrician who became a watchmaker, and educated at Nottingham High School, an independent day school, and Gonville and Caius College, Cambridge. In 1964 he married the Cambridge mediaevalist Gillian Edwards, who became an important influence

on his political views. They had two children. He was called to the Bar at
Gray's Inn in 1963, became MP for the Rushcliffe division of
Nottinghamshire in 1970, and took silk as a Parliamentarian in 1980. In 1993
he became Chancellor of the Exchequer. He was very fond of his Club, the
Garrick, where he was much liked and admired as a wide-ranging conversa-
tionalist and a man of generous sympathies.

Clarke was the commanding Conservative politician of the 1990s, and
lacked cant. By 1997 he had been in the Cabinet continuously for twelve
years, first as Paymaster-General from 1985 to 1987, then as Chancellor of the
Duchy of Lancaster from 1987 to 1988, Secretary of State for Health from
1988 to 1990, Secretary of State for Education and Science from 1990 to 1992
and Home Secretary from 1992 to 1993. Clarke's public popularity in the
mid-1990s obscured his earlier battles with the public services. Once
resolved, conflicts with the ambulance workers' and nurses' unions, and then
with the teachers', earned him Tory plaudits as a courageous Minister.

Clarke's politics were defined by 'Europe' and by an advertised belief that
European integration was the inevitable solution to the continent's past
conflicts. Clarke enraged his Party's Euro-sceptics by dismissing their views as
the ranting of an insecure minority. They were, he thought, culpably ignorant in
their failure to recognize European inevitability. Perhaps their closest cousins,
in his view, were the obscurantist Empire Loyalists of an earlier generation.
Both he and his wife, by contrast, developed an open-minded curiosity about the
continent, its history and its future. He was an apolitical Chancellor whose
custodianship of the Treasury was marked by caution and by an aversion to
using taxation as a way of influencing personal conduct. Although prepared to
lead his Party, he was not prepared to be led by its atavism, for he had immense
self-confidence and pride. These qualities were obscured by his deployment of
the mannerisms associated with a highly successful, professional provincial.
The piping tones of the cut-glass youth who addressed the Cambridge Union
had been displaced long since by the crescendo of eliding Midlands vowels that
marked the speech of the mature man.

Clarke gave every appearance of being at home in the world, if not in the
Parliamentary Party. Mastery of the canons of classical jazz completed the
democratic picture. Some thought the artistry of his 'bloke-ishness' lay in its
artful display. In this judgement, the professionally hard-bitten displayed the
naivety of cynicism. Clarke, though complex, was in the happy position of
deriving political advantage from a life lived as authentically as a public man
could manage. In 1997 he was the clear choice of the non-parliamentary
Conservative masses for the leadership of their Party. After his defeat, Clarke
displayed realism about his Party's desuetude, and developed a lucrative and
varied City and business career. Doubtless he echoed the musical sentiment of
the late Ray Charles – 'It Should've Been Me' – but wasted little time in
reflection on that fact.

Dorrell, Rt Hon Stephen James

Stephen Dorrell, who was born in 1952, belonged to the younger generation of Conservative politicians. He was educated at Uppingham School and Brasenose College, Oxford. Married with two children, he was MP for Loughborough from 1979, transferring in 1997 to the safer delights of Charnwood, also in Leicestershire, when redrawn constituency boundaries made his original seat a Labour one. He had served on the Board of Christian Aid and was interested in flying.

In the mid-1990s Dorrell was a promising Conservative politician with Christian convictions and European belief. He had entered politics under the patronage of Peter Walker (Lord Walker of Worcester), in whose Worcester constituency Dorrell's merchant family owned a department store. The Thatcher 1980s were not the Dorrell decade, and he waited until 1987 for recognition. Following three years in the Whips' Office, the 1990s started promisingly when Major gave him a junior post in the Department of Health in 1990. From 1992 to 1994 he was a distinguished Financial Secretary to the Treasury, but treated his promotion to the Cabinet as Secretary of State for National Heritage, a job he disliked, with an ill-concealed bad grace. As Secretary of State for Health from 1995 to 1997, he succeeded in containing the endemic political difficulties inherent in that post. He had personal charm but, realizing that he needed to adopt a thoughtful manner, succeeded instead in displaying a grim and gaunt Cromwellian mien. From 1995 onwards he made unconvincing and maladroit attempts to divest himself of his Euro-phile reputation, and kept his ears to the ground straining for the sounds of the imminent leadership battle. It was a conflict from which he was compelled to flee in its opening stage when he found meagre support among Conservative MPs.

Garel-Jones, Rt Hon William Armand Thomas Tristan
(Lord Garel-Jones)

Tristan Garel-Jones was born in 1941 in Llangennech, a semi-industrial village on the South Wales coast near Llanelli. His mother, Meriel Williams, was a notable singer of Eisteddfod-ic distinction, but disliked her compatriots. Her son inherited a full measure of this ancestral hatred. He was educated locally and at The King's School, Canterbury, where he played rugby football. He left school to help his family to run a language school in Madrid. After working as a merchant banker, he was elected MP for Watford in 1979, a seat he had nursed constantly since his first attempt at election there in 1974. From 1982 to 1990 he was a Government Whip, subsequently serving as Minister of State for Foreign and Commonwealth Affairs from 1990 to 1993. He was a member of the Beefsteak Club, smoked vigorously and drank little. His wife was Spanish, and they had five children. When in London they lived in Catherine Place, an attractive Westminster backwater. It was here, according to Thatcher's circle, that disaffected Ministers met to plot the post-Thatcher future once her fall had become inevitable in the November 1990 leadership contest. Garel-Jones did not stand in the 1997 general election, and was made a life peer on Major's recommendation.

Garel-Jones was too obvious a Machiavel to be a consistently successful one. He enjoyed his demonization by Euro-sceptics and other insurgents as he lurked in corridors over-hearing conversations. He vigorously served Margaret Thatcher, with whose instincts he was out of sympathy, latterly as Deputy Chief Whip. He spoke Spanish fluently and with a Mediterranean ease that may have owed much to his childhood bilingualism in Welsh and English. He was the Tories' man of Maastricht since his Foreign Office brief was European affairs, and he gave every appearance of enjoying the imposition of that legislation on the Parliamentary Party. Like many who were close to Major, he did not advance as much as he had hoped, and never became a Cabinet Minister. Major had been prepared to appoint him Secretary of State for Wales, and asked Garel-Jones why a Welsh-speaker should not crave the office. 'Because, Prime Minister,' he replied, 'the two things are not related. What the Welsh like is for a clever Englishman to be in charge.' Like Clarke, he lacked cant, and he attributed lunacy too easily to Euro-sceptics whom he thought noisy and fractious. When he looked at them he could have echoed the Duke of Wellington: 'What is the meaning of a Party if they don't follow their leader? 'Damn 'em; let 'em go.' The problem was that the Conservative Party lacked leadership. Garel-Jones' future included his return to the City of London as it prepared for the introduction of the euro.

Gummer, Rt Hon John Selwyn

John Gummer, known originally as John Selwyn Gummer, was born in 1939, the son of a Canon of Rochester Cathedral. His brother, Peter, to whom he was close, was Chairman of Shandwick plc, a public relations company, and the recipient of much Tory political patronage, he was made a life peer on Major's recommendation in 1996. Gummer was educated at King's School, Rochester and Selwyn College, Cambridge, which in the late 1950s remained a largely Anglican and confessional enclave. From 1970 to 1974 he was MP for Lewisham West, and returned to the House of Commons in 1979 as a Suffolk MP, representing Eye until 1983, and subsequently Suffolk Coastal. He first enjoyed public attention as Chairman of the Conservative Party from 1983 to 1985. There followed two posts as a Minister of State, at the Ministry of Agriculture, Fisheries and Food and then at the Department of the Environment, before Thatcher allowed him into the Cabinet as Agriculture Minister in 1989. He remained in that office until 1993, when he became Secretary of State for the Environment. He was married to a former secretary to Sir Edward Heath and they had four children.

Gummer was a vigorous survivor in office and, although much mocked, was important because he illustrated the survival of a threatened style of Anglican Conservatism. His advance on the path to Rome in the 1990s did not alter the public view that he offered a type of ethical, Church-of-England earnestness. Like Bottomley, Gummer believed in the regenerative capacity of Government, and enjoyed his imperial powers of central planning at the Department of the Environment, where he vigorously enforced the norms of the quango state. But he was no Fabian, and he had no belief in the perfectibility of man. His Conservative politics were rooted in the political recognition of the consequences of the Fall and the reality of Original Sin. He had deep-seated, if rarely advertised, beliefs in European unification as an aspect of the defence of Christendom. He understood the coherence of Europe's Christian culture and how all Europeans are the legatees of Charlemagne. Gummer was a Carolingian Conservative.

Hague, Rt Hon William Jefferson

William Hague was born in 1961 in Yorkshire, where his parents ran a soft-drinks company. He was educated at Wath-upon-Dearne Comprehensive School and Magdalen College, Oxford, where he read PPE. His presidency of the Oxford Union was much admired, and his debating skills widely recognized. He joined McKinsey and Co. in 1983 and trained as a management consultant. In February 1989 he succeeded Sir Leon Brittan, a friend and mentor, as the MP for Richmond, North Yorkshire, on the latter's translation to Brussels as a European Commissioner. In 1993 he became a Junior Social Security Minister and subsequently Minister of State in the same Department. Two years later he joined the Cabinet as Secretary of State for Wales following John Redwood's resignation. In 1997 he was elected leader of the Conservative Party and thus became Leader of the Opposition. He subsequently married the daughter of a former BBC Wales newsreader. He gave no indication of enjoying a life either of the mind or of the spirit, and was entirely absorbed within the institutional structures of his Party.

Hague had a pleasingly polite personal manner allied with an ambitious understanding of men and institutions. Whether he understood modern Britain was another matter. He was the master of a fine, if mannered, Oxford Union style of debate which scored points but somehow missed the heart of the matter. Like Neil Kinnock, another Opposition leader, he understood his task to be that of an effective modernizer of his Party's decayed structures, and set about their reform. Talk of 'decentralization' and 'involvement' obscured the extent to which his changes entrenched his position as leader and made him more secure in his office than either Thatcher or Major. However, Kinnock's reforms presaged a doctrinal revolution in Labour Party belief. Although undeniably good at central control, Hague lacked creative political imagination and surrounded himself with a tight circle of close friends.

Heath, Rt Hon Sir Edward Richard George ('Ted')

Edward Heath was born in 1916 in Broadstairs, Kent, the son of a local carpenter; his mother was a housemaid before her marriage. He was educated at Chatham House School, a local grammar school, and Balliol College, Oxford, where he was an Organ Scholar. He was proud of his association with such an historical nursery of progressivism, and was an Honorary Fellow of his College. As an undergraduate he went cycling on the continent with Madron Seligman, one of his few close friends, who later became a Member of the European Parliament. Heath became convinced of the centrality of Europe to Britain's late-imperial and then post-imperial prospects. The rise of National Socialism and the consequences of war, he believed, transformed the nature and extent of Britain's sphere of political interest. Heath served in the Royal Artillery during World War II, was mentioned in despatches, and rose to the rank of Lieutenant-Colonel. He became an administrative civil servant in 1946, but resigned to become the prospective parliamentary candidate for Bexley. He was elected in 1950, and held the seat thereafter.

Heath spent the 1950s in the Whips' Office, serving as Deputy Chief Whip from 1953 to 1955 and then as Chief Whip until 1959 – Sir Anthony Eden thought him 'the best Chief Whip the Party has ever had'. He entered the Cabinet as Minister of Labour in 1959, and as Lord Privy Seal from 1960 to 1963 spoke on Foreign Office matters in the House of Commons. In this latter capacity he was in charge of negotiations for Britain's entry to the European Economic Communities. From 1963 to 1964 he was President of the Board of Trade. In 1965, he was elected leader of the Conservative Party, and thus became Leader of the Opposition. After the unexpected Conservative victory in the 1970 general election he took office as Prime Minister. Following the Conservative defeat in February 1974, he again served as Leader of the Opposition until his replacement, which he greatly resented, by Margaret Thatcher a year later. Never a politician to cultivate the backbench mind, he had lost the support of the Parliamentary Party.

Heath was a 'Church of England man' of a decidedly old-fashioned kind. Music and sailing, both self-absorbed activities, were important to him. He was a bachelor and in his latter days lived in splendour, which some found inexplicable, in a Georgian house in the Cathedral Close at Salisbury. In 1992 he became a Knight of the Garter – a signal distinction that he greatly valued, since he had a high regard for his Sovereign.

Heath was fundamental to the Conservative decline and fall. His interventions in the politics of the 1990s remained lethal and vigorous. He criticized Major's handling of the Nolan Report as an interference with the privileges of the House of Commons. He judged the Back to Basics campaign to be an incoherent regression and considered Major's European policy, in so far as he had one, a contemptible betrayal of his own legacy. By the end of the century it looked as if Heath had got his way. Britain's New Labour Government approached his own in its European-mindedness. As it became clear that 'Thatcherism' had been an epiphenomenon in Britain's wider political life, it was also evident that Heath's long-term European artillery had been more powerful than Thatcher's firework display. The enduring irony of Heath's position was that it was he, rather than Thatcher, who killed the tradition of Tory liberalism he claimed to represent.

Heath's managerialism of the spirit failed to arouse European ardour in the British. The Government over which he presided had been elected on the promise of modernizing Britain and her institutions. Trade union legislation, reformed industrial relations and the recovery of market disciplines were advocated as the path towards greater prosperity and self-reliance. But the coal-miners' strike of early 1972 destroyed the Government's authority, and it had to accede to a 32 per cent pay increase. Rising unemployment in the case of Upper Clyde Shipbuilders, and fear of the loss of a national asset in the case of Rolls-Royce, forced the Government to return to the post-war tradition of nationalization, while the Industry Act promoted substantial State intervention. Britain's 'one-nation Tory' Prime Minister presided over a period of industrial and social conflict. Heath may not have believed much of the free market rhetoric he espoused in the late 1960s as a way of getting into Government. Nonetheless, his return to the post-war norms of economic management proved just as effective in engendering social conflict as had the original abandonment of those norms. Both the broad and the narrow way had been attempted and were thought to have failed. Heath's liberal Toryism became associated with an illiberal regime of State control and doomed policies on prices and incomes.

The collapse was largely the result of Heath's abrasive personality. He treated his Party extremely roughly and in this respect was strangely like Major. They both had a similar training in the Whips' Office. Both shared the inability to understand, and therefore to manage, dissent that could be produced by the harsher application of such a training. They also had in common a preoccupation with Party loyalism that always seems to plague those of uncertain social origins. The difference between them lay in Europe. Heath had a very clear vision of where he was going, and was prepared to drag his Party with him. By contrast, to survive in office Major relied on the artful cultivation of his Party's European divisions. Both broke their Party's spirit, and Heath made Thatcher possible.

Heseltine, Rt Hon Michael Ray Dibdin

The Conservative Party's Great Gatsby was born in Swansea, the son of a structural engineer who had been an officer in the Royal Engineers. He was educated at Shrewsbury School and Pembroke College, Oxford. In 1962 he married Anne Williams, who entertained artistic interests, and they had three children, one of whom, Annabel, was a society journalist. Heseltine, formed perhaps by the louche and mercantile brashness of his native heath, understood money and how to make it. His fortune was based on the Haymarket Press, which he founded and built up into a major magazine-publishing group. From 1966 to 1974 he was MP for Tavistock, moving in that year to Henley, which he represented thereafter. From 1972 to 1974 he served Edward Heath as Minister for Aerospace. In 1979 Margaret Thatcher appointed him Secretary of State for the Environment and subsequently, in 1983, Secretary of State for Defence, a post he held until his resignation in 1986. Four years later he challenged Thatcher for the leadership of the Conservative Party. Although he succeeded in deposing her, he was defeated by John Major, who brought him back to Cabinet as Environment Secretary once again. From 1992 to 1995 he served as President of the Board of Trade, and from 1995 to 1997 he held the posts of Deputy Prime Minister and First Secretary of State. In the 1997 leadership election, when arriving to cast his vote at the third ballot, he told the crowd assembled outside the Committee Room, 'I'm here to vote for – Redwood.' A romantic-materialist, Heseltine had no religion and was resolutely unintellectual.

Heseltine liked, and appreciated, Government as a grand managerialist enterprise to be administered in the spirit of a large public company. He had an intuitive flair for understanding issues of policy, and preferred conversation to documentation as a way of clarifying and deciding such issues. He had little knowledge of, or feel for, the politics, culture and history of other European countries; for him, the European Union was a business consortium. His imperial longings were ill adapted to the quotidian life of a medium-sized European power. The usefulness of 'Europe' to Heseltine was that it provided him with a platform on which such longings might be expressed and gratified. However, it also had another purpose. In January 1986 he resigned from the Cabinet and accused the Prime Minister of intriguing against him in the matter of Westland Helicopters. The Defence Secretary had wanted a group of European manufacturers to take over the ailing firm, rather than the American United Technologies Corporation. Margaret Thatcher's reputation for veracity was tarnished, and she was consequently a less effective Prime Minister from 1986 to 1990 than she had been earlier.

Heseltine's advocacy of Europe in what remained of the 1980s, rather like Winston Churchill's espousal of rearmament in the 1930s, was an aspect of his belief that he should be leader of the Conservative Party. That ambition had been his lodestar since young manhood, although in temperament and belief he was akin to a Lloyd George Liberal. In the early 1980s he had been a vigorous believer in the sale of council houses and associated social changes. But Heseltine believed less in 'capitalism' than in 'enterprise'. As 'Minister for Merseyside' for twelve months after the riots in Toxteth, Liverpool, in 1981, he showed administrative vigour in the nineteenth-century municipal tradition of Joseph Chamberlain.

What remained of the Tory patriciate regarded Heseltine with suspicion as a Swansea tradesman. But Thatcher's island-state and small-business ethic were equally alien to him. When his star shone bright, he could command the House of Commons with his manufactured contempt for the Labour Party, and his Welsh oratory stirred the Conservative Party's Conferences. But in truth he was a reserved and shy figure, whose pursuits were solitary. He was a fisherman, and spent much of his time on his estate on the Oxfordshire-Northamptonshire border, where he gardened passionately and worked on the development of his arboretum. Heseltine attracted intense loyalty among his dwindling band of admirers, and there was some pathos in his enforced withdrawal from public life during the first weekend after the general election, when he suffered an angina attack.

Hogg, Rt Hon Douglas Martin

Douglas Hogg was born in 1945, the son of Quintin Hogg, who became better known to posterity as Lord Hailsham of Marylebone, Lord Chancellor under both Heath and Thatcher and a High Tory theorist concerning the rule of law, the centrality of Christianity and the nature of modern Conservatism. He was educated at Eton, where he was an Oppidan Scholar, and Christ Church, Oxford. He was called to the Bar at Lincoln's Inn in 1968, and took silk as a Parliamentarian in 1990. In 1968 he married Sarah Boyd-Carpenter, daughter of Lord Boyd-Carpenter (see Sarah Hogg); they had two children. In 1979 he was elected MP for Grantham. From 1986 to 1989 he was a Junior Home Office Minister. In 1989 he was appointed Minister of State at the Department of Trade and Industry, and then became a Minister of State in the Foreign and Commonwealth Office in 1990. His elevation to the Cabinet was delayed while his wife held high office in Number 10. He joined the Cabinet as Minister for Agriculture, Fisheries and Food in 1995.

Like his father, Hogg was an amalgam of cleverness and foolishness – and found himself destroyed by the 1996 BSE crisis. He confronted Britain's democratic masses with a pinched, self-righteous irritability that became an essential part of the public view of the Conservative Party in its latter days. Dorrell's escape from responsibility for the administrative chaos revealed by the crisis was an adroit achievement. By contrast, Hogg bore the brunt of the blame, and so qualified as a 'clever fool' who, owing a debt of gratitude to the Prime Minister for their survival, could be relied upon to give him uncritical support.

Hogg, Sarah Elizabeth Mary (Baroness Hogg)

Sarah Hogg was born in 1946, the daughter of Sir John Boyd-Carpenter, later Lord Boyd-Carpenter, who served as Chief Secretary to the Treasury under Macmillan and Home. She was educated at St Mary's, Wantage and Lady Margaret Hall, Oxford. She worked as a journalist, first on *The Economist* and subsequently on the *Sunday Times*, and then in 1982 embarked an unhappy period in television, where her progress was plagued by a speech lacking in mellifluousness. In 1983 she returned to print journalism, working in succession on *The Times*, the *Independent* and the *Daily* and *Sunday Telegraph*, and developed a voice as a powerful and wide-ranging economic commentator. In 1990 she was appointed to run the Prime Minister's Policy Unit at Number 10, where she served until the end of 1994. She was made a life peer on

Major's recommendation in 1995. In 1968 she married Douglas Hogg (q.v.), who later became a Tory MP and Minister for Agriculture, and they had two children.

Hogg was Bottomley with brains, but most Tory MPs thought she was hell on toast. She used her power-base in Number 10 to aggrandize herself and her position, and it suited her that the Political Office in Number 10 was staffed by weak men. Having previously concerned itself with medium- to long-term thinking, under her leadership the Policy Unit became a feeble, limping response force absorbed in the daily minutiae of political crisis management. She enjoyed unique, daily access to the Prime Minister. Every Prime Minister needs his Richelieu, but not his Hogg. Sarah Hogg's particular problem was her narrowly ideological *idée fixe* about the virtues of the Exchange Rate Mechanism and the much-prophesied 'golden scenario' it would inaugurate of low inflation, low interest rates and stable currencies. Major owed much of his own obsession with the ERM to Hogg's partisan advocacy. She was also responsible for the narrow and suspicious cast of mind that enveloped Number 10, especially from 1992 onwards, and which survived her departure.

Howard, Rt Hon Michael

Michael Howard was born in 1941 and brought up in Llanelli, the South Wales coastal town whose liltingly genteel accent formed his own distinctive speech. His father, Bernat Hecht, a Romanian-Jewish immigrant, ran a local clothes shop. Howard was educated at Llanelli Boys Grammar School and Peterhouse, Cambridge. In 1975 he married Sandra Paul, a celebrated 1960s model; they had two children and a stepson by a former marriage of Mrs Howard's. He was called to the Bar at the Inner Temple in 1964 and took silk in 1982. In 1983 Howard was elected MP for Folkestone and Hythe, a near-marginal seat whose cultivation he took seriously. From 1985 to 1987 he was a Junior Minister at the Department of Trade and Industry, and subsequently served as a Minister of State at the Department of the Environment from 1987 to 1990. In 1990 he joined the Cabinet as Secretary of State for Employment. He was Environment Secretary from 1992 to 1993, and Home Secretary from 1993 to 1997.

Howard's first patron at the Bar was Lord Elwyn-Jones, who was Attorney-General in Harold Wilson's 1964–70 Labour Government and then Lord Chancellor under Wilson and Callaghan from 1974 to 1979 and who shared Howard's Llanelli upbringing. As a young man, Howard was thought to have flirted with the right-wing Labour Campaign for Democratic Socialism. During the 1970s Howard established himself in the Chambers of Geoffrey Rippon, the former Conservative Cabinet Minister, and specialized in dull but lucrative planning issues. He had a cultivated and smoothly Welsh personal manner that advanced his career at the Bar. However, many who worked with him afterwards in the political arena regarded him as obsessive, manipulative and opportunistic. Anti-European convictions only came his way slowly, solidifying at the same time as Margaret Thatcher hardened her position in the late 1980s. As Home Secretary he rode the horse of populist opinion extremely hard, thought that prison worked, undermined the right to silence, shortened the terms for early remission, and led calls for mandatory minimum sentences for third-time burglars. The judiciary, invariably 'liberal-minded' in Howard's parlance, believed that he had undermined their independence and read the tabloids rather than Blackstone's *Commentaries on the Laws of England*. While the Conservative Party approved of Howard's vigour, the pursuit of populism failed to bring him wider popularity, and he became a much disliked public figure. For all the vigour and consistency of aim he showed for over a year in pursuit of the Tory leadership, Howard gained the least number of votes in the June 1997 contest.

Lamont, Rt Hon Norman Stewart Hughson

Norman Lamont was born in Lerwick, Shetland, in 1942. While the Scots pronunciation of his surname would emphasize the first syllable, he chose to adopt the anglicized stress on the second syllable. Lamont was educated at Loretto, a minor Edinburgh public school, and Fitzwilliam College, Cambridge, an institution which was beginning to establish itself as a College in its own right. At Cambridge, he was a contemporary of Kenneth Clarke, who succeeded him as Chancellor, and of Michael Howard; Howard and Lamont each acted as the other's best man. He worked as a merchant banker with Rothschilds but, in the words of Sir Michael Richardson, then a director, was 'not partnership material'. He married Rosemary White in 1971, and they had two children.

In 1972 Lamont was elected MP for Kingston-upon-Thames. He was in office continuously from 1979, first as a Junior Minister in the Department of Energy until 1981, then as a Minister of State at the Department of Trade and Industry until 1985. Posts as Minister of State for Defence Procurement (1985–86) and Financial Secretary to the Treasury (1986–89) followed. Thatcher was unpersuaded by the case for Lamont's advance into Cabinet, but finally relented and made him Chief Secretary to the Treasury in 1989. In 1990 he acted as John Major's campaign manager in the Conservative Party leadership election, and Major rewarded him with the Chancellorship. In 1993, he rejected Major's offer of a move to the Department of the Environment. After this effective dismissal, Lamont waxed furious on the backbenches, re-emerging in 1995 to back John Redwood's campaign for the leadership. After his constituency disappeared under new boundaries, he was adopted for Harrogate in Yorkshire, but the combination of his public unpopularity and local Liberal activism meant that he lost the seat in 1997. He subsequently supported William Hague's campaign for the Party leadership from outside the House of Commons. He was a member of the Garrick Club and was interested in ornithology.

Lamont was emotional and thin-skinned. Part of him was the effective machine politician associated with the Oxford and Cambridge Unions. Indeed, he admired those one-dimensional qualities, and it was no surprise that William Hague served as his PPS while Lamont was Chancellor. In other respects, however, although not intellectual, Lamont did have an interestingly romantic streak of political adventurism in his make-up. Like many Tories, he entertained a sentimental view of de Gaulle and of Gaullism. Once removed from office, he began to develop a broader and more informed view of the constitution and of Unionism than was current in his Party. Lamont was one of the more spectacular casualties of the politics of the media age, for he combined the furtive appearance of the Artful Dodger with a talent for deploying maladroit phrases – he detected green shoots of economic recovery, and regretted *rien*. His political career was ruined both by John Major and by his own unwillingness to resign in the autumn of 1992 and accept responsibility for the collapse of the Government's central economic strategy. While his personal convictions may well have been set against the Exchange Rate Mechanism, his evident glee at its collapse compounded his problems. To most commentators, his Euro-scepticism seemed a political mechanism designed to eject the Prime Minister.

Lilley, Rt Hon Peter Bruce

Peter Lilley was born in 1943, the son of a BBC personnel officer, and brought up in Hayes, Kent. He was educated at Dulwich College, a south London independent boys' day school with a tradition of scholarship, and Clare College, Cambridge, where he read natural sciences. He married a portrait painter, Gail Ansel, in 1979, and they had no children. In the 1970s he worked as an oil analyst, at a time when that industry was expanding. In 1983 he became MP for St Albans. His early experience of ministerial office was at the Treasury, where he was Economic Secretary from 1987 to 1989 and Financial Secretary until 1990. In 1990 he entered the Cabinet as Secretary of State for Trade and Industry, one of the last beneficiaries of Thatcher's patronage. From 1992 to 1997 he served as Secretary of State for Social Security.

Lilley's experience of Government placed him at the Gradgrind end of things, where modern politics became a matter for desiccated calculators and dry-as-dust economists. Lilley was aware of the danger of being thought to be concerned solely with the nicely calculated lore of less or more – especially since he considered himself a future leader of the Conservative Party. He needed a wider front, and so he encouraged media discussion of his house in Normandy where his wife painted, he made Calvados and they both entertained their friends. In the Tory fashion, he was also an admirer of de Gaulle, who emerged in such platitudinous Tory accounts as the equivalent of a rather high-minded chairman of a local Conservative Association. Slight and fair, thoughtful and cautious, Lilley lacked scepticism about his own immortal political longings. His presentation of pension reform in the 1997 general election allowed Labour to claim that the State pension was not safe in Tory hands. He was a reasonably serious-minded Anglican. He and his wife liked society, though not as vigorously as Michael and Sandra Howard and Michael and Carolyn Portillo.

Major, Rt Hon John Roy

John Major was born in 1943 in Worcester Park, south London, the son of elderly parents. His father, who had worked in a circus, made garden ornaments. Indigence forced the family's move to Brixton, and Major left Rutlish School, a local boys' grammar school, at the age of sixteen. He joined Standard Chartered Bank, where the demands his emerging political interests made on his time confined him to the marketing side of the Bank's work. He was a Lambeth councillor from 1968 to 1971, and in 1979 was elected MP for Huntingdonshire, renamed Huntingdon in 1983 – a town whose new housing estates contained many London émigrés of the 1960s and 1970s. Major served as a Whip from 1983 to 1985, a Junior Minister from 1985 to 1986 at the Department of Health and Social Security and subsequently a Minister of State in the same department. He entered the Cabinet in 1987 when Thatcher appointed him Chief Secretary to the Treasury. He served as Foreign Secretary for three months in 1989, and from 1989 to 1990 was Chancellor of the Exchequer. From the 28th of November 1990 to the 1st of May 1997 he was Prime Minister. His wife, Norma, liked opera, and they had two children.

Posterity, seeking a mystery, would shroud Major and his intentions in ambiguity and secretiveness. But the reality was neither mysterious nor complicated. He was a master of detail; while his contemporaries whiled their time away in sociability, gossip, drink and dining, he spent long, lonely hours with the minutiae of Civil Service submissions. He showed how far a politician can get simply by not talking too much and by giving every impression of listening carefully. After his insecure upbringing, the Conservative Party gave him the only safety he had ever known and he familiarized himself completely with its inner workings. He had no political convictions other than the desirability of sustaining a Conservative administration, and himself, in office. 'Convictions' may be undesirable commodities in, and for, most politicians. They may even become dangerous in the hands of some. But Major failed to convince the British people that the Conservative Party was anything other than a sectional grouping whose prime object was to secure jobs for Tories. Judged even by that low standard he failed for, by the end of his leadership, his Party's parliamentary representation had been halved. He had much self-importance and liked to consider the question of how history would remember him. Doubtless he would have been unhappy with the prospect of an epitaph on a Huntingdonshire tombstone: 'The Conservative Party's last Prime Minister'.

Mawhinney, Rt Hon Brian Stanley

Brian Mawhinney, an Ulsterman, was born in 1940 and educated at the Royal

Belfast Academical Institution and Queen's University, Belfast. In 1965 he
married Betty, an American who shared his Christian and evangelical views.
Mawhinney was a medical scientist who held higher degrees from the
University of Michigan and the University of London. He was therefore
entitled to be called 'Dr' Mawhinney – a right he chose to exercise, although
when some others deployed the title irony was never far from the surface. He
was Assistant Professor at the University of Iowa from 1968 to 1970, and
subsequently lectured at the Royal Free Hospital School of Medicine in
London. In 1979 he became MP for Peterborough, where he remained until
1997 when unhappy boundary changes led him to depart for the contiguous
pastures of Cambridgeshire North West. The mature Mawhinney veered from
the rebarbative dissent of his upbringing and embraced the Church of
England, and from 1985 to 1990 he was a member of the General Synod of
that Church.

For a while, it looked as if Ulster's politics might claim Mawhinney
permanently and deny him the wider stage he rather obviously craved. From
1986 to 1992 he served in the Northern Ireland Office, initially as a Junior
Minister and then, from 1990, as a Minister of State. He asserted his
personality vigorously, and officials would mutter 'The ego has landed' when
he reached Belfast from London. John Major, who represented the next-door
constituency, extricated him, and from 1992 to 1994 he was a Minister of
State at the Department of Health. Here he enjoyed an uneasy coexistence
with Virginia Bottomley, and was not unhappy at press reports that
Mawhinney was the Minister whom Health Service 'professionals' valued and
the one who got things done. In 1994 he entered the Cabinet as Secretary of
State for Transport. The following year, he replaced the hapless Jeremy
Hanley as Chairman of the Conservative Party.

Mawhinney combined a reputation for a brutal professional style with a
surprising degree of administrative indecision. This was most evident during
his brief period as Transport Secretary, when he found rail privatization and
bus deregulation particularly difficult issues. It was never satisfactorily
explained why he had become a politician at all, or a Conservative, and he
could not be identified with any set of ambitions or views within his Party.
Civil servants found him difficult to work for, since he attempted to establish
a reputation for effectiveness through public displays of bad temper at their
expense. In 1995 Major decided to put a self-advertised 'hard' man into
Central Office to replace Jeremy Hanley, whose supposed geniality and light-
comedic touch had failed to restore the Party's fraying nerves. Hanley's own
political nerve had deserted him as the Prime Minister's loss of faith in his
Party's Chairman was advertised with increasing obviousness.

In the two years that remained to the general election, Mawhinney, as
Party Chairman, counselled against Heseltine's proposal that all Conservative
MPs should endorse the Government's ambiguities on the Single Currency,
and won the day. He understood that the Government's position was
impractical and that it was impossible for Central Office to take on the role of

censor of individual candidates' election manifestos. Recognizing the need to mollify, he acquired an unnervingly fixed smile whose silent malice disturbed many. Mawhinney was also Chief Executive at Central Office, but failed to clarify the confusions, both administrative and intellectual, that characterized that organization in the dying months of the Major administration. He relished the violent imagery of the 1996 'demon-eyes' poster, but remained blind to its self-proclamation of Tory despair.

Portillo, Rt Hon Michael Denzil Xavier

Michael Portillo was born in 1953, the son of a Spanish intellectual father, Luis Gabriel, whose Republican sympathies had led him to a north London exile. He was educated at Harrow County Boys Grammar School and Peterhouse, Cambridge. He liked to tell the story of how, at his admission interview, Maurice Cowling, his future College supervisor in history, had looked at him wearily and asked, 'Tell me, exactly how Italian are you?' He was placed in the First Class of the Tripos, of which he was very proud. In 1982 he married Carolyn Eadie, a childhood friend who rose in the world of head-hunting and executive search. They had no children and later lived in Victoria Square, a late Regency square in Lower Belgravia. Portillo had a brief experience in commerce, which he did not enjoy, before joining Central Office's Research Department in 1976. He subsequently worked as a special adviser to a number of Cabinet Ministers.

Portillo was elected for Enfield Southgate in the December 1984 by-election that followed the death of the previous MP, Sir Anthony Berry, in the bomb attack by the IRA at the Conservative Party Conference two months earlier. He became a Junior Whip in 1986 and a Junior Minister in the Department of Health and Social Security in 1987. From 1988 to 1990 he was a Minister of State at the Department of Transport, and then served as Minister of State for Local Government in the Department of the Environment until 1992. In 1992 he entered the Cabinet as Chief Secretary to the Treasury. From 1994 to 1995 he was Employment Secretary, and in 1995 he became Secretary of State for Defence. On the night of the 1st of May 1997, he became the most spectacular Conservative casualty when he lost his seat on a swing of 17.4 per cent. He was an admirer of the operas of Richard Wagner, and he and his wife were a sociable couple. He gave no sign of being interested in religion, and was indeed a heavily secular figure.

For a politician who gave every sign of understanding that, in politics, personality is more important than policy, Portillo was strangely compliant in accepting the labels of 'leader of the Right' and 'Thatcher's Crown Prince'. He later said that during the mid-1990s he had not been very good at explaining himself. The truth was that Portillo had no particularly distinctive credo to advance other than the limping *idées reçues* of a fast degenerating 'Thatcherism'. In the quest for a definition of 'post-Thatcherism', he remained absorbed in the acquired certitudes of his early development. He had

become convinced at a very young age that he should become a very considerable person in the Conservative Party, and he learnt the rules of the game
extremely well. He immersed himself thoroughly in the milieu and customs
of his chosen Party. A House of Commons taste, Portillo purveyed a romantic
view of Britain's history and her institutions – a loyalism of the spirit that
appeared to be fixed in its unchanging essentials. He enjoyed the apparent
paradox of one who was so obviously 'European', and who spoke Spanish
fluently, resisting European integration. Fortitude and some humour were
displayed as he bore jibes about 'Portillo the Caudillo' and 'Portillo the cruel-
lipped Castilian'. He possessed great personal dignity and bearing – which
came to the fore on the night of his General Election defeat – and a richly
melodious voice that cracked when he pushed his oratory too hard and started
to rant.

After 1995 questions of political judgement crowded in upon him. He
appeared indifferent to the wider political questions raised by Britain's social
worries and institutional decay – perhaps, being so grateful to be born British,
he did not wish to change anything. When he attempted to discuss political
themes on a general level, he revealed a thinness of thought that embarrassed
his many admirers. Like Margaret Thatcher, he aroused strong visceral
feelings. His friends loved him. In the public mind he came to embody
modern Conservatism's heedless arrogance, and his political difficulties arose
from an insensitive ear for the cadences of Britain's mass democracy.

Redwood, Rt Hon John Alan

John Redwood was born in 1951 and spent his early years in a council house,
a fact whose political advantages he refused to manipulate. He was educated
at Kent College, Canterbury and Magdalen College, Oxford, as well as,
briefly, at St Anthony's College. In 1972 he was elected a Fellow of All Souls
College by examination. In 1974 he married Gail Chippington, an Oxford
contemporary and lawyer who shared his modest background; later she
worked as company secretary to British Airways under the patronage of Lord
King, the BA Chairman. She became the most important personal influence
on his views and urged him onwards in his increasing detachment from John
Major's administration. Both took a high view of the dictates of truth and
liked scholarly clarity. They had two children. In 1973 he started his career as
an investment adviser with Robert Fleming and Co., moving in 1977 to N. M.
Rothschild and Sons, where he became a director. From 1983 to 1985 he ran
the Prime Minister's Policy Unit, and raised the status of his post to the
equivalent of a Permanent Secretary, an important achievement in a hierar-
chical and deferential world. He was an Oxfordshire County Councillor from
1973 to 1977.

In 1987, after some difficulty, Redwood succeeded in gaining a parliamentary seat at Wokingham, Berkshire, where he was admired for his
integrity, energy and dedication. He was appointed a Junior Minister in the

Department of Trade and Industry in 1989, and promoted to Minister of State in the same department in 1990. From 1992 to 1993 he was Minister of State for Local Government at the Department of the Environment, succeeding Michael Portillo, his later rival. In 1993 he entered the Cabinet as Secretary of State for Wales. He resigned in 1995 to challenge John Major for the leadership of the Conservative Party. He was a conventional Anglican with a regard for social propriety and an indifference to theology. He disliked the late Diana, Princess of Wales and, having shared a railway carriage with her on a journey to watch a rugby football international in Cardiff, regarded her as skittish and manipulative in her relations with the press. From 1985 to 1989 he was a director of Norcros plc, a conglomerate of domestic goods manufacturers, and served as its non-executive Chairman from 1987 to 1989.

Redwood was a dominating influence in Conservative, and so in British, politics from 1995 to 1997. Until 1995 his ambition had been to become Chancellor of the Exchequer. However, the strange events of the summer of 1995 changed his life, and from 1995 to 1997 he pursued the Tory crown with a characteristically political combination of opportunism and principle. In private he could display a laconic and sardonic wit – qualities he shared with the late Nicholas Ridley whom he had greatly admired as his chief at the Department of Trade and Industry – but he thought that publicly expressed humour harmed a politician, since it divided and offended as much as it amused. In its stead he communicated, in the first half of the 1990s, an angry and neurotic tension. The qualities he most disliked in the Major administration were its propensity to lie, its pronounced intolerance of debate within Government and its equally pronounced tolerance of, as he put it, 'sloppiness'. He liked working in tight little gnostic groups, and was highly suspicious of the times in which he lived. His much remarked English 'populism' was a matter of carefully constructed words rather than deeds. He served English table wine from the Thames Valley, but himself drank vintages bought on account from St James' wine-merchants. He sighed for the bone china of Rothschilds when civil servants placed mugs of morning coffee in front of him. He had poor posture and a scholar's stoop, the tensions of his mind displaying themselves in his physical awkwardness. He liked cricket, a game he played vigorously rather than elegantly.

Redwood brought vigour and clarity to a dying Party, but disliked working with others in the enforced mediocrity of political life. The schoolboy who made fun of his masters behind their backs and imitated their gait was never far from the adult Redwood. He liked his own reputation for 'honesty', but his Party thought he had bought that reputation at their expense. His comments on social policy and on single mothers contributed to the pharisaic stench surrounding his Party in its decline. He was intolerant on Europe and was convinced that in the future the overwhelming majority of his Party would be sceptical. 'If that young man wants a Tory political future,' he once said of an evasive parliamentary candidate, 'he'd better be Euro-sceptic.' He had a very great love of his country, England, and realized that the 1997 general election had settled the question of her independence. His friends esteemed him for his valour and his love of liberty. He was the Tory Cato.

Thatcher, Rt Hon Margaret Hilda (Baroness Thatcher)

Inclined to describe herself, inaccurately, as 'Margaret, the Lady Thatcher', Margaret Roberts was born in 1925 in Grantham, Lincolnshire, the daughter of Alfred Roberts, a local grocer. Her closeness to her father, an alderman and an important local politician, and indifference to her mother spawned much psycho-analytic fantasy. She was educated at Kesteven and Grantham Girls' School and Somerville College, Oxford, where she read chemistry. After a period as a research scientist, she was called to the Bar at Lincoln's Inn in 1954. In 1959 she became MP for Finchley, and in 1961 was appointed a Junior Minister at the Ministry of Pensions, serving until the 1964 general election. She advanced during her Party's Opposition years, and in 1970 held office as Secretary of State for Education and Science under Edward Heath.

In 1975, Margaret Thatcher won the leadership of the Conservative Party, and after four years as Leader of the Opposition became Prime Minister following the 1979 general election. In November 1990 her own Parliamentary Party forced her out of office; her handling of the contentious community charge, or 'poll' tax, had convinced them that she had ceased to understand or respond to public opinion. In 1992 she left the House of Commons and became a life peer. In 1951 she married, as his second wife, Denis Thatcher, an affluent and shrewd businessman who reinforced her fundamental philistinism and materialism. They had twin children whose progress through life caused them occasional concern. Denis Thatcher was created a Baronet in 1991. Raised a Methodist, Margaret Thatcher turned towards the Church of England, but the asperity and individualism of the dissenting tradition in its classical form left a marked impression on her mind and, in secularized mode, survived strongly within her character. She was elected a Fellow of the Royal Society in 1983, and became a member of the Order of Merit in 1990. In 1995 she was invested as a Lady of the Garter.

For much of her career, Margaret Thatcher was a conventionally opportunistic Conservative politician. Until she became Party leader at the age of fifty, she gave no sign of being interested in the advanced tenets of 'Thatcherism'. As leader she was tutored in the advanced simplicities of free-market economics by Sir Keith Joseph, her chief intellectual mentor. Even at the height of her power, she was a more cautious politician than her rhetoric suggested. Her most important contribution to her Party was to convince it of the inevitability and of the rectitude of its rule. The social and economic forces unleashed by what she called the 'Thatcher Revolution' would underlie and guarantee her new order. She had an impersonal but vulgar conception of herself as a historical force, and felt herself to be both the incarnation of that force and the servant of it, hence her habit of referring to herself in the first person plural. She talked a lot about freedom and wanted the British to become more capitalist than they themselves wished to be. She understood the temper of the USA extremely well, and was the dominant partner in her relationship with President Ronald Reagan. When she laid siege to a host of British institutions in the 1980s, it was not yet clear that her legacy would undermine another British institution, the Conservative Party.

Many of her causes, such as the humbling of the trades unions, were popular, but she herself was not, and the public view of her was formed by the shrill certitudes that marked her entry into the first ranks of British public life in the early 1970s. The size of her parliamentary majorities masked the reality of the Tories' tenuous hold on public approval, and the undoubted strength of her personality attracted and repelled in equal measure. Through deploying such phrases as 'the enemy within' to describe striking miners, Thatcher used a naturally divisive temperament to strengthen her hold on power. Her own Party liked her very much indeed and regarded her as one of them; she neglected her own inheritance, and her active intervention ensured the election of John Major in 1990 and of William Hague in 1997. In all probability she regarded her legacy as more than adequately protected by the premiership of Tony Blair, whom she liked personally and for whom she had a far higher regard than for either of her two successors as Conservative leader.

Throughout the 1990s, Thatcher's interventions in British politics were closely watched, and she was a zealous editor of her own texts – especially on the European issue. For instance, she claimed not to have anticipated that the Single European Act, a measure designed to ensure the free movement of goods within the European Community, could be used to justify increasing regulation and intervention. However, she had been advised to argue for so-called 'sunset clauses' designed to shorten the Act's life and limit its applicability. In office she encouraged a cult of leadership that emasculated her Parliamentary Party and, by the late 1980s, threatened to detach her from reality as she became a disembodied international icon. When she left office, her cult degenerated into a sentimental veneration that prevented the Tories from looking British reality in the face.

APPENDIX

The following are transcriptions and reproductions of documents referred to in the text.

Document A

This document is an excerpt from a 'progress summary' prepared by the Secretary of State for Wales and his special adviser and sent to the Head of the Policy Unit and, through him, the Prime Minister in March 1995. It was the first substantial response to the Prime Minister's letter of 22nd of December 1994, in which Mr Major asked all Cabinet Ministers to establish policy groups early in the new year. The aim was, in his words, 'to generate ideas for the next manifesto well in advance of the actual election campaign'. The Prime Minister's conception of a balanced membership for such groups included back-benchers, Party members (on the advice of the Party Chairman), peers, Central Office staff and representatives of the Number 10 Policy Unit. This created some bureaucratic difficulties. Mr Major said in his original letter that he 'would hope to have an interim report from each group by the summer recess'. In the case of the Welsh Office, two such meetings of 'policy groups' were held. John Redwood took the opportunity to present what was effectively an embryo manifesto for the Conservative Party and Government covering most Whitehall departments. In this document, therefore, for 'Wales' read 'Britain'. The paper illustrates a pragmatic administrative and political mind at work.

MANIFESTO FOR WALES

EDUCATION

The Education debate should be more about leadership and motivation and less about money. We need to show how schools in similar circumstances achieve different results because of the quality of leadership among those who teach and inspire. Education is now a strong suit for the Conservatives. We have established that parental wishes are important, that Local Management of Schools works and that an increased knowledge about schools in the form of league tables and exam results is popular with parents. These developments have made education more democratic and a previously bureaucratic system more open to scrutiny. Conservative aims for a shareholding, property owning democracy have been extended to include the way we run our schools, colleges and universities. We now need to build on our general themes of more opportunity, more choice, higher standards and more parental pressure.

In Wales we will be building on the "People and Prosperity" document – we will set demanding and realistic targets for individual schools.

1. Extend the range of delegated powers under local management in schools to all schools, including school meals and transport. Offer schools 100% of their money. They can choose which council services to buy.

2. Expanding the range of powers to grant maintained schools including powers to borrow and wider delegation over finance, admissions and other matters.

3. Expand popular schools initiative, so that more parents can obtain their first choice of school.

4. As part of raising standards, intensify efforts to combat truancy and use powers under the Education Act to improve poor performing schools.

5. Improve teaching of the basics in primary schools by inspection, tests, example.

6. Strengthen religious and moral education in schools.

7. Headteacher contracts to specify minimum time teaching and schools to teach at least the minimum hours.

8. Improve training for governors, show them comparative information on schools costs and achievement and advise them to spend a substantial proportion of their time on academic standards.

9. Maximum limit for reserves, unless earmarked for a specific improvement.

10. Governors to expect evidence of good work before awarding higher grade or extra money to teachers. They should not sanction early retirements in normal circumstances.

11. Prizes or certificates to recognise improvements in schools.

12. Value added to be spelt out in the league tables.

13. Council nominated governors to be proportionate to council membership.

14. Publish figures for teacher assistants as well as teachers in ratios.

15. Encourage system of university funding based on student choice with less emphasis on central control and educational bureaucracy.

HEALTH

Conservatives are committed to providing the people of Britain with first class public services. Competitive tendering, market testing, league tables of performance are designed to ensure that more money is spent on the patient and less on the administrators. A war on waste and a war on jargon should both be part of a Conservative campaign against mindless manageralism.

1. Bring health promotion under the control of general practitioners and hospitals. Thereby abolishing a quango.

2. Give more genuine patient and GP choice over hospital consultant through access to good quality information. Make real the ability to refer outside the area of the given district authority.

3. Complete the amalgamation of FHSAs and DHAs and complete the change from 17 to 5 health authorities. Use this to make a further substantial reduction in paper work, administration and management in the hospitals as well as in the health authorities.

4. Arrest the closure of smaller community hospitals and older facilities where the local communities support retention and encourage the provision of more beds including intensive care beds. These will be needed despite the growing trend towards more day surgery.

TRANSPORT AND ROADS

Communications are a key to prosperity. Privatisation and the deregulation of air travel and bus services has meant competition, lower prices and better services. Privatisation needs to be re-launched as the key Conservative contribution towards democratising our public services. Privatisation puts the customer first. He can choose a greater range of services. Companies eager to run a profitable business have to respond to a world where the customer is king and the monopolist a conspirator against the public interest.

1. Encourage the restoration of rail freight through expanded rail freight facilities and active marketing by the private sector companies.

2. Build a new railfreight terminal.

3. Encourage more rail passenger travel through privatisation and private sector policies being adopted.

4. Complete the strategic network of roads by completing the A55 across Anglesey, the improved M4, M48 in South Wales and the A465 Heads of the Valleys Road. Complete the links to this network from South Gwynedd and from Pembrokeshire.

5. Encourage greater choice and diversity of service including secure car-parking at railway stations, park and ride schemes and better provision for cycling.

HOUSING

The former council house with a neo-Georgian front door opened the way to the Conservative successes of the 1980s. In the 1990s we now need to build on this legacy and extend it. We should now aim for 80% home ownership compared with 72% today in line with people's wishes as expressed in recent surveys.

The most "social" form of housing is the one where you own your own house. There is nothing social about having to pay in rent an increasing amount of your disposable income at a time in your 60s and 70s when you are most vulnerable.

1. Give Right to Buy in housing association developments. Housing associations in Wales are now prohibited from buying houses on the open market, thereby causing artificial house inflation in local areas. They are encouraged to continue with building.

2. Develop further low-cost ownership schemes and DIY and shared ownership.

3. Continue work on 6 new settlements including making land available at realistic prices for low-cost home ownership. Develop further policies for shared ownership and do-it-yourself self build.

WATER

The monopoly industry is widely disliked for high and rising prices and insufficient improvement in quality and service. As with Gas and Telecom, we need to inject real choice and competition.

1. Make the pipe network a common carrier.

2. Open up water supply to other suppliers in each area.

This should cut prices and solve problems like the shortage of water in dry summers.

Document B

This note from the Secretary of State for Wales, undated and unsigned, was sent to the Head of the Policy Unit and, through him, to the Prime Minister, at the same time as Document A. Its contents were not discussed with any 'policy group'. By 1995, taxation had long since become the Tory albatross. The background to this document was one of electoral scepticism about the government's declared long-term desire to resume its policy of cutting the standard rate of Income Tax. These proposals sought to rebuild confidence in the short term by reconnecting fiscal policy with Conservative values. The first paragraph of the original document was deleted from the final version sent to Number 10.

Many people are quietly angry about Conservative tax increases. They thought they voted for a party that would cut taxes. They believe the government has broken its word.

What we need to do is to cut taxes as part of a concerted strategy to achieve other policy goals: so the tax reduction is more widely 'accepted' as well as privately welcomed. Cutting taxes on motoring is not 'politically acceptable', yet cutting duty on unleaded petrol was the most popular green measure taken by a long way. Similar proposals that would stand a good chance of popularity include:

1. *Restoration of family life* Propose tax reduction for married couples with children to help with the costs of traditional family life. Many former Conservative supporters feel all the dice are now loaded in favour of the less conventional family.

2. *Freeing the negative equity generation* Propose a higher mortgage tax relief level for those moving out of a house where the proceeds are less than the mortgage, to help them with the extra loan they need.

3. *Encouraging mobility for those seeking new jobs* Raise the Stamp Duty threshold. Give tax breaks to rented housing investment trusts.

4. *Helping the prudent pensioner* Many pensioners regret the fall in interest rates which has cut their income from deposits. They also feel penalised for saving because it rules out income related benefits for them. Offer a much more generous tax free National Savings investment for them, or offer them higher tax relief on the income from their savings.

5. *Backing green action*
a. Exempt building works that improve insulation and heat retention from VAT, up to a limit for each household;
b. offer two years freedom from VAT on a household's electricity or gas bill if the consumer sends in a receipt for a specified product that will increase their

insulation (tank lagging, roof insulation packs etc)

6. *Backing self employment and small business*
a. Raise the VAT threshold higher.
b. Allow the first 'employee' to be self-employed if they wish to reduce the small business's paperwork.
c. Delay the introduction of higher business rates until recovery is that much stronger.

How should this be paid for?

Much of this can be paid for out of the fruits of economic growth and the consequences of past budgetary actions. The City would be reassured if there were some public spending reductions to help pay for these measures. Suggested compensation of £1,000m includes:

a. Sale of empty defence and health houses (£100m)
b. Transfer of more capital items to risk bearing private finance eg rented housing (£350m)
c. Reduce the numbers and overheads of quangos (£200m)
d. Cut the number and costs of consultancy in government (£350m)

Document C

A letter to the Prime Minister, April 1995, in which John Redwood, once again, tries to elicit interest in, and support for, his proposals.

PRIME MINISTER

Following our discussion on Thursday 20th I thought I would sketch three ideas to you which may be of interest.

The first is to relaunch ourselves as the party of home ownership and to set ourselves new targets for spreading ownership more widely. We need to win the argument that a home of your own is true social housing. It is much cheaper to buy a house on a 20 or 25 year mortgage and live in it for the rest of life rent free than to rent even a subsidised property over 50 or 60 years. It also gives you greater freedom, it means that in retirement you face the smallest bills for your housing rather than the largest bills which happens if you are renting.

A recent survey in Wales [showed] that 8 out of 10 want to own their own home. Currently just a little over 7 out of 10 do. This survey is despite the fall in house values of the early 1990's and the well publicised problems of negative equity. The country does need reassuring that home ownership is the right thing and especially that this Government supports and backs home owners in the way it always used to. There are a number of things we can do:

(i) *Victims of negative equity:* we could target a package of tax reliefs to help those whose mortgages exceed the sale value of their properties. When moving we could give them extra mortgage interest relief on the mortgage they take out to buy the new home. Give them full relief at the standard rate of income tax rather than a reduced rate of relief. Give them a more generous allowance perhaps adding to the £30,000 standard allowance the amount of the negative equity up to say a maximum of £10,000.

(ii) *Giving housing association tenants of all new housing association properties to be built and rented an automatic right to buy* as part of the condition of the housing association grant for the new construction.

(iii) *Encouraging Housing Associations to offer right to buy for existing properties* by making sure that there are arrangements to reinvest the money freed by the tenants sale along with protection of the Housing Association's underlying investment position.

(iv) *Give tax breaks to investors wishing to build and offer property to rent* if they will include a right to buy clause in any rental agreement for suitably qualified tenants. The tax relief could be built around a business expansion scheme type fund or could be an income or corporation tax concession to investment trusts.

(v) *To accelerate a programme of urban villages with emphasis on low cost housing for sale.* The land price is typically 25% of the price of the finished home in many parts of the country. In urban villages in more difficult areas it would be possible to achieve a much lower land cost thereby improving the saleability of the properties.

(vi) *Extend the tenants' incentive scheme* to offer people capital help with the down payment on a home of their own where they are prepared to move out of subsidised rented accommodation.

Secondly, we need to win back those who feel that the privatised utilities are not delivering a good package for the customer. In the case of telephones we need to sell the achievements better. There has been a decline of more than one third in telecom prices, coupled with a massive expansion of choice of equipment and service offered. The time it takes to install a phone and to have a phone repaired has reduced and the reliability of phone boxes has improved.

At the other end of the spectrum, people are understandably unhappy about the quality, standard and price of the service provided by the water monopolies. It is bizarre that as soon as you get a dry spell in the summer the water industry tells you not to buy its product and introduces hose pipe and garden watering bans. It is worrying that gold plated investment has been encouraged by the price control formula and prices have risen more than is desirable. The water industry needs a healthy injection of competition which would very rapidly transform its productivity and encourage proper appraisal of its investment programmes to get good value. We should make the water pipeline system a common carrier as with the gas and oil pipelines and encourage competitors to come in to offer water to towns, housing estates and industrial parks. There is now a competitive market at the very large end for industry. We could extend it downwards in the way that we are extending gas competition downwards from the large industrial users ultimately to the retail level.

We need to highlight the advantages of a competitive gas market, underlining the message that prices have been falling and reminding people that there will soon be a further major increase in competitive pressures likely to increase the quality, choice and price competitiveness of the service.

Thirdly, we need to associate ourselves more prominently with multi-media technology and give a higher profile to the undoubted successes of our media and telecom policies. Multi-media policy is wide reaching. In education we need to make sure that all children are familiar with the new technologies and that we use the strengths of the new technologies to get the best teaching materials into every school and college. In employment we wish to make sure that the new technology is used for our training programmes and that trainees are fully conversant with it. The lead department is clearly the DTI who are doing excellent work on the regulatory and industrial aspects of the new technology. Heritage is involved particularly with the impact the media industry itself has on the new technology and the use they can make of it. Every other department can make use of the new technology for the provision of their own services, the training of their own staff and communication with the users and electors.

I have tried to draw together the threads in Wales. The results of this work are two fold. I have produced a speech setting out the general themes. I have planned a series of announcements over the next few months translating the speech into an action programme for multi-media in Wales. The announcements include a new cable franchise for South Wales Valleys and in due course for North East Wales: discussions with the industry about microwave and other technologies to extend into rural West and Mid Wales: the cabling of industrial parks and the Cardiff Bay development; the development of the Cymru Net Service: attempts to secure investment in a video cafe demonstration project, a tele-working demonstration project in West Wales and a series of important investors in the media and technology areas into Cardiff Bay itself. Sky have now approached me offering a free dish and receiver for satellite TV for every Welsh school.

April 1995   JR

Document D

A letter from the Prime Minister's Principal Private Secretary which was sent to the Private Offices of all Cabinet Ministers, 6th of February 1995. Recent speeches, especially perhaps that of John Redwood at Winchester (p. 98), suggested the need for such an enjoyable reminder of prime ministerial control.

CLEARANCE OF SPEECHES, ARTICLES AND INTERVIEWS

In my letter on Friday in which I circulated the Prime Minister's speech I drew attention to what the Prime Minister said at Cabinet last week and to the guidance in Questions of Procedure for Ministers (QPM). It may help if I amplify what is required of private offices and press offices.

First, QPM notes in paragraph 87 that Ministers "should ensure that their statements are consistent with collective Government policy and . . . should exercise special care in referring to subjects that are the responsibility of other Ministers." The Prime Minister attaches importance to all Ministers adhering to this guidance. The views of the other Ministers concerned should be sought through their private offices before any commitment is given to make a speech or write an article on a subject outside a Minister's own departmental responsibilities, or which deals with subjects that are the responsibility of other Departments.

Second, where it has been agreed that a Minister should make a speech or write an article dealing with a subject which is the primary responsibility of another Department, the draft must be cleared *at private office level* so that Ministers in the other Department have an opportunity to comment personally. This applies to any statement about Government policy, even if it is to be issued via Party sources. It may also be appropriate to clear drafts at official level or among special advisers, but that is no substitute for clearance through the private office. For the time being, please could any speech or article about European policy be cleared via the Number 10 Private Office as well as with the Foreign Office (and Treasury or other department as necessary).

Third, QPM notes in Paragraph 91(d) that "In the interests of effective co-ordination of Government policies, Ministers should ensure that No 10 Press Office is informed of their intentions [to give interviews or otherwise take part in radio and television programmes.]" This should be done *before* any commitment is made to the broadcasters concerned.

I should be grateful if you and other secretaries could personally ensure that these procedures are followed within your departments. I am copying this letter to the Private Secretaries of all Cabinet Ministers, to Juliet Wheldon (Law Officers' Department), to Murdo Maclean (Chief Whip's Office) and to Melanie Leech (Cabinet Office).

INDEX